Statistics and the Public Sphere

Numbers and the People in
Modern Britain, c. 1800–2000

Edited by
Tom Crook
and Glen O'Hara

Routledge
Taylor & Francis Group
New York   London

First published 2011
by Routledge
711 Third Avenue, New York, NY 10017

Simultaneously published in the UK
by Routledge
2 Park Square, Milton Park, Abingdon, Oxon OX14 4RN

Routledge is an imprint of the Taylor & Francis Group, an informa business

© 2011 Taylor & Francis

The right of Tom Cook and Glen O'Hara to be identified as the authors of the editorial material, and of the authors for their individual chapters, has been asserted in accordance with sections 77 and 78 of the Copyright, Designs and Patents Act 1988.

Typeset in Sabon by IBT Global.

Library of Congress Cataloging-in-Publication Data
    Statistics and the public sphere : numbers and the people in modern
Britain, c. 1800–2000 / edited by Tom Crook and Glen O'Hara.—1st ed.
       p. cm.—(Routledge studies in modern British history ; 6)
    Includes bibliographical references and index.
    ISBN 978-0-415-87894-4
  1. Great Britain—Statistics. 2. Great Britain—Social conditions. I. Crook, Tom,
1977– II. O'Hara, Glen, 1974–
    HA1134.S727 2011
    314.1—dc22

ISBN13: 978-0-415-87894-4 (hbk)
ISBN13: 978-0-203-81867-1 (ebk)

Statistics and the
Public Sphere

Routledge Studies in Modern British History

Contents

Tables

Figures

Acknowledgements

This volume arises from a conference held at Oxford Brookes University in September 2008. The editors would like to acknowledge the financial support of the following institutions and associations: the Economic History Society; the Centre for the History of Welfare, Oxford Brookes University; and the Institute for Historical and Cultural Research, Oxford Brookes University. Thanks also to Stephen Byrne for help in preparing the final typescript, and to all those who attended the conference.

1   The 'Torrent of Numbers'

Statistics and the Public Sphere in Britain, c. 1800–2000

Tom Crook and Glen O'Hara

Modern political life would be unthinkable without statistics. Politicians use statistics to track public opinion; numbers proliferate in the media; academics, state bureaucrats, and corporations provide an 'informed public' with a steady stream of facts and figures. The public thus defines itself and its fortunes in terms of statistics and statistical norms: among others, growth rates, house prices, and crime indices. As the historian Adam Tooze has observed, 'a torrent of numbers accompanies both the bureaucratic communication and the public discourses that are characteristic of modernity'.[1] Yet statistics are hardly free of controversy. One reason numbers loom so large in today's public sphere is that they often elicit debate regarding their veracity. It is widely acknowledged that numbers, like words, can be 'spun', and their circulation among members of the public, experts, and politicians is often attended with suspicion. Statistics are rarely consumed these days without important questions being asked regarding their origins and the categories and temporal boundaries used to order them.

Meanwhile, among observers of the public sphere, philosophers point to the hegemony of statistics and the way numbers immobilize, through their sheer profusion, any proper critical engagement with the present. In the introduction to *Number and Numbers*, the philosopher Alain Badiou notes the abundance of statistics in contemporary Western societies, adding: 'The ideology of modern parliamentary societies, if they have one, is not humanism, law or the subject. It is number, the countable, countability.' 'We live in the era of number's despotism', something which means we have become incapable of posing more abstract questions concerning freedom, justice, and the true nature of citizenship.[2] Evidently numbers, though they may enable debate, also arouse debate in themselves. They may even, as the likes of Badiou contend, close down debate, turning the very idea of the public into nothing more than a shifting statistical aggregate.

It has been the intention of the authors who have written for this volume to explore the interrelations of statistics and the public sphere in the context of modern Britain, from roughly 1800 through to the post–Second World War era. The volume arrives in the wake of at least three decades of scholarship dedicated to tracking the governmental use of numbers. Britain has been especially well-served, partly because it was home to a variety of crucial innovations. Established in 1837, the General Register Office (GRO), for instance, pioneered the collection and dissemination of 'vital statistics', now an essential part of any developed state's bureaucratic infrastructure. But the existing historiography also encompasses many other countries and governmental projects. To name only a small sample, histories now exist which examine perceptions of population growth in *ancien régime* France; the British authorities' attempts to enumerate the Indian Empire; and the Nazis' use of the census to regulate the racial world they wanted to build.[3] Few, if any, Western states lack some account of their dependence on numbers, and the historiography of statistics and modern governance is an immensely crowded one.

It is also immensely varied in terms of the kinds of numbers and practices that have been engaged with. Two areas might be highlighted. On the one hand, historians have traced key developments in the history of statistical reasoning, including, most notably, the gradual application during the nineteenth century of observational error analysis to concrete phenomena in the social, biological, and physical sciences.[4] The evolution of the more technical, mathematical side of statistics, such as biometrics, econometrics, and experimental sampling, is now a significant field in itself.[5] On the other hand, historians have examined the organization of 'official statistics', as well as those which appeared in surveys produced outside of the state. From government censuses and 'blue books' to works of urban exploration and social reportage, the use of statistics to classify and discipline given populations has been meticulously documented.[6] Twentieth-century developments such as market research and opinion polling have also been subject to critical scrutiny, especially in recent years.[7]

Yet there is a further area of scholarship worthy of mention, one which complements, but also departs from, the history of statistics and modern governance, namely the fledging genre of 'information history'.[8] One aim of this promising new field of inquiry is to reconstruct the myriad ways information was utilized and negotiated in everyday arenas such as the home, street, and workplace. Numerical and tabular forms of information have already been scrutinized with these aims in mind. We now know, for instance, of the struggles endured by middle-class Victorians as they got to grips with the mass-produced train timetables which began to appear in the 1840s.[9] Other works have begun to broach the 'media ecology' of nineteenth-century Britain and how the new postal and telegraphic networks reconfigured people's understanding and consumption of knowledge.[10]

This volume thus contributes to an already rich and expansive historiography. Yet its subject matter remains neglected. This might be summed up as the interrelations of statistics and the public sphere, but it encompasses a series of research questions. Four in particular might be highlighted. First, how and to what extent was the generation of statistics complicated by the existence of governmental centres and peripheries, and the need to rely on and inform the public? Secondly, in what representational forms did numbers circulate among the public, and how did they enable the public to be imagined in new ways? Thirdly, how and to what extent did statistics inspire public trust and transform public conceptions of authority and accountability? Finally, how and when did numbers and statistics begin to permeate political debate, frame political issues, and generate new forms of political reasoning?

Of course, these questions have not been entirely overlooked in the existing historiography. Various accounts might be invoked which attend to one or two of the above questions: Theodore Porter's *Trust in Numbers*, for instance, deals directly with the relations of statistics, authority, and public life.[11] As ever, it is a matter of shifting the angle or emphasis of inquiry: a question of developing a hitherto only latent or scattered research agenda, and in the case of an edited collection, also drawing together scholars, all with their own distinct specialisms, to contribute towards this task. This new angle or emphasis is indicated in the title of the volume, and the principal purpose of this introduction it to sketch some key developments in the history of statistics and the public sphere in modern Britain. But first a few more words are in order by way of situating the aims of the volume as a whole.

AIMS AND RATIONALE

Certainly the present volume differs from those histories mentioned above that deal with the development of mathematical statistics. None of the essays contained in this collection deal with innovations of this sort. Rather, they deal with the place of statistics within political reasoning and the function of numbers in relation to considerations of public debate, authority, trust, and representation. Yet the volume also differs from those histories that deal with statistics in relation to state administration. Partly owing to the immense influence of Michel Foucault and the various models of power he outlined (especially his 'bio-political' and 'disciplinary' models), particular attention has been paid to how statistics facilitated the fabrication of society as an 'object of rule': how, that is, statistics classified, ordered, and standardized society according to a medley of norms and categories regarding health, wealth, class, and domesticity. It is a preoccupation which can be seen in the work of Ian Hacking, Mary Poovey, Patrick Joyce, and Nikolas Rose.[12] All are sophisticated Foucauldians, and they weave the insights of Foucault into those of science studies and discourse analysis. Yet the dominant concern remains with how numbers 'objectified' society, thereby furnishing the epistemological 'conditions of possibility' for the emergence of the modern state and bureaucratic power.

Dominant, however, but by no means total: Rose, for instance, also explores the role of numbers in relation to democratic reasoning. He notes how statistics provided nineteenth-century American citizens with a means of critiquing and assessing government, thus empowering society just as much as the state. He also notes the egalitarian thrust of numbers. The quantifiable nature of modern society, he suggests, also means that everyone within a given territory lives according to the same spatial dimensions, weights, and monetary values—in short, according to exactly the same standards and units of measurements: a mile of road, a kilogram of food, and the exchangeable worth of cash, for instance.[13]

More recent work shares a similar sensitivity to the complex dynamics of power inscribed in the use and dissemination of statistics and numerical information. Although concerned with the generation of government-sponsored inquiries in nineteenth-century Britain and the United States, Oz Frankel's *States of Inquiry* is at pains to stress their contested genesis and reception. In Britain, the inspectors who gathered information for the various royal commissions which emerged in the 1830s and 1840s often met with suspicion. Similarly, the findings of subsequent reports were often fiercely denounced in the press, as in the case of the 1833 Factory Commission report, which was lambasted by the Tory-radical agitator Richard Oastler, among others. In Frankel's reading, what he terms 'print-statism' was always provocative of debate, resistance and controversy. As he notes, 'The state could not exercise full mastery over the process of inquiry, the behaviour of its emissaries as investigators or authors, or the fate of its printed reports once they were issued and promiscuously circulated.'[14]

It is the aim of this volume to develop this emerging current of interest and to probe further the intersections and transformations of statistical reasoning and numerical information on the one hand, and public authority and political debate on the other. Intersections, transformations: the plural is entirely appropriate. As the volume demonstrates, numbers complicated and transformed political debate on a number of levels and in a variety of scenarios, and the same applies to considerations of public trust and authority. To give just one example, statistics always addressed a broad, mixed constituency. Much like today, skilled practitioners, politicians, and members of the public debated statistics, albeit with varying degrees of sophistication. Furthermore, not only were there various kinds of statistics to debate (financial, vital, criminal, etc.), emerging from various sources, state and non-state; the very use of statistics in relation to political matters was questioned. If it is possible to speak of a series of 'interfaces' between numbers, public administration, and political life, then they were—and still are—decidedly ragged and complex, characterized as much by contestation, doubt, and confusion as rational communication and disciplinary power.

In general, historians of political culture have shied away from engaging with the role of statistics in public life. In recent decades, owing to the 'linguistic turn', considerations of language and identity have tended to dominate discussion, though there is growing interest in the visual dimensions of political culture.[15] There has, however, been a longstanding interest in the question of the public sphere, especially among historians of the eighteenth century. The key text here is Jürgen Habermas's *The Structural Transformation of the Public Sphere*, first published in Germany in 1962 but translated into English only in 1989.[16] Habermas defined the public sphere as that 'realm of our social life in which something approaching public opinion can be formed', and he clearly distinguished it from the state. It was, he further clarified, 'a sphere which mediates between society and the state', forming a 'principle of public information which once had to be fought for against the arcane policies of monarchies and which since that time has made possible the democratic control of state activities.'[17]

Yet Habermas's account was also a critical one. The public sphere, he argued, first flourished in the eighteenth century in countries such as Britain and France, where new sites and media—notably the salon, the coffeehouse, and the popular press—opened up a space of political reflection outside of existing state structures and channels of communication. What was termed 'public opinion' was increasingly invoked by statesmen and politicians as a form of authority distinct from property, social status and familial ties. This early variant of the public sphere—the 'bourgeois public sphere'—represented, for Habermas, an effective, if by no means democratic, means of critical reflection on government and society. Yet, as it developed subsequently, this initial potential was lost. Over the course of the nineteenth and twentieth centuries the public sphere 'decayed', to quote Habermas, splintering into a series of sectional battles between interest groups.[18] At the same time, it was colonized by big business, mass political parties, culture industries ('mass entertainment'), and mechanisms of welfare, all of which positioned the public as a passive, rather than an active, social and political agent. Instead of engaging in rational-critical political debate, members of the public were forced to become consumers of 'manufactured' forms of opinion, culture, and publicity.

For two decades now historians have by turns rejected, affirmed, and complicated Habermas's thesis. It has been gendered, pluralized, and re-periodized.[19] British historians have pushed back the genesis of a functioning public sphere to the sixteenth century, whilst its eighteenth-century incarnation is now recognized to have been far more exclusionary than Habermas allowed.[20] Furthermore, rather than speak of one public sphere, historians are now more inclined to point to a series of competing public spheres distinguished by gender, political affiliation, and class. Similarly, historians have argued that even the bourgeois public sphere idealized by Habermas was not just about rational communication and discourse; it also involved a variety of performative and dramaturgical modes of address.[21] Like that regarding statistics and modern governance, the historiography of the modern public sphere is rich, expansive, and theoretically sophisticated.

In looking at statistics and numerical information, this volume does not seek to pit Foucault against Habermas—or vice versa. It does, however, make up for the neglect of numbers by historians of the public sphere. This partly reflects the chronological bias of the historiography, which has tended to focus on the seventeenth and eighteenth centuries, a time when numbers had yet to 'go public' in any significant or systematic way; but it also seems to reflect the fact that statistics are still associated with the state and not those forms of reasoning and discussion which are thought to lie beyond its bounds. It is certainly the case that Habermas viewed the application of numbers to the public sphere—as in something like opinion polling—as part of its degeneration during the twentieth century, but he did not take up the theme with any rigour.[22] Even so, in making up for this neglect, the volume does lend credence to recent historiography in the sense of highlighting the complex nature of the modern public sphere. One thing it demonstrates is that numbers have multiple functions, changing—and challenging—perceptions of the public sphere as a whole just as much as the forms of reasoning practiced within it.

If anything, the volume suggests the need to move beyond both Foucauldian and Habermasian perspectives. The overriding concern, however, is empirical rather than theoretical. As the final section of this introduction will set out, the essays contained in this collection represent a series of detailed case studies with respect to particular debates, institutional locales, and forms of statistical representation. Taken together, they point to an antagonistic field of governance composed of multiple forms of authority and representation. They also suggest that the development of a bureaucratic, numerate state and a critical public sphere need not be considered in isolation.

The one exception is the chapter by Theodore Porter, which follows this introduction. Here Porter engages with something of the 'bigger picture' by tracing the changing ambitions and organization of statistical science and its relationship to public life. Ranging over two centuries and a number of countries—Britain, France, Germany, and the United States—Porter notes how for much of the nineteenth century practitioners of statistics were very much embedded within the public sphere, self-consciously seeking to transform, and speak to, society at large. Only with the development of mathematical statistics around the turn of the twentieth century did statistical science begin to develop an ethos of detachment rather than engagement. As the essay makes clear, statistical science has transformed the very meaning of 'public reason', both its limits and its possibilities.

In terms of mapping some of the key developments and transformations which have occurred from roughly the middle of the eighteenth century up to the present, Porter's essay can be usefully read alongside this introduction. But before turning to these developments, it should be emphasized that this volume, like most edited collections, by no means exhausts its subject matter. As the concluding chapter will suggest, much work remains to be done on the history of statistics and the public sphere, and the chapters collected here serve to open, rather than resolve, a series of potentially fruitful lines of future inquiry.

THE MEANING OF 'STATISTICS'

One key development concerns the meaning of the term 'statistics'. Today the term connotes numbers and the mathematical manipulation of data. The *OED* defines it as 'the practice or science of collecting and analysing numerical data in large quantities'.[23] This understanding only became widespread during the twentieth century, however. Prior to the development of mathematical statistics during the fifty years between 1880 and 1930, the term referred to an ill-defined science of 'states' and 'conditions'. Statistics always promised clarity and precision; yet, as scholars such as Porter, Poovey, and Libby Schweber have shown, during the nineteenth century there was in fact much confusion regarding its status as a scientific discipline and its precise domain of application.[24]

'Statistics' derives from the German term 'statistik', first used in 1749 by the Göttingen professor Gottfried Achenwall.[25] Yet at this point it referred to the art of describing a given country or state. Historical and geographical facts might also be considered statistical in this sense. There was no necessary connection to numbers, which may have been used only to the extent that they helped to provide a fuller description. The anglicized form of the German term was introduced to Britain by the MP Sir John Sinclair in his twenty-one volume *Statistical Account of Scotland*, published between 1791 and 1799. Sinclair gave the term a new connotation: whereas German statistical inquiries, he suggested, were concerned with considerations of 'political strength' and 'matters of state', his inquiries were designed to ascertain the 'quantum of happiness' enjoyed by the inhabitants of a country and 'the means of its future improvement'.[26] It was with Sinclair's work in mind that the *Encyclopaedia Britannica* defined statistics in 1797 with no reference to numerical expertise or information. It was simply 'a word lately introduced to express a view or survey of any kingdom, country or parish'.[27]

Quite when the term became associated with the use and application of numbers is difficult to locate with precision. As Porter writes, the transition took place 'almost subconsciously, and with a minimum of debate.'[28] Nonetheless, the transition seems to have been complete by the late 1820s. In 1829, the doctor Bisset Hawkins defined 'medical statistics' as 'the application of numbers to illustrate the natural history of man in health and disease', and pointed to an analogous statistical field in political economy. In its opening *Prospectus* published in 1834, the Statistical Society of London declared that it would 'confine itself to facts—and, as far as may be possible, to facts which can be stated numerically and arranged in tables.'[29] Just a few years later, in 1838, the Society clarified the disciplinary demands of statistics as follows: 'it is simply required that all conclusions shall be drawn from well-attested data, and shall admit of mathematical demonstration.'[30]

Three points are worth emphasizing at this juncture. First, though the 'science' of statistics was now associated with the use of numbers, it was not exclusively so. Mathematically speaking, techniques were still rudimentary, certainly when compared to those pioneered in the twentieth century, and up until the 1880s it remained largely a descriptive science concerned with the collection and presentation of facts. Whilst these facts may have been numerical, they were often embedded in extensive narrative descriptions of the 'condition' of a particular parish or town, for example, or of the progress of a particular field of governance, such as education. Secondly, as Poovey in particular has demonstrated, there was great contention regarding the status of statistical facts and their relation to theory and *a priori* reasoning, especially during the 1830s. Whether statistics could really divorce itself from the world of politics and speculative opinion, as its practitioners claimed, was questioned in various quarters, including by members of the British Association for the Advancement of Science.[31]

Finally, as its practitioners affirmed time and again, though statistics entailed the use of numbers, it also concerned a particular object of study, namely society, and for much of the nineteenth century it considered itself solely a 'social science'. That there remained scepticism about its ability to dissociate itself from politics was partly because practitioners affirmed its utility to government. 'Man in society is the subject of our study', declared the *Fifteenth Annual Report* (1849) of the Statistical Society of London, adding: 'inductive reasoning from phenomena observable and observed with mathematical precision [is] our method'. It went on to note that whilst 'statesmanship and government are equally beyond our region', the Society would prove eminently 'useful in supplying evidence to aid the legislatorial labours' of parliament.[32] Similarly, in 1865, a paper which sought to clarify the meaning of the term 'statistics' argued that the foremost function of the Society was 'to collect and preserve facts illustrating the past and present condition and probable future prospects of States and their territorial divisions, and of the several classes of their inhabitants.'[33]

The enduring, if modified, meaning of the original German term is also apparent in the name given to statistical practitioners: 'statists'. It seems that the term 'statistician' was in use from the time of the mid-nineteenth century, but it would not be commonly employed until the turn of the twentieth. By this time, 'statistics' was coming to assume its current meaning, as practitioners began to assert their common use of 'the statistical method', as it was termed, and mathematical procedures of analysis and manipulation. Libby Schweber's *Disciplining Statistics* suggests that the turning point came in the 1880s, when statistical pioneers such as Francis Galton, Francis Edgeworth, and Alfred Marshall began presenting papers to the Statistical Society of London (known as the Royal Statistical Society from 1887).[34] Unlike their predecessors, they had no qualms about foregrounding the technical nature of their work, in particular the innovative use they were making of the mathematical calculus of probability.

Over the course of the twentieth century, mathematical statistics was fully institutionalized as a scientific discipline with a particular repertoire of numerical techniques and methods. It lost its connection with any particular object of study and was gradually applied to all manner of phenomena, from fluctuations in the price of gold and the behaviour of gases, to the measurement of intelligence (intelligence quotient testing) and the variable form of football teams. During the interwar period, books began to appear offering 'introductions' to the use of applied mathematical techniques, most notably R.A. Fisher's *Statistical Methods for Research Workers*. First published in 1925, it was in its seventh edition by 1939 and its fourteenth by 1970.[35] Similar books continue to appear today, all of them incorporating the key innovations made during the late nineteenth and early twentieth centuries: among others, regression and correlation analysis, random sampling, and 'goodness-of-fit' testing. The figure of the statistician was also given a further institutional home. In 1948, the Institute of Statisticians was founded and within two years it had established its own journal, *The Incorporated Statistician*. In 1993, the Institute merged with the Royal Statistical Society, now the principal professional association within Britain.[36]

THE GROWTH OF STATISTICS AND THE PUBLIC SPHERE

Evidently statistics was—and remains—a dynamic field of study, and its meaning and scope should not be taken for granted. The same applies to the public sphere, as the scholarship noted in the second section suggests. The genesis of both can be traced back to the seventeenth century—and perhaps before in the case of the public sphere—yet it was not until the Victorian period that numbers began to circulate in the public domain on a properly systematic basis. There are, however, some crucial intermediate developments which might be noted. One of these regards the development of 'political arithmetic', a discipline often thought of as the forerunner of modern statistics. The term was coined by one of its first practitioners, William Petty, during the late seventeenth century, and was linked to a broadly mercantilist conception of statecraft.[37] One key variable was the size of the population, which was thought to bear a direct relation to the strength of the state. More people entailed higher tax revenues and a higher number of men able to bear arms in the event of war. Some of the first works on 'rates of mortality' were carried out with this premise in mind, including works by Gregory King and Edmund Halley.[38]

Yet throughout the eighteenth century accurate numbers regarding the size of the population were hard to come by, and political arithmetic failed to evolve into a state-sponsored enterprise. As late as 1800 'estimates' of the population of Great Britain and Ireland were still being published.[39] Even so, it is during this period that we can locate some of the first incursions of numbers into the public sphere. On the one hand, attempts to place political arithmetic on a systematic footing were resisted. During the 1750s two census bills were introduced to the House of Commons. Both would have provided for the collection of information on births, deaths, and marriages, as well as the number of people receiving poor relief. The measures were discussed extensively in the press and in parliament, but both were defeated, partly on the grounds that they represented a threat to 'English liberties'.[40] On the other hand—and precisely because of the absence of any official statistics—debate flourished regarding the exact number of people inhabiting the British Isles. During the 1770s and 1780s in particular, numerous pamphlets were produced on the subject, each seeking to correct and contest the claims of those that had gone before. One of them, published in 1781, was tellingly entitled *Uncertainty of the Present Population of this Kingdom*.[41] Only after 1801, with the execution of the first state-sponsored census, was the matter finally laid to rest.

Political arithmetic was eclipsed by the discipline of statistics around the turn of the nineteenth century. The term 'political arithmetic' was seldom used thereafter, and it was during the 1820s and 1830s that statistics began to pour forth on a range of topics. These years witnessed what Ian Hacking has dubbed 'an avalanche of printed numbers', and they mark a threshold with respect to the breadth of issues deemed suitable for enumeration.[42] Population remained a crucial preoccupation, but statistics were also collected with respect to the full gamut of modern administrative domains: judicial, military, economic, educational, medical, and so on. Arguably, the key innovation was the establishment of specialized statistical offices. The GRO is perhaps the best known of these, but others might be mentioned. In 1832, the Board of Trade set up what it termed a 'statistical department'. By the 1860s it was collecting detailed economic data relating to industrial and agricultural wage rates, and publishing monthly accounts of domestic and foreign trade. As this latter activity suggests, there was not only a step-change in the range of subjects dealt with; there was also a step-change in the regularity with which numbers were collected and disseminated. Annual statistical statements were common in a variety of fields: in 1839, for instance, the GRO began publishing annual reports. Yet yearly statements were often abstracts of data that had been collected on a quarterly, monthly, and even weekly basis. Doubtless the reform of the penny post system in 1840, together with the development of the railways, helped to enhance the flow of information from local peripheries to administrative centres.

As has been noted above, for much of the nineteenth century statistics was defined by a specific commitment to investigating social (as opposed to natural) phenomena. Whether explicitly or implicitly articulated, the underlying premise was that society was a complex entity, composed of multiple laws and logics. As the likes of Porter and Hacking have argued, if political arithmetic was underpinned by a broadly mercantilist conception of statecraft, then nineteenth-century statistics was underpinned by a broadly liberal one.[43] It took for granted the idea that society possessed a degree of autonomy—or at least a certain kind of density—which meant that the state had to proceed cautiously, in due deference to its intricate workings and self-propelling, self-governing dynamism. In this way, the increased flow of statistical data at once reflected and encouraged the evolution of an increasingly complex, but also self-reflexive, society. Whether numbers were used to argue for or against state intervention, they were now instruments of critique and the recurrent, ongoing questioning of government.

One source of social dynamism was thought to lie in what was referred to as the 'public mind' or 'public opinion'. In terms of the development of a recognizably modern public sphere, the key medium was the newspaper. The British newspaper press underwent considerable expansion over the course of the eighteenth century, and it continued to expand during the nineteenth. Then, as now, London was the centre of the newspaper trade, and in 1750 there were eighteen newspapers circulating in the capital, including six dailies. By the mid-Victorian period, there were ten dailies, the most popular of which was *The Times*, established in 1785. Overall, it has been estimated that between the early eighteenth and mid-nineteenth centuries the number of newspapers in circulation increased twenty-fold.[44] But further growth was still to come. Following the repeal of various newspaper taxes between the 1830s and mid-1850s, self-consciously popular titles in particular prospered. In the 1880s, *The Star* quickly established a circulation of 200,000, and in 1911 the *Daily Mirror* became the first paper to reach a circulation of one million.[45]

The newspaper was undoubtedly the most important vehicle of public expression during the late Georgian and Victorian periods; but other media enjoyed considerable growth during this time as well, including pamphlets, periodicals, and novels, making for a print-dominated public sphere. Crucially, this was paralleled by the emergence of new conceptions of political authority. References to 'public opinion' had been made as early as the 1730s, but it was not until the 1780s that it was invoked with any regularity.[46] Following Habermas, it is certainly true that public opinion came to form a new source of political authority, though there was never any consensus over its precise role or usefulness.[47] Both the press and the public opinion it was thought to articulate were regarded with suspicion, especially among the political elite. Notwithstanding these complexities, two general points might be made. First, by the Victorian period, the press was widely recognized as a significant source of popular accountability. As the former factory owner W.R. Greg wrote in 1844: '[P]erhaps one of the most necessary and practically important functions of the Daily Press is the opening it affords for the exposition of individual grievances and wrongs. It is a surer guarantee against injustice and oppression than any institutions or any forms of government could be.'[48] Secondly, the authority of public opinion altered the practice of political leadership. The art of statesmanship, for instance, was increasingly conceived as one of careful accommodation and balance. The successful statesman, so the likes of William Gladstone and

Walter Bagehot claimed, was about leading public opinion, while also taking care not to override its ruder, more conservative instincts.[49]

Other changes might be noted, including changes in how the relation of the press and the public was conceived. As Mark Hampton has argued, during the mid-Victorian period, the press was conceived as an instrument of popular enlightenment. It aspired to what he terms an 'educational ideal'. By the late Victorian and Edwardian periods, however, this had been displaced, if not entirely, by a 'representative ideal', based on the assumption that it was the role of the press to appeal to, rather than improve, public opinion. This was partly driven, Hampton argues, by an ascendant ethos of cutthroat commercialism, but it also reflected an increasingly pessimistic outlook regarding the possibilities of rational communication.[50] The complexion of the press, then, changed towards the end of the century, assuming a more populist, tabloid form. Yet of more importance, certainly in terms of thinking about very general developments, was that which remained in place, namely the temporal intensity with which news was gathered and disseminated. The 'dailiness' of modern news has been traced back to the seventeenth century, but it became an entrenched, taken-for-granted aspect of political life only in the late eighteenth and early nineteenth centuries.[51] In short, just as the flow of statistics gradually intensified after roughly 1800, so too did the flow of news items. Numbers, facts, the news: all were now subject to systematic collection, circulation, and consumption.

Yet these flows were not only confined to the nation-state; increasingly they crossed borders. The British press had been relaying news of global events since the time of the eighteenth century, if not before. Its global reach, however, was placed on a new technological footing during the nineteenth century with the development of electrical telegraphy. International news agencies such as Reuters, established in Britain in 1851, quickly seized on the possibilities opened up by the telegraph, and by the end of the century events abroad could be relayed within hours, not days or weeks.[52] It is also possible to point to an internationalization of statistical knowledge from the middle of the century. The pivotal figure was the Belgian statistician Adolphe Quetelet. In the 1830s Quetelet had been instrumental in setting up the Statistical Society of London; later he helped with the design of the British census of 1841, the first to be conducted by the GRO. Quetelet was always eager to promote the transnational exchange of statistical innovations, and his efforts in this respect came to fruition in 1853, with the staging of the first International Congress of Statistics in Brussels. It met nine times before its dissolution in 1878. By bringing together the heads of statistical bureaus from across Europe, the congress aimed to standardize administrative procedures and produce internationally comparable data.[53] It was succeeded in 1885 by the International Institute of Statistics, a professional body which continues to meet today.

NUMBERING MASS DEMOCRACY AND THE WELFARE STATE

During the twentieth century, with the development of the welfare state and the advent of mass democracy, the interrelations of numbers and the British people became still more complex and intense. The state's new and more interventionist social programmes depended ever more heavily on the collection of data on each individual citizen. The National Insurance legislation of 1911 created a number, as well as a numbered card, for each skilled worker.[54] The modern idea of 'unemployment' as a single figure recording those seeking work and for whom work might or ought to be found—the very basis of the Keynesian management of the economy in the middle years of the twentieth century—can be traced to this new system.[55] The flow of National Insurance numbers into the Ministry of Labour became, as Sarah Igo has argued, 'a powerful, if covert, kind of nation-building', one of those means by which 'it has now become nearly impossible to know the modern public *apart* from opinion polls, surveys, and social statistics'.[56]

This numerical outlook also found its expression in 'ground level' sociological and market research. Social scientists and economists such as Arthur Bowley pioneered the use of standardized questions and random sampling, as exemplified by Bowley's pre–First World War studies of Reading.[57] These techniques were further popularized between the wars, when they were adopted by British businesses as part of their marketing campaigns. The American advertising agency J. Walter Thompson was one pioneer in the 1920s.[58] Mark Abrams, later to become the Labour party's private pollster and an influential political thinker in his own right, founded a rival research department for the London Press Exchange in 1934.[59]

The British government was not averse to drawing on the efforts of private organizations, and it made great use of the evidence provided by the Mass Observation group (M-O) during the Second World War. From its founding in 1937, M-O made great play of its public reach. The cover of its best-selling survey *Britain*, published in 1939, claimed that 'some two thousand' people had sat on its national panel (though the actual number was probably closer to 400).[60] The information gathered by this unofficial social movement—for this was how its founders, Tom Harrisson, Charles Madge, and Humphrey Jennings, imagined it—was much used by the Ministry of Information (until 1941), as well as a number of other government departments. The effects of bombing, the 'fairness' or otherwise of rationing, and the way demobilization should work were among the many topics on which the group reported.[61] The long-term effect of these surveys was profound. The need to find out about civilian morale, and to test and understand the effect of government policies, led to the creation of the government's own Wartime Social Survey in 1940.[62] This constitutes a crucial development in twentieth-century governance, for the peacetime Social Survey later became one of the key ways in which successive governments found out about the preferences of 'the people'. Public views of immigration; playgrounds for children; labour mobility; National Service; youth unemployment, training, and 'delinquency': these were just some of the topics that the Social Survey investigated during the 'golden age' of Keynesian economic management in the 1950s and 1960s.[63]

During the middle decades of the century, statistics was also pressed into use as a tool for the new anthropological studies of the British electorate. Here, as elsewhere, innovations made in the United States provided a consistent point of reference and emulation. If the international exchange of statistics and surveying techniques dates back to the nineteenth century, then this intensified considerably during the twentieth, and now encompassed the United States as a respected home of pioneering research. Robert and Helen Lynds's in-depth, 'dynamic' and 'functional' studies of Muncie, Indiana—'Middletown', as they termed it—proved enormously influential.[64] American sociologists such as Lloyd Warner and Conrad Arensberg further showed Europeans what could be done using similar techniques in their County Clare studies of the 1930s.[65]

The work of Paul Lazarsfeld, founder of Columbia University's Bureau for Applied Social Research, was also influential in transmitting American social science to a British audience.[66] His research on 'how the voter makes up his mind' followed the same sample of voters from Erie, New York, during an entire election period.[67] British studies of individual seats published during the 1950s usually cited his influence.[68] Even the work conducted by Michael Young, Peter Wilmott, and Peter Townshend for the Institute of Community Studies (ICS)—such as Young and Wilmott's 1957 *Family and Kinship in East London*—bore a North American imprint.[69] Though usually thought of as peculiarly 'British' in its incorporation of both narrative experience and anthropology, and in its exploration of the abiding importance of class, Young drew extensively on work from the 'Chicago School' of Robert Park and Ernest Burgess.[70] Although both they and their ICS counterparts on the other side of the Atlantic were objects of suspicion among some British theorists, the American influence was unmistakable.[71]

With respect to party politics, however, the development of opinion polling proved much more decisive than the growth of small-scale sociological studies. Indeed, in terms of the relations between political elites and parties on the one hand, and the public and the press on the other, the rise of opinion polling arguably constitutes the central development of the twentieth century. It first began in Britain in 1937, when the American pollster George Gallup conducted surveys under the auspices of the British Institute of Public Opinion. Gallup's polling allowed the Liberal *News Chronicle* to be one of the few newspapers to foresee accurately Labour's 1945 landslide.[72] Thereafter 'the polls' became steadily more important. Oxford's Nuffield College mounted a study of each general election after the Second World War: its first study, which dealt with the 1945 contest, barely mentioned earlier Gallup polls for Westminster elections, but by 1970 an entire twenty-seven-page chapter was devoted to the subject.[73]

The Conservatives were the first political party to make extensive use of the new techniques, conducting private research into 'floating voters' in fifty-two constituencies during 1949, before following that up with research on voting by gender, class, trade union membership, and regional loyalties, during the 1951–55 Parliament.[74] In the years after 1960, when the death of Aneurin Bevan removed from Labour's ranks one of the foremost opponents of opinion polls, the party gradually became accustomed to thinking in terms of polling data.[75] After his death, Labour commissioned work by Abrams on 'target voters' in marginal constituencies, as well as research into the effects of different advertising strategies. Most of Labour's leading politicians continued to ponder publicly available national data rather than their own officials' research; and under Wilson's leadership in the late 1960s opinion polling was subordinated to his own instincts and political gambles.[76] But by the early 1970s it was clear opinion polls were going to be a constant on the British political scene, for both the Left and the Right.

The 'American' nature of opinion polling was sometimes denounced as 'alien' and antithetical to British public life; yet American practices continued to inform British innovations during the postwar years. Donald Stokes, one of the Nuffield researchers, had previously worked on a large-scale University of Michigan study of the 1952 and 1956 presidential elections. The American sociologist Seymour Lipset's 'pluralist' analysis, which posited that electoral competition was one means by which social competition could be expressed, was also influential in the UK, where post–Second World War voting was dominated by class.[77] Labour's Right, in particular, seized on polls as evidence that Labour must head in a more centrist direction. Abrams himself used interviews with 724 voters to show how out of date the party now looked in a survey for *Socialist Commentary* in 1960.[78] Leading revisionists, such as Tony Crosland, became engrossed in polling evidence, obsessively tracking the polls whenever governments made major or controversial decisions.[79]

The consequences of this new fascination with opinion polling were manifold, but foremost among them was the way governments could be painted as 'successful' or 'failing' on an almost day-by-day basis. Some political scientists, such as Richard Hodder-Williams, defended a 'Burkean' analysis of the constitution, in which the views of the *informed* public should be weighed more heavily than those of 'general opinion'.[80] But critics were in a minority. Increasingly, polls began to frame the very nature of electoral competition: they were now part of the political equation, not just a means of reflecting on it. The Orpington by-election of 1962, famously won by the Liberals in a previously safe Conservative seat, was one of the first examples of effective 'tactical voting'. Polls revealed that the Conservative candidate might be beaten if enough Labour voters switched to the Liberals, which they duly did.[81]

The hold of statistical information of all sorts on politics and public life was by now total. During the 1970s and 1980s, it became commonplace among academics, journalists, and the Westminster elite to assert a new theory of electoral success, namely that politics could be reduced to a series of quantifiable economic measurements. It was thought that falls in unemployment and the rate of inflation, for instance, would almost guarantee the re-election of a sitting government.[82] The theory was dealt a blow with the failure of John Major's administration to gain re-election in 1997, when the economy was growing strongly.[83] Yet the success of Tony Blair's Labour party in the 2001 and 2005 general elections, when Britain was enjoying a period of unprecedented economic growth, suggests that the 'feelgood factor' is still an important, if not a decisive, determinant of election outcomes. Either way, facts and figures relating to Britain's 'economic performance' remain a central referent in party political debate and public discourse.

During the 1980s, polling also became central to the formation of party policies, and not just to their assessment when put into practice. The Thatcher manifestoes of 1983 and 1987 were framed only after intense focus group questioning and market research.[84] By the 1990s, with the advent of New Labour, the two techniques—opinion polling and market surveying—had fused into a single and near-hegemonic 'science' of the electorate. Traditional mechanisms of policy formation within the Labour party, such as Party Conference and the National Executive Committee, were marginalized.[85] In their place, inner cliques of 'reformers' and 'modernizers' used focus-group evidence drawn from 'average' voters to dictate what party policy should become.[86] In turn, the evidence gathered and the techniques used fed back into government practice. Introduced in 2007, Citizens' Juries, for instance, were one means by which New Labour hoped to 're-connect' with a public it had been 'listening to' since the early 1990s. Public hearings, local consumer 'panels', and 'community forums' were other mechanisms that bore the unmistakable hallmark of the focus group.[87] So pervasive was this discourse that these ideas became one of the key points around which critics of the Blair and Brown 'project' rallied.[88] For some, government by the polls had reached its *reductio ad absurdum*.

NUMERICAL REASONING AND THE PUBLIC SPHERE

What kinds of reasoning did the relentless circulation of numbers rely on and make possible? A final set of developments relates to the various ways numbers were presented to the public, and how they manifested and made possible new modes of knowing. Of course, words, not numbers, dominated the public sphere between the eighteenth and twentieth centuries. Yet words and numbers were often used in conjunction, much as they are today. On a very basic level, numbers were used to convey a sense of quantitative proportion and change. No doubt examples of this might be found in the seventeenth and eighteenth centuries, but it seems to have become a common feature of the public sphere only during the nineteenth. When, for instance, politicians spoke of the need for sanitary reform during the 1840s and 1850s, they always quoted the rates of mortality (as supplied by the GRO) which afflicted a given town or city, and whether they were getting better or worse.[89]

However, numbers and words combined in more complex ways. Drawing on John Pickstone's *Ways of Knowing*, his revisionist survey of the history of science, technology and medicine, two modes of reasoning might be distinguished. One is classificatory and represents a statistical variant of the natural-historical knowledge pioneered during the Enlightenment. For Pickstone, this was defined by a quest for comprehensive representation and semiotic order; Linnaean taxonomy is one example.[90] Of course, to count necessarily depends upon classificatory procedures; there must be some kind of consensus regarding who or what will be counted and how they will be labelled. Yet, in the case of collecting numbers, the active pursuit of taxonomic order and uniformity has not always been apparent. It was not a distinguishing feature of political arithmetic; only in the nineteenth century, it seems, were concerted efforts made to order the relations of words and numbers, though it would prove to be an ongoing project. In the 1830s, the Home Office standardized the collection and dissemination of criminal statistics according to six categories: offences against the person; offences against property with violence; offences against property without violence; malicious offences against property; offences against the currency; and miscellaneous offences.[91] It was the first of many efforts to place the categorization of crime on a comprehensive footing. Similarly, throughout the nineteenth century the Board of Trade attempted to discipline the categories with which it collected and displayed economic statistics.

The most thorough work of this sort, however, was undertaken by William Farr, statistical superintendent of the GRO. On assuming his position, one of the first tasks he set himself was to organize a uniform nomenclature with which to register causes of death. As he suggested in the GRO's *First Annual Report* published in 1839:

> The advantages of a uniform statistical nomenclature, however imperfect, are so obvious that it is surprising no attention has been paid to its enforcement in Bills of Mortality. Each disease has in many instances been denoted by three or four terms, and each term has been applied to as many different diseases ... The nomenclature is of as much importance in this department of inquiry, as weights and measures in the physical sciences, and should be settled without delay.[92]

Though he was aware it might have been organized differently—and in fact it was subject to reform over the course of the nineteenth century—in the end he opted for a standardized nomenclature comprised of three main divisions: the first contained various epidemic, endemic and contagious diseases (cholera and typhus, for instance); the second contained what he termed 'sporadic diseases' arranged under eight organ systems. The third division was for deaths by violence.

In this way, from the nineteenth century onwards, statistics was inextricably linked to classificatory reasoning and the ceaseless generation of new taxonomies and descriptive categories. This co-existed alongside a second mode of reasoning, what Pickstone terms 'analytical' reasoning. Analytical reasoning turns upon 'decomposing' objects into their constituent elements, which can then be measured and weighed, compared and contrasted. For Pickstone, the exemplar of this particular way of knowing is Antoine Lavoisier's pioneering work in chemistry, which he carried out in the late eighteenth century. Lavoisier's concern was to understand the relations of different chemical elements and how they combined and interacted with one another according to particular variables (heat, for instance).[93]

The use of statistics enabled society to be decomposed in an analogous fashion. First undertaken during the 1830s, statistical investigations of British cities sought to enumerate a series of social elements: marriage, crime, drunkenness, poverty and literacy, among others. The relative frequency or intensity of these elements could then be compared and contrasted according to time (years, months) and space (districts, parishes, streets). In 1847, a paper delivered to the Statistical Society of London stated that the purpose of statistical inquiry was to undertake precisely this sort of analysis. It conceded, quite explicitly, that the statistician, unlike the chemist, was unable to conduct controlled experiments in a laboratory. Yet a kindred mode of reasoning was at stake:

> Analysis, in the sense of the chemist, is absolutely impossible; but by the exhaustive enumeration of facts which are strongly indicative of many others, or are their invariable concomitants, we get a means of detecting the excess or deficiency of certain social elements [crime and education, for instance], in definite classes and localities; and by multiplying these lines of observation, and the combinations in which they are arranged for purposes of comparison, we gradually arrive at higher and safer inductions.

What it referred to as the 'analytical method' was a means whereby the statistician could 'bring several elements into every combination, and detect laws of their coincidence and relationship'.[94]

These days we perhaps take for granted these two modes of reasoning, such is their ubiquity. The media regularly reports on whether crime rates have diminished or increased over time, and in what towns and cities they remain particularly problematic. Unemployment rates, among others, are reported in a similar fashion. Speculation often follows as to their causes, their probable future effects, and their relation to other variables. High unemployment is thought to accompany poor health, for example. This kind of analysis is now part and parcel of the public sphere we inhabit. Similarly, as recent work has argued, we live according to such a dizzying array of classificatory schemas that they have come to seem entirely natural. They are part of the 'infrastructure of everyday life'.[95] We are classified and counted in our status as consumers, patients, voters, homeowners, graduates, workers, taxpayers and parents; and when we die we do so according to the International Statistical Classification of Diseases and Related Health Problems, otherwise known by the abbreviation 'ICD'. Yet these two modes of reasoning—the classificatory and the analytical—are historically specific and date back to the time of the Enlightenment.

The majority of the public is no doubt unaware of the complex decisions which go into the making of classificatory schemes. It is also unaware of—or simply unable to comprehend—the complex mathematical techniques which make possible the many statistical facts which inhabit today's public sphere. Indeed, the complex workings of mathematical statistics—what, in Pickstone's typology, would constitute an 'experimental' form of knowledge—are seldom made available for popular consumption.[96] Even so, rudimentary statistical analysis is presented to the public on a regular basis: figures are compared and contrasted over time and space; problems are measured and isolated. Equally, schemes of statistical classification and their related categories form part of the language of public life. In short, the circulation of numbers means that the public invariably engages in analytical and classificatory modes of reasoning, however basic they may be.

Yet numbers are presented in a variety of forms. They may be quoted in the course of a speech or a newspaper article, for instance. They are also presented in the form of tables. Tables, of course, have been used for various purposes for thousands of years: tabular formatting, as a basic mode of presenting information, has been traced back to 2500 BC.[97] Here especially it is difficult to point to one origin or principal development. According to Judy Klein, however, the seventeenth-century political arithmetic of John Graunt marks something of a modern departure. For Klein, Graunt's work represents an early instance of what is now known as 'time-series analysis', where statistical inferences are derived on the basis of the temporal—and tabular—ordering of uniform data sets.[98] In his 1662 work, *Observations Made upon Bills of Mortality*, Graunt presented various tables detailing, among other things, the number of burials and christenings in metropolitan parishes according to their year of occurrence. Years were listed in a column on the left-hand side, the corresponding figures in a series of columns to the right. Significantly, as Klein stresses, Graunt was a cloth merchant and he used a key, if rudimentary, method of mercantile arithmetic—the 'Rule of Three'—to deduce from his tables such things as population growth and the relative mortality of plagues.

The key innovations in time-series analysis were made during the nineteenth century and were fostered as part of the development of mathematical statistics. Basic tools such as index numbers and moving averages date from this time.[99] By this point tables of numbers were being produced with respect to all manner of phenomena: economic, sanitary, legal, and so on. Hacking's 'avalanche of printed numbers', which began to fall during the 1820s and 1830s, was in part an avalanche of tabulated numbers. Some presented uniform data over a series of years; others presented different sets of figures for the same year. Most featured in either government documents produced by statistical offices or in the publications of professional societies, such as the Institute of Actuaries established in 1848. Quite how many statistical tables, and of what sort, featured in more popular publications has yet to be investigated in depth, though it is clear they were by no means entirely absent. The myriad publications of the Society for the Diffusion of Useful Knowledge, established in 1826, contained tables of numerical data; friendly society magazines published the 'life tables' they used for the purposes of determining subscription rates; while almanacs presented tables of meteorological information. In terms of the economy, the weekly journal *The Economist* seems to have been the key popular organ of tabular data. From its establishment in 1843, it routinely published tables concerning the volume of imports and exports, the prices of commodities and securities, and government revenues and bank returns.[100]

Tables of various sorts would continue to proliferate during the twentieth century and they remain ubiquitous today. The computer 'spreadsheet', first mass-marketed during the 1980s, is one of the more recent developments. As has been noted, tables have a very long history indeed, but the same cannot be said of the other principal means via which statistical data are presented to the public: the graph. Graphs, like tables, correlate two variables, but graphs have a stronger visual dimension to the extent that they 'diagram' the relation, often using a line drawn between points. The father of the modern graph is generally held to be the draftsman and engineer William Playfair. In 1786, he published *The Commercial and Political Atlas*, containing forty-four hand-coloured graphs. Forty-three were line graphs of the same generic design: the horizontal axis represented time, the vertical axis various aspects of the British economy, such as the volume of foreign trade or the national debt. The sole exception was a bar graph of Scotland's imports and exports during the year 1781. Later, in his 1801 work, *The Statistical Breviary*, he presented the first pie chart and circle graph.[101]

Graphs of all kinds were readily developed over the course of the nineteenth century and featured in a range of disciplines. By the middle of the century their use had become widespread in the natural sciences. The astronomer John Herschel, the physicist J.D. Forbes and the polymath scientist William Whewell were all advocates of graphical forms of representation. Beyond the natural sciences, William Farr and Florence Nightingale pioneered the use of graphs with respect to sanitary matters.[102] There was more resistance in the domain of economics, but by the 1880s graphs had become an accepted tool of analysis, largely thanks to the efforts of William

Stanley Jevons.[103] There is also evidence that efforts were made to promote their understanding among the public: during the Edwardian period, for instance, books were published entitled *Elementary Graphs* and *Graphs for Beginners*.[104] As yet, however, the public consumption and production of graphs remains a neglected subject of research, and still awaits a full-length book study.

ORGANIZATION OF THE BOOK

The above is just a sketch and is intended to provide a broad narrative framework in which to situate the chapters that follow. The complexities which have been overlooked will become immediately apparent. It should also be noted that the volume adopts a broad understanding of statistics, embracing a range of representational forms, as well as rudimentary types of numerical information, which, as Porter notes in his chapter, can be consumed without recourse to sophisticated analysis. Finally, the editors have opted for a thematic, rather than a chronological, organization, in order to focus attention on the research questions mentioned in the opening section of this introduction.

The volume is thus organized into four parts. The chapters presented in the first part, entitled Governing Numbers, explore the role of what we might call bureaucracies in generating and disseminating numbers about and for the public. It is this part which comes closest to the state-oriented historiography noted above. However, in their own ways, each chapter seeks to evoke the complexity which characterizes the circulation and generation of governmental numbers. Like other chapters, they point to the need to develop a more dynamic, interactive appreciation of the relations between numerical centres and peripheries, and between politicians, administrators, and members of the public.

It opens with an essay by Steven King, which looks at the growing utilization of financial information and accounting practices under the Old Poor Law. The period in question—roughly 1790 to 1840—is often associated with developing discontent regarding the economic expense of the poor law, partly as a result of its 'statisticalization' as a national numerical entity. Yet, as King suggests, there are good reasons to question any linear, causal link between the demise of the Old Poor Law, the 'objectification' of paupers, and the rise of financial transparency and bookkeeping. In fact, the circulation of numbers may have enhanced, rather than diminished, the administrative robustness of the Old Poor Law, making it less, not more, susceptible to reform and public critique. Equally, paupers maintained agency. Like their social superiors, who administered the poor law, they were not averse to mobilizing basic numerical information and a language of financial probity, albeit in their case to make claims on the system.

The following chapter by Edward Higgs examines the statistical output of the GRO in light of the competing communicational theories of Habermas and Niklas Luhmann. In line with Porter's account, Higgs suggests that around the turn of the twentieth century the GRO abandoned its initial aim of seeking to empower the public sphere, and more particularly ratepayers, with information relating to the sanitary effectiveness of local authorities. However, Higgs argues that there was always a tension between providing statistical information to the public, on the one hand, and the need to manage informational complexity on the other. If the former fulfilled (at least in part) Habermas's ideal of a rational public sphere, then the latter imposed restrictions on what the public might know, bearing out Luhmann's claim that knowledge of the social world must always be partial if it is to be provided at all. Yet, as Higgs suggests, it was not only practical constraints which restricted the available flow of knowledge; so too did ideological assumptions about the nature of society.

The struggles and complexities of building statistical pictures of the world beyond government are also apparent in Glen O'Hara's chapter, which looks at the various attempts made during the 1950s and 1960s to capture the economic reality of Britain's industrial training capacities and regional growth patterns. Elsewhere, the United States provided investigative models for emulation (not least in the field of consumer research, as explored in Schwarzkopf's chapter); but here, in another instance of the transnational dimensions of modern statistics, it was France. Even so, the process of reforming the statistical bases of economic planning proved messy and contentious. Did a clear statistical picture of the public emerge? O'Hara sounds a sceptical note, emphasizing policymakers' struggles to secure the cooperation of various groups and individuals, both at the centre and at the peripheries. Here certainly the statistical eyes of the state were always blinkered and obscured, as it ventured into a public world of vested interests and partisan perspectives.

The part of the book which follows, entitled Picturing the Public, seeks to recover the multiple forms through which the public was imagined and depicted using statistics and statistically based forms of representation, including graphs and consumer surveys. The need to recognize a plurality of statistical users is once again very much in evidence, rendering problematic any neat distinction between state and society. Yet what is most striking is the plurality of ways in which the public was pictured as a national statistical entity. In fact, it was depicted via a medley of representational forms and each form, furthermore, was open to multiple uses, depending on one's political affiliation and social sympathies. The 'public' of the public sphere was thus always in movement, as it found form in the shifting, and often contested, claims of various representational technologies.

The opening chapter by Maeve Adams examines the epistemological affinities of nineteenth-century statistics and social realist novels, or more simply numbers and narratives. To be sure, there was a definite tension between the two, one which was recognized and explored at the time, including by Charles Dickens, as the chapter demonstrates. Yet, as Adams argues, both statistical and narrative accounts imagined the public as an aggregate 'whole' comprised of distinct 'parts', thus evincing a common commitment to what she terms 'aggregation'. The chapter, then, explores the tensions but also the affinities between genres often considered separately. In the process, it blurs any neat, disciplinary division between the two, bringing into relief a theme already registered in Porter's chapter: namely, the descriptive nature of nineteenth-century statistical 'science' compared to its later, more mathematical and experimental variants.

However, the public also found representational form in numbers-as-pictures, or rather as graphs, tables, and 'pictograms', among other possibilities. This is the subject of James Thompson's chapter, which seeks to recover something of the rich and varied visual culture of numbers in late Victorian and Edwardian Britain. As well as considering the neglected topic of public numeracy, Thompson brings together the history of numerical-graphical forms of representation and the history of popular politics, shedding some much needed light on how the former informed the latter (something also explored in Edmund Rogers's chapter). Evidently, as the chapter makes clear, the Liberal and Tory parties were not averse to drawing on pictorial forms of numerical representation to help simplify and dramatize what in reality were decidedly complex issues. Similarly, the very realm of partisan struggle was now mapped, quite literally, in terms of the numerical distribution and turnover of seats. As Thompson concludes, numbers and images of numbers were firmly enmeshed in the fractious world of late Victorian and Edwardian party politics.

Thompson's chapter is a useful reminder that numbers, as a 'language', are capable of being 'translated' into various forms and genres. But these forms and genres are also capable of embodying more than one vision of the public, as Stefan Schwarzkopf demonstrates in his exploration of consumer surveying in interwar and postwar Britain. Although pioneered in the United States, by the interwar period consumer research had become an established part of British culture and corporate enterprise. Yet, as Schwarzkopf demonstrates, advertisers and market researchers found various, and often conflicting, uses for consumer surveys and statistics. This is an argument he develops by examining the research activities of two key agencies: the American-owned J. Walter Thompson agency and the British-owned London Press Exchange. There was no one political logic underpinning the 'statisticalization' of the consumer during the 1920s through to the 1960s. On the contrary, as the case of the London Press Exchange, and especially the work of Mark Abrams, demonstrates it could also serve more 'progressive' agendas.

The next part of the volume, entitled Numbers and Public Trust, comprises two chapters, the first by Tom Crook and the second by James Taylor. Was there ever a time when statistics were trusted? Both chapters help to recover something of the history of what is now a matter of ongoing public comment: the disputation and even confusion surrounding the reception of statistics and numerical forms of information. There is no question that the circulation of statistics and numbers has reconfigured understandings of what constitutes public authority: as Porter notes in his chapter, statistics have helped to establish the technical authority of experts. Yet, as these two chapters attest, the authority of numbers cannot be readily disentangled from other forms of authority, not least that associated with the 'character' of those who provide them. Numbers may enhance public authority, but they can also detract from it, prompting suspicion and critical questioning, just as much as trust and confidence.

Crook's chapter focuses on Victorian England and begins by surveying the persistence and reworking of traditional forms of trust, in particular the trust invested in the figure of the gentleman. As Crook acknowledges, gentlemen were not averse to drawing on numbers to bolster the authority of their social status. However, the use of numbers often sat uneasily with the disinterest associated with their background, making for a hybrid— and highly unstable—form of authority. Indeed, both the morality and the political neutrality of those who used them were called into question. Yet, as Crook suggests, numbers could be put to multiple uses, including as instruments of state critique, thus working with, rather than against, the new premium placed on public accountability. Thus, even if trusted as such, numbers might be wielded as instruments of governmental distrust. In short, Crook argues against linear readings of the history of trust, numbers and public authority, offering instead a richer, more complex story in which numbers functioned as technologies of both trust and distrust, while also intersecting with established forms of authority.

Kindred complexities are apparent in Taylor's chapter, which presents a detailed case study of early Victorian financial fraud. Using the example of a fictitious joint-stock company established in 1836, the Independent West Middlesex Fire and Life Assurance Company, Taylor examines the interplay of older and newer forms of trust. Statistics and numbers had a place, he suggests: they were central to actuarial forecasting, as well as practices such as accounting, by which members of the public could monitor their investments. However, in terms of securing trust, traditional notions of character, status, and respectability remained central, and continued to provide the bedrock on which economic decisions were made. Though investors may have looked at the numbers presented by companies, they attempted to gauge the reliability of these numbers by evaluating the character of those who published them. Company strategies for encouraging trust thus focused on proving—or simulating—the gentility and respectability of the directors. Much like Crook, Taylor argues for the emergence of hybrid forms of authority and trust, with older forms still very prominent.

The final part of the volume, entitled The Politics of Statistics, focuses on the political use of numbers and their place and function in political debates and party electioneering. Two themes, both apparent elsewhere in the volume, are affirmed: first, that numbers were capable of being put to use in multiple ways, in this case by different parties and party agents; and secondly, that statistics were always attended by criticism and suspicion. But this part of the volume also affords a glimpse of some of the ways numbers have come to *frame* party conflict and to constitute our sense of what 'the political' is and should be. If 'representation' is a key feature of modern democracy, then it is a feature mediated by the power of numbers. Parliamentary seats, MPs, voters, and ultimately votes: all are counted, measured, and reckoned with on the basis that, numerically speaking, they are of equal value. It might be argued that appealing to the electorate and predicting its behaviour is now nothing more than an elaborate numbers game; but it might be countered that it could hardly be otherwise.

S.J. Thompson's chapter takes a fresh look at a key milestone in modern British history, the 1832 Reform Act, and explores the first steps made towards a feature of political life we now take for granted: that parliamentary constituencies contain roughly equal numbers of eligible voters. In late eighteenth- and early nineteenth-century Britain, however, political representation was determined by the grant of ancient privileges and immemorial custom, rather than the size or distribution of the population. As Thompson shows, reforming this system involved the application of statistical information gathered in blue books and collected since 1801, the year of the first national census. Drawing on ministerial and parliamentary papers and contemporary periodicals, Thompson argues that population statistics were integral to the Whigs' scheme of reform, which was finally enacted in 1832. Yet no blueprint unfolded: on the contrary, developing and applying the 'principle of population' was thoroughly contested and owed a great deal to ministerial improvisation and negotiation.

In 1831–32, the very principle of basing political reasoning on statistical reasoning was in question. But as Edmund Rogers demonstrates in the following chapter, the place of statistics within economic reasoning could prove just as controversial, even among those who accepted the basic premise of 'inductivist' economics. In particular, the chapter examines the use of numbers in the context of the late Victorian and Edwardian tariff reform debate, demonstrating how statistics were used to bolster rival claims for competing fiscal policies in two domains: first, in the debate among 'educated' Britons carried out in newspapers and learned journals; and secondly, in the arena of mass electoral politics, where statistics were presented in a populist fashion, strong on visual impact and 'key' facts. Rogers's chapter can usefully be read alongside James Thompson's in terms of grasping the visual culture of numbers evident at the time. But Rogers's chapter also illuminates the transnational nature of statistical debate, which in this case embraced information relating to New World colonies, Germany and the United States. Here, as elsewhere, numbers were productive not of clarity and communicational rationality, but of conflict and the fractious—and arguably confused—exchange of claims and counterclaims.

Evidently, by the Edwardian period political parties had become accustomed to contesting electoral issues in statistical terms. But what of the statistical standing of parties with the electorate? This is something explored by Laura Beers in the final chapter of this volume, where she examines the first tentative forays into the art of electoral prediction undertaken by the Tory party during the interwar period. As Beers notes, these years were very much transitional ones in terms of 'knowing' the electorate. The often corrupt and violent world of mid-Victorian politics had long passed, with voting now conducted secretly, rather than publicly, meaning that parties no longer knew precisely who had voted for which one. Equally, the postwar world of obsessive opinion polling and focus-group research was still to come. In this context, pundits, punters, and parties repeatedly misread the intentions of the mass electorate. Occasional polls, newspaper speculation, and the shifting odds of political bookmakers were all that could be relied upon. Even so, it is also possible to discern the emergence of a new kind of language and a new way of reckoning with the electorate. Already there was talk of 'floating voters', while the concept of 'electoral swing' was in evidence, as party agents mused on which bits of the electorate had turned for or against them, and to what degree. The chapter presents a vivid picture of a political culture not wholly foreign to our own, yet still free of 'polling gurus' and twenty-four-hour media monitoring.

NOTES

1. J.A. Tooze, 'Trouble with Numbers: Statistics, Politics and History in the Construction of Weimar's Trade Balance', *American Historical Review* 113 (2008), p. 678.
2. A. Badiou, *Number and Numbers* [1990, trans. R. Mackay] (Cambridge, 2008), pp. 3 and 1.
3. C. Blum, *Strength in Numbers: Population, Reproduction and Power in Eighteenth-Century France* (Baltimore, MD, 2002); C.A. Bayly, *Empire and Information: Intelligence Gathering and Social Communication in India, 1780–1870* (Cambridge, 1996); G. Aly and K.H. Roth, *The Nazi Census: Identification and Control in the Third Reich* (Philadelphia, PA, 2004).
4. Key works here include S.M. Stigler, *The History of Statistics: The Measurement of Uncertainty before 1900* (Cambridge, MA, 1986); T.M. Porter, *The Rise of Statistical Thinking, 1820–1900* (Princeton, NJ, 1986); and I. Hacking, *The Taming of Chance* (Cambridge, 1990).
5. See, for instance, A. Desrosières, *The Politics of Large Numbers: A History of Statistical Reasoning* [trans. Camille Naish] (Cambridge, MA, 1998); G. Gigerenzer, Z. Swijtink, T.M. Porter, L. Daston, J. Beatty and L. Krüger, *The Empire of Chance: How Probability Changed Science and Everyday Life* (Cambridge, 1989); M.S. Morgan, *The History of Econometric Ideas* (Cambridge, 1990); E. R. Weintraub, *How Economics Became a Mathematical Science* (Durham, NC, 2002); T.M. Porter, *Karl Pearson: The Scientific Life in a Statistical Age* (Princeton, NJ, 2004).

6. Among others, D. Englander and R. O'Day (eds.), *Retrieved Riches: Social Investigation in Britain, 1840–1914* (Aldershot, 1995); M. Bulmer (ed.), *Essays on the History of British Sociological Research* (Cambridge, 1985); M. Bulmer and K. Kish Sklar (eds.), *The Social Survey in Historical Perspective, 1880–1940* (Cambridge, 1991); E. Higgs, *The Information State in England: The Central Collection of Information on Citizens since 1500* (Basingstoke, 2004).

7. See, for instance, R.M. Worcester, *British Public Opinion: A Guide to the History and Methodology of Political Opinion Polling* (Oxford, 1991) and C. McDonald and S. King, *Sampling the Universe: The Growth, Development and Influence of Market Research in Britain since 1945* (Henley-on-Thames, 1996). More recent works include L.D. Beers, 'Whose Opinion? Changing Attitudes Towards Opinion Polling in British Politics, 1937–1964', *Twentieth Century British History* 17 (2006), pp. 177–205, and J. Moran, 'Mass-Observation, Market Research and the Birth of the Focus Group, 1937–1997', *Journal of British Studies* 47 (2008), pp. 827–51.

8. See D.R. Headrick, *When Information Came of Age: Technologies of Knowledge in the Age of Reason and Revolution, 1700–1850* (Cambridge, 2000); T. Weller and D. Bawden, 'The Social and Technological Origins of the Information Society: An Analysis of the Crisis of Control in England, 1830–1900', *Journal of Documentation* 61 (2005), pp. 777–802; Toni Weller, *Information History—An Introduction: Exploring an Emergent Field* (Oxford, 2008).

9. M. Esbester, 'Nineteenth-Century Timetables and the History of Reading', *Book History* 12 (2009), pp. 156–85; M. Esbester, 'Designing Time: The Design and Use of Nineteenth-Century Transport Timetables', *Journal of Design History* 22 (2009), pp. 91–113.

10. R. Menke, *Telegraphic Realism: Victorian Fiction and Other Information Systems* (Stanford, CA, 2008).

11. T.M. Porter, *Trust in Numbers: The Pursuit of Objectivity in Science and Public Life* (Princeton, NJ, 1995).

12. I. Hacking, 'Bio-power and the Avalanche of Printed Numbers', *Humanities in Society* 5 (1982), pp. 275–95; Hacking, *The Taming of Chance*; M. Poovey, *Making a Social Body: British Cultural Formation, 1830–1865* (Chicago, 1995); P. Joyce, *The Rule of Freedom: Liberalism and the Modern City* (London, 2003), pp. 24–34; and N. Rose, *Powers of Freedom: Reframing Political Thought* (Cambridge, 1999), ch. 6.

13. Rose, *Powers of Freedom*, pp. 221, 207.

14. O. Frankel, *State of Inquiry: Social Investigations and Print Culture in Nineteenth-Century Britain and the United States* (Baltimore, MD, 2006), p. 3.

15. See, for instance, J. Thompson, 'Pictorial Lies?—Posters and Politics in Britain, c. 1880–1914', *Past and Present* 197 (2007), pp. 177–210.

16. J. Habermas, *The Structural Transformation of the Public Sphere: An Inquiry into a Category of Bourgeois Society* [1962, trans. T. Burger with the assistance of F. Lawrence] (Oxford, 1992).

17. J. Habermas, 'The Public Sphere: An Encyclopaedia Article (1964)', *New German Critique* 1 (1974), pp. 49–50.

18. Habermas, *The Structural Transformation of the Public Sphere*, p. 215.

19. Recent reviews include J.L. Brooke, 'Reason and Passion in the Public Sphere: Habermas and the Cultural Historians', *Journal of Interdisciplinary History* 29 (1998), pp. 43–67; and H. Mah, 'Phantasies of the Public Sphere: Rethinking the Habermas of Historians', *Journal of Modern History* 72 (2000), pp. 153–82. See also N. Crossley and J.M. Roberts, *After Habermas: New Perspectives on the Public Sphere* (Oxford, 2004).

20. P. Lake and S. Pincus, 'Rethinking the Public Sphere in Early Modern England', *Journal of British Studies* 45 (2006), pp. 270–92; G. Eley, 'Nations, Publics, and Political Cultures: Placing Habermas in the Nineteenth Century', in C. Calhoun (ed.), *Habermas and the Public Sphere* (Cambridge, MA, 1992), pp. 289–339.
21. J. Plotz, 'Crowd Power: Chartism, Carlyle, and the Victorian Public Sphere', *Representations* 70 (2000), pp. 87–114; E. Hadley, 'The Old Price Wars: Melodramatizing the Public Sphere in Early Nineteenth-Century England', *PMLA* 107 (1992), pp. 524–37.
22. Habermas, *The Structural Transformation of the Public Sphere*, Part VI, especially pp. 216–18.
23. *The New Oxford Dictionary of English* (Oxford, 1998), p. 1817.
24. Porter, *The Rise of Statistical Thinking*; M. Poovey, *A History of the Modern Fact: Problems of Knowledge in the Sciences of Wealth and Society* (Chicago, 1998); L. Schweber, *Disciplining Statistics: Demography and Vital Statistics in France and England, 1830–1885* (Durham, NC, 2006).
25. Porter, *The Rise of Statistical Thinking*, p. 23.
26. Quoted in *ibid.*, p. 24.
27. Quoted in Headrick, *When Information Came of Age*, p. 68.
28. Porter, *The Rise of Statistical Thinking*, p. 24.
29. *Prospectus of the Objects and Plan of the Statistical Society of London* (London, 1834), p. 1.
30. *Journal of the Statistical Society of London* [hereafter *JSSL*] 1 (1838), p. 3.
31. Poovey, *A History of the Modern Fact*, ch. 7.
32. 'Fifteenth Annual Report of the Statistical Society of London', *JSSL* 12 (1849), p. 98.
33. W.A. Guy, 'On the Original and Acquired Meaning of the Term "Statistics", and on the Proper Functions of a Statistical Society', *JSSL* 28 (1865), p. 486.
34. Schweber, *Disciplining Statistics*, pp. 200–7.
35. R.A. Fisher, *Statistical Methods for Research Workers* (Edinburgh, 1925).
36. G. Upton and I. Cook, *Oxford Dictionary of Statistics* (Rev. edn., Oxford, 2008), p. 188.
37. P. Buck, 'Seventeenth-Century Political Arithmetic: Civil Strife and Vital Statistics', *Isis* 68 (1977), pp. 64–84.
38. See the discussion in Porter, *The Rise of Statistical Thinking*, pp. 18–20.
39. Sir F.M. Eden, *An Estimate of the Number of Inhabitants in Great Britain and Ireland* (London, 1800).
40. D.V. Glass, *Numbering the People: The Eighteenth-Century Population Controversy and the Development of Census and Vital Statistics in Britain* (Farnborough, 1973), pp. 17–21.
41. *Ibid.*, ch. 2.
42. Hacking, *The Taming of Chance*, p. viii.
43. Porter, *The Rise of Statistical Thinking*, pp. 23–9; Hacking, *The Taming of Chance*, ch. 5.
44. A useful overview of the development of the press during this time can be found in H. Barker, *Newspapers, Politics and English Society, 1695–1855* (Harlow, 2000), ch. 2.
45. M. Hampton, *Visions of the Press in Britain, 1850–1950* (Urbana, IL, 2005), p. 28.
46. Barker, *Newspapers, Politics and English Society*, ch. 1; J.A.W. Gunn, *Beyond Liberty and Property: The Process of Self-Recognition in Eighteenth-Century Thought* (Kingston, 1983), ch. 7.
47. See, for instance, D. Wahrman, 'Public Opinion, Violence and the Limits of Constitutional Politics', in J. Vernon (ed.), *Re-reading the Constitution: New*

Narratives in the Political History of England's Long Nineteenth Century (Cambridge, 1996), pp. 83–122.
48. Quoted in A. King and J. Plunkett (eds.), *Victorian Print Media: A Reader* (Oxford, 2005), p. 46.
49. H.S. Jones, *Victorian Political Thought* (Basingstoke, 2000), pp. 69–73.
50. See especially Hampton, *Visions of the Press in Britain*, chs. 2 and 4.
51. S. Sherman, *Telling Time: Clocks, Diaries, and English Diurnal Form, 1660–1785* (Chicago, 1996); C.J. Somerville, *The News Revolution in England: Cultural Dynamics of Daily Information* (Oxford, 1996).
52. G. O'Hara, 'New Histories of British Imperial Communications and the "Networked World" of the Nineteenth and Early Twentieth Centuries', *History Compass* 8 (2010), pp. 609–25.
53. Schweber, *Disciplining Statistics*, pp. 31–2.
54. J. Harris, *Unemployment and Politics: A Study in English Social Policy 1886–1914* (Oxford, 1972), pp. 360–3.
55. Higgs, *Information State*, pp. 118–21.
56. S.E. Igo, 'Social Scientific Citizens: Surveys, Statistics and the Public in Modern America', *Princeton School of Social Science Occasional Papers* 24 (2006), p. 2.
57. L.J. Martin, 'The Genealogy of Public Opinion Polling', *Annals of the American Academy of Political and Social Science* 472 (1984), pp. 19–20.
58. C. McDonald and S. King, *Sampling the Universe: The Growth, Development and Influence of Market Research in Britain since 1945* (1996), p. 23.
59. P. Kleinman, *Market Research: Head Counting Becomes Big Business* (London, 1985), p. 9.
60. Moran, 'Mass-Observation', p. 831.
61. A. Calder, 'Mass Observation, 1937–1949', in Bulmer (ed.), *Essays on the History of British Sociological Research*, pp. 121–3; P. Summerfield, 'Mass-Observation: Social Research or Social Movement?', *Journal of Contemporary History* 20 (1985), esp. pp. 444–7.
62. Beers, 'Whose Opinion?', pp. 188–91.
63. See e.g. National Archives of the United Kingdom, Kew [hereafter NAUK], RG 23/262, Enquiry into tenants' views about different types of access arrangements in high blocks, 1957; NAUK RG 23/257, Enquiry into effects of the Rent Act, 1957; NAUK RG 23/379, Enquiry into knowledge and opinions of the general public about crime, 1966.
64. H. Lynd and R. Lynd, *Middletown: A Study in American Political Culture* (London, 1929); S. Igo, *The Averaged American: Surveys, Citizens, and the Making of a Mass Public* (Cambridge, MA, 2007).
65. For the Lynds' general influence see G. Payne, *Sociology and Social Research* (London, 1981), pp. 95–6.
66. A.H. Halsey, *A History of Sociology in Britain: Science, Literature, and Society* (Oxford, 2004), pp. 41–2.
67. P. Lazarsfeld, *The People's Choice: How the Voter Makes up His Mind in a Presidential Campaign* (New York, 1944), pp. 101–4.
68. M. Benney, A.P. Gray and R.H. Pear, *How People Vote: A Study of Electoral Behaviour in Greenwich* (London, 1956), pp. 2, 3. Other examples of this genre include R.S. Milne and H.C. Mackenzie, *Straight Fight: A Study of Voting Behaviour in the Constituency of Bristol North-East at the General Election of 1951* (London, 1954); and M. Stacey, *Tradition and Change: A Study of Banbury* (Oxford, 1960).
69. The methodology of *Family and Kinship* is detailed in M. Young and P. Wilmott, *Family and Kinship in East London* (London, 1957), Appendix I, pp. 167–77.

70. S. Parker, *Urban Theory and the Urban Experience: Encountering the City* (London, 2004), p. 96. For Young's ambivalent view of the United States in general, see A. Briggs, *Michael Young: Social Entrepreneur* (Basingstoke, 2001), pp. 102, 197–8.

71. M. Bulmer, *The Chicago School of Sociology: Institutionalization, Diversity, and the Rise of Sociological Research* (Chicago, 1986), esp. ch. 7, pp. 109–28; M. D'Eramo and G. Thomson, *The Pig and the Skyscraper: Chicago, a History of our Future* (London, 2003), pp. 256–7.

72. R.M. Worcester, *British Public Opinion: A Guide to the History and Methodology of Political Opinion Polling* (London, 1991), pp. 3–8.

73. R.B. McCallum and A. Readman, *The British General Election of 1945* (London, 1947), pp. 203–4, 242; D. Butler and M. Pinto-Duschinsky, *The British General Election of 1970* (London, 1971), ch. 8.

74. A. Taylor, ' "The Record of the 1950s is Irrelevant": The Conservative Party, Electoral Strategy and Opinion Research, 1945–64', *Contemporary British History* 17 (2003), pp. 84, 88.

75. Bevan thought it vulgar and liable to take the 'poetry out of politics'; worse still, polling might encourage politicians to follow rather than lead the people. L. Black, *The Political Culture of the Left in Affluent Britain, 1951–64: Old Labour, New Britain?* (Basingstoke, 2003), pp. 172–3.

76. M. Rosenbaum, *From Soapbox to Soundbite: Party Political Campaigning in Britain since 1945* (London, 1997), pp. 151–3.

77. J. Lawrence and M. Taylor, 'Electoral Sociology and the Historians', in *idem.* (eds.), *Party, State and Society: Electoral Behaviour in Britain since 1820* (Aldershot, 1997), pp. 4–7.

78. M. Abrams, R. Rose and R. Hinden, *Must Labour Lose?* (Harmondsworth, 1960), esp. table 3, p. 16.

79. D. MacDougall, *Don and Mandarin: Memoirs of an Economist* (London, 1987), p. 168. For Crosland's wider use of polls, see A. Crosland, 'The Future of the Left', *Encounter* 14 (1960), p. 5; *idem.*, *The Conservative Enemy: A Programme of Radical Reform for the 1960s* (London, 1962), pp. 149–53.

80. R. Hodder-Williams, *Public Opinion Polls and British Politics* (London, 1970), pp. 75–7.

81. D. Broughton, *Public Opinion Polling and Politics in Britain* (London, 1995), p. 6.

82. See, for example, W.L. Miller and W.M. Mackie, 'The Electoral Cycle and the Asymmetry of Government and Opposition Popularity', *Political Studies* 21 (1973), pp. 263–79; C. Pissarides, 'British Government Popularity and Economic Performance', *Economic Journal* 90 (1980), pp. 569–81.

83. G. O'Hara and N. Ferguson, 'The Myth of the Feelgood Factor', in N. Ferguson, *The Cash Nexus: Money and Power in the Modern World 1700–2000* (London, 2001), pp. 224–52.

84. M. Scammell, 'The Phenomenon of Political Marketing: The Thatcher Contribution', *Contemporary British History* 8 (1994), p. 25.

85. On the powerlessness of the NEC, see A. Rawnsley, *Servants of the People: The Inside Story of New Labour* (London, 2000), e.g. pp. 154, 200, 351.

86. P. Gould, *The Unfinished Revolution: How the Modernisers Saved the Labour Party* (London, 1998), pp. 326–33.

87. S. Driver and L. Martell, *New Labour: Politics after Thatcherism* (1998), esp. p. 143.

88. D. Wring, *The Politics of Marketing the Labour Party* (Basingstoke, 2005), pp. 170–6.

89. An early example is *Sanitary Reform: Speech of Viscount Morpeth in the House of Commons on Tuesday, 30th March, 1847* (London, 1847), pp. 1–15.
90. J.V. Pickstone, *Ways of Knowing: A New History of Science, Technology and Medicine* (Manchester, 2000), ch. 3.
91. C. Emsley, *Crime, Police and Penal Policy: European Experiences, 1750–1940* (Oxford, 2007), p. 119.
92. *First Annual Report of the Registrar General* (London, 1839), p. 99.
93. Pickstone, *Ways of Knowing*, chs. 4–5.
94. J. Fletcher, 'Moral and Educational Statistics of England and Wales', *JSSL* 10 (1847), pp. 194–5.
95. G.C. Bowker and S.L. Star, *Sorting Things Out: Classification and Its Consequences* (Cambridge, MA, 1999); M. Lampland and S.L. Star (eds.), *Standards and Their Stories: How Quantifying, Classifying and Formalizing Practices Shape Everyday Life* (New York, 2009).
96. Pickstone, *Ways of Knowing*, ch. 6.
97. E. Robson, 'Table and Tabular Formatting in Sumer, Babylonia and Assyria, 2500 BCE–50 CE', in M. Campbell-Kelly, M. Croarken, R. Flood and E. Robson (eds.), *The History of Mathematical Tables: From Sumer to Spreadsheets* (Oxford, 2003), pp. 19–48.
98. J.L. Klein, *Statistical Visions in Time: A History of Time Series Analysis, 1662–1938* (Cambridge, 1997), ch. 2.
99. *Ibid.*, chs. 3 and 4.
100. *Ibid.*, pp. 56–7.
101. See E.R. Tufte, *The Visual Display of Quantitative Evidence* (Cheshire, CT, 1983).
102. Headrick, *When Information Came of Age*, pp. 129–30.
103. H. Maas and M.S. Morgan, 'Timing History: The Introduction of Graphical Analysis in Nineteenth-Century British Economics', *Revue d'Histoire des Sciences Humaines* 7 (2002), pp. 97–127.
104. W.M. Baker and A.A. Bourne, *Elementary Graphs* (London, 1903); W. Jamieson, *Graphs for Beginners* (London, 1905).

2 Statistics and the Career of Public Reason

Engagement and Detachment in a Quantified World

Theodore M. Porter

Where in the world do we find reason now? Max Weber interpreted rationality as very nearly synonymous with modernity. He linked the rise of rationality in the West with the expansion of capitalism, but it extended outside of specifically profit-making and capital-accumulating institutions to political ones. Bureaucratic rationalization was for him almost a tautology, and also a teleology, though he was painfully ambivalent about the desirability of this outcome. He regarded the centrality of reason in science, too, as virtually self-evident. Weber is especially pertinent to the topic of public reason because he did not confine scientific rationality to the forms of knowledge most esteemed for their rigour and detachment, such as physics, but explored its emergence in the more mundane worlds of commerce and bookkeeping. To these we can add statistics without distorting his meaning.

Although Weber identified sources of rationalized capitalism in irrational religious doctrines (notably the anxieties of Calvinists), his legacy includes a widespread assumption that rationalization advances relentlessly and more or less autonomously. His sense of its driving force was endorsed by social scientists, especially in postwar America, who celebrated it, as well as by cultural critics who did not. Max Horkheimer and Theodor Adorno, developing his image of the iron cage (or steel-hard shell), interpreted rationalization not so much as the triumph of reason, but as its confinement, the scourge of beauty, wonder, and spontaneous joy. Jürgen Habermas, though reasoning more subtly, has also worked recognizably in the Frankfurt School tradition of critique of the incessant power of Weberian rationalization. He laboured to map out a different form of reason, a product of communication and community rather than of isolation and oppression. His sense of *Öffentlichkeit*, the public sphere, embodies that ambition, but its historical trajectory, as he developed it, gives little ground for hope. Insurgent capitalism created a domain of reasoned discussion and debate in newspapers and coffeehouses that was closed off by mass society in a later phase of political and economic development. It left behind, Habermas suggested, a world operating according to the narrow logic of Weberian calculation, which might be typified by statistics and even accounts. These, as we will see, are often prominent in public discussion, and need not be at odds with communicative action or the public sphere. They arise, however, from a different and often contradictory impulse: to advise administrators and sometimes to inform the public with properly defined measurements, rather than seeking the advance of truth through open, democratic debate.[1]

It would be asking a great deal of statistics, or indeed of any form of knowledge, to provide the foundation of the public sphere as a transcendental place of reason, accessible to every citizen. If we adopt instead a less strenuous standard, we can see that statistics have become ubiquitous in the public circulation of knowledge, information and opinions. The category of 'statistics', however, covers a range of knowledge forms. At one end we have numbers as *information*, which, as Yaron Ezrahi points out, refers to something much shallower, much less in need of analysis or interpretation, than what we call 'science' or even 'knowledge'.[2] Information is presumed to be transparent and unproblematical, fit for do-it-yourself use by almost anyone. Its standing depends on not probing too deeply, for 'anyone' might become wary if alerted to all the choices and manipulations, whether standardized or ad hoc, that go into the definition of such numbers; and still more so if instructed in the ways that economic interests and pressure groups can threaten, inveigle, and bribe to get the numbers they prefer into the media limelight. Information flourishes in a world where such efforts are kept quiet. The consumer of information does not ask about origins, but regards numbers, like sausages, as complete and indivisible, already wrapped up in their casings.

At the other extreme, whole libraries are devoted to the methodologies of measurement and statistical analysis practiced within the natural and social sciences. Here too the numbers often circulate as information, which is to say, without critical scrutiny, but such exchanges are generally made on the presumption that the numbers were competently produced and scrutinized by expert reviewers before they saw the light of day in print. Statistical inference and measurement are widely celebrated as the highest form of empirical knowledge to which humans can aspire, especially in social science fields such as experimental psychology, econometrics, and social surveys. This hubris of modern statistics has been much criticized on the grounds that it narrows inappropriately the domain of social inquiry or silences public discussion with its claims of quantitative rigour.[3]

This analysis seems to imply a divide between technical specialists and a credulous public. And yet expert and popular forms of statistics are not always distinct. Scientists can be credulous too, especially about numbers, whilst statistical claims are sometimes challenged effectively in non-expert public discussion. The religion of science is not really monotheistic if all sorts of numbers, and not only those certified by advanced statistics, are accepted uncritically as information. Sceptics of democratic reason complain that the public draws on statistics the way drunks use a lamppost, for support rather than illumination. They forget, however, that scientists and policy experts themselves often rule out of court any evaluation of a measurement process that goes beyond the details to critique a methodology of calculation, insisting that the standard of a serious participant in the discussion is to come forth with better statistics. The founding figure of the statistical discipline, Karl Pearson, responded to doubts about his calculations with this challenge: 'Statistics on the table, please.'[4] For Pearson and for others, putting aside the available numbers as misleading or unreliable when there was no better method to replace them was not an option.

There are powerful institutional forces at work now tending to draw a line between expert and public discussion. We are encouraged these days to think of science, almost by its very nature, as detached from the mundane and often corrupt concerns of political actors or even ordinary citizens. Science, we say, is 'technical', a word that has come to signify the specialized competence required to produce it and the closed communities that possess this competence. Although the original sense of the term 'technical' refers to trade secrets and crafts skills, including in professional fields such as the law, the word now is understood to apply paradigmatically to mathematical methods in science. Modernist science has largely accepted, and indeed often vaunts, its insulation from the public as a necessary foundation for objectivity.

Statistical mathematics was the most effective means by which the twentieth-century social sciences, including much of psychology, economics, sociology, political science, and geography, as well as parts of anthropology and history, were remade as technical in this sense. As social scientists became increasingly preoccupied with their objectivity, they regarded statistics more and more as a way to manage or manipulate an unreasoning public than to instruct it. Although elite science has always been sceptical of the intelligence of common people, there is still an important contrast here from enlightened ideals of public knowledge. In those campaigns to educate the public that arose in the eighteenth century, and which flourished as never before in the nineteenth, statistics was put forward in an almost utopian spirit as the indispensable foundation of public knowledge, of reason in the public sphere. That dream endured into the twentieth century, yet by 1890 was already beginning to seem unnatural.[5]

The reliance of social science on official numbers did not diminish over the course of the twentieth century. Increasingly, though, the social disciplines treated descriptive statistics, including most official statistics, as background knowledge, the humdrum product of bureaucratic registration processes, and not as a serious form of scientific inquiry. Postwar social science emphasized the assignment of numbers to objects that could not be directly measured, or often whose very existence had hitherto been unacknowledged or dimly recognized, such as collective attitudes, business cycles, the authoritarian personality, biological intelligence, and the slope of indifference curves. Or they laboured to break down the variability of a statistical series, say of crime or birth rates, and to assign different weights to possible causes. More generally, statistical analysis was worked out as the proper basis of inference in the 1920s and 1930s, and was very quickly institutionalized by textbooks and journals.[6] The methods for such analysis were supported by some very serious mathematics, and even if sociologists or political scientists did not usually confront this mathematics directly, the new tools came with unfamiliar concepts involving the measurement and partitioning of variation that had to be mastered. Popular audiences would not know what to make of them.

The disappearance of familiar categories of social understanding in academic work, and the alienation of scholars and researchers from the lay public, might have been taken as causes for regret. Instead, increasingly specialized discourses were welcomed within social science as a mark of objectivity and the ticket to scientific respectability. It is often said, by admirers and critics alike, that in withdrawing from the public sphere and emphasizing mathematics, the social scientists were following the well-worn path of the 'hard' natural sciences. But this claim is profoundly misleading. The very idea that real science is distinguished by its technicality, and that the self-conscious introduction or appropriation of technical tools and concepts is the royal road to scientific status, was solidified if not invented by the modern social sciences. Postwar sociologists, political scientists, anthropologists, and economists developed a comprehensive theory of historical 'modernization', which turned social science itself into a key protagonist in the history of progress. They defined modernity as the rise of complex, interdependent societies, a new and unfamiliar world that could not be grasped by vernacular concepts. The conditions of everyday knowledge and local experience leave unnoticed those remote and complex causes that increasingly shape the world. Real social knowledge and the ability to act effectively on the world required disciplined experts. Theorists of modernization spoke of science and medicine as having been successfully professionalized, and they set themselves the task of professionalizing social science. Like Weber, and invoking Weber, they saw bureaucratic and scientific rationalization sweeping the world, while admitting little of Weber's regret.[7]

Social science in its technical mode has idealized the scientific profession as a closed community which trains up its own members and sets its own standards.[8] But the social sciences also acknowledge, as indeed the idea of modernization requires, that such knowledge should contribute to effective policy. How widely must science be diffused for this to be achieved? Twentieth-century social scientists across a range of fields were typically sceptical of democratic decision making.[9] Voters would act most wisely by endorsing the outcomes of expert investigation. Enlightening the public in the sense of giving them the knowledge to assess the issues themselves did not seem very promising, or necessary. Social science cultivated a different kind of audience, namely the decision makers in those purportedly rational bureaucracies that had risen up in government and business.

This alliance of social mathematics with administration recalls the statistical science of the eighteenth century, referred to by contemporaries as 'political arithmetic' or as 'the calculus of probabilities'. Alexis de Tocqueville described the French *ancien régime* as becoming ever more centralized, and the revolution as not so much a break in this development as an acceleration of it. Yet statistics in the wake of the revolution became more open, whereas absolutist France, like most continental monarchies, was disinclined to make its numbers public. In the decades before the French Revolution, the government of Louis XVI made determined efforts to conduct a census and did in fact keep a tally of birth registrations. Mathematicians, notably that most illustrious of probabilists Pierre Simon Laplace, performed calculations to estimate the French population from birth statistics, and even gave figures for the bounds of probable error. In the same years, Daniel Bernoulli published a mathematical model for the increase of population that could be achieved if every child were required to be inoculated against smallpox. Eric Brian has described an alliance of mathematicians and administrators which supported the use of advanced probability methods to try to manage populations.[10]

The *philosophe* Condorcet is particularly interesting on these points, because he was so strongly committed to the use of mathematics and number to define conditions for public involvement in political decisions. His ideal of a quantified world is nicely exemplified in his vigorous support of the metric system, an enthusiasm shared by the most democratic of early US political leaders, Thomas Jefferson. A uniform system of weights, measures, land surveys, and currency would empower anyone with even rudimentary instruction in arithmetic and measurement to become, for most purposes, self-sufficient in calculation, and hence to look after his own interests.[11] Condorcet's mathematical career was devoted above all to working out the probabilities of elections and judicial decisions in a way that would allow the general will to be revealed (within acceptable limits of error). But could everyman check Condorcet's mathematics and determine for himself that the electoral system was fair? He could not and Condorcet never addressed the public in this way. Rather, for all his commitment to government that would serve the people, he composed most of his work, including many of his mathematical writings, for the Crown, which in practice meant high functionaries of the French state. His highly mathematical programme, which aimed to supplant fallible judgment with rational calculation, as well as the rarified social nexus within which he worked, revealed his doubts about public rationality.[12]

The French Revolution, greatest of the 'democratic revolutions' of the late eighteenth century, heightened the fears of elites about letting the people govern themselves. The statistical institutions it stimulated were designed to provide state information, rather than supplying a basis for liberal government. The proliferation of censuses around 1800 was mainly a reaction to war and to the need for accurate knowledge to help with military conscription and the supplying of military forces. And yet, in Britain and the

United States, and across much of Western Europe, the census soon became a liberal institution, at least in its attachment to public opinion. To be sure, liberal institutions were not at first democratic ones. After all, the right to vote was, until very near the end of the nineteenth century, restricted in most European countries to reasonably prosperous, educated men. The popular classes were more likely to be objects of statistical investigation than informed readers of statistics. Liberalism did, however, mean that normal government activities and accomplishments (or failings) should not be closely guarded secrets of a privileged caste, but open to inspection by the newspaper-reading classes. Almost everyone agreed that the collection and publication of numbers were vital to create an informed public, as well as to guide policymaking.[13]

Indeed, this prosaic domain of bureaucratic rationalization was often the site of sweeping, missionary ambitions. In the French Third Republic, Alfred de Foville made statistics essential to good government. '*Aux armes, citoyens*', he declared, for numbers are weapons in a timeless battle! 'Wherever the struggle resurfaces between the champions of the general interest and that of private interest, you will find us [statisticians] at our post, armed and ready to march.' In Progressive America, Carroll Wright of the pioneering Massachusetts Bureau of Labor Statistics (to which we owe the measurement, and in a way the very idea, of unemployment), spoke of accurate statistics as a sacred duty. He hoped that numbers, rather than violent class conflict, would enable workers to better their lives.[14] Statistical offices in Berlin, Vienna, and other cities published popular statistical journals, as well as official compilations of numbers. An informed citizenry, they supposed, must pay attention to statistics. And in the 1930s and 1940s, American pioneers of public opinion research made the converse argument, always in a tone reflecting the sublimity of their calling, that opinion measures enabled elected officials to gauge the mood of the people and to act in accordance with their wishes.[15]

For much of the nineteenth century, when statistics was very nearly synonymous with social science, it had rather little in common with the Ivory Tower. Statistics, that is, social statistics, was sometimes practiced at universities, especially in nations like Germany, where the professor was a civil servant and where political economy competed with law to train those state functionaries who inspired Weber with the odd idea that bureaucracy is intrinsically a site of rationality. Fields like the *Staatswissenschaften* (state sciences) gave institutional body to the ideal that learning should be put at the service of policy. Statistical directors often had university positions or taught seminars; this was most famously the case with Ernst Engel, in Saxony and then Prussia, who instructed a generation of German historical economists.[16] Further west, as in France, England, and North America, the chief locus of social science until very late in the nineteenth century was voluntary societies. The Statistical Society of London was in some ways the prototype of social science institutions.

A double point is being made here: that so much of nineteenth-century social science was empirical, most often statistical, and also that it was not detached, socially or intellectually, from the public sphere. Now, it is not only empirical social science that could be made and debated in the public domain. The most forbidding theoretical lucubrations by the likes of David Ricardo and Karl Marx were also taken up, adapted and reinterpreted by popular movements.[17] But most political economy too was empirical and statistical during the nineteenth century. This is well known in the German case, where the 'historical school' was still more a statistical school. But a glance at the *Economic Journal* in Britain or the *American Economic Review* or *Journal of Political Economy* in the United States reveals that, at the outset of the new century, most economists continued to examine production or trade or labour movements from a standpoint that was statistical, political or institutional. Usually the papers involved policy issues of concern to the larger public, and—the crucial point—the preoccupation with statistics did not obstruct but encouraged this public engagement. One factor facilitating public comprehension is that the numbers generally referred to countable things, like monetary expenditures, unemployed persons, deaths from cholera, convictions for burglary, or acres of land planted in wheat or rye. It was relatively straightforward to compare different numbers of the same thing to see which was larger, or to look for trends. Increasing use of graphical forms of representation also made the numbers readily accessible to the eye.

Also, no abstruse mathematical manipulations were involved. The nineteenth century overwhelmingly preferred complete counts to probabilistic estimates. In truth, the organization of labour required to tally a national population is at least as troublesome and as vulnerable to manipulation as any statistical procedure to estimate the magnitude of a coefficient or calculate frequencies of error. But a complete enumeration was the gold standard of statistics, perhaps above all because it was built up out of experiences that were familiar to everyone, and analyzable using operations of basic arithmetic. Sampling was rarely employed in public statistics before the very end of the nineteenth century.[18]

Notwithstanding the arguments of an important recent study, which makes the late nineteenth century the high point of self-denying objectivity in the production of scientific images, there was in fact only little of what recent social science defines as objectivity in nineteenth-century statistics.[19] Indeed, this may be the most important reason that the period before about 1880 is generally regarded within the social sciences as prehistory and not as history proper of their fields. We cannot say that the statisticians of that era were unconcerned with objectivity, though the word was little used before 1880. They did want solid knowledge and they did aspire to fair-mindedness, free from the temptations of self-interest. But they put more emphasis on their own moral character than on the inflexible rigour of their methods. It would be less misleading to say that they had a different sense of the requirements of objectivity from twentieth-century ones.

Two differences from social science in our own day might be emphasized. First, the Victorians were not notably reluctant to mix value judgments with their analyses or even with their counts. In Charles Booth's famous survey of London, for example, he had no compunction about using words like 'shiftless', 'degraded', 'degenerate' or 'criminal', and he dismissed a whole stratum of the population as the 'residuum.'[20] Anyone who has opened a work by Marx knows that the pronouncement of sharp moral judgments is not limited to bourgeois social science. Secondly, they did not think that social science had to be made from a neutral or detached position. A good example here is the French mining engineer Frédéric Le Play, who eventually came to the view that the real repository of social science was the knowledge of (traditional) elites, who knew their tenants or employees personally. Le Play himself always came in from outside to prepare his monographic studies of Siberian herders or Norwegian miners, and so he could have claimed independence and distance as a resource had he wanted to. He did not; instead, he consulted local leaders to identify a family to study and to learn about them, and then made free with advice and assistance. For him, the role of social investigator ought, ideally, to incorporate that of the seigneur or manager (*patron*).[21]

In the London Statistical Society, many of the leading contributors were government employees, often statisticians, as in the Board of Trade (G.R. Porter) or the General Register Office (William Farr). Notwithstanding their pose of political neutrality, captured in an early resolution to limit their discussions to facts, which should be 'threshed out by others [*aliis exterendum*],' they were active in movements for public health, insurance for the poor, trade policy and child labour. The Manchester Statistical Society was made up predominantly of urban reformers and Quetelet's International Statistical Congresses, which began in 1853, brought together high government officials. A still more extreme case is the British Social Science Association of the mid-to-late nineteenth century, whose meetings were attended by dukes, prime ministers and bishops, though this body was not so preoccupied with statistics. These were politically involved men and sometimes they had charge of the populations they investigated.[22] By the 1940s, the very idea of social science seemed to exclude the practical knowledge of statesmen and industrialists, cultivated by administrative agencies, business corporations and reform movements. Le Play and his allies, by contrast, regarded practical involvement in public affairs as an advantage or even a necessity for the pursuit of social science. Patronal or administrative responsibility, they reasoned, gave men the capacity as well as the moral obligation to observe, often to quantify, society, and then to act on their knowledge.

Many social issues and many topics of public discussion in the nineteenth century—and this of course has continued—were closely tied up with or even inextricably bound to statistics. Charles Dupin's shaded statistical maps created the line between educated and ignorant France, running from Geneva to St Malo, in the 1820s. New population figures underlay the announcement in 1851 that Britain had become an urban society, and the American census of 1890 was the basis for a celebrated declaration of the closing of the frontier, inspiring the historian Frederick Jackson Turner to work out his eponymous thesis about the frontier and American history. The British tally of 1851, the first to count religious affiliation and church attendance, led to so much anxiety about a weakening of religious faith and relative decline of the Church of England that the religious census was never repeated. Statistics, in many ways, helped to form a sense of what it meant to be British or American, or French, Prussian, Saxon or Italian.[23]

Though questions of belonging and identity were important ones, especially for national statistics, social science was first of all about social problems. In the emerging urbanized, industrial world, there was less regular contact than before across class lines and less opportunity for paternalistic concern of the sort that Le Play idealized. Statistics came in to fill the gap, to provide a larger and more distant view of a more anonymous population, 'the masses'. The statistical idiom made it easier to group labourers or the poor together, easier to talk about them as 'hands' or as ignorant and readily manipulated in crowds. Statistical inquiries and results were used to chart the progress of cholera epidemics and to locate centres of ignorance and thievery. Institutions such as hospitals, asylums, schools, and armies were regularly subjected to statistical tabulation and the conclusions this permitted were often unflattering. The widespread anxiety about degeneration at the end of the nineteenth century was saturated with statistics, as were the eugenic campaigns and health and sanitation campaigns that grew up to combat this degeneration. These efforts enlisted a variety of professionals and reformers, including doctors, businessmen, political leaders, asylum directors, school administrators, actuaries, economists, biologists and statisticians. They were discussed in meetings, public lectures and newspapers, as well as in journals of medicine and social reform. Although only a minority could make their voices heard, these were very much public issues.[24]

By the beginning of the twentieth century, the texture of discussion was changing as claims for technical knowledge became more insistent. In an age of mass society and of growing democratic participation, it was more and more difficult for intellectuals to maintain confidence in the rationality of the public and their capacity to influence it. Practitioners of the new social science did not try, at least not at first, to close down or bypass public discussion, but they did want the public to recognize the proper authority of science in regard to policies that depended, as the scientifically most ambitious insisted, not on what the majority wants, but on how the world works. What should the public sphere be like in an age of science? Would it be enough to encourage free, critical discussion, of the sort defended in

John Stuart Mill's *On Liberty*, or should real experts be empowered some-how to take the lead in such debates?

This question takes on particular poignancy in relation to the individual who perhaps did more than anyone else to create statistics as a mathematical field, Karl Pearson.[25] He carried out his most important mathematical work from roughly 1890 to 1914, and at the same time was forming a vision of the place of statistics in the sciences and in relation to the state. Pearson is known for his remarks that most political issues, such as how to deal with the effects of parental alcoholism on children, are first of all scientific questions, which should depend on competent research, rather than the opinion of the man in the street. This makes sense in terms of the scientific programme he pursued with tireless dedication for the last forty-five years of his life, which was to work out mathematical means to estimate quantities and infer causal relationships from statistical data.

In this he went a long way toward making sciences such as physical anthropology, psychology, medicine, sociology, and eugenics into technical scientific fields. If we are to believe that he understood the social value of statistics in terms of its participation in the public sphere, this cannot be by pretending that he wanted every conclusion to be open to debate, or that unconstrained discussion was the most essential feature of a democratic political order. Like Condorcet, he aspired to raise the tone of public speech and to focus it on questions of truth, rather than letting these debates be hijacked by the ignorant and the self-serving. A good education, he preached, would familiarize citizens with the scientific method, which for him involved some formal methodology, experience in a particular science, and a heavy dose of morality, focused on disinterested impartiality. Workers and shopkeepers would never become truly expert in statistical mathematics, or in any branch of science, but they could learn enough to distinguish real authorities, in whom they could invest confidence, from quacks and pretenders. And the pretenders, he thought, were numerous enough. Pearson was suspicious of almost every popular movement. He never joined the Eugenics Society, for example, though he was among the founders of eugenics as a scientific campaign. His phrase 'in the name of eugenics,' which he used on several occasions, conveys his sense that most of it was false coin. He might have said the same of medicine or economics or biology, and he disputed fiercely with practitioners of these and other fields.

Mathematical statistics seems to make subjective reasoning explicit and rigorous: choose the correct form of analysis, feed in the data and calculate the result. So it is perhaps surprising that Pearson put no faith in mathematical recipes. He refused even to write or rely on textbooks, insisting instead on a combination of lecturing and personal instruction, the cultivation of skills and practices, in his biometric laboratory. This refusal to put the rudiments of statistics in writing looks like a way of keeping the shop door closed, of maintaining a kind of privileged secrecy, akin to the protection of the old craft guilds. Indeed, Pearson wrote admiringly of medieval universities and of these guilds, with their dependence on face-to-face relations. His rejection of textbooks, however, was about the formation of character, not secrecy, for he held skill, wisdom and personal morality to be necessary for the practice of science. Pearson's scheme for objective knowledge involved not the suppression of individuality but its elevation and refinement.

It is revealing that he explicitly associated science with wisdom. This seems implausible in our age, but it was still widely defended in 1900. The famous Victorian advocates of scientific naturalism, such as T.H. Huxley, endorsed the old ideal of an elite made wise and supple through literary instruction, except that the foundation for this good sense and good character would now be formed by science. This is why Pearson called his public lectures on science at Gresham College and his ensuing book of 1892 *The Grammar of Science*. Grammar refers to rudiments, but it also alludes to the role of dead languages in the traditional formation of educated men and wise, cultivated leaders, which should now fall to science and statistics. He always put great emphasis on the intellectual stature and morality of the statesman or scientist, which could never be supplanted by catalogues of factual information. Pearson did not theorize the public sphere, but he endeavored throughout his life to speak to it. He did not believe that science (which for him was almost synonymous with measurement and calculation) closed down the public forum of reasoned debate. On the contrary, science would make it possible. To be sure, his was a highly idealized notion of public discussion, which above all was to be rational. He hoped to achieve this by making the structure of public belief and discussion more hierarchical.

In that sense, Pearson was raising to prominence one of the forces that would tend to dismantle the public sphere. It is almost unthinkable now to endorse his politics. But this founder of statistical mathematics comes to us from a world that has almost disappeared, in which it was still possible to think that science can make us moral and wise. Few now would suppose that Pearson's own public campaigns, especially his preoccupation with eugenics and the calumnies he heaped on any statistician who dissented from Saint Biometrika, bear this out. Crucially for us, his ideals contained a profound internal tension, a tension that was already noticed by some of his contemporaries. He assumed that true science can really be wise and disinterested on matters of public controversy, can refrain from exaggerating the certainty of its knowledge, and will be recognized as such by the public. But Pearson himself was forever frustrated by the pigheadedness of his fellow scientists, even the physicists, who were excellent in their field, but who seemed to forget their scientific method whenever they dealt with anything but physics. How else could so many have been so committed to impossible topics such as psychical research? And he recognized that by 1890 it was becoming very difficult for a scientist to communicate effectively with the public, as Huxley had, while retaining the esteem of his colleagues.

For Pearson, knowledge of statistics was closely allied to scientific method, and for many of his admirers, eugenics also was part of the package, the reconceptualization of social problems as scientific ones. Pearson was as dedicated to empirical measurement as he was to mathematics, insisting always on their alliance, and he believed that statistical methods could bring a scientific perspective to almost any important question. Though he was tireless in his efforts to train statisticians, he also hoped to introduce his field into the general curriculum, so that any educated person would be familiar with statistical reasoning. That is, he opposed the segregation of statistical experts from ordinary citizens, and hoped that mathematics could raise the standard of public discourse rather than bypass it. This remained a common view in policy-relevant sciences in the early twentieth century, and did not disappear even from the field of statistics.

Yet the statistical impulse was becoming better at producing black-boxed results than it was at promoting public understanding. R.A. Fisher, Pearson's bitter rival, moved the field further in the direction of technicality, not only by the power of his mathematics, but also by the particular methods and tools he promoted. The statistical test of significance, which spread like wildfire through the social and biological disciplines in the 1930s and 1940s, was a technique to separate the wheat from the chaff—results that could, at least provisionally, be regarded as valid from those that did not deserve to be registered. The statistical standard for making this division was purely quantitative and even formulaic, with scarcely a thought for the substantive significance of the result.[26] In the disciplines that took them up, Fisher's methods (or those of Jerzy Neyman and Pearson's son Egon, or some combination of the two) were treated as the straight and narrow path to valid scientific results, and the ability to perform these routines as the mark of one who was qualified to participate in a research community. This was at first an American story, but the United States assumed a very powerful position in world science after the world wars. The new statistics implied a rather stiff standard of rationality, for the methods themselves required a good deal of training, and they presumed experimental or sampling setups of a very special type.

Toward the end of the nineteenth century, social scientists began to teach that common sense and intuition were helpless when faced with the complexity of modern societies, which required high-level technical expertise of the sort they possessed. They tried to live up to the ideal of science as they understood it, which meant that they should demonstrate their aloofness from mere opinion by employing rigorous methods leading to conclusions that their expert colleagues would accept. It also entailed that they should hold back from sharing conclusions with the public until the specialists had reached agreement. But even then, would the public understand? In an era of mass society and specialized, technical knowledge, public rationality was almost unthinkable. Social science, however, did not simply turn inward, advancing knowledge for its own sake and for fellow specialists.

Scientific and statistical experts earned credibility and exercised a public function by communicating their results to state agencies, which, in their turn, welcomed the legitimacy that a more rigorous and 'objective' science was able to supply. Democratic politics now required a conspicuously apolitical form of science. Paradoxically, ostensible detachment from politics was sometimes the best politics. The relationship of social knowledge with state administration, which had been in place for centuries, now demanded an ostensible detachment of knowledge from the sites of its application. The public had almost no legitimacy as a participant in making knowledge, or even as an audience for social expertise, though it typically was impossible to exclude the voice of interested groups when the time came to decide and to implement.

Yet it would be a mistake to suppose that the discourse of statistics has come to be controlled by statistical experts. Statistical results in the twentieth century achieved a higher profile than ever before. In the United States, interwar surveys, such as the Middletown studies, the Kinsey reports on sexual behaviour and public opinion polling, attracted huge interest, as Sarah Igo has demonstrated.[27] From the standpoint of public information, the most compelling development in statistics since 1900 has been an increasing fixation on a few iconic numbers to stand in for complex phenomena such as national income, health and well-being, conditions of labour, the character of a population, crime, inequality, and, more generally, what the public thinks. Such numbers are consistent with the typical postwar model of science as public provider of thin descriptions. The gathering of information is generally supposed to be unproblematical, and the calculation of rates and indexes to be a technical matter, of interest only to specialists. A suitably compliant public should not ask hard questions, but only assess whether the number bodes well or ill, and what it implies about the competence of elected or appointed officials, or the acceptability of current policies.

Typically, numbers are assimilated by the public in this rather unquestioning way. But often enough they stimulate more complex, more activist responses. The sustained effort since the late nineteenth century to reduce collective phenomena to a few simple numbers, such as population figures, gross domestic product, and rates of crime, inflation, illiteracy and infant mortality, is typically muddied by the availability of alternative formulas for almost the same thing. There are means and medians, income per person and income per household, people collecting unemployment checks and skilled workers forced to get by on unskilled or part-time labour. Parties to debates can often sustain contradictory positions by a choice of subtly different official numbers. In this case, the typical black-boxing of the process for generating numbers does not enforce consensus, but increases the difficulty of resolving debates.

To interested parties, the collection and calculation of pertinent numbers may be quite visible. Probably the most public statistical operation is the census count. Normally, at least one member of every household will have filled out a form or answered the queries of a census taker, and so can imagine the entire census, albeit rather simplistically, as the repetition of this encounter millions of times. Many numbers are gathered in the process of administering an agency, such as the work of customs and immigration officials, courts and prisons, schools and hospitals. Other numbers are of particular interest to the communities affected. Even if the tally of an entire population is uncontroversial, breakdowns of the population often have ideological or financial consequences: Anglicans versus Dissenters in 1851 Britain; Upper versus Lower Canada in nineteenth-century Canadian censuses; homeless or illegal immigrant populations in modern American cities. Sometimes communities take an active role in registering their own activities and they often struggle to see themselves or their activities properly represented in official numbers.[28] Emmanuel Didier has described a succession of attempts, made during the early twentieth century through the Great Depression and Second World War, to estimate and then measure crop yields, from identifying a knowledgeable and reputable informant to wielding a mechanical measuring device, each drawing on and exemplifying distinctive conceptions of a democratic political order.[29]

The relationship of consumers to the gathering of price statistics is less direct, though the results can affect them personally, and they often have not passively accepted the official figures. Rather, they invoke their own experience—buying food and clothing, finding housing, and operating vehicles, for instance—to claim that the index must be wrong, or at least does not apply properly to their own situation as a family with children of certain ages in a particular income class and a specific city or neighbourhood. In the United States, as Thomas Stapleford has shown, such objections to official price measures were pressed by a considerable movement as early as the 1920s. The cost-of-living index itself depends on the compression of a great heterogeneity of products and circumstances into a single number. Stapleford's history documents the striving through collective action by different sorts of people to disassemble this aggregate. It is no mere record of futility, and public protests sometimes led even to changes of method. Yet the index survived to be deployed again and again in an effort to settle routinely and by calculation what would be immensely complex and contentious for politics.[30]

It would be fatuous to argue that technical statistical methods, or science in general, have shut down public debate, or that social science has fully succeeded in detaching itself from public engagement and political controversy. We should rather say that the sciences have participated in a reshaping of the public sphere and assumed a prominent role within the political discourses of the contemporary world. The power of social numbers arises from the application of uniform, 'objective' standards that seem independent of political pressures, leavened with a touch of hocus-pocus to bring the results within the range of practical and political acceptability. Statistical reason is the beacon of an ideal of impersonal rationality achieved through technical methods, which nevertheless has repeatedly been transformed by the alchemy of politics into an element of rhetorical struggle among institutions and interest groups.

NOTES

1. M. Horkheimer and T.W. Adorno, *The Dialectic of Enlightenment: Philosophical Fragments* (New York, [1944] 1972); J. Habermas, *The Structural Transformation of the Public Sphere: An Inquiry into a Category of Bourgeois Society* [1962, trans. T. Burger with the assistance of F. Lawrence] (Oxford, 1989).
2. Y. Ezrahi, 'Science and the Political Imagination in Contemporary Democracies', in S. Jasanoff (ed.), *States of Knowledge: The Co-Production of Science and Social Order* (New York, 2002), pp. 254–73.
3. G. Gigerenzer, Z. Swijtink, T.M. Porter, L. Daston, J. Beatty and L. Krüger, *The Empire of Chance: How Probability Changed Science and Everyday Life* (Cambridge, 1989); T.M. Porter, 'Statistics and Statistical Methods', in T.M. Porter and D. Ross (eds.), *The Cambridge History of Science, Volume Seven: Modern Social Sciences* (Cambridge, 2003), pp. 238–50.
4. See S.M. Stigler, *Statistics on the Table: The History of Statistical Concepts and Methods* (Cambridge, MA, 1999).
5. T.M. Porter, 'Speaking Precision to Power: The Modern Political Role of Social Science', *Social Research* 73 (2006), pp. 1273–94; *idem.*, 'How Science Became Technical', *Isis* 100 (2009), pp. 292–309.
6. Gigerenzer et al., *Empire of Chance.*
7. T. Haskell's *The Emergence of Professional Social Science* (Urbana, IL, 1977) documents the rise of this perspective in the United States around 1900 and uses it to support a functionalist explanation of change in the social sciences.
8. J. Ben-David, *The Scientist's Role in Society: A Comparative Study* (Englewood Cliffs, NJ, 1971).
9. D.P. Haney, *The Americanization of Social Science: Intellectuals and Public Responsibility in the Postwar United States* (Philadelphia, PA, 2008).
10. E. Brian, *La mesure de l'état: administrateurs et géomètres au XVIIIe siècle* (Paris, 1994); L. Daston, *Classical Probability in the Enlightenment* (Princeton, NJ, 1988); A. Rusnock, *Vital Accounts: Quantifying Health and Population in Eighteenth-Century England and France* (Cambridge, 2002).
11. K. Alder, *The Measure of All Things* (New York, 2002); C.C. Gillispie, *Science and Polity in France: The Revolutionary and Napoleonic Years* (Princeton, NJ, 2004).
12. K.M. Baker, *Condorcet: From Natural Philosophy to Social Mathematics* (Chicago, 1975); C.C. Gillispie, *Science and Polity in France at the End of the Old Regime* (Princeton, NJ, 1980); Brian, *La mesure de l'état.*
13. E. Higgs, *The Information State in England: The Central Collection of Information on Citizens since 1500* (Basingstoke, 2004); T.M. Porter, *The Rise of Statistical Thinking, 1820–1900* (Princeton, NJ, 1986); I. Hacking *The Taming of Chance* (Cambridge, 1990).
14. T.M. Porter, *Trust in Numbers: The Pursuit of Objectivity in Science and Public Life* (Princeton, NJ, 1995); C. Topalov, *Naissance du chômeur, 1880–1910* (Paris, 1994); T.A. Stapleford, *The Cost of Living in America: A Political History of Economic Statistics, 1880–2000* (Cambridge, 2009).

15. S. Igo, *The Averaged American: Surveys, Citizens, and the Making of a Mass Public* (Cambridge, MA, 2007).
16. D. Lindenfeld, *The Practical Imagination: The German Sciences of State in the Nineteenth Century* (Chicago, 1997); M. Labbé, 'Institutionalizing the Statistics of Nationality in Prussia in the 19th Century (From Local Bureaucracy to State-Level Census of Population)', *Centaurus* 49 (2007), pp. 289–306.
17. T.M. Porter, 'The Social Sciences', in David Cahan (ed.), *From Natural Philosophy to the Sciences: Writing the History of Nineteenth-Century Science* (Chicago, 2003), pp. 254–90.
18. A. Desrosières, *The Politics of Large Numbers: A History of Statistical Reasoning* [trans. Camille Naish] (Cambridge, MA, 1998); Martine Mespoulet, *Statistique et révolution en Russie: un compromis impossible* (Rennes, 2001).
19. L. Daston and P. Galison, *Objectivity* (New York, 2007).
20. G. Himmelfarb, *Poverty and Compassion: The Moral Imagination of the Late Victorians* (New York, 1991).
21. T.M. Porter, 'Reforming Vision: The Engineer Le Play Learns to Observe Society Sagely', in L. Daston and E. Lunbeck (eds.), *Histories of Scientific Observation* (Chicago, 2011).
22. V.L. Hilts, '*Aliis Exterendum*, or, the Origins of the Statistical Society of London,' *Isis* 69 (1978), pp. 21–43; M.J. Cullen, *The Statistical Movement in Early Victorian Britain: The Foundations of Empirical Social Research* (Hassocks, 1975); L. Goldman, *Science, Reform, and Politics in Victorian Britain: The Social Science Association, 1857–1886* (Cambridge, 2002).
23. M.J. Anderson, *The American Census: A Social History* (New Haven, CT, 1988); G. Palsky, *Des chiffres et des cartes: naissance et développement de la cartographie quantitative française au XIXe siècle* (Paris, 1996); S. Patriarca, *Numbers and Nationhood: Writing Statistics in Nineteenth-Century Italy* (Cambridge, 1996).
24. G.K. Wolfenstein, *Public Numbers and the Victorian State: The General Register Office, the Census, and Statistics in Nineteenth-Century Britain* (PhD Dissertation, University of California, Los Angeles 2004); D. Pick, *Faces of Degeneration: A European Disorder, c. 1848–1918* (Cambridge, 1989); S. Szreter, *Fertility, Class, and Gender in Britain, 1860–1940* (Cambridge, 1996).
25. T.M. Porter, *Karl Pearson: The Scientific Life in a Statistical Age* (Princeton, NJ, 2004).
26. S.T. Ziliak and D.N. McCloskey, *The Cult of Statistical Significance: How the Standard Error Costs Us Jobs, Justice and Lives* (Ann Arbor, MI, 2008).
27. Igo, *Averaged American*.
28. Wolfenstein, *Public Numbers*; B. Curtis, *The Politics of Population: State Formation, Statistics, and the Census of Canada, 1840–1875* (Toronto, 2001); A. Leibler and D. Breslau, 'The Uncounted: Citizenship and Exclusion in the Israeli Census of 1948', *Ethnic and Racial Studies* 28 (2005), pp. 880–902; P. Schor, *Compter et classer: histoire des recensements americains* (Paris, 2009).
29. E. Didier, *En quoi consiste l'Amérique? les Statistiques, le new deal, et la démocratie* (Paris, 2009).
30. Stapleford, *The Cost of Living in America*.

Part I
Governing Numbers

3 'In These You May Trust'

Numerical Information, Accounting Practices, and the Poor Law, c. 1790 to 1840

Steven King

Statistics on poor relief stand alongside those on trade, national product and land tax as among the first systematic attempts to garner a picture of the economic situation of the country as a whole.[1] Initially collected in an intermittent, patchy and voluntary fashion during the 1770s and 1780s, national figures disappeared in the 1790s.[2] Frederick Morton Eden and a raft of other antiquarians and social commentators partly filled the gap, providing regional snapshots of the character, role and reformability of the Old Poor Law.[3] The turn of the nineteenth century, however, marked a new dawn for the numerical representation of the poor law at national, regional and local levels.[4] Driven by a vigorous debate over the nature of individual responsibility for poverty,[5] and amidst increasing concern about the level of rate expenditure, the government acted in 1802 and 1803 to require 'national returns' on poor law spending, placing a numerical representation of this core function squarely in the public domain.[6] Subsequently these returns became regularized annual events, coordinated by clerks to the Quarter Sessions, but constructed by local agents drawn from the middling sorts. The amount and depth of information required changed with each new politico-legal phase of the Old Poor Law. There were increases in the level of numerical information required in 1812/13, 1818/1819 (the Sturges-Bourne Select Vestry Acts), 1823, and 1829, and many welfare historians have pointed to the immense collection of data that was used to argue for a New Poor Law between 1832 and 1834.[7]

This demand for numerical knowledge was part of the advance of the information state during the early part of the nineteenth century. Indeed, it was arguably part of a wider change in the nature of government, in which numbers became crucial to the framing of social problems and the operation of power at all levels.[8] In turn, quantitative information on poverty and poor relief can be seen permeating middling and even labouring culture (in an extension of popular numeracy) from the early 1800s. To take one example of many, on 26 January 1822, Henry Lomas, a builder from Watford, noted with some dismay that 'From a return made before the House of Commons it appears that the amount of the Poor Rates for 1821 in Great Britain was £7,329,594–7s. What a burthen on Property.'[9]

Significantly, he had culled his information from the *London Gazette* and *The Times*, both of which drew on a compendium of returns of poor law expenditure made under new and more detailed reporting requirements on parish officers instigated in 1818/1819. Their reporting allowed the public to trace the burden of poor relief and in effect widened the realm of public debate about poverty and its relief. Certainly, many commentators had come to share Lomas's sense of dismay at the cost of the poor, while contemporaneously published figures on issues such as illegitimacy, family abandonment and wage allowances fostered heated debate about the prevalence of particular social evils.[10] Numerical information on welfare, it might be argued, redefined the 'problem' of the Old Poor Law from a local one concerning the burden placed upon private ratepayers, to a national one in which questions of the public good and public expense held sway.[11]

Unsurprisingly, welfare historians have come to identify a crisis of the Old Poor Law alongside and arising out of this numerical representation of the costs of welfare.[12] Though they cannot agree on the exact chronology of changing sentiment towards the poor, most would perhaps follow Lynn Hollen Lees, who sees a breakdown of customary support for the claims of the poor from the late 1790s and early 1800s.[13] The last three decades of the Old Poor Law were ones in which the welfare system was re-imagined as a national quantitative entity, wherein a new language of numbers came to be used, in contrast to an earlier language of custom and moral right, and around which official and ratepayer opinion came to coalesce.[14] Looking at early nineteenth-century vestry data, one is struck by the frequency with which officials tried to pare back the number of claimants on relief lists. These attempts were invariably couched in terms of trends in wages and prices that undermined the need for relief; and they were usually accompanied too by a raft of new numbers about the scale and impact of provision elsewhere.

This story is broadly familiar to welfare historians. However, there are good reasons to question any linear link between the quantification of the Old Poor Law and its demise. The first is that whilst national numerical representations of poverty and poor law spending became commonplace, local and regional surveys, whether numerical or narrative, or some mixture of the two, continued to have a significant impact on public opinion. In this sense, it is all too easy to forget that investigations by Frederick Eden, David Davies and John Camfield were just three of more than 140 local and regional surveys of poverty and relief between the later eighteenth century and 1834. Such surveys, precursors to the Victorian social survey, widened the legitimate sphere of public comment and interest, and were disseminated to the middling sorts via vestries, newspapers, society meetings, and pamphlets. They often provided a different, less critical rendering of the nature of poverty and the appropriateness of local responses. To take just one example, the Liverpool accountant William Langstaff's survey of poverty in Lancashire conducted between 1817 and 1821 pointed to the inequities of un- and underemployment, and took issue with newly constructed government tables on matters such as relief per capita. He argued that government statistics were fatally flawed and risked 'setting the ratepayers unjustifiably against their poor brethren'.[15]

A second observation is that numerical knowledge on the poor law was not received in isolation. Local and regional newspapers reported trends in prices, business failures and start-ups, property values, and population figures as keenly as they recorded information on poverty and its relief. As welfare historians have long appreciated, when all of these trends induced economic pessimism, sentiment towards the poor hardened appreciably. However, such 'perfect storms' were relatively rare, and while Henry Lomas complained about the national cost of poor relief, other commentators considering the situation in the round were less severe. Charles Knightley, of Dodford in Northamptonshire, lamented the huge burden that the poor placed on the rates nationally after he saw the same 1821 figures as Lomas. However, when faced by a fourth rate assessment in the year, he mused that 'we may thank god that the value of the property here has risen by so much so that I am scarce worse off'.[16] It is for this reason that while we see periodic drives to slash the relief lists, these attempts were invariably short-lived, as conditions changed or as the composition of vestries altered.

A third observation is that those who considered numerical data on welfare often disagreed about how to interpret it, even at the height of the crisis of the Old Poor Law. Joanna Innes has reviewed the sentiment of much of the pamphlet literature on the national stage.[17] When we also take account of newspapers and magazine articles it is clear that there was a wide spectrum of opinion on how to read the numerical information made available on different aspects of the relief system, and on the changes that might be employed. This backdrop partly helps to explain an important but often overlooked conundrum in British welfare history: namely, not why the Old Poor Law was dismantled and reassembled as a centrally directed system in the period 1832–34; but rather why, when viewed as a compendium of national numbers and in the context of repeated attempts at reform, the Old Poor Law did not fold much sooner. Innes, John Prest and others have offered some explanations for this conundrum—including the fact that there was not a professional political class capable of taking reform all the way through parliament—but the variable interpretation of the numerical basis of the Old Poor Law was also important.[18]

The rest of this chapter is concerned not with national statistics per se, but with the way numerical information and reasoning, and more rigorous accounting practices, came to permeate the local operation of the poor law. In particular, it will suggest that, at the same time as a national quantitative understanding of the costs of the Old Poor Law system undermined its legitimacy, officials and paupers alike came to understand the value of financial information. Indeed, it could be that the language and fact of numbers, allied with new local and regional understandings of the economics of overseeing, actually strengthened commitment to the poor law before 1834. The chapter will explore these matters using vestry minutes, overseers' correspondence and pauper letters, and will focus particularly on the last three decades of the Old Poor Law (when national debate about reform was most intense) and on source material drawn mainly (but not exclusively) from parish archives relating to Berkshire, Northamptonshire and Wiltshire. [19] In general, urban communities had better systems of information sharing and transmission than their rural counterparts. Yet, as these cases demonstrate, the impact and diffusion of better accounting practices extended to rural and provincial areas, suggesting that numbers flowed back and forth at both local and national levels.

PROVIDING AND RECEIVING NUMBERS

How did local overseers and vestrymen, the fulcrum of the Old Poor Law system, receive and understand numerical data? How did they provide it when asked? How did they conceive of the economics of the poor law system? And how did more robust systems of accounting, data collection and distribution underpin support for the early nineteenth-century poor law? These are surprisingly difficult questions to answer, either because sources do not survive or the linking together of multiple sources has not been done to answer them. The problem is magnified by the fact that so few diaries detailing the work and thoughts of Old Poor Law officials survive. [20] There are ways, however, to deepen our understanding of these matters.

That officials came to be acutely aware of their place as providers of numerical information is hinted at consistently in poor law sources. Thus, Quarter Sessions clerks, who were responsible for assembling county-level data on poor relief spending for transmission to London, wrote frequent reminders about the need for timely and accurate figures to local officials. Such letters could be very terse where officials threatened to breach the annual deadline. Charles Truss, clerk of the peace for Northampton, wrote to the vestry of Earls Barton (Northamptonshire) on 26 December 1817 to register his disapproval of their tardiness in providing data, stating that 'Not having received the poor return for your parish I write to desire you will send the same to me without delay as it will be immediately called for by Government.' [21] Even a cursory look at the physical manuscripts of the average poor law archive highlights how parish officials were made aware of their role as providers of numerical information. In the parish of Pangbourne (Berkshire), the overseer pasted into the front of his book a printed circular dated 23 April 1808, which set out who should be relieved and under what circumstances, but whose primary aim was to ensure that overseers kept the right information for annual returns to parliament:

The Instructions and Directions for the Overseers. . . You are to take Care that there be kept in your Parish, a Book wherein the Names of Persons of your Parish who receive Collection, Pay, or relief, shall be registered, with the Day and Year when they were admitted, and the Occasion which brought them under the Necessity; and Yearly in Easter Week (or as often as shall be thought convenient) your Parishioners shall meet in Vestry, before whom the Books shall be produced, and all Persons receiving Collection or Relief shall be called over, and the Reason of their taking Relief examined, and a new List made of such as they shall think fit to receive Collection or Relief . . .[22]

This practice supplemented books of instructions for overseers and can be found in all of the counties considered here. Most commonly parishes followed the practice of the Northamptonshire town of Oundle, which pasted into the front of its vestry minute books the 'Abstract of an Act of Parliament entitled "An Act to Amend the Laws for the Relief of the Poor" (Passed 31st March 1819)'. The abstract set out the new rules governing decision making under the Old Poor Law, as well as the new reporting heads required for government returns.[23] An accompanying instruction sheet told the overseer to distinguish relief recipients by age; to record information in tabular form across the year rather than in simple list form; to calculate per capita relief totals; and to provide information on the number of disabled recipients and the nature of their disability.[24] In short, it seems overseers were ever more aware of the need for strong and standardized accounting forms, and of the potential power of numerical information, however basic, for both state and locality.

A related issue is the question of how officials consumed such data: how they conceived of the Old Poor Law as an economic and numerical system; how they employed numerical data to shape the formulation of parish policy; and how associated accounting procedures fed through into local understandings of the wider poor law system. In these respects, three core developments in the period post-1790 might be noted. First, though it is difficult to find direct commentary by officials regarding the consumption of numerical data—and thereby to trace comprehensively how such data shaped policy—there is much indirect evidence that the second decade of the nineteenth century in particular witnessed a fundamental change in vestry and overseer awareness of the national and regional context to their spending. Two examples stand for many. Richard Harbury, a vestryman of Trowbridge (Wiltshire), on receiving his summary of national poor law spending in aggregate and per capita via a newspaper in May 1822, suggested that the overseer should 'make a listing of all those in receipt of relief and detail their family and other circumstances that we might better know where the parish stands in relation to other places in this county.'[25] The subsequent report on the poor of Trowbridge was received 4 August 1822 and upon examination the vestry wished to 'Convey their thanks to the overseers for their attention to economy, which has placed this parish in the lowest quarter for relief for the County and much below the national figures but without harm to the poor'.[26] This benchmarking of activity against other parishes was an explicit exercise in more refined accounting procedures. It gave an excuse for allowances to be managed, massaged and cut, but equally it gave officials the power to argue that their relief practices constituted good value for money.

Such sentiments are even more forcefully expressed in a second example taken from the rural industrial township of Garstang in Lancashire. Like Trowbridge, Garstang was active in benchmarking itself against other places. From the 1810s, the vestry published an annual digest of statistics, representing both what was spent by the township and where the township stood in relation to other places in terms of yardsticks such as spending per capita. The overseer was to 'take care that the same [digest] shall be distributed to the respective tax payers throughout the township'.[27] As in Trowbridge, the results of this benchmarking were positive, showing that Garstang had a strong control of its relief spending, and thus (to take the example of 27 April 1825) 'the thanks of this general meeting are very sincerely given to the late select vestry and the overseers for their great attention to the interest of the town during their continuance in office'.[28] More fulsomely, the overseer had been praised in July 1821 on the discovery that Garstang was in the bottom third of the table for relief payments per capita, with the vestry and township at large thanking the overseer for 'our commendable position in this County as a whole'.[29] The generation of this comparative (if basic) numerical framework is itself significant, and points to the entrenchment of stronger information-gathering and accounting practices in the local operation of the poor law during its so-called 'crisis' phase. Just as importantly, the use of a comparative numerical framework clearly had the power to transform the meaning of poor law spending for officials and ratepayers. They were enabled to focus not on the 'problem' of spending, but on the economy and humanity of the town and its officials, reducing latent pressure for wider reform of the poor law system.

Popular susceptibility to the power of numerical reasoning was enhanced by a second core development of the post-1800 period: the development of the out-parish system of relief payments to cope with the fact that large numbers of paupers were not in their place of settlement when need struck. Familiarity with the inter-parish accounting, financial instruments, economic contracts and debt management that lay at the heart of the out-parish system meant that officials were increasingly well-equipped to be consumers of numerical information. A brief rendering of the overseers' correspondence for Oundle from 1833–35 suggests the depth of knowledge that officials were expected to have. The Oundle officials in this period dealt with nine different regional banks and were part of a series of financial transactions in which cheques and ready cash were used to pay off debts or to balance the relative liabilities of parishes with whom Oundle was connected in the out-parish system. The officials were well aware of the need for accountability and the absolute requirement for numbers that could be reported to the vestry and thus to the community. They wrote on 10 December 1833 to Mr John Lines, enclosing 'a ck for £5:8:0 for the children's maintenance up to the first of November from May 17th to Nov 1st is twenty four weeks'. The overseer desired (one of many occasions when they expressed the same sentiments) from Lines 'a correct account of them' and a 'true and faithful acct' of the expenditure involved.[30] The wording of this phrase is significant, and exactly mirrors the guidance given by Quarter Sessions clerks on behalf of the government when they sought the annual data for returns to parliament after 1802–3.

Of course, though the overseers paid out cheques, they also received cash. This raised all sorts of accounting problems, from the physical quality of money through to active debt management. The overseer of Oundle wrote to the father of an illegitimate child on 19 December 1833, noting: 'I received by Mr Jenks [a carrier] Seven shillings. One of the shillings so very very Bad [that is, clipped or soiled] that I am certain you must have known when you put it in the parcel I have therefore only given you credit for 6/-'.[31] Nor were bills and notes always paid on time, and overseers needed to keep a tight handle on such issues, while maintaining a wider knowledge of the regulations. Oundle's overseer wrote to his counterpart in Thrapston (Northamptonshire) on 22 September 1835 to note that

> The promissary note by Mr James Flemming in favour of Oundle parish for thirty six pounds bearing your endorsement was due yesterday and was presented for payment but which now lays in my hands unpaid and to which I beg to call your attention. Mrs Flemming states that Mr F will be at Home tomorrow and will pay it but the Law compels me to give you warning being the endorsee Notice of the non payment today I am etc.[32]

Much more evidence of this sort could be employed, but the key point is that the accounting principles embodied here are clear and are not seen in many later eighteenth-century poor law contexts. In a situation where the politico-legal system gave no guidance (or authority) for the out-parish system, basic numerical data and accounting principles provided the bedrock of a developing structure of inter-parish relations. Officials were not just reporters of numerical knowledge; they were also users and constructors of this knowledge. In this way, the generation of national numbers on the Old Poor Law may have tightened local accounting practices, thus making it more robust, rather than more likely to be repealed.

A final development is a change in the linguistic register employed by officials to describe and conceptualize the economic framework of the Old Poor Law. This was partly caused by, but also reflected in, the guidance books for overseers, treatises on the poor law, and schemes for poor law reform that multiplied prodigiously in the early nineteenth century. A consideration of just a sample of these works—in this case Willis, Courtenay, Davison, Halcomb, Nolan, Bird, Bosworth, and Robinson, each of which went through multiple editions[33]—points to a change in both the guidance given on the economics of the poor law (how to raise the rates, how to cope with deficits, the range of measures that could be used to transmit money, liabilities under the law etc., all of which became more central to the advice) *and* the language used to describe the operation of the system.

To develop this line of argument in detail would comprise a chapter in its own right. One example, however, is the language of financial liability and comparability. The term 'liability' was hardly present in earlier versions of guidance books, but those of the 1820s talk of the liability of overseers to provide statistical information, their liability to ratepayers, and their liability to the poor themselves. In terms of making comparisons, neither an anonymous guidance book published in 1774, nor Joseph Paul's manual of 1785, gave much by way of instruction on ensuring comparability with the practices of other parishes, or with reference to national statistics. By contrast, Robinson's manual of 1827 and Bird's of 1828 (the eighth edition) carry admonitions for officials to collect, understand and use comparable evidence from elsewhere.[34] There is clearly more scope for this sort of work, but for now it is important to acknowledge the leaching of this changed linguistic register into the vestry minutes and the correspondence of overseers themselves. To remain with the example of Oundle, vestry minutes by the early 1830s were dwelling on the 'liability' of apprentices and their masters, the parish and its paupers, and the ratepayers and their officials.[35] Equally, as we have seen from the examples of Garstang and Trowbridge, the principle and practice of comparability, and not just its linguistic footprint, had become part of the administrative landscape.

INTER-PARISH RELATIONSHIPS AND THE
NEGOTIATION OF ENTITLEMENT

A deeper sense of how more robust accounting practices and the deployment of a wider corpus of numerical data informed the operation of the Old Poor Law can be constructed from an analysis of the out-parish relief system, dealt with briefly above, and the official and pauper correspondence that it generated. Drawing first on the correspondence of officials, it is notable that the linguistic and functional ground for relations between parishes (over the entitlement of paupers, rates of relief, payment of bills, etc.) shifted after 1800 away from issues of customary duty and past practice and towards a more rigorous rendering of the numerical identity of the Old Poor Law. Though space constraints prevent a full examination, some emblematic cases provide a sense of this distinctive linguistic register.

Widow Naylor and her children were legally settled in Oundle but actually resident in the Cambridgeshire parish of Sawston when they fell into poverty. In response to a letter from Sawston asking for authority to relieve, the Oundle overseer wrote on 12 May 1835 to sanction a one-shilling-per-week increase to the widow's allowance. He warned, however, 'considering that this is in addition to the extra shilling allowed by my letter March 3rd 1835 it is as much as they [the vestry] can possibly can do in Justice to other Applicants you will now please pay her 7/- a week.'[36] The implication that relief for widow Naylor was set out in some comparative numerical formula for all Oundle paupers is validated in a letter of 21 September 1835 enclosing a cheque to cover Naylor's relief, in which the overseer instructed:

> In future you will only pay Widow Naylor & family five shillings per week taking into consideration the price of Bread. Our Paupers have all been reduced and we hear that the Boy does & the Girl can obtain work at the paper mills under these circumstances we shall be allowing widow Naylor 2/9 and -/9 a head for each child per week. This is as much as we can afford and more than would be allowed but we have taken into consideration her not enjoying a very good state of health.[37]

By way of confirmation, the overseer enclosed a table of relief payments showing the majority of Oundle paupers falling into the bottom quartile of payment bands. He wrote across the top, 'Sir, in these you may trust', giving us a clear sense of both the rigour of his accounting but also the implicit authority of the numbers thus constructed.[38]

Sawston and Oundle came to an amicable solution in the case of widow Naylor. Where responsibility for paupers or the allowances for them was disputed, numerical evidence came even more directly into play. Mr Jimson, the overseer of Rothersthorpe (Northamptonshire), was dismayed to be sent a bill for £16 by his counterpart in Reading on 16 May 1821 covering the costs of sickness for the Harrison family, who had a settlement in Rothersthorpe. He wrote that 'according to my table of liabilities, it was agreed by the previous overseer that the bill should not exceed £5', and that he thought the cost of the doctor employed by Reading (£7) 'most excessive compared to this County where no parish of which I have knowledge would pay a doctor more than £3 for the same task'. Berating the Reading overseer for failing to provide him with the names, income and location of the Harrison children, as agreed with the previous overseer, Jimson concluded: 'You account with us very hard and on this matter of Trust I see that we were wrong to step away from our normal counting practice'.[39] Four years later (21 June 1825) a new Rothersthorpe overseer, Daniel Gleadle, was involved in an exchange with his counterpart in Leicester about an allowance for Widow Steele, a Rothersthorpe resident who had fallen into poverty. In response to a suggestion that she receive an allowance of 6 shillings per week for the duration of her sickness, Gleadle wrote that such an allowance 'is something above what we would normally give. Indeed this figure would amount to three times that of other widows from this parish similarly placed'. Instead, he suggested the widow should be given 2 shillings and some extra food and fuel. The response from Leicester does not survive, but it clearly troubled Gleadle, who wrote, 'allowances given in the past will not be a guide for this parish given strained times and a better grasp of practice in other places'. He enclosed a list of 'agreed allowances' for paupers of different sorts, and recommended that his Leicester counterpart 'be not troubled by the custom of the place' but 'be persuaded of the truth' of these allowances.[40] Gleadle's letter demonstrates an interesting fusion of linguistic registers, referring to past practice and custom alongside a numerical understanding of the nature of local allowances, a comparative frame of numerical reference, and an elision of trust with a table of predetermined allowances. Yet, for Gleadle, custom, precedent and the moral economy (which would have placed widows firmly on the deserving side of relief eligibility) were backward-looking constructs, which he urged his counterpart to abandon. More generally, the language of custom and precedent falls off sharply in overseers' correspondence from the 1810s, with numerical evidence and its accounting forming a cornerstone of the out-parish relief system thereafter, as has already been suggested above.

The other side of the out-parish system was the pauper letter, a vehicle through which paupers distant from their parish of settlement hoped to establish their entitlement and to negotiate the form and longevity of their relief. Though such letters present a suite of problems to do with truthfulness, accuracy and authorial voice, those who have used them regard the many thousands of surviving pauper letters as both representative and accurate sources.[41] Their advantage is that they provide at least a partial answer to two important and closely interlaced questions that go to the heart of this chapter: How did the early nineteenth-century entrenchment of formalized accounting practices and the collection, dissemination and utilization of numerical information influence official attitudes towards paupers at local level? And how far were paupers themselves able to use numerical data to enhance the persuasiveness of their appeals for relief?

We return to the first of these questions in the conclusion; but that paupers would have had access to information on poor law spending figures is not now in doubt.[42] There is also increasing evidence of a more widespread base of popular numeracy than has often been allowed.[43] In turn, pauper letters, particularly after the early 1810s, certainly come to contain more numerical information and reasoning. A good, but by no means unusual, example is Jane Buckeridge, writing from Lambeth to her settlement parish of Pangbourne (Berkshire). Her first letter of 20 March 1817 sets the general tone of her entire correspondence, arguing that '[I] Beg to say I expected to Receive one Pound four instead of one Pound one as you will find by your books if you will please to inspect them that the 3rd of April makes two months Pay due to me.'[44] The implications of this letter—that she knew something about the accounting practices of the overseer and that she kept her own records of what was due and when—are important for the argument of this chapter. In turn, Pangbourne was to hear frequently from Buckeridge. Her letter of 7 October 1828 exemplifies the series as a whole. Relaying the death of her mother, she asked the overseers for the costs of her burial, adding, 'I should wish to remind the Gentlemen that the expences of a Funerall in London comes very dear, and I have not got one belonging to me that is able to give me a sixpence towards the burying of her'. To enhance her case she deployed a relatively sophisticated (for a pauper) numerical rhetoric, arguing 'I would wish to Remind the Gentlemen that the expences of the funeral when all is paid will not be a farthing less than six pounds and that will not amount to a years Money at three shillings per week.'[45]

Paupers in the more than 2,000 surviving narratives for the three counties considered in this chapter used numerical evidence, and an associated linguistic register, in similar ways. William Lloyd, for instance, wrote from Oxford to Caversham (Berkshire) on 26 November 1818 to say that

> Understanding that Monday is Parish meeting and that the Business respecting my Rent is to be settled that Evening I think it is proper that the Gentlemen should know my mind on the Subject to prevent aney mistakes. My wife Informs me that Mr Horn & Curtis should say that only 2s per week would be allowed and that no longer than Ladey Day. But I can not concent to That. I think the least the Parish can do is to allow 3s per week How can the[y] think that I can suport a wife and 2 or 3 children with only 8s or 10s per week at such a Dear place as Oxford. I cannot concent to starve my self to favour my Parish . . . I hope the Gentlemen—will no Disaprove my Request for it will only augment the expenses to the Parish to send my wife and family to Caversham.[46]

Written on the back of the letter was a further note informing the overseer that

> I inclose a list of the value of the parish rents payd here that you might see the imposerbility of my meeting all of the rent required and of the general state of things in Oxford at this time you will have seen from the newspapers wich i know as been reported in Caversham from my brother.[47]

In short, William Lloyd felt himself to be using the same vocabulary of numbers as the officials he addressed. Just as overseers used numbers to enhance the trustworthiness of their statements, so did paupers. As Tom Crook has argued elsewhere in this volume, numbers allowed ordinary people to question government; but more than this, even basic numerical information and reasoning might define, convey and facilitate pauper agency in the negotiation of poor relief. This was probably the intention of Elizabeth Fry's letter from her host town of Birmingham to her settlement parish of Rothersthorpe, in which she noted:

> I know full well from the newspapers the burthen of the rates and that others cry for relief as do I, but consider gentlemen what it must be for a mother to see her children starve and no one to offer us friendship but you. I beg that you will place our claims in your hearts and at the top of your lists.[48]

Perhaps more directly, Jonathan Waites wrote from Northampton General Hospital to his parish of settlement in Malmesbury (Wiltshire) on 18 July 1829 to say that he needed relief on the occasion of his wife and several children being ill. Appealing to the overseer almost as a friend, he wrote:

> Consider Mr Hampton the Economy of 5s a week while we get well For yet I Know from the news[papers] that this Would be not a half of the Wages of a Man in this place and you will save at the Least £50 for Were my Wife to Die we must come to You I Know the Rates is Stretched with You but 5s is Not out of the Ordinery up at Mamsbry as You Know from the Report to the Gentlemen.[49]

This deployment of numerical evidence is hardly sophisticated, but it is at the heart of the appeal. Certainly more evidence of pauper numeracy is needed than can be offered here. Nonetheless, considering pauper letters in the round, it is possible to argue that rather than simply losing their legitimacy in the eyes of early nineteenth-century ratepayers, as Hollen Lees suggests, the agency of the poor in this period was re-energized, and perhaps even magnified, by emerging numerical understandings of their position.

CONCLUSION

The post-1800 period was one in which numerical understandings and representations of the Old Poor Law at national and local levels underwent significant development. This can of course be seen as part of the rise of the information state, but it was also specific to the circumstances of the welfare system. An increasing reliance on numerical data and more rigorous accounting procedures created a framework and linguistic register within which disparate parishes could interact as economic units, especially in the out-parish relief system (itself crucial to the mutability of the Old Poor Law). Officials also used numerical data and reasoning more explicitly to locate, amend and validate local practices for vestries and ratepayers. As we have seen, officials consumed numerical data on practices elsewhere with real vigour. In this respect, it is unsurprising that the 1830s saw renewed attempts to generate standardized numerical data, as for instance in the instructions sent to the Bradfield Poor Law Union (Berkshire) in May 1835 which instructed officials that 'In the report, on cases of application for relief to the Board, the ages of the applicant & his children should always be stated, his last employment & the cause of his present necessity as nearly as can be ascertained, & the date of the application as all other particulars relative to the case.'[50]

To be sure, diarists often recorded with dismay the burden of the poor rates, and it is certainly true that the generation and analysis of poor law numbers at a national level drove a politico-legal discourse on the need for welfare reform. Equally, however, the language and logic of numbers provided power, justification and rhetoric to both officials and paupers, serving to keep the Old Poor Law in place for significantly longer than might otherwise have been the case. Against this backdrop, it is also important to note that paupers began to see the importance of numerical information in establishing their case. Subtly, but definitely, pauper letters came to be infused with numbers and rudimentary numerical reasoning. One reading of this trend is that paupers and officials came to inhabit a shared linguistic territory of numbers, in which the exercise of pauper agency and the perceived legitimacy (or otherwise) of their claims were interwoven for the audience of parish ratepayers. Numbers and stronger accounting mechanisms, in other words, changed both the nature of local debate over the Old Poor Law and influenced the way officials and local elites viewed the poor. Though it is often argued that the poor law lost legitimacy after 1800, the fact is that most attempts to slash the relief lists were as ineffectual as they were periodic. The very numbers and comparative data that provided the rationale for cutbacks could serve other functions: they might provide a defence mechanism for paupers; a means for local officials to claim that their activities represented value-for-money; as well as a common linguistic territory in which a shared version of entitlement between pauper and officials could be created, even as older notions of custom, precedent and moral right waned in their potency.

NOTES

1. M. Daunton, *Trusting Leviathan: The Politics of Taxation in Britain 1799–1914* (Cambridge, 2001); D. Eastwood, '"Amplifying the Province in the Legislature": The Flow of Information and the English State in the Early Nineteenth Century', *Historical Research* 62 (1998), pp. 279–94; W. Bisschop, *The Rise of the London Money Market, 1640–1826* (London, 1968).
2. See, for instance, Report from the Committee on the Laws which Concern the Relief and Settlement of the Poor [1775–1788]: Report from Committees of the House of Commons 1715–1803 (x).

3. Local surveys had a rich eighteenth-century history, as for instance in A Country Gentleman, *A Letter to Thomas Gilbert, Esq: On His Intended Reform of the Poor Laws* (London, 1787). However, the surveys became bigger and more numerous from the 1790s. See F.M. Eden, *The state of the poor: or, An history of the labouring classes in England, from the conquest to the present period . . . and many original documents on subjects of national importance* (London, 1797). On earlier extensive Quaker surveys, see P. Morgan, 'Service of the Truth: Quaker Poor Relief in Staffordshire to the Mid-Eighteenth Century', in P. Morgan and A. Phillips (eds.), *Staffordshire Histories* (Keele, 1999), pp. 157–76.

4. This chapter uses the term 'numerical reasoning' to refer to numbers constructed for, or used in support of, narrative arguments and/or used to identify normative standards and comparative contexts. The collection and calculation of recognizably modern 'statistical information' on the poor law was a product of the mid-Victorian period. For a discussion of terminology, see the introduction to this volume and L. Schweber, *Disciplining Statistics: Demography and Vital Statistics in France and England 1830–1885* (Durham, NC, 2006).

5. E.A. Wrigley, 'Malthus and the Prospects for the Labouring Poor', *Historical Journal* 31 (1988), pp. 813–29; D. Collard, 'Malthus, Population and the Generational Bargain', *History of Political Economy* 33 (2001), pp. 697–716.

6. See Abstract of Answers and Returns Relative to the Expense and Maintenance of the Poor 1803/04. Report from Committees of the House of Commons 1715–1803 (xxii).

7. See A. Kidd, *State, Society and the Poor in Nineteenth Century England* (Basingstoke, 1999), ch. 1. For a wider overview, see M. Cullen, *The Statistical Movement in Early Victorian Britain* (New York, 1975).

8. E. Higgs, *The Information State in England: The Central Collection of Information on Citizens since 1500* (Basingstoke, 2004); O. MacDonagh, *Early Victorian Government, 1830–1870* (London, 1977); L. Goldman, *Science, Reform and Politics in Victorian Britain: The Social Science Association, 1857–1886* (Cambridge, 2002). For a broader, European perspective, see N. Randeraad, *States and Statistics in the Nineteenth Century: Europe by Numbers* (Manchester, 2010).

9. J. Knight and S. Flood (eds.), *Two Nineteenth Century Hertfordshire Diaries* (Hertford, 2002), 26 Jan. 1822.

10. D. Eastwood, 'Men, Morals and the Machinery of Social Legislation, 1790–1840', *Parliamentary History* 13 (1994), pp. 197–8.

11. See D. Eastwood, 'Rethinking the Debates on the Poor Law in Early Nineteenth Century England', *Utilitas* 6 (1994), pp. 200–1.

12. On the crisis of the Old Poor Law, see P. Dunkley, *The Crisis of the Old Poor Law in England, 1795–1834: An Interpretive Essay* (New York, 1982).

13. L. Hollen Lees, *The Solidarities of Strangers: The English Poor Laws and the People, 1700–1948* (Cambridge, 1998), pp. 20, 73–114.

14. For a particularly strong rendering of this view (and an excellent counterargument), see S. Sherman, *Imagining Poverty: Quantification and the Decline of Paternalism* (Columbus, OH, 2001).

15. His survey, part of his diary covering these years, is held in private hands. I am grateful to John Sims for access to his family collection. William Langstaff had been obliged to recognize an illegitimate child in 1817. Lancashire Record Office [hereafter LRO] QSP/2716/295, 'Filiation order'.

16. Consulted at Knighton House private muniment room December 1998. I am grateful to Maj. Knighton for access to these records.

17. J. Innes, 'The "Mixed Economy of Welfare" in Early Modern England: Assessments of the Options from Hale to Malthus, c. 1683–1803', in M. Daunton (ed.), *Charity, Self-Interest and Welfare in the English Past* (London, 1996), pp. 139–80.

18. J. Innes, 'The Local Acts of a National Parliament: Parliament's Role in Sanctioning Local Action in Eighteenth-Century Britain', *Parliamentary History* 17 (1998), pp. 23–47; J. Prest, *Liberty and Locality: Parliament, Permissive Legislation and Ratepayers' Democracies in the Nineteenth Century* (Oxford, 1990).

19. On the out-parish system that generated pauper letters, see S. King, '"It Is Impossible for Our Vestry to Judge His Case into Perfection from Here": Managing the Distance Dimensions of Poor Relief, 1800–40', *Rural History* 16 (2005), pp. 161–89.

20. See, for instance, the limited commentary by Thomas Turner in D. Vaisey (ed.), *The Diary of Thomas Turner 1754–1765* (East Hoathley, 1994).

21. Northamptonshire Record Office [hereafter NRO] 110p/138/17, 'Earls Barton letters'.

22. Berkshire Record Office [hereafter BRO] DP 91/18/1, 'Pangbourne Correspondence'.

23. NRO 249P/166, 'Oundle Vestry Minutes'.

24. Interestingly, this sort of guidance and admonition did not yield more accurate statistics. The wider British Academy project on which this chapter is based (SG-43571, 'The Economics of Overseeing') is currently investigating the reliability of 'national' statistics.

25. Wiltshire Record Office [hereafter WRO]. Uncatalogued, 'Diary of Richard Harbury'.

26. WRO 206/68, 'Overseer's Accounts'. The resolution is in the form of a loose flyer.

27. LRO DDX 386/3, 'Garstang Vestry Book'.

28. *Ibid.*

29. *Ibid.*

30. NRO 249p/216, 'Oundle Letter Book', 25 Apr. 1834.

31. *Ibid.*, 19 Dec. 1833.

32. *Ibid.*, 22 Sep. 1835.

33. J. Willis, *On the Poor Laws of England* (London, 1808); T. Courtenay, *A Treatise upon the Poor Laws* (London, 1818); J. Halcomb, *A Practical Measure of Relief from the Present System of the Poor Laws* (London, 1826); G. Lewin, *A Summary of the Laws Relating to the Government and Maintenance of the Poor* (London, 1828); J. Bird, *The Laws Respecting Parish Matters* (London, 1828); J. Bosworth, *The Practical Means of Reducing the Poor's Rate* (London, 1824); J. Davison, *Considerations on the Poor Laws* (Oxford, 1817); M. Nolan, *A Treatise on the Laws for the Relief and Settlement of the Poor* (4th edn., 3 vols., London, 1825); W. Robinson, *Lex Parochialis: Or a Compendium of the Laws Relating to the Poor* (London, 1827). I am grateful to Peter King for this suggestion and for access to his collection of pamphlets and guidance books.

34. J. Paul, *The Parish Officer's Complete Guide* (London, 1785); A Gentleman of Lincoln's Inn, *The Modern Parish Officer; or the Parish Officer's Complete Duty* (London, 1774). See also E. Barry, *Justice of the Peace* (London, 1790).

35. NRO 249p/164–66, 'Oundle Vestry Minutes 1828–35'.

36. NRO 249p/216, 'Oundle Letter Book', 12 May 1835.

37. *Ibid.*, 21 Sep. 1835.

38. *Ibid.*

39. Consulted at Rothersthorpe Parish Church in the parish chest, October 1996.
40. *Ibid.* On statistics and truth, see M. Poovey, *A History of the Modern Fact: Problems of Knowledge in the Sciences of Wealth and Society* (Chicago, 1999). Edward Higgs has suggested to me that there may have been a differential tendency for numerical information and reasoning to be used by urban versus rural officials because of the problems associated with identification of the individual in urban areas. That is, numerical evidence was a substitute for personal knowledge. This does not appear to be the case for Rothersthorpe, though the fact that so many of its paupers were out of the parish might have generated a tendency to use numerical information as a means of controlling liabilities.
41. T. Sokoll, *Essex Pauper Letters, 1731–1837* (Oxford, 2001) provides the most thorough overview.
42. See B. Bushaway, '"Things Said or Sung a Thousand Times": Customary Society and Oral Culture in Rural England, 1700–1900', in A. Fox and D. Woolf (eds.), *The Spoken Word: Oral Culture in Britain 1500–1850* (Manchester, 2002), pp. 256–77; J. Raven, H. Small and N. Tadmor (eds.), *The Practice and Representation of Reading in England* (Cambridge, 1996), pp. 1–21, 175–225.
43. Cash payments at the Bank of England were suspended in 1797, leading to coin hoarding and shortage. Hutter argues that 'a much wider portion of the population, largely illiterate, [were obliged] to use paper money'. This applied equally to overseers and even paupers and forced an extension of popular numeracy. See M. Hutter, 'Visual Credit: The Britannia Vignette on the Notes of the Bank of England', in F. Cox and H. W. Schmidt-Hannisa (eds.), *Money and Culture* (Berne, 2007), pp. 28–9.
44. BRO D/P/91/18/5, 'Letters', 20 Mar. 1817.
45. BRO D/P91/18/2/2, 'Letters', 7 Oct. 1828.
46. BRO D/P/162/18/2, 'Letters', 26 Nov. 1818.
47. *Ibid.*
48. Consulted at Rothersthorpe Parish Church in the parish chest, October, 1996.
49. Northampton General Hospital Archive. I am grateful to Dr Andrew Williams for introducing me to the archive and arranging access.
50. BRO D/P132/19/7, 'Bradfield Correspondence', 14 May 1835.

4 The State and Statistics in Victorian and Edwardian Britain
Promotion of the Public Sphere or Boundary Maintenance?

Edward Higgs

As Tom Crook and Glen O'Hara note in the introduction to this volume, any attempt to examine the relationship between the production and dissemination of statistics and the creation and workings of the public sphere must engage with the monumental work of the German theorist Jürgen Habermas. Habermas's description of the formation of a space for public discourse during the Enlightenment has become the paradigm from which other discussions of the subject take their bearings. The present chapter is no exception in that it attempts to examine the statistical output of a key institution in Victorian and Edwardian Britain, the General Register Office (GRO), in light of Habermas's notion of the public sphere.[1] As will be discussed, the GRO saw itself as contributing towards the formation of informed members of the public who could make sensible decisions about their own mode of life, as well as enter into local debate over issues of sanitation and environmental health. To this extent, the work of the GRO can be seen in terms of the public sphere described and idealized by Habermas.

However, Habermas's ideal of a sphere of public discourse assumed untrammelled communication between social actors, and it will also be argued that this was not what the GRO was helping to enable in the Victorian and Edwardian periods. Given the need to reduce data complexity, the GRO's statistical production inevitably involved processes of information truncation. For instance, only certain questions were asked; replies were grouped under headings in classification systems that structured data in certain ways; and the reporting of the results of these manipulations dwelt only on certain facets of the data. In other words, choices had to be made as to what was considered important and relevant, and these choices precluded the making of other choices. This exercise of power and authority shut off alternative discourses about the social world. It will be argued below that these processes of information truncation can be understood in terms of the systems theory of Habermas's intellectual *bête noir*, Niklas Luhmann.

The chapter is presented in three sections. The first section discusses the contrasting theories of Habermas and Luhmann. Some of Habermas's early work has been incorporated into contemporary historiography, but the true nature and extent of his broader theoretical project has not always been appreciated. The work of Luhmann, by contrast, is hardly known at all to Anglo-Saxon scholars. The second section examines the work of the GRO in terms of Habermas's theory of the public sphere, while the final section looks at processes of information truncation in the light of Luhmann's systems theory.

HABERMAS, LUHMANN, AND THE NATURE OF COMMUNICATIVE ACTION

On the whole, historians in the Anglophone world have engaged more fully with French intellectuals (especially Michel Foucault) than with postwar German theorists.[2] A notable exception is Habermas, especially his early work *The Structural Transformation of the Public Sphere: An Inquiry into a Category of Bourgeois Society*, first published in 1962.[3] Here Habermas describes how a society dominated by a feudal monarchy, and lacking a distinction between state and society, public and private, was replaced during the eighteenth century by a liberal constitutional order that distinguished between a public state and a private realm. Crucially, this shift was also accompanied by the emergence of a bourgeois public sphere for rational-critical debate and the formation of public opinion, and it was here where the bourgeoisie first learned to reflect upon itself and its society. But as Crook and O'Hara note, for Habermas this public sphere 'decayed' during the twentieth century, as it was gradually colonized by big business, state bodies and the mass media. Increasingly the public was posited as a passive consumer, rather than a critical subject.

Habermas's subsequent work, culminating in his *Theory of Communicative Action* of 1981, further developed the theme of rational-critical debate, albeit in more philosophical terms. In this later work, Habermas attempts to give an ontological underpinning to the Enlightenment concept of human rights, based on an examination of what happens when human beings communicate with each other for the purpose of reaching understanding. Following 'speech act' theorists such as J.L. Austin and John Searle, among others, he argues that language has force. It is used to make claims, issue commands, express feelings, and so on, with the expectation that this will affect the consciousness and actions of others. But language can only do this if the participants in a process of communication accept certain things about each other: that they are all competent communicative practitioners who understand the 'rules of the game', and as such are 'rational' and worthy of recognition.[4] Communication of this sort, when unconstrained by force or guile, thus reveals other human beings as free agents of debate, equal participants in dialogue, and common partners united by a shared interest in reaching understanding. In some respects, this is Habermas's reformulation of the concepts of *liberté*, *égalité*, and *fraternité*.

Members of the public sphere must, however, adhere to certain rules for such an 'ideal speech situation' to occur:

1.   Every subject with the competence to speak and act is allowed to take part in a discourse.
2a. Everyone is allowed to question any assertion whatever.
2b. Everyone is allowed to introduce any assertion whatever into the discourse.
2c. Everyone is allowed to express his attitudes, desires and needs.
3.   No speaker may be prevented, by internal or external coercion, from exercising his rights as laid down in (1) and (2).[5]

These are formal rules for a situation and do not say anything about the content of assertions, or where they come from. But in keeping with his earlier work, Habermas clearly believes that modern political and commercial systems are increasingly encroaching on this sphere of discursive rationality, and with detrimental effects, limiting what individuals can speak and think about. Of course, this is a mere sketch of Habermas's arguments, shorn of the erudition and theoretical considerations that give them substance, but it points to the key importance that Habermas places on unconstrained communication in determining what it is to be human.

Communication is also crucial to Niklas Luhmann's theory of social processes, though his understanding of its role is almost diametrically opposed to that of Habermas.[6] Luhmann does not think in terms of autonomous, communicating individuals, but of systems. In brief, a system, whether it is a person, an academic discipline, or a commercial company, is defined by a boundary between itself and its environment. The interior of the system is a space of reduced complexity, and communication within a system operates by selecting only a limited amount of the information available on the outside. Selection generates meaning, and both social systems and psychical (or personal) systems operate by processing meaning; a system that cannot make such choices at its boundary ceases to be a distinct system able to process information and function on its own terms. An academic discipline, such as history, for example, has its own field of facts, which it picks from the vast world of information that exists, according to certain criteria. If it chooses other criteria, for example, those of particle physics, it will cease to be history. Similarly, a person who could not pick or choose what stimuli they considered to be important or relevant in their daily lives would be lost in a babble of communications and would cease to function. For Luhmann, systems have 'evolved' in this manner to allow their limited processing capacities to handle the vast, chaotic flows of information that exist in the environment. As such, unconstrained communication is almost a contradiction in terms, because any entity which cannot control the information it receives from its environment will cease to be an entity. If a system fails to maintain that identity, it ceases to exist as a system, and dissolves back into the environment from which it emerged.

This is a highly abstract theory and not an altogether pleasant one, because it implies that what determines consciousness and meaning is a set of choices programmed into individuals by society. Indeed, individuals can hardly be said to exist for Luhmann: they are really just the bearers of the choices operating at their boundaries, which enable them to order and sift information. Human beings cannot 'know' other individuals; they only attribute certain conventional forms of behaviour to them—that of being the boss, a parent, or a spouse, for instance. This works because others act likewise, drawing on the same social conventions and communicative criteria.[7] In this way, Luhmann's theory also makes for a radical form of relativism, in which Enlightenment values are not the reflection of what it is to be human, but simply conventions that allow us to orientate ourselves in a world of intense complexity and information density. The processing of information does not facilitate genuine communication between sentient individuals; rather, it leads to the creation of similar frames of reference for actors, so that the systems in which they are embedded can function efficiently. A does not need to 'connect' with B; A only needs to assume that B will act in an appropriate manner in a particular social context.

THE GRO AND THE CREATION OF THE PUBLIC SPHERE

In the Victorian period, the GRO, as well as the wider public, saw its activities in terms of providing information to facilitate debate and personal decision making. It certainly harboured what might be termed Habermasian ambitions. The GRO was set up in London in 1837 to administer the civil registration of births, marriages, and deaths. The new system replaced the parochial registration of baptisms, marriages, and burials that had been established in the early sixteenth century, and it was hoped that the improved registration of vital events would protect property rights via more accurate recording of lines of descent. Civil registration also removed the necessity for non-conformists to record such information via the Church of England, and provided data for medical research in the form of a particular cause of death recorded on the death certificates. The whole of England and Wales was divided into registration districts based on the boundaries of the Poor Law Unions, each of which had its own registrar. These officers issued the certificates of birth, death, and marriage, and sent copies of the certificates to the GRO, which created indexes and made them available to the public at a central site in London.[8]

Initially, the GRO was in a position of great constitutional independence. It was nominally responsible to the Home Office, though the department does not appear to have been particularly interested in the GRO. At first the head of the Office, the Registrar General, negotiated directly with the

Treasury over staffing matters. This gave the GRO considerable room for developing its own research agenda.[9] Although the GRO was not set up to undertake statistical research, the early Registrar Generals, Thomas Lister (1836–42) and George Graham (1842–79), built up a Statistical Department to compile medical, demographic, public health and actuarial statistics. [10] Much of this work was undertaken in the period 1839 to 1879 by William Farr, the GRO's Superintendent of Statistics. The *Annual Reports of the Registrar General*, and associated publications, became a vehicle for administrative and social reform.[11] In 1840 the GRO took over responsibility for the decennial census, which throughout the nineteenth century asked householders on one night every ten years to provide information on the marital status, relationship to household head, age, sex, occupation, birthplace, and medical disabilities of each member of their family. This information was collected by local census enumerators and forwarded to a temporary Census Office in London, run by the GRO, where the data were tabulated on a national and local basis, and then disseminated in various published *Census Reports*.[12]

The GRO saw this activity in terms of supplying information for use by the wider public. As Graham put it in his first *Annual Report* in 1842, referring to the published data on births, marriages, and deaths:

> The inhabitants [of each district] will thus learn from authentic documents the relative sanatory state of their neighbourhood; the causes of disease will be discovered, and suggestions which may lead to numerous improvements will be pressed upon the attention of resident proprietors and authorities. The friendly societies will obtain from the local tables the means of adjusting their premiums equitably to the prevailing rate of sickness and mortality, which may be a fourth or a half higher in some districts than in others, and will be found to differ among the same class, so as to affect materially the money value of assurance and the stability and prosperity of the societies.[13]

The publication of data was also intended to enable individual citizens in a liberal polity to make sensible decisions about their lives—to avoid jobs that had high levels of mortality, or districts that were insalubrious.[14] This may have been impracticable, but it reveals a desire to provide citizens with tools to live autonomous lives.

Such data were also to facilitate national political debate and action. Graham noted in his *Annual Report* for 1847, for example, that:

> In successive Reports the births, deaths and marriages have been compared with the population of differing districts; the prevalence of disease has been traced in various parts; and the irrefragable proofs of the high mortality in towns induced the late Government to appoint a commission of inquiry, which resulted in a bill submitted to parliament

by Lord Lincoln and Sir James Graham. A new bill for improving the health of towns has been prepared and brought in by the Viscount Morpeth, Lord John Russell, and Sir George Grey.[15]

In addition, as Simon Szreter has argued, the provision of data on local mortality rates was intended to provide information for local sanitary reformers and to shame local authorities into action. Under the 1848 Public Health Act, local authorities were even compelled to set up local sanitary boards if the annual mortality in their districts was higher than twenty-three per thousand, as measured by the GRO.[16] To this end, in their sections of the *Reports*, both Graham and Farr commented on the statistics produced by the GRO in a tone of exhortation. In the *Annual Report* for 1853, Farr exclaimed:

> What no sceptical philosopher would have dared to propose as an experiment, what no haughty conqueror ever condemned the inhabitants of a subjugated city to endure—this fine English town on the Tyne—the centre of the coal trade—of intelligence of every kind—and of engineering knowledge—has done and suffered. All the excreta, which are thrown into the streets or water closets, are washed down the acclivities of the streets into the river; the fermenting mass is driven up and down by the tides, and has thence since July been pumped by the engine at Elswick all over the town through the water pipes for domestic uses: it has been used for ablution, it has been washed over the floors, it has been drunk as a beverage by many of the children and the wives, as well as large numbers of the higher and middle as well as the working men of the town. This sad fact in the history of Newcastle will be remembered when the loss of 1500 lives [by cholera], by which it was followed, is forgotten.[17]

This is certainly not the tone of a modern government report, and such purple passages are more reminiscent of a writer such as Charles Dickens, than of twenty-first-century statistical publications.

In the *Census Reports* the GRO also expressed its belief that the dissemination of accurate information would allow the various classes of society to come to an agreement about true states of affairs and their respective positions within them. Commenting on their analysis of occupational data in the *General Report* for 1861, the officers of the GRO commented:

> Nothing is accidental in the marvellous economy of society; and the investigations of its laws, while it will dissipate illusions and remove misapprehensions will cherish just hopes, and lead to innumerable improvements. Errors will be dissipated. The workman, when the truth is known, will no longer fancy that he alone is the producer of wealth; and the master will learn that he can best win industrial

victories with the aid of intelligent, healthy, contented men, and not with mere 'hands'.[18]

Public debate was thus to take place in an informed manner through the provision of information.

This exercise in public instruction and opinion forming was carried forward by the ambitious policy of distributing large numbers of *Reports* free to people the GRO wished to inform and influence. Prior to 1858, for example, the Office sent in excess of 4,000 free copies of its *Annual Report* to registration officers in the country, to every clerk in the GRO, to all coroners, as well as to learned societies, medical practitioners, reading rooms, mechanics institutes, the statistical departments of foreign governments, and private individuals. It also distributed 9,000 free quarterly reports and an astounding 65,000 free weekly reports a year. This was an extraordinary exercise in public education, one made possible by the development of railways and the new, cheap postal services established in the early Victorian period.[19]

Other public opinion formers understood the GRO's activities in a similar way. Commenting on the passage of the 1850 Census Act, *The Times* informed its readers that:

> The revelations therefore of our coming census will bear a mighty import, and the more so as they will extend to features of our condition which have not hitherto been so critically investigated. They will reach beyond the mere facts of our actual or proportionate increase to other facts bearing on our sanitary, economical, educational and religious position. We are to lay the foundation next year of a more complete self-knowledge, and apply unshrinkingly the test which alone will satisfy ourselves and confute the prophets of misfortune . . . On the social bearing of such an investigation it is hardly necessary to dwell; it is only by learning what as a people we have been doing that we can learn what remains for us as a people to do. The command of data is the one circumstance which separates our legislation from the legislation on crude or mistaken principles which even great men were compelled to accept in former times.[20]

Similarly, the national and local press throughout the Victorian period carried descriptions, often in great detail, of the national and local data on births, marriages, and deaths in the *Annual Report of the Registrar General*. This could extend to trenchant critiques of the data, as when, in 1864, the *Birmingham Daily Post* carried a lengthy description of a paper presented at the Royal Statistical Society, 'On certain defects of the reports of the Registrar General'. This pointed out that the death rates in a city such as Birmingham depended on the boundaries of registration districts, and might not give a fair picture of the relative salubrity of a place.[21] Census and civil registration data were thus actively disseminated and commented upon as part of ongoing public debate.

These activities fitted into a classical liberal understanding of the role of the central state as educator and facilitator, rather than as executive authority. As John Stuart Mill put it in his *Considerations on Representative Government*, published in 1861:

> The authority which is most conversant with principles should be supreme over principles, while that which is most competent in details should have the details left to it. The principal business of the central authority should be to give instruction, of the local authority to apply it. Power may be localized, but knowledge, to be most useful, must be centralized . . . [Central government] ought to keep open a perpetual communication with the localities: informing itself by their experience, and them by its own; giving advice freely when asked, volunteering it when seen to be required; compelling publicity and recordation of proceedings, and enforcing obedience to every general law which the legislature has laid down on the subject of local management.[22]

'Knowledge', of course, increasingly implied statistical knowledge. Mill's emphasis on the importance of maintaining face-to-face relationships in local political communities, and of informed debate, in part reflected his attachment to the ideals of classical Greek democracy. Even so, the development of a centralized, bureaucratic state could be justified if its role was to facilitate, rather than override, the workings of active citizenship at the local level in the form of ratepayer democracies.[23]

However, the ability of the GRO to function as an independent catalyst for unconstrained public discussion was gradually curtailed over the course of the nineteenth century. In 1858 the Treasury decided that as an economy measure the GRO's lavish distribution of its reports would be curtailed, and in future the Office was only to receive one hundred *Annual Reports*, and one hundred weekly and 150 quarterly reports.[24] By the 1870s the GRO was receiving 350 copies of the *Annual Report*, but its distribution programme plainly never returned to the scale of the 1840s and 1850s.[25] In addition, the institutional position of the Office changed in 1871, when it came under the supervision of the Local Government Board (LGB), an amalgam of the Poor Law Commission and the Medical Department of the Privy Council. The LGB introduced closer scrutiny of the GRO's activities, a process facilitated by the appointment of Sir Brydges Henniker as Registrar General in 1880. Henniker, who was in post until 1900, had been the private secretary to the president of the LGB, and was a somewhat ineffectual head of the Office. Under his leadership the quality of the GRO's publications declined, and the tone of exhortation associated with Graham and Farr was dropped. The recitation of dry statistics became the GRO's forte.[26]

Other state departments also began to intrude into the work of the GRO, increasingly converting it into a research facility for government, rather than a catalyst for public debate. After the deliberations of a Treasury Committee on the Census in 1890, the GRO began to defer to other departments with respect to the questions asked in the decennial enumeration.[27] In 1919 the GRO was absorbed into the Ministry of Health, and was now seen as merely providing statistical data for policy formation to be undertaken elsewhere within the ministry. Indeed, it very nearly disappeared as a separate entity altogether. Under Sir Sylvanus Vivian, the Registrar General from 1920 to 1945, the work of the GRO was closely aligned with the policy of the Ministry of Health. After 1920 the *Annual Reports* ceased as a series signed by the Registrar General, and were replaced by the anonymous *Statistical Review*. The GRO now turned inwards to the state, rather than outwards to the public sphere.[28]

THE GRO AND INFORMATION TRUNCATION

This shift in the activities of the GRO—from being a catalyst of public debate to becoming a provider of technical data for state policy formation—fits Habermas's understanding of the decline of the liberal-bourgeois public sphere, whereby policy debate came to be a function of specialist groups, civil servants, politicians, and NGOs, rather than the outcome of wider debate within an 'ideal speech situation'.[29] Yet even during its 'Golden Age' of public engagement in the early to mid-Victorian period, the GRO's activities placed limits on the nature of public discourse, which was by no means unconstrained. It is here we can appreciate the utility of Luhmann's model of the truncation of information flows across system boundaries in order to reduce complexity.

The processes of collecting and tabulating data inevitably involved the GRO in making decisions about what was important and what was not, what information should be collected and presented, and what could be ignored. As noted earlier, Luhmann suggests that this involves decisions about what information means and what it does not mean. A census schedule or a death certificate in the nineteenth century, for instance, demanded only certain pieces of information about individuals; the rest were regarded as irrelevant to the task at hand. Citizens were not asked what they thought important, or what to them revealed the 'state of the nation'. In addition, the two-way tables given in the GRO's nineteenth-century *Reports* selected merely a few variables to hold up for inspection: occupation cross-tabulated by sex and age, for example, but not by income. Data were grouped in classification systems for ease of manipulation and presentation, according to certain organizing principles. The GRO's officials made decisions about what was 'important' and 'meaningful', and they could do so because they were in a position of authority. The decisions made changed over time, reflecting their changing concerns.

There was nothing necessarily sinister about such processes of trunca-tion, because they may merely have reflected the need to produce data out-put in as efficient a manner as possible. Given the scarcity of the GRO's resources, information collection, analysis, and presentation needed to be curtailed to fit the funds available. However, although selection and truncations may have been necessary, the particular selections made by the GRO also reflected certain ideological predispositions that pushed public understanding in certain directions—only certain forms of analysis were considered meaningful. Luhmann tends to write as if these processes of information selection are 'natural' and value-free, but one might enquire as to whose interests such manipulations may have served.

It is certainly true that the processes of collecting and analyzing census and civil registration data involved the handling of vast amounts of infor-mation, and that the GRO's resources were limited. During the census of 1901, for example, ten pieces of information were gathered for each of a total of 32,527,842 individuals, whilst registered vital events in the same year totalled just over 2,000,000. In order to undertake the work of ana-lyzing this information the GRO had very few clerical resources. For most of the nineteenth century the Office had fewer than ninety staff, and of these never more than a quarter were employed in the Statistical Depart-ment, which undertook the tabulation of data.[30] For the processes of cen-sus tabulation, the GRO had to employ temporary clerks every ten years. Inevitably they were the dregs of the trade, and there was little time to organize and train such staff. During the 1881 census, of the ninety-eight clerks employed, four were so ill that no work could be got from them, two died on the job, and the quality of the majority of the rest was considered indifferent, or worse.[31] It is a testimony to the tenacity, energy, and perhaps ruthlessness of men such as Graham and Farr that the GRO managed to produce statistical reports on a regular basis.

During the Victorian period, the GRO's clerks had only simple, manual technologies to undertake this vast task of data processing. Until 1911 they had to add up and present results via the use of tabling sheets and the 'tick-ing' method. In the case of occupational abstraction by age in the census, for example, the tabling sheets were large pieces of paper with occupa-tional headings down one side and age ranges across the top. These head-ings were then ruled across the sheet, creating a matrix of boxes into which the census clerks were to place a tick for an occurrence in the enumerators' returns of a person of the relevant age and occupation. The ticks in the columns were then added up, and the results placed in another series of col-umns on another sheet, giving the raw numbers of people under particular occupational headings within particular age groups. Sheets were created in this manner for each registration sub-district. In order to create tables for registration districts, the sheets for sub-districts had to be folded at the column to be totalled and then lined up so that they overlapped, and the fig-ures were then read off on to district sheets. Figures were transferred from district to county sheets in a similar manner. This was extremely exacting labour, and constant bending over work surfaces was exhausting for the tabler, necessitating frequent breaks.[32] Similar methods were used for creating other forms of cross-tabulation from civil registration data. In 1856, for example, the GRO reported to the Treasury that an experienced clerk had just completed 'tabling the ages and diseases of the females of Lancashire for 1854, comprising 310 abstract sheets containing an aggregate of 29,063 ticks', and that this had taken him four days.[33] The sheer boredom of such work drove at least one GRO clerk to insanity.[34]

These cumbersome processes, and doubts about the capacity of the public to supply and interpret data, help to explain why the GRO sought to keep the census and civil registration as simple as possible in the nineteenth century, and why its statistical output was restricted, in the main, to tables with simple cross-tabulations. In the case of the census, the questions asked on the forms were almost identical from 1851 through to 1881. Even in the twentieth century the number of questions asked by the British census was always significantly lower than that in the US case.[35] Moreover, the adoption of two-dimensional forms of representation necessitated a simplification of the complex natural and social phenomena which the Office sought to study. The use of simple two-way tables encouraged the Victorian GRO to treat variables as simple undifferentiated entities that could be neatly placed once, and once only, in one of the boxes in the matrices of its ticking sheets. Census respondents, for example, could only have one occupation in the published tables, although they were encouraged to give multiple occupations on their census schedules. Many did so, in forms such as 'Maltster, Brewer and Publican', although the census clerks were instructed to abstract only the 'most important', usually the first, during the processes of tabulation. The wording on the census schedule also spoke of people having a 'Rank, Profession or Occupation', which may have precluded the recording of much casual and seasonal work, especially that of women and children, from the decennial enumeration.[36] Economic activity was thus reduced to the paid activities of men, perhaps reflecting the contemporary belief in 'separate spheres' of activity for men and women.[37]

In a similar manner, the mortality tables in the GRO's *Annual Reports* assumed that everybody died of a 'primary' cause of death, rather than from multiple causes, enabling the dead to appear only once in each tabulation. However, on their death certificates, doctors defined 'primary' in several ways, either chronologically, or in terms of the cause that contributed most to death.[38] The later introduction on the certificate of the concept of a 'secondary' or 'contributory' cause of death caused even more confusion, because it then became difficult to tell whether any 'secondary' cause was regarded as a consequence of the primary, or as of independent origin but contributing appreciably to death. These difficulties led the GRO to begin to doubt the very objectivity of the concept of a primary cause of death.[39] The reduction of death to a single, mono-causal process also oversimplified the train of events at the end of life. Associated with a particular under-standing of causation—which will be discussed further below—this nar-rowed what 'death' itself could mean.

Allied to these issues were the problems arising from the GRO's creation of various classification systems: medical nosologies (classifications of dis-eases), occupational classification systems, and socioeconomic groupings. These all worked by placing reported causes of death, and the occupations provided in the census returns, under broader headings that were then the terms placed on the axes of tables. Such classification systems were essen-tial to prevent the coding sheets becoming too large, or the finished tables being too extensive and complex to present to the public. But the use of such systems inevitably introduced into the tables certain ideological prin-ciples that have bedevilled subsequent analysis.

This has been highlighted by Simon Szreter's work on the development of the GRO's system of socioeconomic groupings in the early part of the twentieth century. T.H.C. Stevenson, the GRO's senior medical statisti-cian from 1909 to 1931, constructed this classification in order to study the fertility of married women from data supplied in response to questions in the 1911 census on completed family size. He assumed that the social status of a family could be determined by assigning it to one of a series of socioeconomic groups based on the occupation of the male household head. The classification was based on the belief in a gradation of skill and intelligence which was assumed to be reflected in occupational biographies, and to be constant both geographically and temporally. Stevenson used this classification to 'show' that marital fertility declined the 'higher' one pro-gressed up the social scale. He saw this as reflecting the gradual diffusion of knowledge of contraception from the middle classes 'downwards' in soci-ety.[40] As Szreter argues, however, this system masks all sorts of local and occupational anomalies in family size, and obscures the dynamics of fertil-ity decline. These cannot simply be read off from occupational titles, but need to be seen in terms of the negotiations which went on between men and women within families over sexual and reproductive matters. It was not levels of 'intelligence' that determined fertility, but more concrete mat-ters such as the availability of work for married women, the relative cost of having children, and the gendered balance of power within marriage. Ste-venson's assumption that the occupational wage of the male 'breadwinner', rather than total family income, determined status has also been criticized by historians.[41]

Similar issues could be raised with respect to the occupational classi-fication systems used by the GRO in the Victorian period. The occupa-tional classification systems developed by William Farr were based on the grouping of occupational titles according to the materials being worked up. These in turn were taken as affecting the morbidity and mortality of those who undertook these occupations. In addition, Farr also appears to have followed classical precedents in believing that working with particular materials affected the character of workmen, which led him to claim of his tenth occupational class—persons employed about animals (including such diverse occupations as vet, horse breaker, stock dealer, gamekeeper, fisherman, and mole catcher)—that they were:

> a peculiar race of men; silent, circumspective, prompt, agile, dextrous, enduring, danger-defying men, generally—but modified variously by the classes of animals which occupy them. They contain the representatives of the hunting tribes of old, when wild animals abounded, and men lived off the produce of the chase . . . By their habits many of the class must be well adapted to the purposes of war; they are sometimes idle, and in a militia they could be turned to account.[42]

Those who failed to indicate the material upon which they worked in the census schedule, or those, such as clerks, who did not shape or tend particular substances or animals, were fitted into the material-based classification in residual categories. Thus 'labourers' who neglected to indicate their branch of employment were abstracted under the heading 'General Labourers'. This occupational category included over half a million men in 1871. Similarly, clerks, warehousemen, and stock dealers were placed in the material categories relating to the establishments within which they worked. Thus a clerk in an iron mill would be abstracted under the heading 'Iron Manufacture Service', rather than under 'Commercial Clerk'.

The retirement of Farr in 1879, and his replacement as Superintendent of Statistics by William Ogle, led to an important shift in the principles of occupational classification used in the 1881 census. Clerks and other tertiary workers were now abstracted under their own distinct headings. This shift may lie behind the apparent tertiary economic 'revolution' in the late nineteenth century.[43] Yet these shifting terminologies, and the implications they had for understanding economic and social structures, were attacked by Charles Booth in a seminal critique of the GRO's work published in 1886.[44]

In addition, the confounding of employers, the self-employed, and employees in Farr's 'material' categories helped to obscure the distinctions between masters and 'hands' that the GRO recognized as being so contentious. In this way, debates over the notion of productive and unproductive labour could simply be elided, and the apparent 'harmony' of economic relations emphasized. The pretensions of manual workers to be the source of all wealth, as Farr had noted, could largely be ignored. The GRO resolutely refused to introduce a column into the 1891 census on 'employment status', despite the fact that this change was sought by the Board of Trade at the 1890 Treasury Committee on the Census. In the end, the GRO had to be ordered to do so by the president of the LGB; but even then the GRO tried to claim that it was not legally bound to collect the data. Although the question was put in 1891, the GRO declined to analyze the results in its subsequent *Census Reports*.[45]

Similarly, although the GRO's activities were intended to foster debate about public health, what the right to life meant in practice was constrained by how the GRO and other public health bodies classified death. As Christopher Hamlin has argued, the early public health movement can be seen as an attempt to constrict what 'health' implied. Traditionally, individual manifestations of disease were viewed in terms of myriad external influences (heat, cold, dampness, aridity, diet, work, and so on) on unique human constitutions made up of a balance of humours. Sanitary reformers such as Edwin Chadwick followed Neil Arnott and Thomas Southwood Smith in seeing disease as the result of the invasion of the body by specific chemical pathogens. This allowed Chadwick to narrow the concept of a right to health to the right to the removal of noxious substances from cities via sewers, and to the provision of clean water supplies. He could thus outflank medical and Chartist claims that health should be seen in the broader terms of access to food, rest, and tolerable working conditions. Health became an administrative issue, rather than an economic and social one.[46]

Farr agreed with Arnott and Southwood Smith that infectious diseases were caused by chemical blood poisoning. As noted earlier, his medical nosologies placed each death in a single category according to the 'primary' cause of death, and this cause was in turn conceived as a specific illness. It was no longer possible to use environmental terms such as 'Cold' or 'Damp clothes (putting on, or sleeping in)' as a cause of death; clinical terms such as 'pneumonia' and 'bronchitis' needed to be used. It thus became difficult to talk in terms of more holistic understandings of ill health. This revolution in medical classification has brought vast benefits in terms of diagnosis and therapeutics, but it has also detracted from the ability to see patients as whole human beings placed in particular social settings.[47]

CONCLUSION

The statistical production of the GRO in the Victorian and Edwardian periods can readily be seen in terms of Habermas's understanding of the creation and decline of a liberal public sphere. Equally, however, the work of the GRO can also be understood in terms of Luhmann's theories of communicative truncation, in which information processing curtails what is meaningful, or indeed possible, to talk about. Perhaps, as Habermas contends, his concept of the public sphere is only an ideal against which social and political phenomena can be measured. One can certainly use the concept to engage in public discourse to indicate how far that same discourse falls short of 'humanity'—a critique that has the potential to create the conditions for its proper fulfilment. However, is an ideal that has never been—and perhaps never can be—realized really a useful model for understanding the history of human development?

Perhaps one can square the circle here by following Michael Mann in seeing modern society in terms of a 'bounded pluralism', in which there is a space for public discussion and compromise, but only within the boundaries delineated by acceptance of the territorial integrity of the state, the operations of a free-market economy, and the workings of parliamentary government.[48] In this respect, it should be noted that Victorian statistics, as with so many statistics today, are *'state*-istics'. Like other state statistical bureaux, the GRO was concerned with creating a quantitative picture of a particular territorial entity. This was inevitable given that the information gathering it undertook, through civil registration and census taking, for instance, presupposed state power. To have done otherwise would have been beyond the GRO's authority and competency. However, this did lead to the creation of a particular 'state-bound' understanding of reality, indeed, the creation of what Benedict Anderson calls an 'imagined community', which underpinned the nationalism of the age.[49] In this way, the Victorian GRO created both a space for public discussion, but also the boundaries which constrained and defined it. The question remains, however, whether this should be seen as a trade-off between idealism on the one hand and the practical requirements for an 'actually existing' public sphere on the other; or whether the constraints placed on free discussion represented the interests of political and economic elites.

NOTES

1. For the standard works on the GRO, see E. Higgs, *Life, Death and Statistics: Civil Registration, Censuses and the Work of the General Register Office, 1837–1952* (Hatfield, 2004) and S. Szreter, 'The GRO and the Public Health Movement in Britain, 1837–1914', *Social History of Medicine* 4 (1991), pp. 454–62.
2. J. Tosh, with S. Lang, *The Pursuit of History* (Harlow, 2006), pp. 194–205.
3. J. Habermas, *The Structural Transformation of the Public Sphere: An Inquiry into a Category of Bourgeois Society* [1962, trans. T. Burger, with F. Lawrence] (Oxford, 1992).
4. J. Habermas, *Theory of Communicative Action, Volume One: Reason and the Rationalization of Society* (Cambridge, 1991), pp. 8–42.
5. J. Habermas, *Moral Consciousness and Communicative Action* [trans. C. Lenhardt and S. Weber Nicholson] (Cambridge, MA, 1990), p. 86.
6. Niklas Luhmann, *Social Systems* [1984, trans. J Bednarz, Jr., with Dirk Baecker] (Stanford, CA, 1995).
7. *Ibid.*, p. 227.
8. Higgs, *Life, Death and Statistics*, pp. 1–89; E. Higgs, 'A Cuckoo in the Nest? The Origins of Civil Registration and State Medical Statistics in England and Wales', *Continuity and Change* 11 (1996), pp. 115–34.
9. Higgs, *Life, Death and Statistics*, pp. 29–32.
10. E. Higgs, 'George Graham', *Oxford Dictionary of Historical Biography* (Oxford, 2007).
11. J.M. Eyler, *Victorian Social Medicine: The Ideas and Methods of William Farr* (London, 1979); Higgs, *Life, Death and Statistics*, pp. 45–89, and Szreter, 'The GRO and the Public Health Movement'.

82   *Edward Higgs*

12. E. Higgs, *Making Sense of the Census: The Manuscript Returns for England and Wales, 1801–1901* (London, 1989), pp. 10–15.
13. *4th Annual Report of the Registrar General for the Year Ending 30 June 1841* (London, 1842), p. 3.
14. E. Higgs, 'Citizen Rights and Nationhood: The Genesis and Functions of Civil Registration in 19th-Century England and Wales as Compared to France', *Jahrbuch Für Europäische Verwaltungsgeschichite* 8 (1996), pp. 285–303.
15. *10th Annual Report of the Registrar General for 1847* (London, 1852), p. ix.
16. Szreter, 'The GRO and the Public Health Movement'.
17. *16th Annual Report of the Registrar General for 1853* (London, 1856), p. 38.
18. *Census of England and Wales, 1861, General Report, Volume Three. Parliamentary Papers* [hereafter *PP*], 1863, LIII, p. 233.
19. National Archives, London: RG 29: GRO: Letter Books: RG 29/1, pp. 551–2.
20. *The Times*, 18 Oct. 1850, p. 4.
21. *Birmingham Daily Post*, 19 Feb. 1864.
22. J.S. Mill, 'Considerations on Representative Government', in *idem.*, *Utilitarianism, On Liberty, Considerations on Representative Government* (London, 1993), pp. 388–9.
23. E.F. Biagini, 'Liberalism and Direct Democracy: John Stuart Mill and the Model of Ancient Athens', in E.F. Biagini (ed.), *Citizenship and Community: Liberals, Radicals and Collective Identities in the British Isles, 1865–1931* (Cambridge, 1996), pp. 21–44.
24. National Archives, London: RG 29: GRO: Letter Books: RG 29/5, pp. 425–6.
25. National Archives, London: STAT 3: Stationery Office Out Letters: STAT 3/16, p. 268.
26. Higgs, *Life, Death and Statistics*, pp. 90–128.
27. *Report of the Treasury Committee on the Census. PP*, 1890, LVIII. See also E. Higgs, 'The Struggle for the Occupational Census, 1841–1911', in R. MacLeod (ed.), *Government and Expertise: Specialists, Administrators and Professionals, 1860–1919* (Cambridge, 1988), pp. 73–88.
28. Higgs, *Life, Death and Statistics*, pp. 188–201.
29. Habermas, *The Structural Transformation of the Public Sphere*, pp. 222–35.
30. Higgs, *Life, Death and Statistics*, p. 46.
31. National Archives, London: RG 29: GRO Letter Books: RG 29/3, pp. 78–81.
32. E. Higgs, *A Clearer Sense of the Census: The Victorian Census and Historical Research* (London: HMSO, 1996), pp. 155–6.
33. National Archives, London: T 1: Treasury Board Papers: T 1/6028B/12646, enclosure.
34. National Archives, London: RG 29/1, p. 311.
35. C. Hakim, 'Social Monitors: Population Censuses as Social Surveys', in M. Bulmer (ed.), *Essays on the History of British Sociological Research* (Cambridge, 1985), p. 41.
36. E. Higgs, *Making Sense of the Census*, pp. 80–9.
37. E. Higgs, 'Women, Occupations and Work in the Nineteenth-Century Censuses', *History Workshop Journal* 23 (1987), pp. 59–80.
38. *First and Second Report of the Select Committee on Death Certification. PP*, 1893–94, XI, p. xvii.
39. *Registrar General's Statistical Review for 1927* [HMSO] (London, 1929), p. 145.
40. S. Szreter, *Fertility, Class and Gender in Britain, 1860–1940* (Cambridge, 1996), pp. 67–282.
41. *Ibid.*, pp. 443–602.

42. *Census of Great Britain, 1851, Population Tables, II. Ages, Civil Conditions, Occupations and Birth-place of the People ... Volume One. PP,* 1852–53, LXXXVIII, p. cxii.
43. Higgs, *A Clearer Sense of the Census*, pp. 161–6.
44. C. Booth, 'Occupations of the People of the United Kingdom, 1801–81', *Journal of the Statistical Society of London* 49 (1886), pp. 314–444.
45. K. Schürer, 'The 1891 Census and Local Population Studies', *Local Population Studies* 47 (1991), pp. 16–29.
46. C. Hamlin, *Public Health and Social Justice in the Age of Chadwick: Britain, 1800–1854* (Cambridge, 1998), pp. 52–66, 110–20.
47. E. Higgs, 'The Linguistic Construction of Social and Medical Categories in the Work of the English General Register Office', in S. Szreter, A. Dharmalingam and H. Sholkamy (eds.), *The Qualitative Dimension of Quantitative Demography* (Oxford, 2004), pp. 86–106.
48. M. Mann, *The Sources of Social Power, Volume Two: The Rise of Classes and Nation-States* (Cambridge, 1993), pp. 82–8.
49. B. Anderson, *Imagined Communities: Reflections on the Origin and Spread of Nationalism* (London, 1983).

5 Numbers, Experts and Ideas
The French Economic Model in Britain, c. 1951–1973

Glen O'Hara

Recent debates about statistical knowledge and 'accuracy' have tended to suggest that contemporary policymakers inhabit an entirely new and complex world of impossibly tangled data. During the late 1980s, for instance, there was a sharp divergence between the three accepted measures of gross domestic product (GDP), based alternatively on output, total income, and expenditure, which caused renewed debate as to the efficacy of government figures.[1] These were brought together in one series from 1990 onwards—though only through adjustment and the use of balancing items—when John Major and Norman Lamont as chancellors in 1990 and 1991 launched another statistical initiative. The so-called 'phase one' and 'phase two' efforts of the 1990s focused on making previously voluntary surveys compulsory, and on widening the net of turnover, profit, stock building, and investment figures so as to see whether those adjustments were realistic. In particular, the growth of service industries, small business, and self-employment meant that governments had constantly to adopt more complicated means of data collection.[2]

Many of these issues are still not settled, for instance, on the problems of accounting for services and calculating regional economic growth. The Labour government that came to power in Britain in 1997 was very interested in both: just like their 1960s counterparts, ministers stressed the need for more and better information. However, in the first years of the twenty-first century the Office for National Statistics (ONS) has come in for unprecedented public criticism. In 2003 alone it was blamed for underestimating GDP growth and the trade deficit, encouraging a monetary relaxation that may not have been required, and for mishandling the introduction of regional income accounts based on business surveys, which had to be withdrawn when it was found that their boundaries did not match the geographical boundaries or analytical categories of other data.[3]

Opinion polling suggests that the public have lost a great deal of their previous confidence in official statistics.[4] Well-publicized debacles have ranged from the 'spurious accuracy' that the Royal Statistical Society divined in school league tables, to the very poor quality of the Office of the

Deputy Prime Minister's (ODPM) house price index.[5] In December 2008, Home Secretary Jacqui Smith was reprimanded by Sir Michael Scholar, the head of the UK Statistics Authority, for her 'premature, irregular and selective' use of statistics when she released injury statistics appearing to show knife crime going down in areas where the government was piloting new police methods. Such incidents have led to a situation in which the former 'Respect Tsar', Louise Casey, has argued that 'public confidence in statistics is so low that it does not matter what happens . . . shock horror, there is another statistics story. It is a shock and horror for newspapers, but not for the public'.[6]

Laggardly or poorly drawn statistics do not only carry consequences for the relationships between the public and successive governments. They have also been seen, with ever more clarity, to undermine effective public policy in an era when 'implementation' has become the mantra of most politicians. The crude nature of immigration statistics has led many local authorities to be underfunded in terms of the number of families in their respective areas.[7] It has also come to seem almost impossible, in an era when individuals move around a great deal and households are increasingly made up of 'unconventional' types, to collect data through the Census of Population. Numbers of young men, in particular, were greatly inflated in the 1990s because the ONS had missed the slow but inexorable emigration of British-born citizens. Close examination of the 2001 census caused statisticians to realize that there were nearly one million fewer young men in Britain than they had previously thought.[8] The Treasury's 2003–4 review of economic statistics pointed out in this vein that official figures still relied too heavily on data from manufacturing industry, and still did not provide regional output figures that are compiled from information actually collected in the regions (rather than worked out 'backwards' and 'downwards' from the overall national income accounts).[9]

In this situation the governor of the Bank of England and its chief economist have referred to the economy as a 'jigsaw puzzle' shrouded in a 'statistical fog', as well as to the need for 'a good dose of judgement' when using 'quantitative economic models'.[10] The Statistics Commission set up in the year 2000 to monitor the ONS has recommended better performance monitoring; more communication with expert 'customers', government departments, and the public; and the use of more data sets to cross-check information and speed up forecasts.[11]

Even so, the collapse in public confidence has led to the establishment of a new UK Statistics Authority, with a Statistics Board to oversee the ONS. The Authority started work in 2008.[12] Needless to say, given the level of public and expert concern, this did not settle the debate over the quality of national statistics. Even the debates leading up to the Board's creation showed the level of scepticism that had built up. The Treasury Select Committee called for the Board's mix of executive and supervisory roles to be split, arguing that independent oversight could not be provided by the same appointees who were actually delivering the data.[13] A previous chief statistician argued that the Board's new powers were vague, with little transparency, and with a very unclear remit when calling the new 'National Statistician' to account.[14] Furthermore, a new split has emerged between 'official' and 'national' statistics. The UK government remains in charge of 'official' statistics, produced by subaltern departments and executives, while the devolved administrations control their own 'lower-level' data as well. The idea of independence for statistics has therefore been dismissed as a 'myth'.[15]

Statistics have thus become a very controversial, but extremely slippery, matter of debate. None of this, however, would come as any surprise to economists and journalists were they more aware of the history and nature of statistical reform. At the very least, it would remind all concerned of the inherent fragility of economic knowledge. Deidre McCloskey and Stephen Ziliak, for instance, have recently reminded economists and economic historians alike of the dangers of constructing cross-sectional data from quite different national data sets, and have recommended that economists should think 'more rigorously about data'.[16] Understanding statistics' history and provenance should help in that process. Statistics in fact have *always* been controversial, as many of the essays in this collection demonstrate: Edmund Rogers, for instance, demonstrates how numbered visions of Britain's imperial colonies were employed and critiqued in political battles over tariff reform, while the chapters by Tom Crook and James Taylor suggest that public trust in numbers has long been fragile. These problems still pertained in late twentieth-century policy debates, when Britain's economic problems were still being drawn in complex ways using contested statistical data and methods.

This chapter examines two postwar instances of the complex entanglement of statistics, the reform of governance, and the public: namely, the various efforts made during the 1950s and 1960s to reform statistics relating to industrial training and regional economies. In both cases France provided the principal model for emulation, attesting once again to the transnational dimensions of statistical reform during the twentieth century (though, as the introduction to this volume observed, this is something which dates back to the latter half of the nineteenth century). But what is most striking is the sheer difficulty of establishing anything approaching a clear synoptic vision of the national economy that Whitehall and Westminster could actually *use*. Successive governments had to contend with subaltern agents and groups that were beyond their control. Even by the 1970s, statistics relating to industrial training and regional economies were still far from systematic, and there remained deep discrepancies between the statistical picture at the centre and the economic reality at the peripheries. Here, as elsewhere, 'seeing like a state', to use James C. Scott's term, proved incredibly messy, compromised, and complicated.[17]

THE FRENCH MODEL AND STATISTICS
ON INDUSTRIAL TRAINING

The French economy was enormously influential in postwar Britain. This fact has long been a matter of comment, though the theme has often been left implicit in broader studies, rather than truly brought to the forefront of analysis.[18] What has also remained unclear is the perceived role of information and statistics in France's economic renaissance. John and Anne-Marie Hackett's *Economic Planning in France*, published in 1963, was extremely influential, promoting as it did the numbers contained in France's national economic plans as an 'optimistic' guide to action in and of themselves. The idea was that optimistic data would promote investment, re-equipment, and then growth itself.[19] Pierre Massé, on a London visit during 1962 as head of the Planning Commissariat in Paris, told a National Institute of Economic and Social Research audience that 'planning consists in integrating . . . interdependent efforts, thus extending to a nation-wide scale the market surveys made by each single firm'.[20] Setting high numerical targets as to what *could* be achieved by each sector if the whole economy was to grow more quickly, so the theory went, would encourage firms to redouble their efforts. The role of numbers in encouraging firms was clearly to the fore. To be sure, this hid to a great extent the true network of tax incentives, purchasing power, and the informal networks of influence that the French state could bring to bear behind the economic scenes. But the rhetoric is instructive as to the supposed power of statistics in helping policymakers choose between different means and ends.[21]

French practices were especially influential at a microeconomic level, not least with respect to industrial training, which had been dominated in post–Second World War Britain by tripartite agreements that were *non*-numerical, at least as far as any central targets were concerned. Trade unions, employers, and governments concurred that each industrial sector should be left to its own devices in the setting up and administration of apprenticeship courses. It made for a system based largely on ad hoc local initiative.[22] But as the policy environment shifted in the early 1960s towards more detailed forms of microeconomic intervention, so industrial training came to be seen as an important way of making good—and more explicitly quantitative—use of scarce resources. Enthusiasm came from some of the same sources as the more general 'planning' fervour of the time. The two main employers' bodies, the Federation of British Industries (FBI) and the British Employers' Confederation (BEC), established a joint committee to look at industrial training in 1960. In 1963, the National Economic Development Council published its influential *Conditions Favourable to Faster Growth*, which compared British skills unfavourably to those of continental Europe.[23]

Gertrude Williams, professor of social economics at the University of London, was one particularly effective propagandist for this case. France had long been thought of as a successful example of state-sponsored and work-based instruction for adolescents. Whereas experts on technical education had been praising Germany for many decades, British enthusiasts for more modern work-based apprenticeships had looked to France since at least the 1890s.[24] An apprenticeship tax had been established for each French industry after the First World War. Employers were enabled to pay into this tax and take advantage of the facilities that training boards for each industry provided. Alternatively, employers could offset the charge against their own training costs, which would be centrally monitored and audited. Williams strongly favoured the training young French people received in technical colleges before they even started work. She agreed with the 1959 Crowther Report that there should be a year of compulsory post-school further education in Britain. Williams, however, added the demand for a nationally coordinated apprenticeship scheme based on the French example, replete as this was with apparently more effective forms of statistical knowledge.[25]

Apprenticeship remained the main element of training in British industry, as it had done for centuries; but that institution was now coming to be seen as time-serving, narrow, and old-fashioned, training workers in specific skills that might not help them get jobs anywhere, except in the particular sector or firm where they were already working. This fear became pervasive in the early 1960s at exactly the same time as more general concerns about 'youth' and 'delinquency' were taking hold. Just as the urban policy of the late 1960s was an important harbinger of change in governments' views of education and the 'dangers' of young people living in cities, so new training policies pointed towards an increased level of government intervention to reform the behaviour of the citizenry early on in their working lives.[26] This was clearest in the creation of the Manpower Services Commission in 1973 and the youth training schemes of the 1970s and 1980s.[27]

In the early 1960s, however, central government still had a very limited role in the actual provision of training courses. The Ministry of Labour's National Joint Advisory Committee had already investigated the possibility of such intervention in 1957 and 1958 under Robert Carr, then a junior minister. The final report bemoaned by-now-familiar technical limits, given that 'there was an almost complete absence of statistics . . . many [industries] were unable to supply any sort of answer at all'. Yet the report still concluded, despite this lack of evidence, that there were no grounds for further government interference.[28] All it recommended was the setting up of a central Industrial Training Council to consult about increasing training provision. Such a council was duly appointed over the following year, and it did at least help to bring together much more data on training and part-time education.[29]

Yet, in general, key figures within the postwar British state and its 'core executive' felt that they did not know enough about the public, and specifically about its economic activities; and that very weakness helped to hold back their ambitions to understand and manage a modern economy via the collection of new data.[30] As Jim Tomlinson has pointed out, in order to 'manage the people' politicians and civil servants were in search of better ways to understand and persuade them, an effort which forms the 'hidden underbelly of postwar corporatism'.[31] But while they turned to the example of other countries for solutions, those states often had much longer histories of intervention and statistical surveillance than did Westminster and Whitehall. Central governments' ambitions thus far outstripped existing capacity. In the event, as we shall now see, effective reform of industrial training was hindered by the power of vested interests and the persistence of established practices.

Following a visit to France in February 1961 to look at the French system, Ministry of Labour civil servants became convinced of the scheme's role in increasing the number of people being trained. Both the chancellor and the Ministry of Education expressed an interest in a 'levy/grant' system, which led to the establishment of an official working party under H.F. Rossetti from the Ministry of Labour.[32] The Inland Revenue, worried as it was throughout the postwar era about the implications to government finances of hypothecation and the earmarking of specific funds for particular programmes, was sceptical. The Treasury too was opposed to 'cumbersome administrative machinery' and the addition to costs. In the interim report that went to ministers in January 1962, the committee therefore concluded that change might do more harm than good.[33] John Hare, the minister of Labour, duly reported this negative result to his colleagues, adopting as lukewarm a manner as he could manage; but other ministers' frustration with the slow rate of progress ensured that a further study was commissioned.[34]

Asked to go back and consider ways in which training levies *might* work, officials on Hare's second working party were split. Ministry of Education officials mounted their own bid to take over the process, and pressed for a large expansion in technical college provision that would provide general training for apprentices on day release (they had earlier issued a circular to English further education colleges on this subject in June 1960).[35] But Ministry of Labour officials, by now convinced of the efficacy of the French example, eventually prevailed. They were able to win the backing of a Treasury that was increasingly interested in the idea of faster growth through industrial training rather than more schooling, partly because the former solution would be cheaper for the government. The second working party's final recommendations therefore adopted the idea of an industry-by-industry scheme under which tripartite, voluntary Industrial Training Boards could be set up, charging levies agreed within the industry. This combined industrial self-government with statutory authority for the new boards.[36] The scheme emerged as the 1964 Industrial Training Act, and by 1970 there were twenty-seven Industrial Training Boards, raising some £208 million yearly in training levies and directly employing over 1,000 training officers.[37]

However, there were crucial flaws in the design. What began as a plan to establish government control over apprenticeship became yet another structure for industrial consultation. The minister would appoint Training Board members and adjudicate on demarcation disputes, but was to act solely on the recommendations of employers and unions; civil servants could attend Training Board meetings, but only as non-voting members. The boards were allowed to exclude firms from any levies they might introduce, but they could do little to increase non-specific training or encourage inter-industry links. Indeed, the boards ended up repaying almost all of the money paid to them, mostly to companies they judged as having adequate training programmes. Few of these boards charged amounts that even remotely reflected the true cost of thorough industrial training. Worse, the increase in training subsidies often helped firms that had a rapid turnover of labour and constantly needed to show new workers how to work in their plants, which was hardly what the government had originally envisaged.[38]

Further problems related to the very numerical basis of the new arrangements. Central statistics on the provision of training were now available, but because the Ministry of Labour and the Training Boards could not see 'inside' each firm, they had no way of knowing what was really happening to training. Companies' submissions often became elaborate exercises in recouping their levy payments. The gap between *national* statistics and numbers at the microeconomic level, where people actually experienced economic life, was never clearer. The new Training Boards were based in individual industries, and therefore could not contribute in any meaningful fashion to inter-industrial labour mobility or reallocation. Indeed, their published reports made little attempt to compare the value of spending in one area, or of the hours of training provided for each apprentice, with similar figures elsewhere.[39] Small firms were disadvantaged by the scheme, because they often could not afford to employ training officers, even with the grants that the Training Boards provided. Firms often failed to qualify for grants, causing relations between the government and employers to decline further. The Confederation of British Industry, created by the merger of the FBI and BEC in 1965, complained that such 'inequities were the main reason for the spread of the attitude that the levy was just another tax'.[40]

The reality of the levy-grant system proved very far indeed from Massé's model, which turned upon the production of national-level statistics in the mould of comprehensive, integrated market surveys. Unions and employers had opted to keep control of their fiefdoms: political parties were distracted by ideological conflicts over secondary education, while different ministries remained responsible for training and education. Despite the fact that many industries showed no *overt* or *macroeconomic* signs of needing more able workers, this does not mean that there were no hidden and subtle costs involved in the failure to integrate well-respected and prestigious training courses into the general education system. Chief among those losses was the ability to maintain—and measure—the quality and relevance of industrial training in the harsher economic times to come.[41] The weakness of existing data, and the strength of entrenched interests and practices (which relied on iteration rather than new information), significantly blunted the drive for reform.

THE FRENCH MODEL AND REGIONAL STATISTICS

How regions are surveyed and represented critically affects how they are perceived, how their problems are defined, and therefore the remedies that are thought suitable for their difficulties. Denis Lineham's work on how regions were imagined during the interwar Depression, and the remedies that were based on those preconceptions, contains a number of cases in point.[42] This link between ideas and actions was especially strong in the 1960s, partly due to the sheer lack of information about regional economies. The paucity of data on the national economy and industrial training was bad enough, but in the field of regional economics the situation was even worse.

The think tank Political and Economic Planning had noted the lack of regional statistics back in the 1930s, but this situation had not changed markedly in the postwar era. The Ministry of Labour did provide local unemployment statistics, which could cause political arguments if they went too high, but that was the limit of government information on local labour markets.[43] The lack of regional or local numbers helped to create a specifically *national* politics of numbers, in which Britons' general failings—in terms of skills, entrepreneurial drive, or even a lack of economic optimism—became vital. More specific spatial or local difficulties, and in particular the struggles of some of Britain's staple industries from her industrial past, could in this way be relegated to the background, especially while they appeared to be 'performing' adequately during Britain's 1950s recovery.[44]

The years following the 1958 recession were to witness a rapid return to regional intervention on the part of central government, partly due to the beginnings of long and drawn-out crises in many of those staple industries (in shipbuilding and cotton, for instance).[45] Monitoring the effects of policy would clearly require a large amount of new information if the new era of regional planning was to prove a success.[46] Ideally, and if the information coming in was to be used to reshape lagging regional economies in the north of England, Wales and Scotland, the data available would have to become much richer. It would have to include estimates of regional GDP, regional 'import' and 'export' flows, income and expenditure figures for individuals as well as families, the costs of congestion in 'crowded regions', and the causes and character of regional unemployment. Inter-regional migration, and the effectiveness of past policies, would also have to be measured as a guide to future action. However, this vital data simply did not exist until at least the late 1960s.

Until it did, the relative costs and benefits of moving industry and people from congested to lagging regions would remain what one contemporary economist termed 'one of the unsolved questions of economics'.[47]

One important strand in this rejuvenation of regional statistics was, once again, an enthusiasm for French theory and practice. The most important regional economist in this debate was the Frenchman François Perroux. His analysis of growth and decline, partly inspired by the Austrian Joseph Schumpeter, focused on the process by which economic activities become locked into 'positive' or 'negative' spirals. 'Propulsive' industries—sectors that were new, efficient and technologically innovative—were portrayed as particularly important. Perroux did not initially refer to geographical, as opposed to theoretical, space. However, his ideas were eventually interpreted as an advocacy of growth 'poles' or spatial 'clusters' that would make up for the backwardness of a surrounding region, sucking up labour and investment that would establish self-sustaining industrial regeneration.[48] Nicholas Kaldor, James Callaghan's Special Adviser as chancellor between 1964 and 1967, implicitly cited Perroux's influence (and explicitly mentioned that of the Swede Gunnar Myrdal) when he came to defend the Labour governments' regional policies in 1970.[49] That same year, the University of Glasgow economist Gavin Cameron referred to Perroux's strategy as 'one of the most fashionable and persistent forms of conventional wisdom'.[50]

French regional planning had by this point made a deep impression in the international planning community. Articles poured from academic presses to detail what Stanislaw Wellisz of the University of Chicago termed 'a vigorous policy of economic decentralization'. Wellisz was sceptical about the efficacy of aid to the 'decentralizing' regions. But he was enthusiastic about the value of improved statistics for both 'people' and 'government', on very similar positive lines to those put forward by Massé. Not only was 'social overhead capital' thereby increased in the regions; 'studies of the economic potential of the various regions of France' were also being made that would encourage both business and government to invest there.[51] The American regional economist Niles Hansen singled out the use of public opinion polls—for divining, for instance, what French people really thought about living in Paris and the regions—as a subject of special interest for the reform of regional policy.[52] The British regional planner, Peter Self, praised the way in which data from French regional planning were brought together with the central National Plans, and at the local level with local government, businesses, and farmers.[53]

Some British civil servants were deeply unconvinced. One told a meeting of Board of Trade Regional Controllers in 1961: 'in the postwar years the French had suffered from inflation [and] balance of payments difficulties and had been forced on a number of occasions to devalue their currency. All this seemed to have been forgotten and some planners now described France as a "model" economy'.[54] One of the reasons for their scepticism focused on the role of numbers as a guide to policy. The whole thrust of official advice in the early 1960s was that government should try to get away from automatic triggers for intervention, such as the unemployment rate (it was suggested, for instance, that the unemployment rate was no real guide as to where or when investment or subsidy should be considered). Collecting more data threatened the introduction of that more discretionary system.[55]

But by the time Labour came to power in 1964, 'French' theories and methods were entrenched in the regional planning fraternity. This was once again due to the institutionalization of international numbers. Labour's analysis of the EEC's apparently spectacular growth rate, encapsulated in the usual international league tables, was that Britons worked harder, but less efficiently and to less effect, than their continental neighbours. The country needed to draw on new industrial techniques, perhaps in areas where they would be more readily accepted. One way of achieving this would be to implement an 'effective regional policy based on the introduction of new industries into areas of above-average unemployment'.[56] Perroux's idea of 'propulsive industries' was by now widely accepted among interventionists of all political stripes.

As with macroeconomic policy, French regional policy was in fact little understood by British 'planners', and it was certainly very far from the objective process that some enthusiasts imagined. French regional policy did not have a very long lead on the British; it was only the Third Plan of 1957 that turned seriously to regional issues. Previous work had really been limited to the social and geographical surveys that Wellisz and Hansen so admired.[57] If it is clear that the British system lacked central coordination, then the French system was divided between inter-ministerial committees under the prime minister's Delegation for Regional Action, the regional committee of the Planning Commission, regional prefects appointed by the Ministry of the Interior, and those ministries involved in providing various social and economic services.[58] These divisions served only to perpetuate the powers of central government over the localities, for no entrenched regional machinery was created. Indirectly elected Regional Councils had a similar lack of legitimacy and power, as did the regional Economic Planning Councils that Labour introduced in 1965.[59]

Lack of statistics on subjects ranging from the future growth of cities to very basic figures for regional economic aggregates was also a problem in France throughout this period. Many figures in the Fifth Plan of 1965 were provided, not for the twenty-one planning regions that had been set up, but for a threefold division of the country into West, East and Paris, thus saving on statistical resources. It was only in the early 1970s that a comprehensive regional economic model was set out by official planners.[60] The extensive literature on French regional planning thus makes quite clear that many criticisms of the British system could be extended to the French. Whatever the level of technical ability and close cooperation exhibited, it remains unlikely that such techniques could on their own have resolved general policy dilemmas as to where citizens chose to live and work, or where businesses chose to start up or relocate to.[61]

The inherent flaws in the idea of 'regional economies' per se were soon apparent in the British planning system. The first regional GDP and import-export figures for Britain did begin to emerge in the 1950s, in studies of the Welsh economy. However, reliable figures were not available even for that part of the UK before the mid-1960s. Only then could input-output tables— a crude way of measuring the linkages between demand and final output in different sectors of the economy—be constructed for even that small constituent part of the UK's economy.[62] Regional Phillips curves, demonstrating the sensitivity of each region to national demand changes in terms of unemployment, were similarly not available until the late 1960s.[63] Work conduced by the National Institute of Economic and Social Research on the extent of structural unemployment, as against joblessness that resulted from deficient demand, was first published even later.[64]

Without information that went down to the level of the individual firm, generalizations were extremely hazardous. The 'minimum list heading' system of industrial classification could hide very large variations within each sector of the economy: the printing category, for instance, included photo-development firms that were growing much more quickly than the list heading average. Arguing on the basis of this list that a region was growing more or less quickly than its mix of different industrial groups suggested it should—so-called 'shift and share' analysis—was crude, to say the least.[65] This necessarily coarse and agglomerative approach helps to explain many of the flaws in British economic policy during these years. Unable to break down the categories their own officials had created, it was impossible to see which parts of the manufacturing sector, for instance, might have the most potential for future growth. Long debates on the supposed productivity benefits of encouraging *all* manufacturing ensued, at a highly abstract level, and involving Kaldor as a central controversialist.[66]

When the Conservatives in government turned to regional statistics in the early 1960s, with the setting up of an official inter-departmental group in late 1963, the lack of information was painfully obvious. Inter-regional migration estimates 'would have to rely to a considerable extent on guesswork' before the 1961 Census and a new wave of regional surveys were complete.[67] On the effects of government policy, planners had to rely on the Board of Trade Regional Controllers' reports on the number of Development Certificates they had issued. But right up to the 1964 general election, officials admitted privately that they had 'no comprehensive information' about what happened when a firm was refused a Development Certificate, a fact that made it all the more difficult to estimate policy impact.[68]

Labour attempted to plug these gaps as part of a more general statistical reform effort. Harold Wilson was particularly involved, as befitted his long experience of and interest in statistics as a wartime civil servant and postwar president of the Board of Trade.[69] He complained, for instance, when civil servants' initial 1964–65 review of statistics failed 'to revolutionise statistics based on *regionalisation*'.[70] Other politicians, with those from poorer regions more influential in parliament and Whitehall after Labour's electoral victory in 1964, also became more interested in the state of regional knowledge. The House of Commons Estimates Committee singled out regional statistics for their attention, labelling them just as 'inadequate' as contemporary manpower and wage information. The Census of Production, for instance, did ask questions of individual companies, but did not require them to break down their answers for their regional branches, apart from asking questions about employment at plant level.[71] This failure to regionalize statistics properly was one of the reasons the prime minister set up a high-level Cabinet Statistical Policy Committee in the first place.[72] That committee's enthusiasm for a common register of business units had an obvious bearing on regional policy, for this might end the statistical reliance on crude and overgeneralized minimum list heading data.[73]

The Wilson government did have a number of successes when it came to regional statistics. Notable among this progress was the creation of Standard Regions that had the same boundaries for all departments, and the creation of the *Abstract of Regional Statistics*, published yearly and containing a wealth of material relevant to regional planning. The *Abstract* also grew in ambition as more data became available. Its first issue, in 1965, contained forty-four tables; its sixth, in 1970, contained seventy-six. The first gave figures for inter-regional migration, but only for one year, and only in total; for public spending, though only for capital expenditure; and for earnings, though only average figures for men in manufacturing.[74] By 1970 migration and earnings figures from the New Earnings Survey were broken down by age and gender, and earnings figures were given for services as well as manufacturing—though regional public spending data was still limited only to investment.[75]

However, these advances did not represent the type of decisive breakthrough that Wilson had hoped for. Absorbed in creating the *Abstract of Regional Statistics* and bringing together data on the basis of the new standard regions, staff shortages again meant that little more could be done in the short term.[76] The Statistical Policy Committee's attention tended to move away from regional statistics as time went on, and larger issues of national economic and social statistics demanded attention. The pressures of managing demand over the whole economy made some reforms politically impossible: no regional price indices were to be published, for instance, because ministers feared the political opprobrium of showing high inflation in some parts of the UK as compared to others. If workers in South East England discovered that prices were rising more quickly in that region, the reasoning went, they might demand higher pay settlements than were the norm elsewhere in Britain.[77] Details on regional productivity, output, investment, and manpower were lacking. The 'data bank' based on individual establishments, one of the Statistical Policy Committee's key ambitions, was still some way away by the time Labour left office in 1970, and it was not expected to cover services and distribution for some years, if ever.[78]

CONCLUSION

The preceding survey, provisional as it is, should be enough to outline the contribution that transnational perceptions, in this case of France, played in British economic policy and statistical reform during the postwar 'golden age'. Massé on macroeconomic planning; Perroux on regional 'growth poles'; Williams on industrial training: all three made vital contributions from outside, or in Williams's case by looking outwards. This was perhaps inevitable given the ongoing 'back story' of British economic decline at the time; the Continent naturally seemed to offer more attractive visions of reform. However, these views of France were often inaccurate, or at least failed to grasp the true nature of the French state's involvement in the wider French economy and society. Policymakers' perceptions of France were often muddled and confused (something also evident in their understanding of 'Scandinavian' governance, as this author has argued elsewhere).[79] Yet this was but part of a broader fabric of confusion and contestation, both between government and the public, and *within* the state, as different experts, interest groups, officials, and politicians jostled for place and influence. Statistical reform was always slow, patchy, and uneven. There never has been anything like a state-driven statistical panopticon, and this was certainly true in the 1950s and 1960s with respect to the British national economy.

Arguably, it is these complexities, rather than the entry of the masses and consumer techniques into politics, that helped to confuse, coarsen, and separate public and professional spheres during the twentieth century. Indeed, this forms an insight at the heart of historians' recent utilization of 'policy learning' theories drawn from the social sciences, which are thought to provide a better means of understanding the manner in which governments 'puzzle' as much as 'power' their way forwards.[80] These complexities should also inform recent debates about the malleability of statistics, for economic data have always been political, often vague, and usually capable of manifold interpretations. And yet this is partly what gives 'epistemic communities' of experts, academics, and interested officials their unique power and influence.[81] Their apparent access to the nature of economic and social 'reality', as well as the character of possible or desirable reforms, allow such groups to guard, demonstrate, and reinforce their power and influence. Ministers thus often have to grope forwards, relying on their intercession. Rarely, if ever, are ministers afforded a clear statistical picture of the public.

NOTES

1. C. Johnson and S. Briscoe, *Measuring the Economy* (Rev. edn., Harmonds-worth, 1995), pp. 25–7.
2. D. Caplan and D. Daniel, 'Improving Economic Statistics', *Economic Trends* 460 (1992), pp. 87–8.
3. S. Briscoe and A. Fifield, 'Chief Statistician Defends Practice of Data Revisions', *Financial Times*, 16 Oct. 2003; F. Nolan, 'Report on the Review of Regional Accounts', Office for National Statistics Report (ONS), Aug. 2003.
4. Statistics Commission, 'Legislation Must Transform Public Trust in Official Statistics', press release, 15 Nov. 2006.
5. N. Timmins and S. Briscoe, 'League Tables Give "Misleading Picture"', *Financial Times*, 24 Oct. 2003; R. Jones, 'Prescott's Figures May Add to Homebuyers' Confusion', *Guardian*, 13 Jan. 2004.
6. T. Whitehead, 'Top Crime Adviser Admits Public Do Not Trust Figures', *Daily Telegraph*, 24 Apr. 2009, p. 5; A. Travis, 'Deaths on Rise as Government Anti-Knife Crime Strategy Fails', *Guardian*, 22 July 2009, p. 3.
7. P. Wintour, 'Inaccurate Migrant Numbers May Lead to Rise in Council Tax', *Guardian*, 8 Aug. 2006.
8. ONS, 'Why Census Shows Fewer Men', National Statistics Online, www.statistics.gov.uk/census2001/implications.asp, accessed 6 Apr. 2008.
9. C. Allsopp, *Review of Statistics for Economic Policymaking: First Report* (2003), pp. 5–6, 92–102, 122–5.
10. M. King, 'East Midlands Development Agency/Bank of England Dinner', speech delivered at Leicester, 14 Oct. 2003, p. 2; C. Bean, 'Economists and the Real World', lecture delivered at the London School of Economics, 29 Jan. 2003, p. 12.
11. Statistics Commission, 'Forecasting in the National Accounts at the Office for National Statistics', *Statistics. Commission Reports* 12 (2003), pp. 3–5, 7–8, and Statistics Commission, 'Reliability Study: Report', *Statistics Commission Reports* 11 (2003), p. 12.
12. HM Treasury, *Independence for Statistics* (Nov. 2006); 'Statistics and Registration Service Bill', *House of Commons Papers*, Nov. 2006.
13. S. Briscoe, 'MPs Attack Proposals for Statistics Office', *Financial Times*, 26 July 2006.
14. House of Commons Treasury Select Committee, *The Appointment of the Chair of the Statistics Board: Ninth Report of Session 2006–2007* (2007), p. 3.
15. W. McLennan, 'Statistics and Registration Bill Is Simply a Huge Step Backwards', *Financial Times*, 18 Jan. 2007.
16. D. McCloskey and S. Ziliak, 'The Standard Error of Regressions', *Journal of Economic Literature* 34 (1996), p. 112.
17. J.C. Scott, *Seeing Like a State: How Certain Schemes to Improve the Human Condition Have Failed* (New Haven, CT, 1998).
18. See, for instance, the brief mention of the subject in J. Foreman-Peck and L. Hannah, 'Britain—from Economic Liberalism to Socialism—and Back?', in J. Foreman-Peck and G. Federico (eds.), *European Industrial Policy: The Twentieth-Century Experience* (Oxford, 1999), pp. 36–8.
19. J. Hackett and A.-M. Hackett, *Economic Planning in France* (London, 1963), pp. 358, 369.
20. J. Leruez, *Economic Planning and Politics in Britain* (London, 1975), p. 88.
21. On this, see J. Sheahan, *Promotion and Control of Industry in Post-War France* (Cambridge, MA, 1963).

22. W. Richardson, 'In Search of the Further Education of Young People in Post-War England', *Journal of Vocational Education and Training* (2007), pp. 385–418.
23. H. Pemberton, 'The Keynesian-Plus Experiment: A Study of Social Learning in the UK Core Executive, 1960–1966' (PhD thesis, University of Bristol, 2001), p. 178; NEDO, *Conditions Favourable to Faster Growth* (London, 1963), pp. 7–9.
24. M. Sanderson, 'French Influences on Technical and Managerial Education in England 1870–1940', in Y. Cassis, F. Crouzet and T.R. Gourvish (eds.), *Management and Business in Britain and France: The Age of the Corporate Economy* (Oxford, 1995), pp. 115–19.
25. G. Williams, *Apprenticeship in Europe: The Lesson for Britain* (London, 1963), pp. 80–91.
26. For the fear of delinquency, see A. Wills, 'Delinquency, Masculinity and Citizenship in England 1950–1970', *Past and Present* 187 (2005), pp. 157–85; and for the links between these concerns and urban policy in an Anglo-French context, see P. Booth and H. Green, 'Urban Policy in England and Wales and in France: A Comparative Assessment of Recent Policy Initiatives', *Environment and Planning C: Government and Policy* 11 (1993), pp. 381–93.
27. D. King, *Actively Seeking Work? The Politics of Unemployment and Welfare Policy in the United States and Great Britain* (Chicago, 1995), pp. 113–15, tables 4.1–4.2, pp. 134–5.
28. P.J.C. Perry, *The Evolution of British Manpower Policy* (London, 1976), p. 66.
29. L.M. Cantor and I.F. Roberts, *Further Education in England and Wales* (2nd edn., London, 1972), pp. 8, 81.
30. For a discussion of the apparently growing power of the 'core executive', see R. Heffernan, 'Prime Ministerial Predominance? Core Executive Politics in the UK', *British Journal of Politics and International Relations* 5 (2003), pp. 347–72.
31. J. Tomlinson, 'Managing the Economy, Managing the People: Britain, c. 1931–1970', *Economic History Review* 58 (2005), p. 581.
32. National Archives of the United Kingdom, Kew [hereafter NAUK] LAB 18/729, Rossetti to Helsby, 17 Feb. 1961.
33. NAUK LAB 18/874, Treasury and Inland Revenue memorandum to Training Levy Working Party, 8 Sept. 1961; interim report, 22 Jan. 1962.
34. NAUK CAB 134/1693, Economic Planning Committee minutes, 7 Mar. 1962.
35. Perry, *Manpower Policy*, p. 82.
36. NAUK CAB 129/111, Hare memorandum to Cabinet, 23 Nov. 1962.
37. R.M. Lindley, 'Active Manpower Policy', in G.S. Bain (ed.), *Industrial Relations in Britain* (Oxford, 1983), p. 344.
38. D. Lees and B. Chiplin, 'The Economics of Industrial Training', *Lloyds Bank Review* 96 (1970), p. 34.
39. D. Robinson, 'Labour Market Policies', in W. Beckerman (ed.), *The Labour Government's Economic Record 1964–1970* (1972), p. 317.
40. NAUK LAB 18/1572, DEP, CBI meeting, minutes, 7 Nov. 1968, and CBI memorandum, July 1968.
41. J. Chandler, 'Interpreting Vocationalism: Youth Training and Managerial Practices', in C. Wallace and M. Cross (eds.), *Youth in Transition: The Sociology of Youth and Youth Policy* (1990), pp. 96–112.
42. D. Lineham, 'Regional Surveys and the Economic Geographies of Britain 1930–1939', *Transactions of the Institute of British Geographers* 28 (2003), pp. 96–122.
43. PEP, *Report on the Location of Industry* (1939), pp. 202–3.

44. A link made explicit in S. Woolf, 'Statistics and the Modern State', *Comparative Studies in Society and History* 31 (1989), pp. 603–4.
45. On cotton, see J. Singleton, 'Showing the White Flag: The Lancashire Cotton Industry, 1945–65', *Business History* 32 (1990), pp. 129–49; on shipbuilding, see A.G. Jamieson, *Ebb Tide in the British Maritime Industries: Change and Adaptation, 1918–1990* (Exeter, 2003), pp. 51–84.
46. P. Hall, *Urban and Regional Planning* (2nd edn., Harmondsworth, 1982), pp. 274–5.
47. B. Balassa, *The Theory of Economic Integration* (Homewood, IL, 1961), p. 209.
48. G. O'Hara, 'A Journey Without Maps: The Regional Policies of the 1964–70 Labour Governments', *Regional Studies* 39 (2005), pp. 1183–95.
49. N. Kaldor, 'The Case for Regional Policies', *Scottish Journal of Political Economy* 17 (1970), p. 340.
50. G.C. Cameron, 'Growth Areas, Growth Centres and Regional Conversion', *Scottish Journal of Political Economy* 17 (1970), p. 19.
51. S. Wellisz, 'Economic Planning in the Netherlands, France and Italy', *Journal of Political Economy* 68 (1960), p. 281.
52. N.M. Hansen, 'Regional Planning in a Mixed Economy', *Southern Economic Journal* 32 (1965), pp. 181–2.
53. P. Self, 'Regional Planning in Britain', *Urban Studies* 1 (1964), pp. 63–4.
54. NAUK BT 173/12, Regional Controllers conference, minutes, 11 Aug. 1961.
55. See NAUK CAB 130/165, Eccles memorandum to GEN 692, 3 Sept. 1959.
56. Labour Party Archives, John Ryland Archive and Study Centre, Manchester. NEC sub-committee files, LPRD memorandum to home policy sub-committee, 'Common Market: The Way Ahead', 1963.
57. K. Allen and M.C. Maclennan, *Regional Problems and Policies in Italy and France* (London, 1970), pp. 169–70; P. Gremion and J.-P. Worms, 'The French Regional Planning Experiments', in J. Hayward and M. Watson (eds.), *Planning, Politics, and Public Policy: The British, French, and Italian Experience* (Cambridge, 1975), p. 316.
58. D. Liggins, *National Economic Planning in France* (Farnborough, 1973), pp. 385–97; V. Wright, *The Government and Politics of France* (London, 1978), p. 96.
59. Estrin and Homes, *French Planning*, pp. 112–13.
60. Liggins, *Planning in France*, pp. 234–5, 243, 315–21.
61. P.A. Hall, *Governing the Economy: The Politics of State Intervention in Britain and France* (Cambridge, 1986), pp. 167–78.
62. E.T. Nevin, A. Roe and J.L. Round, *The Structure of the Welsh Economy* (Cardiff, 1966), pp. 11–16.
63. K. Cowling and D. Metcalf, 'Wage-Unemployment Relationships: A Regional Analysis for the UK, 1960–65', *Bulletin of the Oxford University Institute of Statistics* 29 (1967), pp. 35–8.
64. A.J. Brown *et. al.*, 'Regional Problems and Regional Policy', *National Institute Economic Review* 46 (1968), pp. 43–5.
65. T.W. Buck, 'Shift and Share Analysis: A Guide to Regional Policy?', *Regional Studies* 4 (1970), pp. 445–50.
66. N. Kaldor, *Causes of the Slow Rate of Economic Growth of the United Kingdom* (Cambridge, 1966); R.E. Rowthorn, 'What Remains of Kaldor's Law?', *The Economic Journal* 85 (1975), pp. 10–19.
67. NAUK CAB 134/2399, MOL memorandum to Official Committee on Population and Employment, 7 Mar. 1963.
68. NAUK CAB 134/2436, MOL memorandum to Committee on Regional Development, 8 July 1964.

69. P.G. Moore, 'Obituary: James Harold Wilson 1916–95', *Journal of the Royal Statistical Society. Series A (Statistics in Society)* 159 (1996), pp. 165–73.
70. NAUK PREM 13/1432, Wilson note on Trend memorandum, 9 Sept. 1965.
71. House of Commons Estimates Committee, *Fourth Report* (1966), xxxvii–xxxviii.
72. NAUK CAB 134/3274, SPC minutes, 14 Apr. 1967.
73. NAUK CAB 134/3275, Secretaries' memorandum to SPC, 'Developments in Official Statistics', 13 Apr. 1967.
74. *Abstract of Regional Statistics* 1 (1965), tables 3, 17, 35, pp. 8, 25, 41.
75. *Ibid.*, 6 (1970), tables 8, 35, 61–6, pp. 12, 46–7, 81–4.
76. NAUK CAB 134/3277, Secretaries' memorandum to SPC, 'The Role and Development of the Central Statistical Office: A Progress Report', 26 Sept. 1969.
77. R. Ward and T. Doggett, *Keeping Score: The First Fifty Years of the Central Statistical Office* (London, 1991), p. 149.
78. J. Stafford, 'The Development of Industrial Statistics', *Statistical News* 1 (1968), pp. 7–10.
79. G. O'Hara, '"Applied Socialism of a Fairly Moderate Kind": Scandinavia, British Policymakers and the Post-War Housing Market', *Scandinavian Journal of History* 33 (2008), pp. 1–25.
80. See in particular the discussion in H. Pemberton, *Policy Learning and British Governance in the 1960s* (Basingstoke, 2004), pp. 17–24.
81. A concept usually taken to emanate from P.M. Haas, 'Epistemic Communities and International Policy Coordination', *International Organization* 46 (1992), pp. 1–35; recent commentary can be found in P. Clavin, 'Defining Transnationalism', *Contemporary European History* 14 (2005), pp. 427–9.

Part II
Picturing the Public

6 Numbers and Narratives
Epistemologies of Aggregation in British Statistics and Social Realism, c. 1790–1880

Maeve E. Adams

In its 1834 'Prospectus', the Statistical Society of London (SSL) promised to gather and publish 'a body of numerical facts . . . most conveniently collected, which may properly enter in a common publication and will afford safe grounds for comparing the present condition and future progress of different parts of the empire.'[1] In this particular articulation of the SSL's mission, the work of the statistician was to manage a part-whole relationship: the 'different parts of the empire'—its diverse people and discontinuous geography—which belonged, in quantitative fact, to the political whole of the empire. Yet, as Benedict Anderson long ago argued, the problem with entities such as nations and empires is that their wholeness must be imagined; their wholeness, that is, requires an abstract conception of unity that is not concretely or immediately observable in the world of everyday life.[2] Anderson examined nineteenth-century maps and censuses as two representational means via which nations might be imagined as coherent wholes comprised of discrete parts. As the latter example suggests, statistics offered one means of making wholeness manifest and visible, and in the case of the SSL, in a 'body of numerical facts . . . enter[ed] in a common publication.' Indeed, 'different parts', such as people and places, might be dispersed over a large and scattered territory, yet the statistical text might *embody* those parts, containing them within its tidy pages of numerical data, thus projecting an image of unity and wholeness.

Nineteenth-century statistical writing deployed a host of containment strategies, most notably the provision of numerical charts and tables. Charts and tables, of course, were put to work to represent an incredibly diverse array of social variables, yet their textual form nonetheless reflected an underlying epistemological preoccupation with what might be termed aggregation: namely, the classification of individual people into homogeneous groups (or aggregate wholes) defined by geographical location, occupation and other socio-demographic features. This chapter explores the many, and often overlooked, valences of this preoccupation, and demonstrates how it informed not only numerical but also narrative genres. In fact, aggregation constituted an underlying representational epistemology, and is crucial in terms of grasping the distinctiveness of nineteenth-century statistics in relation to its later, more mathematical manifestations.[3] The chapter thus sheds further light on the public character of statistical science for much of the nineteenth century, something Theodore Porter argues for in his contribution to the volume. As Porter notes, statisticians during this time were relatively forthcoming about the moral and reforming ambitions of their work. The various aggregative techniques explored in this chapter help to contextualize this claim by pointing to the common epistemology they shared with literary writers, who were also concerned to engage the public and enlist public opinion in the service of reform.

The proliferation of aggregative methods during the nineteenth century came about partly because writers could not agree over what form statistical evidence should take. The objective of statistics, as encapsulated in the original meaning of the word, was still to account for the 'state of the state'.[4] But though statistics became increasingly numerical over the course of the nineteenth century, it did not become exclusively so until the turn of the twentieth. In the meantime, numerical and narrative genres continued to share strategies of representation, including, in the case of statistical accounts, the incorporation of narrative elements. Nineteenth-century writers certainly distinguished between numerical and narrative forms—between 'figures of speech' and 'figures of arithmetic' in one formulation from the 1830s.[5] However, in attempting to depict social conditions and to persuade the public about the objects of reform, numerical and narrative forms *jointly* developed and deployed an aggregative epistemology—a way of knowing the world in terms of aggregates, and of framing social problems in terms of parts and wholes. Aggregation presumed that to know features of the collective was to know something meaningful about each and every individual, and vice versa. It thus had both an epistemic and a normative function, encouraging readers to know the social world while simultaneously knowing themselves as parts of larger collectives.

The nature and significance of aggregation has not gone entirely unnoticed. Mary Poovey has shown that statistical methods of accounting helped to make the poor visible by subjecting them to 'ocular inspection, quantification and calculation.'[6] Caring for the poor required that they be accounted for as constituent parts of the whole nation, a project that had two (seemingly contradictory) effects: at the same time that quantification underscored the differences between rich and poor, it also, in accounting for their membership of a larger social collective, had the effect of flattening those differences and homogenizing the social world. In general, however, scholarly work which considers statistics and literature together describes their relationship in one of two ways: either it shows how theories of statistical reasoning provided models for fictional representation, or it shows how fictional representation was antagonistic to statistical representation.[7] This chapter, by contrast, describes a more complex relationship of mutual influence, elaboration and contestation, one which comprised multiple variants of aggregative techniques. Indeed, the fact that the modern social sciences eventually privileged numerical techniques over narrative techniques has had the effect of obscuring the extent to which numerical and narrative genres together contributed to a distinctive, if variously expressed, aggregative epistemology.

In what follows, three different kinds of writing that relied on methods of social aggregation are examined. The chapter first discusses the genre of statistical accounting and statistical journalism. It shows that even these numerical forms of writing continued to rely on certain narrative techniques, ones which modern scholars might be more inclined to associate with social realism. The chapter then examines the didactic tracts of Hannah More, who incorporated features evident in numerical genres, including the national census, to substantiate her arguments about moral reform. Both of these sections show that a complementary relationship persisted between numbers and narratives as vehicles of persuasion. Finally, the chapter explores the antagonism between numerical and narrative modes of aggregation which became manifest in forms of social realism. Using Charles Dickens's *Oliver Twist* as an example, it examines the tension that formed between numbers and characters: that is, between the impersonal aggregate of numerical writing and the representative characters of social realism whose deeply affective experiences personalized the aggregate.

STATISTICS AND NARRATIVE

The 1834 'Prospectus' of the SSL is one of the earliest, and most explicit, attempts to place statistics on a numerical footing. As its founders declared, the SSL would 'confine its attention rigorously to facts—and as far as it may be found possible, to facts which can be stated numerically and arranged in tables.'[8] In the first issue of the *Journal of the Statistical Society of London*, inaugurated in 1838, the editors reiterated this expectation in their 'Introduction', claiming that the 'Statist commonly prefers to employ figures and tabular exhibitions, because facts, particularly when they exist in large numbers, are most briefly and clearly stated in such forms, and because he is not satisfied with giving deductions, which admit of question.'[9] The concern was thus to provide evidence that would not 'admit of question': convictions about 'the condition of mankind' and 'the progress of society' would, according to the journal's editors, henceforth rely only on trustworthy numerical facts.[10]

These declarations were misleading not only because they failed to consider the multiple and competing ways in which other writers continued to represent social aggregates but also because the articles published by the SSL did not strictly adhere to the editors' initial rules. In fact, throughout the century the Society published formal addresses and papers which debated the nature of statistical knowledge, some of which argued that numerical content was not necessarily its defining feature. In 1872, William

Stanley Jevons, at that time president of the Statistical Section of the British Association for the Advancement of Science, insisted in his yearly address (subsequently published in the SSL's journal) that his colleagues should acknowledge non-numerical forms of statistical evidence:

> The name Statistics, in its true meaning, denotes all knowledge relating to the condition of the State or people. I am sorry to observe, indeed, that many persons now use the word statistical as if it were synonymous with numerical; but it is a mere accident of the information with which we deal, that it is often expressed in a numerical or tabular form. As other sciences progress, they become more a matter of quantity and number, and so does our science; but we must not suppose that the occurrence of numerical statements is the mark of statistical information.[11]

For Jevons, what defined a statistic was not strictly *how* it informed its readers, or what it looked like in print, but rather *what* information it conveyed. Statistics did not have to be numerical as long as it informed readers about 'the condition of the state'. While associated with the use of numbers, the association was not yet total, and as a term 'statistics' continued to signify information relating to 'the state', including both numerical and narrative forms of representation.

Deploying an aggregative epistemology, statisticians (or 'statists' as they were then more commonly known) frequently drew on narrative details to substantiate their claims. In particular, papers in the *Journal of the Statistical Society of London* often contained a feature now regarded as a hallmark of the social realist novel: the use of an individual character or scene, by which the writer could move from the social aggregate, understood and imagined as a whole, to the more intimate details of the lives of those who made up the aggregate. Indeed, in its first year of publication—when we might imagine the journal's editors to have been especially vigilant about adhering to the promise 'that all conclusions [contained in the journal] shall be drawn from well-attested data, and shall admit of mathematical demonstration'—numerous articles focused on individual characters or scenes by way of enhancing their evidential basis.[12] Lieutenant-Colonel W.H. Sykes, in an article entitled 'Statistics of Cadiz', quoted the moving testimony of a group of female prioresses, which provided evidence of extreme poverty in some outlying nunneries.[13] Sykes offered this evidence by way of correcting, and adding nuance to, the otherwise prosperous picture generated by the economic statistics of Cadiz and its environs.

In this case, the narrative provided by individual testimony was used to qualify the evidence provided by numerical aggregates. More commonly, however, narrative details were used to confirm, rather than contest, the general picture generated by statistics. Yet they did so in various ways, although most served to make further explicit the reforming ambitions of the text and author. In another article published in 1838, entitled 'On the

State of Agriculture and Condition of the Agricultural Labourers of the Northern District of Northumberland', the author L. Hindmarsh implored the reader as follows:

> Look into one of our north-country cottages during a winter's evening, and you will probably see assembled the family group round a cheerful coal-fire . . . you will see the females knitting or spinning; the father, perhaps, mending shoes . . . and contrast this with the condition of many young men employed as farm-servants in the southern countries.[14]

Hindmarsh also provided statistical evidence of the superior conditions of north-country cottages, but in this passage he seeks to bring these conditions to life, while simultaneously elevating them into a normative ideal. A speculative account of what the reader would 'probably see'—here performed by imagining an act of 'look[ing] into one of our north-country cottages'—also doubles as a statement of what the condition of southern farm servants *should* be. The narrative element contains a clear reforming thrust: evidently the author would like all farmers to enjoy the domestic living conditions apparent in the superior north-country cottages.

In these and other ways, statistical accounts shuttled back and forth between the abstraction of numbers on the one hand and the narrative particularity of descriptive details and individual characters and scenes on the other. In some instances, statistical accounts provided itemized descriptions of individuals which, while brief, nonetheless conveyed details regarding their peculiar life history and personal character. In a 'Statistical Notice of the Asylum for the Blind in Newcastle-upon-Tyne', published in October 1838, the Reverend Joseph M'Alister described six inmates, quoting the number given to them by the asylum, but also taking care to convey something of their singularity as individuals. For example, we read of

> No. 2—S.R., aged 34, a native of North Shields; born blind; was 4 years, 9 months at Liverpool, where he learned to make baskets; has some taste for literature; and occasionally preaches in the Methodist connection. He is an inmate of the asylum, and receives 13s per week, as a workman and teacher of his trade; he would like to hear readings from the periodicals; has never been instructed to read.[15]

Each individual is at once a bureaucratic-numerical unit—abstract, anonymous, a simple part of an aggregate of the blind—and a unique case, with particular desires, tastes, habits, and so forth. Homogeneity and difference are simultaneously evoked and remain in tension with one another.

The use of narrative details to embellish the picture provided by numerical and tabular representations of aggregates would continue up until the late nineteenth century. In the March 1886 issue of the journal, the Scottish statistician and later economist Robert Giffen combined extracts from Benjamin Disraeli's *Sybil* (1845) and Elizabeth Gaskell's *Mary Barton* (1848) with numerical charts in his 'Further Notes on the Progress of the Working Classes in the Last Century'. After quoting from *Sybil* and *Mary Barton*, Giffen stated that he was 'anxious to impress that these are descriptions intended to apply to large masses of workmen'. He added: 'If we turn to the blue books, we find ample facts telling their own tale.' [16] In Giffen's view, numbers and narratives each told 'their own tale'; yet they could also work together to form a meaningful representation of 'large masses of workmen' and how their condition had progressed over the past fifty or so years.

The concept of statistical evidence, then, continued to refer to various kinds of non-numerical knowledge and it remained flexible in this way through most (if not all) of the nineteenth century. Writers did not necessarily restrict themselves to unimpassioned accounts of mere numerical aggregates, or to a rigid definition of statistical knowledge as exclusively numerical. Furthermore, when it came to detailing social conditions, there was a sense in which the authority of numerical and narrative accounts might reinforce one another, as parts of the same project. Authors of social realist novels might lean on the authority of government blue books to enhance their credibility, pointing to the 'authentic' evidence they contained, much of which was statistical. In the '*May Day, 1845*' 'Advertisement' to *Sybil; or The Two Nations*, his *roman à thèse* about the Chartist movement, Disraeli did just this, stating:

> The general reader whose attention has not been specially drawn to the subject which these volumes aim to illustrate, the Condition of the People, might suspect that the Writer has been tempted to some exaggeration in the scenes which he has drawn . . . He thinks it therefore due himself to state that he believes there is not a trait in his work for which he has not the authority of his own observations, or authentic evidence which has been received by Royal Commissions and Parliamentary Committees.[17]

To be sure, it would not be possible to mistake the characters of statistical writing for those of social realism, even if, on occasions, statisticians directly incorporated social realist representations (as in the case of Giffen in 1886). In statistical accounts, the individual was essentially a duplicate of every other individual in the aggregate. Numerical tables might illuminate the individual, and vice versa, but only because the individual was thought to be a typical example of the aggregate in question; and of course, social realist novels were, by definition, wholly narrative, developing at length and in great detail the story of a restricted set of characters. Even so, the inclusion of narrative elements is significant. It might be argued that the use of narrative testifies to the limits of numerical representation, and there was certainly a tension between the abstraction of the latter and the more intimate particularity of the former. However, given the still fluid and relatively expansive definition of what constituted statistical knowledge, numbers and narratives are better seen as complementary: as kindred, if certainly not identical, means of elaborating an underlying aggregative understanding of the social world.

HANNAH MORE AND THE MORAL IMPERATIVE OF AGGREGATION

Prior to the establishment of the SSL and its journal, state-sponsored national censuses gave official shape to emerging aggregative epistemologies. The printed *Abstract* of the 1801 census, the first of its kind, offered an example of how numerical representation brought order to the population by dividing it into three socioeconomic categories: Agriculture; Trade, Manufacture or Handicrafts; and 'All the persons not comprised in the Two proceeding Classes'.[18] Between 1801 and 1841, the census *Abstract* became more elaborate. Whereas the 1801 Census depicted three occupational categories, the 1841 Census depicted twelve: Commerce; Agriculture; Labourers; Military; Naval; Professionals; Miscellaneous; Civil Service; Police and Legal; Domestic Servants; Independent; and Alms people.[19]

This occupational variant of aggregation was also performed by novels, something evident in their *full* titles. Modern editions of these texts typically exclude the subtitles of these novels, thus obscuring the conceptual affiliations between narrative genres and numerical ones like the census. Among other examples: Charles Dickens's *Oliver Twist, or A Parish Boy's Progress* (1837–1838); Frances Trollope's *Michael Armstrong, the Factory Boy* (1839–1840); and Charles Kingsley's *Alton Locke, Tailor and Poet* (1850). Each character was thus synecdoche for a larger socioeconomic aggregate which they were thought to exemplify. Not only did novels like this further help to consolidate the social categories used in statistical accounts; through their fictional plots, they also moved readers to align themselves with the plight of particular groups, lending aggregation a fully affective dimension, one which tended to be more restrained in the work of statisticians.

Yet there were significant precedents to the kinds of aggregation evident in early and mid-Victorian novels. In the late eighteenth century, writers like Hannah More used fictional characters to represent social aggregates. Her pathos-laden stories about shopkeepers, shepherds, shoemakers and farmers were not simply character-driven for the sake of narrative convention; they also used characters to signify the same kinds of social aggregates which provided the organizing principle of the census. Her characters extended the epistemological work of aggregation by explaining and arguing for its moral imperative: the character's good character (in a moral sense) helped readers to see the justice of extending philanthropic work to the poor; at the same time, a character's story enabled readers to identify the kinds of people who were in need of aid, placing them in a larger—and ordered and hierarchical—social whole.

Significantly, the representation of these characters received the sanction and encouragement of the state. In 1796, soon after government officials began to draft legislation for the census, members of the elite began to sponsor the writing and distribution of cheap, fictional narratives which they believed would help to persuade readers about the moral importance of social reform. Daughter of a Bristol schoolmaster and friend of William Wilberforce, More was well-connected, and was one of the first writers approached to help with this project. More had already attracted attention by publishing and distributing her extremely popular 'moral tracts'. In 1795, Hannah and her sister Martha began composing the tracts as pedagogical materials, which they used in the twelve schools they had established in Somerset for extending literacy and religious instruction to the poor. They also distributed these tracts among poor-relief societies, manual laborers, military personnel and poor folk.[20]

Although the tracts were initially part of a broad pedagogical mission, they soon became instrumental in the government's social reform projects. Financial sponsors of More's tracts included eminent figures such as Wilberforce, William Pitt, and the Archbishop of Canterbury. Like the Census *Abstract*, More's tracts were divided into occupational types, which also served as their titles: among others, 'The Shepherd of Salisbury Plain', 'Two Shoemakers', 'Two Wealthy Farmers', 'The Cottage Cook', and 'John the Shopkeeper Turned Sailor'. Whereas the 1801 census only contained three occupational categories, the 1831 'Census Schedule' expanded to include a list of occupations that resembled the more detailed classifications contained in More's tracts (including 'Shopkeeper', 'Cook' and 'Ship-Wright'). In this way, More's tracts joined forces with official accounts to generate, refine and deploy a concept of aggregation that gave form (numerical and narrative) to knowledge of the state.

But whereas census documents relied on numbers, More's tracts were able to elaborate in a narrative fashion the moral importance of social taxonomy. In one of her early tracts published in 1798, entitled 'John the Shopkeeper Turned Sailor; or, the Folly of Going out of Your Element', More argued that knowledge of social aggregates was itself a kind of moral knowledge—in this case, that it is 'Folly' for a shopkeeper to try his hand at sailing, because, in so doing, the shopkeeper abandons his occupational 'element'. Social classification allowed writers and readers to distinguish between the parts or 'elements' of shopkeepers and sailors. Yet, as More's title suggests, classification was also governed by moral, not just epistemological, imperatives, suggesting, as it does, the dangers which follow when people stray from their allotted social positions.

Like others, this particular tract took the form of a ballad and it narrated the story of a once-virtuous and successful shopkeeper, John, who foolishly decides to take his family sailing. When the sailor lets the shopkeeper man the rudder, tragedy ensues. A storm overturns the boat and the shopkeeper's wife and daughter drown. More's claim is not simply practical—that shopkeepers are probably not very skilled sailors. Her point is also moral: every Briton has a social position that he or she is duty-bound to keep and the narrator is didactically explicit about this responsibility:

> When Britons, wearied with their lot,
> Grow wild to get they know not what,
> And quit, through love of Revolution,
> Our good old English Constitution . . .
> When Coblers [sic] meet in grand debate,
> And little folks feel vastly great;
> When each forsooth would quit his station,
> And Jack and Will would rule the nation . . .
> Help! Britons, help! we sink, we drown!
> They've turn'd our vessel upside down.[21]

The narrator thus equates the shopkeeper's tragedy with revolutionary upheaval by invoking a ship-of-state metaphor. The shopkeeper's crime is no isolated accident, but rather the sign of a disordered society in which citizens do not recognize or maintain their social positions.

In the final lines of the ballad, the narrator shows the reader how social order might be restored:

> Oh! would ye stop the nation's fall,
> Then every cobbler mind your awl;
> You labouring lads push home your spade;
> Ye trading Johnnies mind your trade;
> Ye seamen fight and don't debate;
> Watch statesmen well the helm of state . . .
> You'll trim the boat by sitting steady:
> Instructed thus by Johnny's case,
> Let ev'ry Briton mind his place.[22]

According to the narrator, the state can avoid dangerous upheaval if citizens retain their appropriate occupational positions. An aggregative epistemology provides a means not simply of knowing the social world, but of maintaining its order as well. In this instance the poetic lines describe what the world would look like if 'ev'ry Briton mind[ed] his place'. The logical structure of the lines and their predictable meter and rhyme also echo and reproduce that rational order, with each line separated by a semicolon containing a class of individuals and a kind of labour. Indeed, the lines thereby *put* every Briton in 'his place', smoothing over the social anarchy evoked by the poem. The categories in More's text have a clear normative function:

they enforce the ideal social order through a representation of it. The lines restore these figures to their correct socioeconomic positions, returning them to their proper aggregates and persuading readers of the virtues of a well-ordered society.

CHARLES DICKENS AND THE AFFECTIVE AGGREGATE

The epistemological affinities of early nineteenth-century writers and reformers met resistance in 1834, when the SSL declared that authoritative accounts of the social world should restrict themselves to numerical facts. They also met resistance in the work of those writers who believed that persuasive arguments about reform should rely on more than numbers alone. Charles Dickens questioned the impersonal quality of numbers over realist characters. He objected to the disinterestedness of numbers because he evidently believed that reformers should be very interested in the objects of reform. The serialized version of *Oliver Twist*, published in *Bentley's Miscellany* between February 1837 and April 1839, showcases these concerns, while also demonstrating the significant extent to which both numerical and narrative genres continued to rely on aggregation as a way to make knowledge about the social world.

In the opening sentence of the novel, Dickens's narrator invokes the impersonal nature of numerical forms:

> Among other public buildings in the town of Mudfog, it boasts of one which is common to most towns, great or small: to wit, a workhouse; and in this workhouse was born: on a day and date I need not trouble myself to repeat, inasmuch as it can be of no possible consequence to the reader, in this stage of the business at all events: the item of mortality whose name [Oliver Twist] is prefixed to the head of this chapter.[23]

The fictional town of Mudfog refers explicitly to another text that Dickens wrote and published alongside *Oliver Twist* in *Bentley's Miscellany* between 1837 and 1838: namely, *The Mudfog Papers*, a lesser-known satire of the British Association for the Advancement of Science in which Dickens lampoons statisticians and their proof-making practices. The satire appeared in the first issue of *Bentley's Miscellany* in the month prior to the first installment of *Oliver Twist*. Before readers met Oliver, in other words, they were introduced to his birthplace of Mudfog. Installments of *The Mudfog Papers* appeared in every subsequent issue that did not feature an installment of *Oliver Twist*. The two texts were, in a way, interleaved with one another, each taking the other's place in the periodical when one was absent.

In *The Mudfog Papers*, Dickens satirizes the kind of 'information' that statisticians gather: instead of gathering data about the population at large or about pressing social issues, the Mudfog statisticians collect data about irrelevant minutiae such as their own drinking habits.[24] The statisticians are likewise lampooned for their pointless efforts at social reform. Instead of targeting the poor and orphaned, the Mudfog statisticians develop projects to improve the conditions of fleas.[25] In Mudfog, animals and insects replace the typical human objects of statistical accounting and social reform. Workhouses and orphanages for fleas also parody the tragically ineffectual ones for children that are described in *Oliver Twist*.

Dickens's satire of statistical societies alternated with his novel about a poor orphan and helped to make sense of the novel's critique of numerical writing that we first encounter in the opening sentence. By calling Oliver an '*item* of mortality' instead of using his name, Dickens's narrator invokes the itemized nature of numerical writing. In doing so, however, he also invokes the aggregative epistemology that takes a very different form in the novel's subsequent pages. Nineteenth-century statistical writing typically itemized the population by listing categories and corresponding numerical values. As an 'item', Oliver could stand in for a larger trend of poverty and mortality. He could thus also constitute a kind of statistical evidence, representing a condition of the state and persuading readers of the problems of child mortality and labour. In the opening pages of the novel, then, the narrator dispenses with numerical representation but not with aggregation per se.

The narrator extends his critique by stating that Oliver must become something more than an enumerated and abstract 'item of mortality' if he is going to remain the novel's protagonist and thus constitute an effective (and affective) piece of evidence:

> For a long time after it was ushered into this world of sorrow and trouble, by the parish surgeon, it remained a matter of considerable doubt whether the child could survive to bear any name at all; in which case it is somewhat more than probable that these memoirs would never have appeared; or, if they had, that being comprised within a couple of pages, they would have possessed the inestimable merit of being the most concise and faithful specimen of biography, extant in the literature of any age or country.[26]

If Oliver had died in infancy, there would be very little story to tell. Sadly, the novel's plot would never come to fruition and would remain instead 'the most concise and faithful specimen of biography, extant in the literature of any age or country.'

In this passage, Dickens describes another problem with statistical representation: it is too abstract and impersonal to generate a coherent or moving narrative. Its capacity to produce knowledge in meaningful and useful ways is impoverished when compared to realist forms of aggregation. We see the incoherence of numerical aggregation manifested in the use of the pronoun 'it', which does not retain a clear referent over the course of the sentence.

At first, 'it' refers to Oliver, who has 'just been ushered into this world of sorrow and trouble.' In the next two clauses, 'it' refers to abstract ideas: 'it remained a matter of considerable doubt' and 'it is somewhat more than probable that these memoirs would never have appeared'. In these clauses, 'it' no longer refers to Oliver. Oliver has disappeared from the text just as he might have disappeared from the world if he had remained an 'item of mortality'. The fact that Dickens's novel opens with such a strange and confusing first sentence suggests that the epistemological problems writers faced in trying to convey knowledge about poverty were, in some ways, just as important as the problem of poverty itself. In his formulation of the aggregate, however, Dickens takes issue with the epistemology of number, despite implicitly registering the fact that numbers and narratives share a common concern with aggregation.

The progression of the opening sentence suggests that abstraction is the result of numerical itemization. By presenting Oliver as a mere example— an 'item of mortality'—the narrator has made him into an abstraction: an 'it' rather than a fully formed character. Yet abstraction also corresponds figuratively to death: if Oliver had remained an 'item' or 'it', he would have died, failing to become the protagonist of a *bildungsroman* and fail- ing to effectively (and affectively) move readers to do anything about the problems for which he stands. Luckily for the novel's reader, Oliver does not die and instead goes on to become something more than a mere 'item of mortality'. By the chapter's closing paragraph, Oliver has become a recognizably realist character, with human emotions and will: 'Oliver cried lustily. If he could have known that he was an orphan, left to the tender mercies of churchwardens and overseers, perhaps he would have cried the louder.'[27] This final paragraph makes a transition from a satire about statistical representation to a sentimental narrative—an emotion- ally moving narrative that seeks to convince its readers about the plight of its orphaned protagonist and, by extension, all such orphans for which Oliver stands. Dickens's novel thereby continues to rely on a strategy of aggregation, while rejecting the 'disinterested' form of aggregation used in numerical writing.

Dickens's novel thus makes an explicit transition between two kinds of knowledge about poverty that nonetheless both rely on aggregative tech- niques: the kind of knowledge that relies on itemized data and the kind of knowledge that relies on emotional experience. The former offers an item- ized representation of an impersonal and abstract aggregate, whereas the latter offers a *personalized* representation of the aggregate. In the chapter's final sentences, the narrator implies that Oliver would cry louder if only he knew more about his situation, or if he knew as much as we (reader and narrator) know. In other words, more knowledge equals more tears—more affect and deeply personalized subjectivity. *Oliver Twist* thus relies on a kind of affective aggregation whereby readers are encouraged to identify with a social group in the terms of an affective narrative that chronicles the suffering of an exemplary character. Here, affective aggregation stands in contrast to the impersonal aggregates of numerical accounting.

This progression from numerical itemization to sentimental narration, however, does not simply oppose one to the other. Rather, it suggests that the sentimental narration has developed progressively out of numerical itemization. The narrator implicitly compares two kinds of development: the potential development of the child, who will grow up to be more than an 'item of mortality', and the development of the novel, which will likewise become more than an abstract form of numerical representation. Just as the child grows up into a morally mature form of himself, so too does the text. Oliver's maturation is as much about his moral development as it is about the way he outgrows his abstract and impoverished statistical form by taking the fleshier shape of a deep-feeling realist character. Statistical representation also grows up, becoming the morally mature form of the social problem novel. Dickens's novel thus offers not simply a narrative of Oliver's improvement, but of the improvement of aggregation itself.

As if to remind the reader of this progress, the novel repeatedly invokes statistical genres and their conventional features, representing numerical forms in increasingly pejorative terms. Dickens's novel refers to the kinds of 'accounts' and 'printed reports' that dominated official social-accounting efforts. In *Oliver Twist*, however, these official genres are often cited by the novel's corrupt poor law officials when justifying Oliver's mistreatment:

> the board then proceeded to converse among themselves [and] the words, 'saving of expenditure', 'look well into accounts', 'have a printed report published', were alone audible. These only chanced to be heard, indeed, on account of their being frequently repeated with great emphasis.[28]

Throughout the novel, forms of official numerical accounting are associated with the novel's most inveterate criminals, and their inarticulate speech reflects what Dickens's novel treats as the central problem of numerical statistical writing: it misrepresents its subject and as such could never effectively persuade the public about the urgency of reform. Their speech conveys no substantive meaning, just as the reports contain no real evidence of social problems. The men and their reports commit crimes against two victims: humanity and persuasive representation. The men have no interest in actually ensuring Oliver's safety because the types of writing/speech that they deploy have already condemned him to remain a mere 'item of mortality'. The novel supplements this impoverished numerical form with its moving narrative account, making up for what numerical writing lacks.

In doing so, the novel does not simply pit statistical misrepresentation against novelistic representation. It asserts a relationship between them such that the novel appears to offer a better, more sophisticated form of representation: rather than a numerical misrepresentation of the poor, the novel offers a fuller and more accurate narrative representation. Put another way, it offers to improve upon the aggregative epistemology that dominated the statistics of the time. The novel reveals this relationship in part by relying heavily on the language and form of statistical writing, even as it also lampoons its ineffective abstractions. In satirizing the system of social investigation practiced by poor law officials, the narrator describes the reasoning of these 'experimental philosopher[s]' in the following terms:

> at the very moment when a child had contrived to exist on the smallest possible portion of the weakest possible food, it did perversely happen in eight and a half cases out of ten, either that it sickened from want and cold, or fell into the fire from neglect, or got smothered by accident, in any one of the cases, the miserable little thing was usually summoned into another world.[29]

Here Dickens invokes the language of counting and probabilistic speculation. Treating children numerically allows for a callous representation of mortality that cites as evidence fractional units ('eight and a half') of people. The syntax of the sentence also obscures the fact that it is anyone's responsibility to protect these children: the phrase 'it did perversely happen in eight and a half cases' makes it seem that the perversity of these deaths is a result of statistical odds rather than neglect. The unfeeling enumeration of potential causes of death reveals how unlikely it is that this system can properly account for these children or persuade the public of their plight. The novel absorbs those methods and transforms them, remaking the ways by which contemporaries could know the poor and imagine the improvement of their conditions.

   While critiquing these practices of speculation, the narrator also describes the novel as a vehicle for another, more believable kind of speculation. At the end of the first installment, the narrator juxtaposes the two kinds of speculation. First, the narrator reports speculations about Oliver's fate voiced by 'the gentleman in the white waistcoat', one of the novel's 'experimental philosophers': '"That boy will be hung," said the gentleman in the white waistcoat. "I know that boy will be hung." Nobody controverted the prophetic gentleman's opinion.'[30] Directly after reporting this prophetic speculation, the narrator informs the reader, 'As I purpose to show in the sequel whether the white-waistcoated gentleman was right or not, I should perhaps mar the interest of this narrative (supposing it to possess any at all), if I ventured to hint just yet, whether the life of Oliver Twist had this violent termination or no.'[31] The narrator contrasts the gentleman's speculation to the reader's speculation about the novel's plot: 'the interest of the narrative' allows the reader to speculate about 'whether the life of Oliver Twist had this violent termination or no.' The novel's interest—unlike the gentleman's callous, scientific disinterestedness—generates a different kind of speculation about Oliver's probable survival, a different (albeit related) way of making knowledge about all poor orphans. The narrator offers this guarantee to the reader of the serialized novel. By continuing to read subsequent installments, readers could participate in an alternative speculative practice that admitted the possibility of a happy ending. Yet these two kinds of speculation are nonetheless related to one another. Mathematical reasoning and novelistic representation share the practice of aggregation and speculation. Only novelistic representation, however, is truly persuasive and effective.

CONCLUSION

Rather than view a novel like *Oliver Twist* as merely debunking the authority of numerical accounting, we might do better to understand the way in which it was grappling with epistemological questions that gave shape to a range of numerical and narrative genres. Aggregation took many different forms as writers attempted to find the most persuasive way of generating knowledge about social wholes and their constituent parts. In seeking to secure the future progress and welfare of Britain's citizens, the SSL insisted that numerical forms of evidence would provide the only sure basis of social knowledge. Following the empirical thrust of Enlightenment sciences, societies like the SSL sought to make statistics into a distinctive discipline by declaring the disinterestedness of numerical facts. It is certainly true that statistics became increasingly numerical over the course of the nineteenth century. Statistical societies and institutions dedicated themselves to systematizing the science of statistics and they articulated rules about the numerical form of statistical writing. Yet this was a long and drawn-out process. The meaning of statistics was still in movement, and it would be wrong therefore to regard the incorporation of narrative elements as intrinsically anachronistic or idiosyncratic to a particular writer or text; only from the perspective of the twentieth- and twenty-first centuries does it appear so. In fact, while the development of numerical statistical writing certainly created new strategies for representing the population and its socioeconomic condition, there were other kinds of writing that developed alongside and collaborated with these numerical genres, all contributing to the decidedly uneven formation of an aggregative social epistemology.

The account offered here, while necessarily brief, offers a corrective to the way in which modern disciplinary formations mediate our understanding of the past. Jevons was right to anticipate that statistical writing would 'become more a matter of quantity and number' over time. That process was not, however, complete until the twentieth century. In the meantime, numerical and narrative features jockeyed for readers' attention in the works of writers who were undecided about how to represent statistical evidence, especially as a persuasive tactic. What we glimpse in the foregoing account are just some of the ways in which different genres sought to account for the social world long before modern disciplines had fully routinized and codified empirical sociological methods. For writers and reformers such as More and Wilberforce, who were concerned with social conditions around the turn of the nineteenth century, different genres of social accounting could take on different and complementary tasks in deploying an aggregative epistemology. Whereas the census could offer a numerical account of social groups, More's didactic tracts could elaborate the moral importance of these same aggregates, with each genre contributing to a larger body of social knowledge.

The SSL and its journal sought to take over the task of producing that body of knowledge in the form of the statistical text. They did not, however, do so without the aid of narrative techniques that gave force to arguments about social reform. The SSL did not feel the need to call on the services of writers like More to make the moral case for aggregation. Statisticians could perform the labours of both counting and narrating without necessarily seeing the two as opposed. Interestingly, according to the material examined above, it was not statistical writing itself, or even statisticians (like Jevons), that demonstrated an eager desire to divide (or re-divide) that labour and thus make statistics exclusively numerical. Novels like *Oliver Twist* demonstrated a much greater insistence that the work of social realism—despite sharing an interest in aggregation—was distinctive and more persuasive than the work of numerical accounting. Dickens had to dispense with numbers in order to offer a more complete and persuasive narrative account.

Why these once complementary forms of aggregation became incompatible must remain an issue for further research. The fact that Dickens's novel was published in the same years that the SSL's journal was founded offers a starting point. We might also entertain a few other unexamined possibilities: that without the development of social realism sociological methods may not have developed in exactly the way that they did. In other words, the codification of social scientific methods was dependent not merely on the founding of institutions, or on disciplinary developments, but also on the emergence of an antagonist in the form of the narrative genre of social realism. At any rate, it is certainly worth considering the role that narrative forms played not just in defining and deploying an aggregative epistemology, but also in granting a more discrete and disciplined shape to statistical methods through an opposition to them. Statistics and political economy (later 'economics') did indeed 'become more a matter of quantity and number' over time, but this was an incredibly complex process, one which involved the working out of epistemological conflicts *and* affinities.

NOTES

1. Quoted in Royal Statistical Society, *Annals of the Royal Statistical Society, 1834–1934* (London, 1934), pp. 26–7.
2. B. Anderson, *Imagined Communities: Reflections on the Origin and Spread of Nationalism* (Rev. edn., London, 1991), ch. 10.

3. As Libby Schweber argues, early Victorian statisticians 'spent little time reflecting on the hierarchy of knowledge, the boundaries between disciplines, and the status [of statistics] as a science. It was only in the late 1870s that social statisticians began to invest in the type of rhetorical work' that conceived of statistical inquiries as a 'disciplinary activity'. L. Schweber, *Disciplining Statistics: Demography and Vital Statistics in France and England, 1830–1885* (Durham, NC, 2006), p. 94.

4. The eighteenth-century genre of the statistical account was chiefly a descriptive genre, reflecting the fact that the term 'statistical' had previously meant 'of the state' and typically referred to prose descriptions of the state's political and geographical parts. For an account of the transition between descriptive and numerical statistics, see F. De Bruyn, 'From Georgic Poetry to Statistics and Graphs: Eighteenth-Century Representations and the "State" of British Society', *Yale Journal of Criticism* 17 (2004), pp. 107–39.

5. The distinction was drawn by the London Statistical Society in 1838. In *A History of the Modern Fact*, Mary Poovey describes the relationship between 'figures of arithmetic' and 'figures of speech' in early nineteenth-century social accounting. Whereas 'figures of speech' were associated pejoratively with rhetoric (along with pathos, fiction and mere deduction), 'figures of arithmetic' were viewed as facts, trustworthy and the privileged material of scientific inquiry. As Poovey notes, 'the word "statistics" seems to have carried connotations of both substance (statistics recorded the kind of information about national resources that would be useful to the state) and form (statistical information was sometimes, though not inevitably, conveyed in numbers and tables).' M. Poovey, *A History of the Modern Fact: Problems of Knowledge in the Sciences of Wealth and Society* (Chicago, 2008), p. 308. As this chapter demonstrates, the fact that statistical reports did not take an exclusively numerical form meant that adjacent concepts (such as social aggregation) remained ill-defined and open to many representational expressions.

6. M. Poovey, *Making a Social Body: British Cultural Formation, 1830–1864* (Chicago, 1995), p. 36.

7. See I. Bernard Cohen, *The Triumph of Numbers: How Counting Shaped Modern Life* (London, 2005), ch. 8; S. Sullivan, 'Dickens's Newgate Vision: Oliver Twist, Moral Statistics, and the Construction of Progressive History', *Nineteenth Century Studies* 14 (2000), pp. 121–48; and E. Courtemanche, '"Naked Truth Is the Best Eloquence": Martineau, Dickens, and the Moral Science of Realism', *ELH* 73 (2006), pp. 383–407.

8. Quoted in *Annals of the Royal Statistical Society*, p. 22.

9. 'Introduction', *Journal of the Statistical Society of London* [hereafter *JSSL*] 1 (1838), p. 3.

10. *Ibid.*, p. 1.

11. Prof. W.S. Jevons, 'Opening Address of the President of Section F (Economic Science and Statistics), of the British Association for the Advancement of Science', *JSSL* 33 (1870), p. 309.

12. 'Introduction', p. 3.

13. W.H. Sykes, 'Statistics of Cadiz', *JSSL* 1 (1838), p. 353.

14. L. Hindmarsh, 'On the State of Agriculture and Condition of the Agricultural Labourers of the Northern District of Northumberland', *JSSL* 1 (1838), p. 411.

15. J. M'Alister, 'Statistical Notice of the Asylum for the Blind in Newcastle-upon-Tyne', *JSSL* 1 (1838), p. 377.

16. R. Giffen, 'Further Notes on the Progress of the Working Classes in the Last Century', *JSSL* 49 (1886), pp. 47–50.

17. B. Disraeli, *Sybil; or the Two Nations* [1845] (London, 1920), p. ii.

18. Great Britain, *Abstract of the Answers and Returns Made Pursuant to . . . An Act for Taking an Account of the Population* (Great Britain, Parliament, House of Commons, 1802), p. 4.
19. Great Britain, *Abstract of the Answers and Returns: Occupations* (Great Britain, Parliament, House of Commons, HMSO, 1844), pp. 10–11.
20. On the reforming ambitions of More and the political and cultural milieu in which these developed and were applied, see in particular Susan Pedersen, 'Hannah More Meets Simple Simon: Tracts, Chapbooks and Popular Culture in Late Eighteenth-Century England', *Journal of British Studies* 25 (1986), pp. 84–113.
21. [H. More] *Cheap Repository Tracts: Moral, Entertaining and Religious* (2. vols., London, 1798), II, pp. 446–7.
22. *Ibid.*, p. 450.
23. *Bentley's Miscellany* 1 (1837), p. 105.
24. C. Dickens, *The Mudfog Papers* [1837–38] (New York, 1880), pp. 24–6, 42.
25. *Ibid.*, pp. 88–93.
26. *Bentley's Miscellany*, p. 106.
27. *Ibid.*, p. 107.
28. *Ibid.*, p. 220.
29. *Ibid.*, p. 108.
30. *Ibid.*, p. 115.
31. *Loc. cit.*

7 Printed Statistics and the Public Sphere

Numeracy, Electoral Politics, and the Visual Culture of Numbers, 1880–1914

James Thompson

This chapter seeks to reconstruct the role of numbers in British political culture in the late nineteenth and early twentieth centuries. Substantial studies now exist charting the development of statistical techniques; the increasing role of mathematics in the social sciences; and the role of the state as a source of quantitative data.[1] The history of mathematics is itself a burgeoning field which has increasingly sought to understand the mathematical in a broad social and cultural context.[2] The focus here, though, is upon the visual language of public numbers. It is now almost a quarter of a century since Keith Thomas noted the relative neglect of numeracy by comparison with literacy in studies of the early modern world.[3] Recent quantitative work has evaluated the spread of numerical skills in the modern world as a means of understanding human capital formation and long-term growth trends.[4] Histories of work have also addressed the role of numerical skills in professional life, whilst historians of leisure—not least gambling—have detailed the uses of numeracy beyond the workplace.[5] However, as the introduction to this volume notes, we still know too little about the circulation and consumption of statistically derived imagery in the public sphere, especially in the form of graphs. This chapter builds on these historiographies in order to start the task of considering the reception, as well as the production and visualization, of numbers in British political culture.

The chapter is in three sections. The first outlines the graphical cultures of late nineteenth- and early twentieth-century Britain. It locates graphical representation in a visual culture where hybrid forms, notably narrative painting, political cartoons and the illustrated book, occupied a privileged place.[6] The second section turns to the visual representation of political numbers. It shows how the changing appearance of newspapers, and the rise of the large-scale pictorial poster, presented new opportunities for the figuring of politics.[7] The final section moves to numeracy, briefly examining both the breadth and depth of numerical skills within the population. It ends with some reflections on what the visual representation of the numerical tells us about late nineteenth- and early twentieth-century British political culture.

GRAPHICAL CULTURES

In his pioneering history of 'the graphical representation of statistical data' published in the 1930s, H.G. Funkhouser termed the period from 1860 to 1900 'the age of enthusiasm'.[8] *The Times* rarely missed an opportunity to proclaim the nature of the zeitgeist, and duly declared in 1874 that this was 'an age of timetables'.[9] New technologies were eagerly exploited for the propagation of graphical material: lantern slides were embraced by lecturers, for example, while developments in printing facilitated the visual representation of numbers within political posters. Graphical methods spread through a range of disciplines: the Mason College engineering professor Robert H. Smith insisted on their business value; Alfred Marshall's deployment of curves in the notes to his *Principles of Economics* was one, albeit highly influential, instance of the adoption by British economists of graphical techniques.[10] The celebrated physicist James Clerk Maxwell also made significant use of diagrams, notably in his work on statics, and wrote the entry on 'diagrams' for the authoritative *Encyclopaedia Britannica*.[11] This section reconstructs Britain's graphical cultures by relating shifts in particular fields to wider cultural developments. It starts, however, with the place of visual representation in late Victorian mathematics.

The recent turn towards less 'internalist' histories of mathematics has served nineteenth-century Britain well. As Joan Richards has noted, though the mathematical research community in nineteenth-century England might have been relatively small, the number of those studying the subject at university level was considerably more impressive.[12] Training in mathematics at university was not principally animated by the agenda of research, but rather was shaped by an ideal of a universalistic liberal education in the exercise of thought. Within this conception of mathematical learning, geometry was accorded a special significance for securing knowledge of the world and of God, and was hymned for its capacity to penetrate the spatial mysteries of reality.[13]

The increasing presence of mathematics within nineteenth-century science has often been portrayed primarily as a process of growing abstraction and formalism. It is undoubtedly true that some 'hard' sciences, notably physics, made significant use of highly technical developments within mathematical analysis. However, mathematical physics could also privilege visual representation through diagrams. Historians of science have illuminated the theoretical and philosophical differences between the two gods of nineteenth-century physics, Lord Kelvin and Clerk Maxwell, arguing that the former's more mechanical approach, anchored in the realities of 'steam-engines, vortex turbines, and telegraph lines', lost out to the more abstract conceptions of the latter.[14] Yet, for all their methodological divergence, both Kelvin and Clerk Maxwell were apostles of the diagram: Kelvin sharply criticized French mathematicians for their neglect of 'diagrams and examples'; Clerk Maxwell placed diagrammatic representation at the heart of his force-based physics.[15] Indeed, as John Roche has suggested, the imaginary spaces of nineteenth-century physics were often interpreted in more literal terms, in part through the seductive powers of the diagram.[16]

More generally, it can be argued that the role of illustrations in nineteenth-century science went well beyond mere representation. In a pioneering article in the mid-1970s, Martin Rudwick excavated the visual language of geology, proclaiming that the dominance of numerical and literary thinking among historians of science had obscured the role played by visual thinking in the development of the discipline.[17] Historians of botany, but also of chemistry and geography, have paid increasing attention to visual languages.[18] In these accounts, evident especially in histories of chemistry, visual language is recognized as growing in potency but increasingly distanced from visual culture more broadly.[19] For students of other disciplines, however, such as geography, visual representation emerged as a means of marrying the popular with the professional in an era in which science was becoming both more specialized and more culturally resonant.[20]

Graphical cultures were rarely discrete; techniques and devices were borrowed and adapted for different purposes. In the introduction to his study of *The Theory of Political Economy*, W.S. Jevons noted his debt to the work of Kelvin, while Marshall, who was often circumspect about the role of mathematics in economics, commended the presentation of time series data as a 'historical curve', rather than a table, as its 'geometrical form . . . brings it one step nearer the language of mathematics'.[21] The sources for the new language of curves were, however, multiple, owing much to the mathematics in which many economists were initially trained, but also to meteorology and engineering, as evident in the pioneering graphical representation of supply and demand by Fleeming Jenkin.[22]

The early history of graphical representation within statistics was also strongly marked by complex borrowings and exchanges. The eighteenth-century efforts of Joseph Priestley and William Playfair owed much to the conventions of mapping, apparent in the former's use of colour in his chronological tables and the latter's comparison of 'lineal arithmetic' with the geographical rendering of a river.[23] Playfair noted how 'copper-plate charts' had benefited historical researches but also advertised mathematical ambitions, claiming to apply 'the principles of geometry to matters of finance'. Playfair tended to lean heavily on the notion of mapping, and even to present his charts as physically embodying the data. He claimed that while figures and letters might be accurate, they could not represent numbers or space.[24] Playfair's Humean language about the imprinting of distinct ideas provided an impeccably empiricist justification for his work, but his championing of the power of the graphical to capture quantity and space celebrated the commonalities between graphical representation and geometry.[25]

Even so, despite the efforts of Priestley and Playfair, only in the latter half of the nineteenth century was there a significant expansion in the use of graphical representations in statistics. Funkhouser identified this process with developments in anthropometry and economics.[26] The records of late nineteenth-century statistical societies bear out his claim. Reviewing the history of the Royal Statistical Society in 1896, John Martin highlighted the recent explosion of graphical methods in the pages of its journal, and figures like William Farr and Marshall featured prominently in his account.[27] In seeking to explain this efflorescence, a number of largely internalist factors have been suggested. Beniger and Robyn have highlighted the problem of continuous distributions as a driver for graphical innovation in the late nineteenth century.[28] Evidence supporting this view is not in short supply. In his *Principles of Economics*, Marshall emphasized that 'our observations of nature, in the moral as in the physical world, relate not so much to aggregate quantities, as to increments of quantities', and noted the value of diagrams for expounding these observations.[29] Judy Klein has identified a move from employing graphs to present information to adopting the graphical as an investigative tool.[30] From the 1860s onwards, Jevons championed the insights supplied by graphical means, attributing his understanding of the periodicity of commercial crises to the contemplation of statistical diagrams.[31]

It is important, however, to characterize accurately the trajectory of graphical culture in these years, and to do so we need to acknowledge both continuity and change. As anthropologists and historians of printing have long argued, we should recognize the conventional and graphical qualities of the tables which proliferated throughout the century in publications from blue books to calculating aids for shopkeepers.[32] In his presidential address, Martin noted that the objectives of the Statistical Society centred on the provision of 'facts being for the most part arranged in tabular forms'.[33] The noted statistician and Society member Robert Giffen devoted a whole chapter in his posthumously published volume on statistics to 'the construction of tables'.[34] Tables continued to appear more frequently than curves in the pages of the Society's journal. The prevalence of the table had important implications, not least in encouraging binary categorizations, though the emergence of multivariate analysis was beginning to mitigate this, at least within more mathematically high-powered contexts.[35] Massed ranks of digits in tabular arrays accorded with the widespread aim of capturing the totality of facts, but also matched the dense, ink-laden presentation of contemporary newspapers. The heavy vertical lines that corseted the data in nineteenth-century tables reflected the dominance of the grid evident in the ubiquity of squared paper.

Towards the end of the century, innovations in newspaper design encouraged the adoption of new means of displaying quantitative data. Here too, though, the story was not one of stark discontinuity. Early attempts to add visual interest to the page departed relatively little from the hegemony of the grid. Illustrations appeared adjacent to blocks of text, rather than breaking up the flow of text. From the 1870s especially, it was maps, especially of wars such as the Franco-Prussian conflict of 1870–71, that spread within newspaper layouts. In turn, and in keeping with the earlier vision of Playfair, quantitative data came to be displayed through statistical maps, not least those showing the distribution of seats in parliament. It was not, in other words, primarily the more abstract conceptions of space evident in the graphical constructions of figures like Jevons and Karl Pearson that permeated the visual language of newspapers, but rather an older approach, which anchored statistical space much more closely to physical space through the conventions of geographical mapping.

The popularity of graphical forms was rising at the close of the nineteenth century, with innovations such as the stereogram, credited by Palgrave in his influential *Dictionary of Political Economy* to Irving Fisher.[36] In tracing the popular dissemination of graphical language, the pictogram, usually attributed to Michael Mulhall, looms larger. Historians of statistics have often taken a dim view of Mulhall's output, recalling contemporary charges of exaggeration and guesswork.[37] Mulhall was certainly a prolific producer of pictorial statistics, whose work, presented as apolitical and scientific, was littered with comparisons between nations in which Britain fared well, as Asa Briggs has noted.[38] Mulhall was also, though, a member of significant statistical associations, and he published widely in leading periodicals, especially the *Contemporary Review*.[39] His *Dictionary of Statistics* was regularly raided by contemporaries for relevant data, as it has been by historians. The *Dictionary* combined sustained scrutiny of comparative literacy rates with anecdotes about the capacity of dogs to survive without food.[40] Illustrations were at the heart of the marketing of the *Dictionary*.[41] Throughout his publications, Mulhall utilized pictorial diagrams, filled with circles and triangles of varying hues. This often introduced an ambiguity about whether the images were meant to be proportionate to the quantities represented, and, if so, whether the proportionality obtained in terms of height or area. More important, however, was Mulhall's use of iconicity, in which arms expenditure was represented by bullets of varying sizes, or meat production by pictures of cows (see Figure 7.1).[42] Whilst Mulhall was not a statistician with the technical skills of a Pearson, his use of pictograms is not best understood as merely naïve or antiquated. Mulhall, with his background successfully editing a newspaper in South America, recognized the potential of pictograms for communicating with a broader audience in an era witnessing rapid shifts in visual culture.

In his famous study of *Human Nature in Politics*, Graham Wallas reflected upon the efficacy of the method of curves, arguing that graphing enabled more data to be grasped, especially when presented as a black line on a white surface. Much of Wallas's argument fits with a familiar story about political science seizing on the techniques of economics. His citation of Marshall on the passage from qualitative to quantitative thinking in economics matches this template. It was striking, however, that he applauded marginalist approaches for their greater realism in embracing human variety rather than relying on abstract notions of economic man.

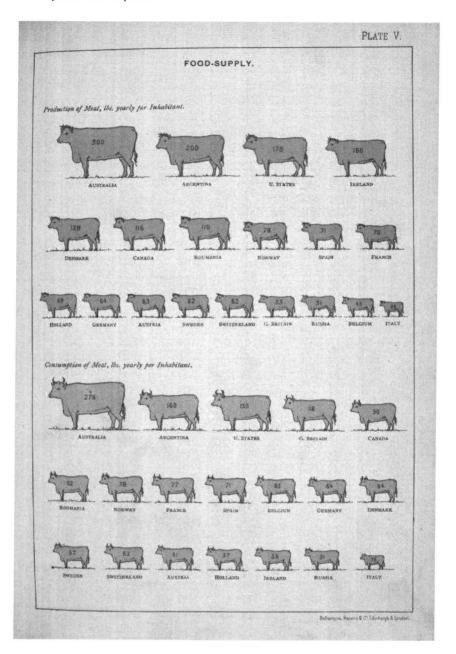

Figure 7.1   'Food-Supply', Mulhall, Plate V, *Dictionary of Statistics*, 1892. © The British Library Board.

More striking, though, from our perspective, are the terms in which he advocated a graphical turn in politics. Noting, doubtless optimistically, the increased understanding of the numerical in an age when 'every newspaper reader is fairly familiar with the figures in the Board of Trade monthly returns', Wallas went on to insist that 'a picture ... may be sometimes nearer to quantitative truth, more easily remembered and more useful for purposes of argument and verification than a row of figures'. He developed the point by observing that 'the most exact quantitative political document I ever saw was a set of photographs of all the women admitted into an inebriate home', claiming that 'it would have been easily possible for a committee of medical men to have arranged the photographs in a series of increasing abnormality, and to have indicated the photograph of the "marginal" woman'.[43]

Wallas's confidence about the possibilities of photography was not unusual in Edwardian England. Nor, as we have seen, was his sense of the value of visual representations of the numerical. Within a range of disciplines and in a variety of contexts, graphical imaging of statistical data was on the rise. The expansion of graphical presentation needs relating to changes in technology and the media. It is perhaps developments within the illustrated media of newspapers and periodicals that are most familiar, but the growing use of pictorial posters and lantern slides also increased the visibility of numbers. The ambiguities of scale generated by Mulhall's pictograms were more than matched by the 'big loaf' posters of the 1906 election, something explored in Edmund Rogers's chapter. It is to the specifically political use of the graphical that we now turn.

FIGURING POLITICS

In 1885 the Liberal Central Association published a poster entitled 'Liberal and Tory Finance No. 1', with a diagram of taxation remitted by central government over the previous twenty-one years (see Figure 7.2).[44] Unsurprisingly, red bars representing taxation lessened by Liberals exceeded blue bars of reduced Conservative taxation. The poster was a response to a previous Conservative image portraying diagrammatically the levying of income tax, and sought to argue that a focus on one kind of taxation was misleading. This poster exchange from the start of our period reveals the willingness of political parties to employ graphical means to communicate their messages. It was not an isolated instance: the Liberal Central Association (LCA) swiftly followed up with a poster purporting to demonstrate the party's superior record in paying off the national debt, illustrated with another boldly coloured bar chart.[45] Clear connections with the graphical cultures sketched earlier are evident in these and other posters from the 1880s. Both LCA posters adopted the grid presentation familiar from the squared paper notebooks that became standard in the nineteenth century.

In both posters, words continued to play a crucial part, occupying at least a third of the space. Interestingly, both images included exact figures adjacent to the bars of colour, suggesting perhaps self-consciousness about their mode of presentation, and a desire at least to appear precise. These kinds of relationships to wider graphical cultures will recur in our examination of the visual representation of statistics within politics.

In July 1886, *The Times* announced the publication of two electoral maps 'showing the distribution of party strength', so enabling readers 'to realize very clearly the nature and localities of the victories that have been won for the cause of the Union'. It went on to suggest that the 'instructive and impressive' maps 'tell the eye better than words or figures the result of the battle up to this hour'.[46] The language of war was perhaps even more conventional than that of sport in late Victorian election coverage, though nonetheless revealing for that. There was, however, a particular significance in linking it to an electoral map, for the demands of war reporting had done much to encourage the inclusion of maps in nineteenth-century newspapers. The alterations to the electoral franchise and the distribution of seats in 1884–5 are often described as 'redrawing the electoral map' in the light of the improved performance of the political right in the last decades of the century. The phrase can be taken in a more literal way, for the changes of the mid-1880s led to a boom in the production of electoral maps, detailing the new constituency boundaries. Home Rule in turn encouraged the mapping impulse, both because of the obvious geographical and political issues it raised about the identity of the United Kingdom and the internal divisions within Ireland, and because of the dramatic impact of the 1886 election upon the distribution of seats.

It is striking, then, that it was an Ulster Roman Catholic convert and unionist, J.F.G. Ross-of-Bladensburg, who compiled the innovative 'Simplex' charts that appeared at successive elections from 1892 to 1910, and which *The Times* adopted from the 1895 election.[47] Earlier electoral maps reproduced counties, at their usual 'atlas' size, and recorded electoral outcomes through labelling. The Simplex chart was built around the constituency, which was represented as a square, and the evenly sized squares were artfully arranged to mimic the familiar atlas map of the United Kingdom, whilst reflecting the actual number of seats in different regions. A series of markings within the squares distinguished county divisions, boroughs, metropolitan boroughs and university seats.[48] In its use of squares, the Simplex accorded with established conventions of graphical representation. Its spatial layout, especially in its larger foldout forms, encouraged attention to the electoral significance of the key battlegrounds, such as Lancashire and London.[49] Whereas newspaper reproductions presented party differences quite literally in black and white, the foldout versions came in colour, or un-shaded to be coloured in as results emerged (adverts noted that crayons were available from the publisher). Attempts to relate scale on the printed page to the distribution of seats both reflected and fostered the heightened

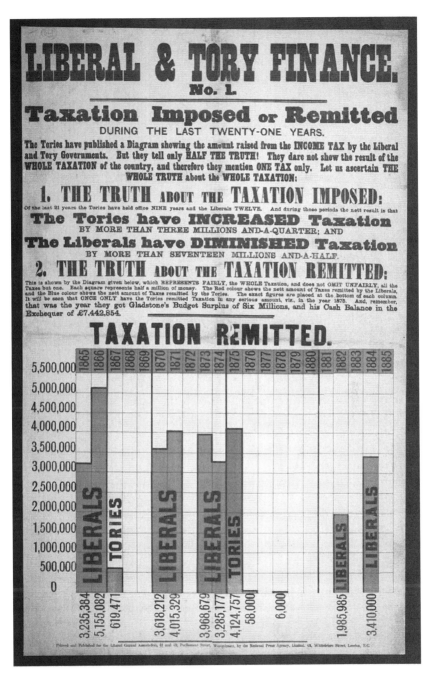

Figure 7.2   Liberal Central Association, 'Liberal and Tory Finance No. 1' LSE, BLPES, Coll. Misc. 519/75. Reproduced by kind permission of the British Library of Political and Economic Science.

sensitivities about electoral arithmetic aroused by the changes of 1884–5, and exacerbated the character and severity of party competition in this period.

In employing black and white to symbolize party affiliation, *The Times* necessarily dichotomized political allegiances, contrasting Conservatives and Liberal Unionists with Liberals and Nationalists. The underlying sentiment behind this approach was made plain in one 1895 version of the chart where the legend labelled the white square 'Unionists' and the black 'Separatists'—scarcely an evenhanded approach to terminology (see Figure 7.3).[50] This really was politics reduced to black and white, with the dark 'Celtic fringe' visibly distinguished from the white metropolitan 'core'. In 1900, *The Times* commented that 'the usefulness of [the Simplex] has now been proved by experience during several general elections'.[51] Its graphic of 'the present state of the parties' on the eve of the 1900 election adopted more neutral terms for describing parties, but the tables framing the map offered comparative statistics on population per seat for different areas contiguous to figures for 'representation in proportion to population' (see Figure 7.4).[52] The implied message was emphatically that of the overrepresentation of the 'periphery', with the nine counties of Ulster helpfully appearing as the only part of Ireland represented at the appropriate weight. After the election, the paper used the Simplex to picture the persistence of Unionist dominance. Here, again, its choice of labels was intriguing if problematic. In the chart recapitulating the pre-election situation, squares were either black or white; in the post-election graphic grey hatching signified the third way of liberal unionism. In both cases, additional statistics were supplied disaggregating the forces of darkness into 'liberal imperialists', 'radicals and labour' and 'nationalists'.[53] This had the convenient effect of both suggesting the incompatibility of the separatists, and of indicating the liberal unionists and the liberal imperialists as the only groups strengthened by the election. The diptych construction recalls the composition of many political posters in the period. Lastly, the availability in 1900 of the Simplex in a poster-sized version for a shilling (or two shillings if coloured) reminds us of the hobbyist interest in politics apparent in this period, further testified to by the existence of electoral toys, such as pendulums for showing the electoral swing.

Electoral maps were an increasingly common device for presenting numerical data. The 'skeleton map', a variant on the Simplex, was employed to display predicted unionist losses in 1905 in both the *Daily Mail* and the *Review of Reviews*.[54] In *The Graphic*, electoral mapping incorporated considerable variety of scale, and greater tonal range conveyed through shading, in keeping with the traditions of the illustrated newspaper.[55] Unmistakably politicized, mapping made electoral trends, or the lack of them, starkly visual. Surveying the electoral landscape in 1900, the *Daily News* proclaimed that 'Ireland is the one place in the United Kingdom where electoral maps are always the same'.[56] Statistical mapping was not

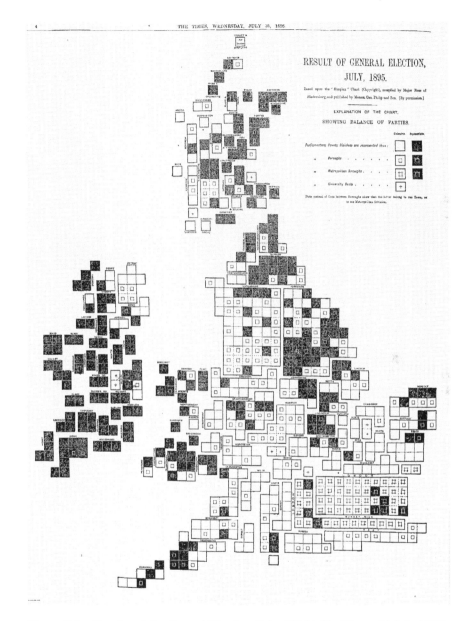

Figure 7.3 'Results of the General Election, July, 1895,' *The Times*, 31 July 1895.

confined to information about elections. Just as some atlases included a range of cartograms, so newspapers found maps appealing for a variety of purposes.[57] Geography and the politics of numbers were intrinsic to

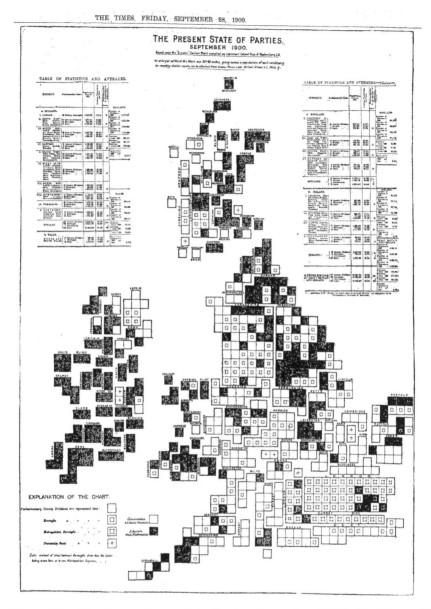

Figure 7.4 'The Present State of the Parties, September 1900', *The Times*, 28 September 1900.

the Irish question. In 1912, *The Times* printed a map of Ireland recording the 'percentage and distribution of non-Catholics' in which the awkward issue of Catholic domination in much of Ulster was made very apparent.

By 1914, the paper was providing political maps of Ireland that supplied constituency-level data on confessional allegiances.[58] Recovering the visual representation of numbers illuminates the construction of 'the Irish problem' in late nineteenth- and early twentieth-century politics.

Political maps drew upon established conventions, and operated at a lower level of abstraction than more technical graphs. The rise of more mathematical forms of representation is discernible from the 1890s. As in earlier periods, the price of wheat was a prime candidate for graphing. Line graphs with quantity on the y-axis and date on the x-axis were also employed to analyze electoral trends, as in the *English Review* in 1910.[59] Graphical tracing of electoral outcomes was not confined to British politics, with the heavily discussed 1896 presidential contest between McKinley and Bryan attracting notable efforts. The *Review of Reviews* was eager to add visual interest to the page, and much concerned with what W.T. Stead revealingly termed 'electoral meteorology'.[60] In 1904, the *Review* plotted by-election results against those for the same constituencies in the 1900 general election for both major parties, and claimed, in an oft-used phrase, that 'the accompanying diagrams speak for themselves'.[61] In keeping with the meteorological analogy, the *Review* had in 1890 already pictured by-election results as subdivided bars of which the white section symbolized liberal successes, the black part Conservative victories.[62] It would, however, be misleading to focus solely on instances where more mathematical conventions were deployed. In 1892, the *Pall Mall Gazette* adopted the popular metaphor of the steeplechase to show 'Hawarden', ridden by Gladstone, having cleared three hurdles in the lead from 'Hatfield', mounted by Salisbury. A ruler was used to show the liberals rubbing off the Tory majority at the dissolution; a pyramid of squares helped visualize the liberal majority. Here, visual representation of election results was anchored in the familiar.[63]

The 1890s witnessed a notable upsurge in the political use of lantern slides. Fintan Cullen has discussed Maud Gonne's nighttime lantern slide Jubilee protest in which 'eviction scenes were interspersed with statistics of the numbers of Irish who had died from starvation in Victoria's reign'.[64] Lantern use was not confined to Irish nationalists. Missionaries and educationalists made concerted use of the lantern, and political organizations adopted an increasingly systematic approach to its deployment. By 1900 the Liberal Publication Department had six lectures on offer, including a treatment of 'the taxes and how they are spent'.[65] In 1904, the Primrose League noted the determined efforts of the Hanley liberals, involving slides of 'F.C.G's cartoons, Liberal statistics, [and] famous quotations from speeches etc'.[66] The casual inclusion here of statistics within this litany suggests the frequency of their deployment. In listing statistics and quotations alongside cartoons, the League reflected the mixed visual economy of British political culture, in which word, image and number jostled for attention in a crowded public sphere.

Further evidence of this pluralism is provided by political posters. The fiscal controversy undoubtedly led to the production of a multitude of posters incorporating statistical claims, but such imagery predates Chamberlain's crusade for tariff reform. Taxes and the national debt were mainstays of political debate, both receiving graphical treatment in the posters of the 1880s. The combination of tariff reform and inflation in the 1900s provided a particular incentive for the creation of images like 'How the Tories have increased the cost of living' in which the working-class staples of tea and sugar were presented as proxies for the price level in general.[67] Numbers had, though, already proliferated in British politics, energetically propagated by organizations like the National Association for the Promotion of Social Science, and were far from confined to debates about the economy. In 'The Great Naval Eclipse', the National Union of Conservative and Constitutional Associations portrayed visually the changing relative size of the British and German fleets, arguing that 'a vote for the Radicals is a vote against the British Navy'.[68]

Pictorial, especially iconic, representation of quantity was a common device in political posters. Such images were seldom constrained by strict respect for proportion. In 'The Worker's Burden *as the Tories would make it*', a worker was bent double under a vast scroll of paper promising 'taxes on food, coloured materials & everything'.[69] The poster provided further numbers on food taxes, but the scale of the emblematic gargantuan scroll was determined rather more by the visual logic of cartooning than the rigours of Cartesian geometry. Personification was a common technique in posters, and it could be used in conjunction with numerical data. In the Budget League's 'Tax the loafer—not the loaf', the respectable worker on 30/- a week appeared as the embodied 'tax payer' contrasted with a mad, senile 'Lord' on £20,000 a year.[70] The juxtaposition of isolated numbers, with representativeness implicitly asserted rather than explicitly established, was frequent. The deployment of statistics reflected broader trends in poster design, notably in terms of integrating numbers more fully into the overall composition.

In his defence of liberal pictures of the 'big' and the 'little loaf', Carruthers Gould argued that such imagery was 'a symbol and was not intended as a prophecy, or a promise'. He did note, however, that 'comparisons are not complete without the ceteris paribus condition, and that cannot be pictorially suggested'.[71] Gould's comments remind us of the highly contested nature of statistical claims, perhaps particularly those made through images. One Edwardian poster saw a ruddy-faced workman rebut the Chamberlainite claim of tariff reform and work for all by pointing to posters giving statistics for unemployment in Germany and the United States.[72] Posters, like lantern shows, could be displayed indoors, but they were primarily part of the vibrant world of outdoor politics in which contestation might take the form of defacement or destruction rather than elegant refutation.

Contemporary champions of statistics in general and the graphical method in particular were often keen to distance their activities from the simplifications and distortions inherent in politicized uses of statistics. As the tariff reform controversy illustrates, however, such assertions of scientific authority could founder upon engagement with partisan political debates. Many recognized, though, both the inescapability and the potency of numbers within the public sphere. In the eleventh edition of the *Encylopaedia Britannica*, Wynnard Hooper, financial editor of *The Times*, acknowledged the intimate relationship between word and number, observing that 'false "statistical" facts which obtain a hold of the public mind may often be traced to some widely circulated table, to which, either from stupidity or carelessness, an erroneous or inaccurate "heading" has been affixed.'[73]

This section has scrutinized the relationship between number and image in turn-of-the-century political culture. It has argued that picturing was a significant means whereby statistics entered the public political sphere in these years. In *Elements of Statistics*, A.L. Bowley described diagrams as 'auxiliary rather than essential', and confined the use of 'lines, triangles, squares, circles, even pictures, of different sizes to assist the presentation of . . . relative magnitude' to 'popular lectures and hand-books'.[74] The popularizing of numbers in politics drew heavily upon the kind of visual devices to which Bowley referred, and it needs to be placed within the broader graphical cultures traced in the previous section. The role of statistical maps in imagining the new electorate after 1884–5 exemplifies this relationship between political and visual cultures. Rather than viewing the visual representation of the numerical within politics as mere simplification and distortion, we need to analyze the complex interactions between word, image and number through which statistics were projected and interrogated within the public sphere. In order to begin reconstructing the reception of statistics, we need to consider the nature of numeracy in late nineteenth- and early twentieth-century Britain.

THE USES OF NUMERACY

For many foreign observers, late Victorian Britain was the archetypal commercial, industrial and numerate society. The nation of shopkeepers and workshop of the world was surely not short of numerical nous. This was a country in which the annual announcement of the senior wrangler in mathematics at Cambridge could receive extensive press coverage. Yet one prominent strand of historiography has emphasized the decline of the industrial spirit and the dominance of gentlemanly values in late nineteenth-century Britain.[75] These interpretations may not necessarily be incompatible with recognition of the prominence of mathematics in elite education. Mathematics might be defended as a liberal pursuit, and pure mathematics in particular could be distinguished from the grubby realities of laboratory science.[76] A growing body of recent work, though, has drawn attention to the interconnectedness of arts and sciences in nineteenth-century Britain, drawing a picture of cross-fertilization rather than mutual estrangement.[77] Estimates of British economic performance in the period prior to 1914 have become notably more optimistic, and the reputation of industry especially has risen considerably.[78] Arguments about the pastoral turn in British culture primarily focus upon the elite. For much of urban Britain, the demands of industry continued to shape their lives throughout the period. In terms of occupational structure, the service sector grew markedly throughout the Victorian period, but then industry was already significant by the 1840s, and the growth of services cannot be equated with anti-entrepreneurial attitudes.[79] Late nineteenth-century Britain was evidently a highly complex and developed capitalist economy in which the calculating spirit was ubiquitous.

The realities of working-class life in late Victorian Britain definitely placed a premium on numerical skills. Juggling weekly wages and rental payments against a background of insecure employment and economic uncertainty required the constant exercise of numeracy. As Paul Johnson has insisted, the vast range of formal and informal mechanisms of plebeian saving, from insurance policies to tick books, testify to the efforts of ordinary people to mitigate irregularity and unpredictability of income.[80] The development of wage bargaining scales, piecework payment and complex arrangements between different kinds of workers: all required calculation from the participants. Trade union newspapers and congresses addressed the relative advantages of differing payment schemes. Similarly, the collaboration of workers in industries with high levels of workshop autonomy, such as shipbuilding, raised challenging questions about relative productivity and wages.[81] Trade union engagement with, and involvement in, the labour department of the Board of Trade reflected the view that the widespread publicizing of economic statistics would reveal the value of association to the working classes. The prevalence of numerical reasoning in popular culture is apparent in the world of consumption and spending, as well as production and saving. Before turning to the evidence for this, it is important to examine the fruits of recent quantitative work on numeracy.

Influenced by the revival of growth theory, economic historians have recently turned to numeracy as an indicator of human capital. Building upon insights from the 1950s, econometricians have increasingly used age-heaping—the tendency to round up or down in giving one's age—as a proxy for numeracy in studying long-term comparative growth patterns.[82] Drawing on census data, along with a variety of other source types, relative numeracy rates have been constructed for a number of countries over time. These approaches produce very high estimates of the incidence of numeracy in late nineteenth- and early twentieth-century Britain in both absolute and relative terms.[83] It is, however, evident from comparing age-heaping studies with measures of literacy that the former provides very much an entry-level assessment of numerical skills.[84] Some comparative work suggests schooling rather than market involvement or state activity was the key driver in reducing age-heaping.[85] This finding might appear hard to reconcile with the wide spread of numeracy in Britain, but relative evaluations of nineteenth-century British education have become much more favourable.[86] Some work on human capital in fact argues that numeracy was more important than schooling for assisting future life chances.[87] What is clear is that the quantitative work accords with other evidence in suggesting high levels of numeracy in Britain. The age-heaping approach is at its most effective in considering the shift from fairly low levels of numeracy. Its focus on gauging the breadth rather than the depth of numerical accomplishment sheds less light on more developed societies.

It is clear that evaluating the scale and character of popular numeracy is a challenging task, and this is an excellent example, to borrow a traditional academic cliché, of an area in which more work is needed. While recent efforts to quantify numeracy are better at measuring low- rather than high-level skills, more qualitative approaches can struggle to deliver the precision and potential for the comparisons we seek. If we consider the analogy with literacy studies, we can recognize the opportunities for future work on the uses of numeracy in the worlds of work, politics, leisure and consumption. Here, it is only possible to glance at these vistas, and we do so by turning to the history of gambling.

Many contemporary commentators were appalled by the scale of popular gambling, and convinced of its ruinous character. These voices were, though, contradicted by large swathes of popular opinion. As the history of popular gambling has come into sharper focus since the 1980s, a growing body of writing has argued that wagering was generally moderate rather than excessive, and that for many punters betting was, as the chief constable of Manchester accepted in the 1920s, 'a studied art'.[88] In an influential essay, Ross McKibbin strongly emphasized the rational and controlled nature of the vast majority of working-class gambling. McKibbin's pioneering picture of working-class gambling has received considerable support in the work of Chinn, Clapson and Davies.[89] Though much of McKibbin's evidence was drawn from observers of popular pastimes, much subsequent writing has used oral history to document popular attitudes. Davies argued that popular morality distinguished sharply between moderate and excessive betting, with only the latter attracting censure.[90] In his thorough work on racing, Mike Huggins has revised some of McKibbin's chronology, and noted the persistence of less 'rational' forms of betting like sweeps, but endorses the broad picture of widespread and moderate betting involving millions advised by a blossoming sporting press.[91] The heyday of 'the pools' came later, but Nicholas Fishwick has noted that football betting was already well established before the First World War, and similar in character to betting on horses or hares.[92]

The vibrant, albeit illegal, world of street betting before 1914 that emerges from the historiography was thus one of mass participation with perhaps four million betting regularly. Examination of the contemporary sporting press suggests the importance of careful consideration of form and odds. Evidence of conscious budgeting is not hard to find, apparent, for instance, in the depressed sales in shops prior to races.[93] As better-informed observers recognized, betting involved intensive scrutiny of relative odds. It is, of course, important not to overstate the degree of sophistication involved, but it would also be wrong to neglect the evidence of popular gambling in assessing the distribution of numerical skills within the population. As we have seen, political coverage could draw heavily upon sporting analogies. This tendency, oft noted but rarely properly explored, has complex origins and effects. Both sport and politics were highly gendered, frequently cross-class pursuits in which ritual and spectacle loomed large. Coverage of both was characterized by numerical analysis, and the sporting analogy reflected and encouraged the application of a calculating, but also playful, spirit to politics.

CONCLUSION

It has only been possible here to offer a brief snapshot of the quantifying spirit in late nineteenth- and early twentieth-century Britain. We are a long way from securing a proper understanding of popular numeracy. This chapter has argued that enhanced attention to the popular consumption and uses of statistics is required to achieve a full assessment of the place of numbers in the public sphere. The case has also been made that it is necessary to recognize the range of ways in which the numerical could be represented. Graphical and pictorial images were a key part of the process whereby statistics entered and circulated within the public political sphere. The intimate relationship between word and image has been central to, perhaps even constitutive of, the field of visual culture over the last three decades.[94] Comprehending the role of statistics within public politics requires attending to word, image and number. Relating the pictorial representation of statistics to broader graphical regimes clarifies the connections between politics and culture, undermining facile attempts to equate quantification with rationality, or to treat visualization as synonymous with irrationality. The rise of quantification in politics has often been treated as a state-centred, rationalizing, even alienating, process. In charting the visual representation of statistics, a different picture has emerged here, one which emphasizes the pluralism and the pleasures of public numbers, and which places statistics firmly within the late nineteenth- and early twentieth-century public sphere.

The close of the nineteenth and the start of the twentieth century have long been seen as an era of transition in British politics. These changes have frequently been characterized as a process of modernization. Modernization narratives take a variety of forms, of course; but as Theodore Porter notes in his chapter, quantification is almost always seen as part of, sometimes as constitutive of, such processes. The story of the pictorial representation of statistics in politics certainly embraces change, and is closely allied to technological developments in printing, as well as technical innovations in statistics. It is, though, also an account that complicates easy assumptions about the direction and nature of change in British political culture, including its modernization. Statistics cannot be seen as a wholly distinct medium, injecting the cold rationality of quantification into public debate. Rather, statistics were often pictured, and their impact depended upon historically embedded ways of looking and knowing. The imaging of number often drew upon established convention, evident in the importance of statistical maps, which rooted abstraction in comprehensible forms developed for the rendering of physical space. Images of commodities themselves were used to represent quantities, whether of items or price. Continuity, as well as change, was thus apparent, and novel technologies could be used to convey familiar motifs. The fondness for utilizing maps to present electoral data reminds us of the salience of distributional questions in debates about political representation, and of how such discussions revealed deep, albeit conflicting, attachments to place and community. In other words, numbers and images of numbers were firmly enmeshed in the bustling, often noisy, disputatious world of late nineteenth- and early twentieth-century public politics; to neglect this dimension is to overlook a crucial means of imagining, contesting and representing the political nation.

NOTES

1. On statistics, see especially T.M. Porter, *The Rise of Statistical Thinking, 1820–1900* (Princeton, NJ, 1986). On mathematics in social science, examples include M. Schabas, *A World Ruled by Number: William Jevons and the Rise of Mathematical Economics* (Princeton, NJ, 1990). For pioneering work on the state and statistics, consult R. Davidson, *Whitehall and the Labour Problem in Late Victorian and Edwardian Britain: A Study in Official Statistics and Social Control* (London, 1985).
2. J.L. Richards, *Mathematical Visions: The Pursuit of Geometry in Victorian England* (Boston, MA, 1988).
3. K. Thomas, 'Numeracy in Early Modern England', *Transactions of the Royal Historical Society* 37 (1987), pp. 103–32.
4. J. Baten, D. Ma, S. Morgan and Q. Wang, 'Evolution of Living Standards and Human Capital in China in the 18–20th Centuries: Evidences from Real Wages, Age-Heaping, and Anthropometrics', *Explorations in Economic History* 47 (2010), pp. 347–59; D. Crayen and J. Baten, 'Global Trends in Numeracy 1820–1949 and Its Implications for Long-Term Growth', *Explorations in Economic History* 47 (2010), pp. 82–99.
5. B. Marsden and C. Smith, *Engineering Empire: A Cultural History of Technology in Nineteenth-Century Britain* (Basingstoke, 2005); R. McKibbin, 'Working-Class Gambling in Britain', *Past and Present* 82 (1979), pp. 147–

78; M. Huggins, *Flat Racing and British Society, 1790–1914: A Social and Economic History* (London, 2000); N. Fishwick, *English Football and Society, 1910–50* (Manchester, 1989).

6. M. Meisel, *Realizations: Narrative, Pictorial and Theatrical Arts in Nineteenth Century England* (Princeton, NJ, 1983); G. Curtis, *Visual Words: Art and the Material Book in Victorian England* (Aldershot, 2002); J. Thomas, *Pictorial Victorians: The Inscription of Values in Word and Image* (Athens, OH, 2004); J. Thompson, '"Pictorial Lies?": Posters and Politics in Britain, 1880–1914', *Past and Present* 197 (2007), pp. 177–210.

7. Thompson, 'Pictorial Lies?'; K. Rix, '"The Elimination of Corrupt Practices in British Elections"? Reassessing the Impact of the 1883 Corrupt Practices Act', *English Historical Review* 123 (2008), pp. 65–97.

8. H.G. Funkhouser, 'Historical Development of the Graphical Representation of Statistical Data', *Osiris* 3 (1937), p. 329.

9. *The Times*, 29 Aug. 1874, as cited in M. Esbester, 'Designing Time: The Design and Use of Nineteenth-Century Transport Timetables', *Journal of Design History* 22 (2009), p. 96.

10. R.H. Smith, *Graphics, or the Art of Calculation by Drawing Lines Applied Especially to Mechanical Engineering with an Atlas of Diagrams* (London, 1889); A. Marshall, *Principles of Economics, Volume One* (London, 1890).

11. J. Clerk Maxwell, 'Diagram', *The Encyclopaedia Britannica* (11th edn., Cambridge, 1910), pp. 146–8.

12. Richards, *Mathematical Visions*, p. 7.

13. *Ibid.*, p. 9.

14. C. Smith and M. Norton Wise, *Energy and Empire: A Biographical Study of Lord Kelvin* (Cambridge, 1989), p. 491.

15. Smith and Wise, *Energy and Empire*, p. 471; Clerk Maxwell, 'Diagram'.

16. J.J. Roche, 'The Semantics of Graphics in Mathematical Natural Philosophy', in R.G. Mazzolini (ed.), *Non-Verbal Communication in Science Prior to 1900* (Florence, 1993), p. 229.

17. M.J. Rudwick, 'The Emergence of a Visual Language for Geological Science', *History of Science* 14 (1976), pp. 148–95.

18. See the essays in Mazzolini (ed.), *Non-Verbal Communication*.

19. D.M. Knight, 'Pictures, Diagrams and Symbols: Visual Language in Nineteenth-Century Chemistry', in Mazzolini (ed.), *Non-Verbal Communication*, p. 344.

20. J.R. Camerini, 'The Physical Atlas of Heinrich Berghaus: Distribution Maps as Scientific Knowledge', in Mazzolini (ed.), *Non-Verbal Communication*, p. 482.

21. W.S. Jevons, *The Theory of Political Economy* (London, 1871), p. 5; A. Marshall, 'On the Graphic Method of Statistics', *Journal of the Statistical Society of London* (Jubilee Volume, 1885), p. 256.

22. On graphing in economics, see J.L. Klein on 'The Method of Diagrams and the Black Art of Inductive Economics', in I.H. Rima (ed.), *Measurement, Quantification and Economic Analysis: Numeracy in Economics* (London, 1995), pp. 98–140.

23. J. Priestley, *A Description of a Chart of Biography* (Warrington, 1765); W. Playfair, *The Commercial and Political Atlas* (3rd edn., London, 1801), p. xi.

24. Playfair, *Commercial and Political Atlas*, p. xiii.

25. *Ibid.*, p. viii.

26. Funkhouser, 'Historical Development', p. 343.

27. J. Martin, 'On Some Developments of Statistical Research and Methods During Recent Years', *Journal of the Royal Statistical Society* 59 (1896), p. 621.

28. J.R. Beniger and D.L. Robyn, 'Quantitative Graphics in Statistics: A Brief History', *The American Statistician* 32 (1978), p. 1.

29. Marshall, *Principles*, p. x.
30. Klein, 'The Method of Diagrams', p. 100.
31. W.S. Jevons, *Investigations in Currency and Finance* (London, 1884), p. 224.
32. J. Goody, *The Domestication of the Savage Mind* (Cambridge, 1977); M. Twyman, 'Articulating Graphical Language: An Historical Perspective', in M.E. Wrolstad and D.F. Fisher (eds.), *Towards a New Understanding of Literacy* (New York, 1986), pp. 210–14.
33. Martin, 'On Some Developments of Statistical Research', p. 618.
34. R. Giffen, *Statistics* (London, 1913), pp. 458–79.
35. E. Higgs, 'The General Register Office and the Tabulation of Data, 1837–1939', in M. Campbell-Kelly, M. Croarken, R. Flood, and E. Robson (eds.), *The History of Mathematical Tables: From Sumer to Spreadsheets* (Oxford, 2003), p. 227.
36. R.H.I. Palgrave, 'Graphic Methods', in R.H.I. Palgrave (ed.), *Dictionary of Political Economy, Volume Two* (London, 1896), p. 254.
37. Funkhouser, 'Historical Development', p. 346.
38. A. Briggs, *Victorian Things* (London, 1988), p. 38.
39. T. Seccombe, 'Mulhall, Michael George (1836–1900)', rev. P.A. Hunt, *Oxford Dictionary of National Biography* (Oxford, 2004), online edn., May 2010 (http://www.oxforddnb.com/view/article/19510, accessed 16 Aug. 2010).
40. M.G. Mulhall, *Dictionary of Statistics* (London, 1892), pp. 237–57.
41. Advert for Mulhall's *Dictionary of Statistics* in *Athenaeum* (Jan., 1891), p. 66.
42. M.G. Mulhall, *Balance-Sheet of the World for Ten Years* (London, 1881).
43. G. Wallas, *Human Nature in Politics* (London, 1908), pp. 134, 143, 160, 162.
44. LSE, BLPES, Coll. Misc. 519/38, LCA, 'Liberal and Tory Finance No. 1' (1886).
45. LSE, BLPES, Coll. Misc. 519/75, LCA, 'Liberal and Tory Finance No. 3' (1886).
46. *The Times*, 10 July 1886.
47. On the life of Ross of Bladensburg, see the obituary in *The Times*, 12 July 1926.
48. *The Times*, 11 July 1895; *The Times*, 28 Sep. 1900.
49. *Philip's Simplex Chart of Parliamentary Representation* (London, 1892); *Philip's Simplex Chart of Parliamentary Representation* (London, 1900); *Election Results Chart Based on the Simplex Chart Designed by Lt-Col Sir J.F.C. Ross of Bladensburg* (London, 1906).
50. *The Times*, 31 July 1895.
51. *The Times*, 3 Oct. 1900.
52. *The Times*, 28 Sep. 1900.
53. *The Times*, 19 Oct. 1900.
54. 'The Progress of the World', *Review of Reviews* 33 (1906), p. 115, reproduced from *The Daily Mail*.
55. *The Graphic*, 30 July 1892.
56. *Daily News*, 31 Oct. 1900.
57. *Stanford's Handy Atlas and Poll Book of Great Britain and Ireland 1886* (London, 1886); *Stanford's London Atlas of Universal Geography* (London, 1887) included maps of population, death, disease, religion and language use.
58. *The Times*, 16 Sep. 1912; 16 July 1914.
59. H. James Robinson, 'The Weight of the Electorate', *English Review* (1910), p. 176.
60. W.T. Stead 'Introduction' in 'Accountant', *What Will Be the Liberal Majority at the General Election* (London, 1905), p. 6.
61. *Review of Reviews* 29 (1904), p. 136.
62. *Review of Reviews* 2 (1890), p. 415.

63. *Pall Mall Gazette*, 14 July 1892.
64. F. Cullen, 'Marketing National Sentiment: Lantern Slides of Evictions in Late Nineteenth-Century Ireland', *History Workshop* 54 (2002), p. 163.
65. National Liberal Federation, *Annual Report* (1900).
66. *Primrose League Gazette* (Oct., 1904), p. 5.
67. LSE, BLPES, Coll. Misc. 519/37, 'How the Tories Have Increased the Cost of Living' (1906).
68. Bodleian, John Johnson Coll., Posters, NUCCA, 'The Great Naval Race' (1910).
69. Cambridge University Library, Political Poster Collection, Budget League, 'The Worker's Burden *as the Tories Would Make It*' (1910).
70. People's History Museum, CPGB Klugmann Collection, Budget League, 'Tax the loafer—not the loaf' (1910).
71. Francis Carruthers Gould unpublished autobiography, HLRO, Ms. 37b, ch. 16, fols. 389–91.
72. CUL, Political Posters Collection.
73. W. Hooper, 'Statistics', *The Encyclopaedia Britannica* (11th edn., Cambridge, 1910–11), p. 809.
74. A.L. Bowley, *Elements of Statistics* (London, 1901), pp. 144, 156.
75. M.J. Wiener, *English Culture and the Decline of the Industrial Spirit, 1850–1980* (2nd edn., Cambridge, 2004); P.J. Cain and A.G. Hopkins, *British Imperialism: Innovation and Expansion, 1688–1914* (London, 1993).
76. C.G. Jones, *Femininity, Mathematics and Science, 1880–1914* (Basingstoke, 2009).
77. M.J. Daunton, *State and Market in Victorian Britain: War, Welfare and Capitalism* (Woodbridge, 2008); B. Rieger, *Technology and the Culture of Modernity in Britain and Germany, 1890–1945* (Cambridge, 2005); G. Beer, *Open Fields: Science in Cultural Encounter* (Oxford, 1996); A.B. Schteir and B. Lightman, *Figuring It Out: Science, Gender, and Visual Culture* (Hanover, NH, 2006).
78. R. Floud and P. Johnson (eds.), *The Cambridge Economic History of Modern Britain, Volume Two: Economic Maturity, 1860–1939* (Cambridge, 2004); S. Broadberry, *The Productivity Race: British Manufacturing in International Perspective, 1850–1990* (Cambridge, 1997); S. Broadberry, *Market Services and the Productivity Race, 1850–2000: British Performance in International Perspective* (Cambridge, 2006).
79. R. Floud, *The People and the British Economy, 1830–1914* (Oxford, 1997), pp. 79–83.
80. P. Johnson, *Saving and Spending: The Working Class Economy in Britain 1870–1939* (Oxford, 1985), p. 217.
81. A.J. Reid, 'Employers' Strategies and Craft Production: The British Shipbuilding Industry, 1870–1950', in S. Tolliday and J. Zeitlin (eds.), *The Power to Manage? Employers and Industrial Relations in Comparative Historical Perspective* (London, 1991).
82. R. Bachi, 'The Tendency to Round Off Age Returns: Measurement and Correction', *Bulletin of the International Statistical Institute* 33 (1951), pp. 195–221.
83. Crayen and Baten, 'Global Trends in Numeracy 1820–1949', p. 85.
84. B. A'Hearn, J. Baten, and D. Crayen, 'Quantifying Quantitative Literacy: Age-Heaping and the History of Human Capital', *Journal of Economic History* 69 (2009), p. 789.
85. Crayen and Baten, 'Global Trends in Numeracy 1820–1949', p. 91.

86. G. Sutherland, 'Education', in F.M.L. Thompson (ed.), *The Cambridge Social History of Britain, 1750–1950, Volume Three: Social Agencies and Institutions* (Cambridge, 1990).

87. J. Long, 'The Socioeconomic Return to Primary Schooling in Victorian England', *Journal of Economic History* 66 (2006), p. 1046.

88. Cited in R. McKibbin, *The Ideologies of Class: Social Relations in Britain, 1880–1950* (Oxford, 1990), p. 124.

89. McKibbin, 'Working-Class Gambling'; C. Chinn, *Better Betting with a Decent Feller: Bookmaking, Betting and the British Working Class, 1750–1990* (Hemel Hempstead, 1991), p. 152; M. Clapson, *A Bit of a Flutter: Popular Gambling in England, c. 1820–1961* (Manchester, 1992); M. Clapson, 'Playing the System: The World of Organised Street Betting in Manchester, Salford and Bolton, c. 1880 to 1939', in A. Davies and S. Fielding (eds.), *Workers' Worlds: Cultures and Communities in Manchester and Salford 1880–1939* (Manchester, 1992); A. Davies, 'The Police and the People: Gambling in Salford, 1900–39', *Historical Journal* 34 (1991), pp. 114–15.

90. Davies, 'The Police and the People', p. 115.

91. M. Huggins, *Flat Racing and British Society, 1790–1914: A Social and Economic History* (London, 2000), pp. 102, 105.

92. Fishwick, *English Football and Society, 1910–1950*, p. 117.

93. Huggins, *Flat Racing*, p. 92.

94. W. J. T. Mitchell, *Iconology: Image, Text, Ideology* (Chicago, 1986); W.J.T. Mitchell, *Picture Theory: Essays on Verbal and Visual Representation* (Chicago, 1994); W.J.T. Mitchell, *What Do Pictures Want? The Lives and Loves of Images* (Chicago, 2004).

8 The Statisticalization of the Consumer in British Market Research, c. 1920–1960

Profiling a Good Society

Stefan Schwarzkopf

> You can imagine, perhaps, a story so crammed with human interest that it might have been something a photographer had posed. Here is poor little "C", fagged out after a hard day's ditch digging, dropping in for a chat with his friend "B" and maybe a free read of the latter's evening paper. "B" is a small shop-keeper—a tobacconist say; and what with the chain stores, the snack bars that sell cigarettes, and what not, he has a stiff struggle to make the £4 to £10 a week that will qualify him for his statistical status. There they sit in the gloaming . . . when in stalks "A". Now "A" is a bully and class-conscious. But the class struggle, to him, is not something Marxian, it is a success story. He believes, not in the equality of the classes, but in the inviolability of the upper classes.
>
> Charles W. Stokes, '"A", "B" and "C"',
> *Advertising World* (September, 1939).

The role of the consumer in the public sphere is now an intensely debated subject. In particular, historians and sociologists have become interested in the various ways the act of consumption establishes and at times reifies the public sphere. Yet, in order for consumers to participate in the public sphere, the consuming public must be produced and defined as such. Surveys and survey data, compiled by advertising agencies, market research companies, and state organizations, do just this: they help produce and reproduce the consuming public as part of the practices and institutions that make up the public sphere. Because of its constitutive role in this process, statistical knowledge about consumers is not only about brand choices, market niches, and retail price floors. Ultimately, it connects the idea of who, or what, the consumer is to political visions of the public. Nikolas Rose claims that 'the exercise of politics depends upon numbers' and that all 'acts of social quantification are politicized'.[1] This is certainly true of consumer surveys, which shape, as much as they reflect, what the public is, and what interests and motivates it.

The statisticalization of the consumer is largely a twentieth-century achievement. Whereas early modern and even nineteenth-century commercial actors often based their transactions upon personal knowledge of traders and consumers, the advent of mass production, mass retailing, and mass marketing demanded more and more knowledge about general patterns of consumer behaviour. This knowledge was provided by the science of statistics and what came to be called 'market research'. A number of historians, notably Harm Schröter and Victoria de Grazia, have argued that the statisticalization of the consumer first occurred in the United States during the first three decades of the twentieth century, and then influenced European societies after the Second World War.[2] Others, such as Liz Cohen, have contended that the statistical observation of consumers in interwar and postwar America led to the creation of information asymmetries in favour of corporations, which used the power of numbers to shape markets to suit their own interests, not those of consumers.[3] Indeed, for these historians, the rise of statistical reasoning in marketing and consumer research during the early to mid-twentieth century had wider and largely detrimental effects for society as a whole. In particular, as consumers became more and more the object of observation, measurement, and surveillance, public concerns for social equality and collective welfare were sidelined in favour of a market-driven obsession with the behaviour of people as *individuals* in various commercial environments.

Yet in Britain, as this chapter demonstrates, during the interwar and immediate postwar periods advertisers and market researchers found various and often conflicting uses for consumer surveys and statistics. The chapter explores two case studies which demonstrate how different visions of the good society popularized and legitimized the statisticalization of the consumer during the 1920s through to the 1960s. The first section looks at the research activities of the largest American-owned advertising agency in London, the J. Walter Thompson agency; the second section examines the work of the then largest British advertising agency, the London Press Exchange. Through their consumer research both agencies developed competing political visions of the role of consumption in the public sphere, and between them they demonstrate that the relationship between market investigations and the rise of affluent consumerism was perhaps less straightforward than is often suggested. In fact, the proliferation of market and consumer research surveys did not necessarily lead to the production of an individualized, consumer-oriented vision of the public. Rather, numbers, data, and surveys lent themselves to varying purposes and varying visions of the public, depending on the socio-political assumptions embedded in their collection, use, and presentation.

JWT LONDON AND THE CONSUMER AS COMMODITY

The J. Walter Thompson (JWT) agency, founded in New York in 1878, followed a management-oriented approach to the creation of advertising campaigns. Whereas many interwar European advertising agencies prided themselves on their high standards of creative output, the JWT agency was locked in a perennial search for an advertising 'formula' which would guarantee that advertisements were read and acted upon by their target audience. During the 1920s, the then agency CEO Stanley Resor sought to turn JWT into a 'University of Advertising', where high-profile academics would create foolproof advertising designs.[4]

As part of this strategy, Resor attracted the 'Father of Behaviourism', the psychologist John Broadus Watson, to the agency in 1921, as well as the former Harvard Business School professor Paul T. Cherington in 1922. Watson conducted market research for JWT, trained personnel, and headed several advertising campaigns in the 1920s. During his career at JWT, Watson directly applied his theories of behavioural conditioning to consumer advertising. Watson believed that through the careful selection of the right stimuli (fear, motherly care for a child, sexual desire, etc.), consumers could be 'conditioned' to buy a certain brand. For Watson, consumers' habitual buying behaviour was nothing more than a reflex, and thus consumers' reflexes could be trained like those of laboratory rats.[5]

Cherington's influence on JWT's global advertising strategy was similarly profound. Somewhat in competition to Watson's narrowly applied behaviourism, Cherington researched the way consumers read, interpreted, and used advertisements. Based on his research, the former marketing professor advised the agency to create advertisements which gave people reasons to be interested in and eventually buy an advertised product. In contrast to Watson's approach, Cherington saw consumers as rational and active. Advertisements needed to convince consumers that the advertised product helped them to solve a problem better than a competitor product. Adverts also had to show new uses of a product in order to keep consumers interested over the course of a product's life cycle. Successful advertisements thus had to take consumers through consecutive stages, beginning with problem recognition, the outlining of extensive product information, exemplification of product use, and finally the suggestion to try the product, often through a coupon enclosed in the advertisement.[6]

Crucially, Cherington taught the JWT agency to think in statistically defined categories, particularly in the categories of social class. According to Cherington, for whom advertising had the singular task of making the consumer a 'more competent buyer', retail distributors needed 'well-defined class markets'.[7] Because classes constituted ordered divisions in a society whose members shared similar values, interests, and behaviours, it was vital for the agency to be able to separate its audience according to socioeconomic classifications. For the purposes of market segmentation and targeted advertising, Cherington adapted the American Census Bureau's system of classification, which took into account both income and professional status. What had been a statistical tool of demography and government planning thus became the first tool to categorize consumers according to their socioeconomic status.

After Cherington, consumers were grouped into the four major classes of 'A' (well-off, landowning), 'B' (middle class, higher professions), 'C' (lower middle classes, skilled workers), and 'D' (occasional labourers and the poor).[8] From the mid-1920s, British and American marketeers applied the A-B-C-D classification schema, and though it remained open as to how to draw exact lines between the four groups, it provided the first system for stratifying consumers according to standardized and measurable categories such as income and employment status.[9]

During the interwar years, JWT began to expand globally. The agency had set up an office in London in 1919 that serviced a small number of American clients. By 1927, JWT London had developed into a full-blown service agency that put a tremendous emphasis on market and consumer research. In 1933, JWT set up its own market research subsidiary, the British Market Research Bureau. In 1950, JWT, for the first time, had larger billings than its closest rival, the London Press Exchange agency, and both agencies began in the 1960s to use computers for the calculation and interpretation of market research findings. The attitude with which JWT researchers in London looked at the market and at consumers in the interwar years somewhat pre-empted the arrival of the postwar affluent society. JWT London executives, like their American colleagues, held the belief that if the right product features were pointed out to consumers, and additional uses for a product were properly communicated, then the fixed class position of certain products could be overcome. In the agency's professional imagination, mass consumer affluence could be anticipated despite its absence in reality. Consumer statistics were a key tool in this very political act of anticipation.

This can be seen from a series of advertisements which JWT published in trade magazines from the mid-1930s in order to attract more clients. One of these advertisements introduced readers to the way JWT used the A-B-C-D classification system. The agency argued that the key to successful salesmanship in advertising was statistical knowledge and the ability to press consumers into measurable norms and categories, especially regarding income, social status, product purchase behaviour, and media usage:

> How can you sell things to people unless you understand them? Unless you know something about their ambitions, their dreams and their desires? How can you sell them soap flakes unless you know not only the way they wash their clothes, but the way they wear their clothes and the sort of clothes they wear? How can you sell to them through the press, the radio, the film, the poster, unless you know which newspapers they read, which features in those newspapers they like best, which radio programmes they listen to, what types of film please them most?[10]

Precisely what consumers bought, read, listened to and watched was a type of knowledge which, for the JWT agency, could only be based on numerical data collected from large samples of consumers. But this also generated something of an epistemological and methodological dilemma (one which also features, albeit in a different context, in Maeve Adams's chapter in this volume): namely, that between the generalizing nature of statistics and statistical categories on the one hand, and the particular, personal nature of the individual consumer on the other. In order to balance this dilemma, the agency developed visual-descriptive consumer profiles which allowed it to 'picture' a given consumer household or family within a pre-defined grid of more abstract classifications. In practice, both forms of knowledge about consumer behaviour—both abstract-general knowledge and personal (or family-specific) knowledge—reinforced one another, through a strategic path that focused on the distillation of consumer categories and profiles from statistical data.[11]

In the JWT universe, every aspect of consumer behaviour had to be measured and the agency attempted to convince its clients that only careful and statistically oriented research allowed an advertising agency to discover 'real' people behind the seemingly chaotic complexity of the mass market. The A-B-C-D classification also allowed the agency to position itself as a key interpreter in the communication process between manufacturers and consumers: because the agency, literally, knew its A-B-C-Ds, it was able to find the right audiences for its clients and communicate product messages in the right language. Statistical categories like the A-B-C-D classification system thus allowed the agency to commodify consumers as 'taxonomic collectives' and derive a profit from giving manufacturers access to this commodity.[12] This newly created commodity, the consuming public, had again to be attractively packaged and marketed by the ad agency in order to make them appealing to advertising clients. The JWT trade advertisement noted above thus continued: 'It has taken us many years to perfect the technique of Market Investigation—to get to know our A.B.C. & D. classes—not as algebraic formulae, but as warm, living, emotional human beings.'

Spread across two pages, the advertisement presented numerous examples of these 'warm, living, emotional' human beings—people, that is, who fitted these socioeconomic categories and exemplified their underlying lifestyles. It ranged across the social spectrum, from the 'stately home of England', which could be sold large cars and refrigerators, to 'Comfortable Kensington' and 'John Citizen', who lived an average lifestyle around mainstream products like Rinso-washed curtains and Horlick's malted drinks, all the way down to casual labourers, who surprised the JWT market researcher with how much they could buy on an income of less than 55 shillings a week ('Can't do much on that? It's staggering what they actually *can* do!'). The consumer classifications used by JWT both necessitated large-scale social statistics (because they were originally derived from official population surveys) and invited further statistical research that pinned down consumer behaviour around standardized categories, such as income, circadian rhythms of behaviour, occupation, place of residence and dwelling type. Statistics based on such data allowed for consumer profiling, which in turn was vital to segmenting mass markets and then targeting these segments more efficiently. The invention of typical consumer profiles, like John Citizen or the workingman's housewife (see below), required an agency with a data-driven outlook on consumers.

A follow-up to this trade advertisement appeared a few weeks later, now with a focus on the daily life of a typical housewife in the C-D class, 'Mrs. Green'. Once again, the agency stressed that knowledge about the socioeconomic groupings of A-B-C-D consumers was vital for manufacturers and marketeers. Equally, the agency also sought to give this statistical average of a 'C-D class housewife' an individual human face:

> This is Mrs. Green. Probably three-quarters of the advertisements a copywriter writes are addressed to her. Mrs. Green is, in effect, the copywriter's public—the radio-writer's audience. . . . We are not going to suggest that every copy-writer should have a framed photograph of Mrs. Green on his desk, but we do insist that any copywriter who writes advertising to Mrs. Green must meet her face to face, and make a study of her—get to know her, not merely as a "C-D class housewife", but as a living person.[13]

The advertisement followed a typical day in the life of Mrs. Green, from early morning housework to Friday-night cinema. After her husband had left the house, to work in a factory for £3 per week, and the three children had been sent off to school, Mrs. Green read newspapers, cleaned the house while listening to a continental radio station, and had a chat with her neighbours. During the day, advertisements in papers, on the radio and on posters suggested to Mrs. Green which products to buy. Though Mrs. Green's interests were 'dulled by economic limitations', inside her was an eager spender waiting to be set free: 'The housework starts. One of these days she may be able to afford a vacuum cleaner, but it's a long way off at the moment . . . Friday night is the bright spot. For two and a half hours Mrs. Green lives in a world of dramatic incident and luxurious settings.'

The advertisement brings out the tension noted above, which stemmed from the reliance of the JWT agency people on statistical survey data. Given the intrinsic abstraction of standardized consumer categories and statistics, the JWT agency had to assure its clients that it had not lost touch with the circumstances that ultimately made each individual consumer unique, different, and 'real'. Yet the firsthand experiential knowledge of JWT copywriters about the lives of people in the lower classes was often limited. Because JWT recruited mainly from the educated, professional middle classes, the agency needed statistical information about the lives of low-income mass consumers, with whom JWT copywriters both in New York and in London had in fact rather little contact.[14] Because the C and D classes made up some 80 percent of the mass market in Britain, and JWT copywriters came from the remaining 20 percent, statistics were needed to make vast swathes of the market intelligible and manageable for the agency. Advertising to the masses meant the copywriter left his 'home ground': 'This is our visualization of the C & D classes—the great mass market. As for the A & B classes—the copywriter is in contact with them every day. We have no fears about that angle of approach. The copywriter is on home ground.'[15]

In addition to 'cold' statistics, then, the JWT admen realized that they had to be socially attuned to often subtle differences of lifestyle. Through the visualization and profiling of income and other socioeconomic statistics, 'class' consumers received an individual face. Yet, for the American agency JWT, this individual face seems to have had an acquisitive physique, one which merely demanded more and more material goods. It is important to understand how JWT gathered statistical information about consumers, and which facts about consumer preferences they chose to emphasize. Other contemporary social and consumer surveys—such as those conducted by Mass Observation and the Rowntree Foundation; Liverpool University's 1934 'Social Survey of Merseyside'; John Boyd-Orr's 1935 survey on food and consumption; the Ministry of Labour's 1937–38 cost of living index; and later the Nuffield Social Reconstruction Survey from 1941—all showed that British working-class people were interested in myriad more things than simply owning a vacuum cleaner. By contrast, JWT's visual representation of the statistically averaged mass consumer, in the form of 'John Citizen' or 'Mrs. Green', made it look as if the C and D classes had nothing else in mind than affluence in the narrow sense of the term, namely cinemas and fridges.[16] Thus, while trying to give the statistically average consumer an individual face, JWT also denied this consumer any aspirations beyond material wants and desires. In other words, market and consumer research surveys were being used by JWT in order to assess the ways in which lower-middle-class, and particularly working-class, consumers could be 'rewired' and made much more brand-conscious.

It was above all statistical information that was deemed necessary in order to rewire the public in this fashion. From the mid-1920s, the London JWT branch channelled resources into gathering statistical information about consumer habits and interests across classes and regions in Britain. The amount of consumer surveys and interviews conducted, and the technical efforts made to turn these surveys into statistically useful information, is impressive, given that consumer research was still virgin territory for many advertisers in the mid- and late 1920s. One of JWT's earliest and most demanding clients in this respect was Lever Brothers, later named Unilever. In order to find a better marketing strategy for a number of Lever's products, such as Lux soap flakes and Rinso soap powder, JWT interviewed tens of thousands of housewives each year.

In one survey in 1928, JWT interviewed some 3,200 British housewives about their habits, including attitudes towards washing and their use of soap products.[17] The principal aim of this research was to find out more about what factors were responsible for the rather limited use of soap in British households. After the research results had been analyzed, it was concluded that the new advertising campaign for Lux soap flakes had to overcome the chief resistance to the brand—the high price—and give housewives from lower income backgrounds a clear set of reasons as to why buying the rather high-end Lux brand made sense economically. JWT made it clear to Lever Brothers that statistical research work was necessary in order to find a 'wedge' into the working-class market and open it up to the more expensive products such as Lux soap flakes, Lux toilet soap, and Lux shampoo. In order to create such a 'wedge', JWT cooperated with the Good Housekeeping Institute to establish a figure for how much an average household in each class segment spent on soaps and detergents.[18]

Speaking to the individual faces behind the consumer categories was the advertising agency's daily job, but in order to speak in the tongues of its various target groups, JWT needed an astonishing amount of data. Between 1928 and 1931, for Lever's Lux brand alone, JWT interviewed some 14,334 consumers on, among other things, methods of washing stockings, hair, and dishes; opinions on soap bars; the levels of knowledge about artificial silk; the impact of price reductions; and the uses of perfumes in soap powders and flakes.[19] These detailed interviews yielded crucial information about weak spots in the consumer's psyche and his or her resistance to certain brands. Earlier surveys had found that 53 percent of all interviewed women used soda ash for various cleaning tasks in the house, and that a majority of them did not know that this was harmful to their skin and to the fabrics they washed. JWT's marketing strategy was to increase demand for Lux despite its high price, so the agency concentrated on scaring women about the ageing skin on their hands; about the damage that hard soaps and soda ash did to their most precious garments; and about the harm done to children when washing their clothing with anything else but soft Lux soap flakes.[20]

The strategy proved largely successful: JWT began advertising Lux in 1928, and by 1931 48 percent of all British women were using Lux soap flakes at least occasionally. Yet new targets and new anxieties were spotted immediately. JWT's research on people's washing behaviour found that although 43 percent of all British women used shampoo, they used it only once a fortnight, and did not seem to know why shampoo was necessary and what it did for their hair. This lack of knowledge threatened the position of the recently introduced Lux Shampoo, which female consumers once again found too expensive.[21] Through its ongoing consumer surveys on soaps, shampoo, and washing, the agency also learned that questionnaires had to be adjusted for each consumer and product category. Two women from the same A-B-C-D classification group could show vastly different reactions to shampoo, for example, depending on whether they had long or short, light or dark hair.[22]

JWT's hunt for data about the mass consumer continued throughout the 1930s. In 1933 alone, JWT London conducted 35,000 consumer interviews for their clients on specific aspects of consumer behaviour.[23] From these surveys and from the more general social surveys that became available at that time, the agency learned that the C and D class constituted around 80 to 90 percent of the British population and that this mass of people read specific papers and mostly listened to radio stations other than the BBC.[24] Women in these two categories, the great army of British housewives and shoppers, were now found to follow very similar, almost homogeneous lifestyles: 'After having despatched their husbands to work and the children to school', they normally listened to the radio between eight and nine o'clock in the morning before doing their shopping. Accordingly, JWT advised its clients to sponsor radio shows and develop morning commercials.[25]

JWT translated the statistical data it gathered into more implicit knowledge about the behaviours and lifestyles of consumers from various income groups. This knowledge, in turn, fed directly into JWT's advertising campaign strategies for Unilever, Rowntree's, Horlicks, and other clients. In particular, the consumer categories that emerged during the interwar years allowed JWT to put its media planning decisions on a sounder basis. It was well-known, for example, that the C and D class did not listen to the BBC, but tuned into continental radio stations that allowed commercials and sponsored shows. Knowledge of readership and consumer preferences was equally important when it came to the press. In 1934, JWT de-listed the *News Chronicle* from its campaign schedule for a number of products that targeted the C-D class. Although JWT's media department acknowledged that the *News Chronicle* was perhaps the 'soundest' and 'most dignified' of all national papers, it failed to produce the same 'pull' among the lower income groups, and the paper therefore had to be dropped. The *Daily Mail* met the same fate, because its readership was also found to consist of too many A and B readers.[26]

The categorization and the statisticalization of the British consumer by the JWT agency thus contributed to the reshaping of the British media landscape. Rothermere's *Daily Mail* and the *Daily Mirror* went through a deep crisis in the mid-1930s as both papers failed to develop what advertising agencies like JWT wanted most, namely well-developed and attractive women's pages that were intellectually accessible for lower income groups. Facing a similar lack of advertising support, the *News Chronicle* finally ceased publication in 1960.[27] Defining the consumer according to income statistics and product purchase preferences also limited the range of consumer attitudes and concerns that could potentially be of public interest. In the JWT surveys, people had no voice to raise concerns about better and more affordable food and water supplies.[28] Instead, their anxieties about skin, hair, and beauty began to take centre stage, long before the advent of postwar affluence. The immense statistical detail about the usage of products and shopping behaviour that was gathered in these surveys was in reality highly filtered information as tens of thousands of consumers were surveyed using the very narrow parameters of owner-ship of consumer goods and material aspirations. JWT's studies into the uses of media were equally narrow, and focused on people's capacity for taking in advertisements, not on the social and political uses of news-papers and the radio for the formation of informed citizens. One survey in June 1936, entitled 'Investigation among housewives to determine the extent to which they listen to radio whilst washing', exemplifies this.[29] By observing housewives' and families' media use, JWT worked out vari-ous promotional ideas, such as the invention of the 'Ovaltineys' or the 'Rinsoptimists', which featured on commercial radio programmes that sidestepped the cultural authority of the BBC.[30]

JWT began as early as the 1930s to conceptualize Britain as a poten-tially 'affluent society' to be modelled on the image of an American mass market made up of individualist, aspirational, self-actualizing consumers. In other words, there was no such thing as society for JWT, only individual consumers as part of measurable market segments. Statistical categories played an important role in this makeup and it is important to note that some of these categories at least were imported from the United States dur-ing the interwar years. JWT's head office in New York put people in charge of larger subsidiary offices like JWT London who had a firm grounding in concepts like a product's market share and an advertisement's 'pulling power'. Within JWT as a global organization there circulated norms and assumptions about the importance of such statistical models. These were handed down to the executive officers at the London office in the form of scripts. One such script, the 'Blue Book' compiled by Sam Meek, the American who led JWT's London office in the crucial half-decade between 1925 and 1930, used example campaigns and advertisements in order to lay out precisely how an advertising campaign had to be conducted. All started with the gathering of statistical evidence about consumers' needs and habits, and led to the formulation of advertising copy which projected new solutions and new uses for products to consumers of different classes.[31] Monthly letters from the New York headquarters ensured that the London office followed the global JWT blueprint.[32]

Wherever the necessary statistical data for successful consumer categori-zation were not available, JWT officials pressed local business and govern-ment leaders to make such data available. In London, members of the JWT agency on many occasions pressed the General Register Office to conduct a Census of Distribution so that measurements of products' market shares and their distribution channels would be possible.[33] In the absence of such data, the London office often slavishly followed advertising policy devel-oped in the American market for products in Britain, such as the adoption of the film-star appeal for the advertising of Lux Soap ('9 out of 10 Hol-lywood Stars use Lux'), introduced in 1925 and 1926.[34]

THE LONDON PRESS EXCHANGE AND
THE CONSUMER IN SOCIETY

Between the late 1920s and the 1950s, however, there existed important differences between JWT's research activities and those of the London Press Exchange (LPE). Whereas JWT focused on individual consumer attitudes and behaviours, the LPE was much more interested in the general state of the market for consumer goods, the attitudes of groups of consumers in Britain, and in readership and media surveys. This more collective outlook on the consumer market was developed by the head of LPE's market research unit, Mark Abrams. Born in 1906 into a north London family of Jewish and Latvian immigrants, Abrams studied economics and sociology under R.H. Tawney and others at the London School of Economics at a time when the institution was known for its social radicalism, left-wing student societies, and Fabian professors. In his 1929 PhD thesis, Abrams analyzed a theme in early modern English economic history, the gold and silver thread monopoly of James I, but he connected his analysis to more current concerns about the effectiveness of the state as an entrepreneur and the responsibilities of entrepreneurs for communal social welfare.[35] In the early 1930s, Abrams published a number of socialist economic treatises, for example, on the role of money and the business cycle in capitalist economies.[36] From 1931 to 1933, Abrams worked at the Brookings Institution in Washington, DC, a centre-left political and economic research institution where he learned how to apply basic statistical and demographic research methods to public policy analysis. Having returned to Britain in 1934, his first job was with the LPE, where, as a twenty-nine-year-old, he was put in charge of what was to become Britain's largest ever readership survey.

Abrams's *Survey of Reader Interest in the National Morning and London Evening Press* became a landmark with respect to the scope and detail of media and advertising research.[37] Conducting memory interviews and in situ studies with more than 20,000 readers from various classes and geographical areas, Abrams's team studied which parts of a newspaper readers from different social backgrounds read. The team also examined which advertisements they looked at, which parts of the advertisements they studied (headline, illustration, product description, and manufacturer details), and which advertising positions on the newspaper page were most likely to attract sustained attention. Using this data, Abrams demonstrated that advertising positions in the top-right corner were read by more people than those in the bottom right, followed by positions in the top-left corner, and so on. Abrams also worked out how many thousands of readers could be reached per pound sterling of advertising expenditure on display advertisements in various newspapers, relative to the sections in which they featured and their positions on the page. For example, the survey stated that the average daily circulation of the *Daily Mirror* was 2,030,000, with its leader page being seen by 84 percent of the readers, which equalled an effective circulation for the leader page of 1,692,000. An advertising position in the bottom right corner of that page was seen by 9.7 percent of readers, meaning that 197,000 people were reached by that particular advertisement. Because the cost of a 'solus position' on that page was £44, the advertisement's 'visibility value' (that is, the circulation it reached per pound) was 4,480, some 12 percent above the average visibility value of advertisements in the *Daily Mirror.*[38]

Findings such as these must have bedazzled marketeers and advertisers in the early 1930s: Abrams was able to show for each page, each position on the page, for each newspaper, for each sex, class and age group how much exposure the advertiser got for his message per pound sterling. Such statistical data turned guesswork and convention—beer adverts were often placed on the sports pages, for instance—into a strategic activity called 'media planning'. By the early 1930s, the consumer had thus finally emerged as a statistical entity and as a statistical construct surrounded by and based on standardized, measurable categories like visibility and attention value (for advertisements), and class, income, age, and gender. This view of a statistical, categorized consumer now extended into areas of media use, as advertising campaign planners increasingly began to rely on data from readership and attention surveys like the one conducted by Abrams in 1934.

In this 1934 survey, Abrams followed a research agenda laid out by the organization that commissioned the survey from the LPE, the Incorporated Institute of Practitioners in Advertising. In its research design and outlook, the survey also followed very closely two American pioneers who had made their name with readership analysis and advertising attention studies: Frank Starch and George Gallup. The Starch and Gallup surveys established a way of looking at consumers' media use which suited the interests of advertising agencies and corporate clients. Instead of looking at the way people understood and engaged with political information in newspapers, Gallup and Starch merely tested which advertisements attracted most attention. What became 'descriptively' standardized and calculated was not readers' engagement with information, but their mere exposure to it. This factor was thus normatively standardized as well: what mattered was not a newspaper's informational value or political standpoint, but simply its readership size and attention value.[39]

Yet, although Abrams had received some training in the United States, the way he imported and adapted American techniques and systems of consumer categorization was very different from that of the JWT agency. In the interwar years, there existed at least two 'Americas' whose standards in market and consumer research became revered, but also reworked, in the British context. The 'America' of the JWT agency, with its corporate outlook and its emphasis on the aspiring, individualist consumer, was a very different 'America' from that of the Brookings Institution, which focused on public policy research and social reforms that enabled greater collective welfare and enhanced international cooperation. The latter outlook very much chimed with Abrams's own socialist background, especially because it allowed him to connect a more equality-oriented outlook on the commercial sphere with a redefinition of consumers' interests in fair prices, product information, and market efficiency as worthwhile political aims for a social democracy.[40] Abrams's own work on consumer surveys thus fused American trends, particularly in the area of audience and polling research, with the British social research traditions he had encountered at the LSE.

By the time Abrams embarked on his next major market research job, the revision of the LPE's market and consumer survey *The Home Market*, Abrams was able to give it a style that was different from the more acquisitive orientation of the JWT surveys. Abrams's survey focused on aspects that went beyond the now common focus in market research on individual consumers and their product choices and shopping behaviour.[41] The 1936 and the 1939 editions of the *Home Market* included diagrams that visualized the social pyramid of Britain through the lens of family and work, not income alone. Whereas JWT's visualization of the A-B-C-D classes centred on individuals as spenders, Abrams's income pyramid was based on the symbolism of the family as a consumption unit. Abrams also eliminated the 'D' classification and instead grouped all low-income-earning families under either 'C1' (£2 10s–£4 per week) or 'C2' (below £2 10s per week).[42] When grading families of the 'B' and 'C' income grades more specifically, Abrams employed a subdivision of four grades in 'C' families (C I-IV) and two grades in the 'B' class (BI-II), mainly in order to detect better the moment of transition between upper-working-class and lower-middle-class families.[43] Although Abrams and the statistical staff at the LPE still used the results of the occupational classification exercises of the General Register Office as a body of evidence to confirm their own classification system, the statisticalization of people as consumers—based on income and spending patterns—had by now developed its own standing as a construction of social reality.[44]

Visually speaking, Abrams's income pyramid and the redefinition of the income groups created a stark contrast between about 8.9 million working-class families at the bottom of society and some 3.2 million middle-class and upper-middle-class families at the top. Whereas JWT's A-B-C-D consumer classification provided a key to the problem of which products one simply could not sell to the 'D' class, and which products were at least occasionally affordable to the masses in the 'C' class, Abrams's classification system focused less on what products could be sold. In *The Home Market*'s visualization, the 'C' and 'D' class were all workers and all deserved a better life. In the JWT surveys, these workers were visualized as shoppers.[45]

After reading Abrams's surveys of the British consumer market, it would have been difficult for political and social commentators to defend policies that were likely to make some 60 percent of the population worse off and privilege the top third of society. *The Home Market*, for example, also included statistics which showed that between 1924 and 1930, 57 percent of Britain's wealth was concentrated in the hands of only 0.8 percent of the population.[46] Abrams's surveys therefore also need to be understood as policy statements in disguise: as manifestos, in fact, for a coming political era. During the Second World War, Abrams worked on the government's National Food Survey, and he provided statistical measurement techniques which allowed the government to manage more effectively food and fuel supplies to the population. In 1946, Abrams returned to the LPE and set up its market research unit as a subsidiary company known as Research Services Ltd., which continued to grow quickly during the 1950s and 1960s. In the early 1960s, it handled over 300 research jobs a year, some of which involved the interviewing of over 100,000 people. As company director, Abrams oversaw the work of ninety-three full-time research staff and some 160 interviewing staff, which put it in the same league as JWT's market research subsidiary, the British Market Research Bureau.

Abrams's Research Services and the British Market Research Bureau competed not only on purely economic terms but also in terms of their different approaches to the consumer and to Britain as a consumer society. Abrams's research, whether for government or for corporate clients, implicitly or explicitly related to social policy concerns. His studies on consumption patterns in Britain were always focused on maintaining necessary balances in a capitalist society, for example between exports and imports, and between public and private consumption. His training at the LSE and the Brookings Institution, and the political circumstances of an economy managed by the Labour party, now allowed Abrams to rework 'American' research techniques for the purposes of a socialist welfare state based on nationalized industries and controlled consumer expenditure. Various publications by Abrams, such as *The Condition of the British People* (1945), *The Population of Great Britain* (1945), and *British Standards of Living* (1948), bore witness to his ideal of using market research techniques for the purpose of encouraging government and private industry to produce products that were 'right' and good for people at a collective level.

In his 1947 pamphlet *The State of the Nation,* Abrams used social survey and market research methods to review the economic state of Britain. Market research here became redefined as a tool that helped society make the right decisions for the future, such as recognizing the need to consume less, import fewer foreign products, work more hours, and spend less money on attractive but costly consumer goods that had to be imported from abroad for dollars which Britain did not own. This approach to the social functions of market research continued with a book published in 1951 which outlined the history of social and market research in Britain under the title *Social Surveys and Social Action.* The title itself made clear that for Abrams consumer and market research were part of an ongoing investigation into the collective and social nature of the market.[47]

Finally, Abrams's 1959 study entitled *The Teenage Consumer* won him credit for having isolated a new facet of the mass market. Yet large parts of

the study read like a detached social survey; there is little sense of excite-
ment at having discovered a new segment of consumers that could be sold
a bundle of shiny commodities. Abrams's study of the teenage consumer
was characterized by insights into the social and psychological problems
of postwar teenagers. More importantly, it alerted readers to the pressures
teenagers were facing in a modern world, such as rising violence among
rival teenage groups, the abuse of alcohol, and social isolation.[48] In this
research, Abrams for the first time developed the concept of the 'vulnerable consumer', a perspective on the market which he continued to develop
in his later studies on the old-age consumer.[49] By looking at the market
from the perspectives of groups of consumers that were in danger of being
marginalized, Abrams developed an understanding of social relationships
in market societies which was surprisingly forward-looking; only now is
market research beginning to incorporate concerns about consumer vulnerability, sustainable marketing, an ageing society, and the uses of market
regulation for the sake of social cohesion. For Abrams, consumer democracy and social democracy were not opposed. Whether in his role as advisor
to the Labour party and the Consumers' Association, as director of the Survey Research Unit at the Social Research Council, or as research director of
Age Concern, Abrams's statistical research was always guided by the belief
that consumer democracy and social democracy were mutually reinforcing
ways of restructuring capitalism. In his submission to the Reith Commission of Enquiry into Advertising of 1966, Abrams summarized his vision
of what consumer and market researchers could and should deliver for a
social democracy as follows:

> . . . as specialists, they can only concern themselves with the problems
> they are asked to solve, and can only report within the limits laid down
> by their clients. The strictly commercial orientation of most of their work
> means that they cannot, unless asked, provide the widest and most so-
> cially orientated view of the situation they investigate. Being employed
> largely by advertisers, their scope is inevitably limited . . . But there is no
> reason why the scope of their work should not be widened. There is a
> mass of socially useful information which they could gather, were their
> skills and services more fully exploited on behalf of public as well as of
> commercial interests . . . For if market research has a social function, it is
> to provide for all concerned such an objective view of the problem situa-
> tion as will lead to more rational and socially desirable decisions.[50]

CONCLUSION

Whereas Mark Abrams's professional agenda for market research was
guided by the ideal of helping the masses get the right products at the right
cost for society as a whole, J. Walter Thompson's long-term policy from

the mid-1920s was to develop and expand the British working classes' consumption capabilities and make them more accessible for semi-luxury and traditionally middle-class products. In order to follow these competing professional agendas, consumer categorization was necessary. JWT's categories broke down society into the four subdivisions of A-B-C-D, and laid emphasis on constructing a growing centre of mass consumers that had their eyes only on material goods and aspirations. The LPE agency, under the socialist Abrams, broke down society into the categories of A and B, and the two sub-categories C1 and C2, and its emphasis was to showcase the numerical strength of the working classes.

Although market and consumer research services helped advertising and market research agencies to attract and retain corporate clients, the research function also gave some of these agencies room to reflect on their wider role within society. In the 1950s and 1960s, LPE and JWT became almost icons for two alternative political visions of British democracy. The market researchers at the LPE and other market research organisations, such as the government's Social Survey unit and Mass Observation, attempted to re-embed market and consumer statistics in the *politeia*, whilst JWT disembedded consumer surveys from social-political concerns and turned the statisticalization of consumers into an exercise purely for the benefit of their corporate clients. Abrams aimed to create market research data that served public policy purposes as well as clients. Accordingly, the LPE's market research results were often published for the benefit of a much wider readership, for example, in the form of pamphlets issued by *Current Affairs* and the agency's own series of pamphlets, the *L.P.E. Papers*. What the JWT market researchers tried to achieve, in contrast, was the private enclosure of statistical knowledge about consumers. For JWT, data had to be gathered purely to turn advertising agencies into monopoly suppliers of statistical knowledge about consumers.

Thus, after the first two decades of the twentieth century had been characterized by the state capture of statistical knowledge about markets and the economy, the 1930s and 1940s saw strong attempts on the part of commercial organizations to emulate this capture.[51] This capture also functioned to produce new visions of the public: here too there occurred a complex and varied synthesis of statistical reasoning on the one hand, and public and political reasoning on the other. Moreover, the contrasting visions explored in this chapter were also competing visions. JWT's approach to the challenges and opportunities of affluence, consumerism, and the market was by no means more successful than that of the LPE. Both agencies continued to compete fiercely for advertising clients, and often—such as in the case of the Ford advertising account in 1960—the LPE beat the JWT agency.[52]

During the 1960s, the LPE agency was swallowed up by the American Leo Burnett advertising agency. At the same time, the slow decline of the JWT advertising agency began to set in. By the late 1960s, JWT's advertising creations had come to be seen as formulaic and unattractive by many

British and American clients, who also found the decision-making processes much too influenced by boards and committees. This places a question mark over assertions that the history of British consumer culture in the twentieth century is merely that of its 'Americanization'.[53] As a sweeping assumption, it prevents historians from looking closely at the specific social and cultural contexts within which different techniques of making consumers statistically intelligible compete with another. In the case explored in this chapter, the competition was not between 'Europe' and 'America', as suggested by Victoria de Grazia, but between different political interpretations of what a consumer is, and what he or she might become.

NOTES

1. N. Rose, 'Governing by Numbers: Figuring Out Democracy', *Accounting, Organizations and Society* 16 (1991), pp. 673–92.
2. V. de Grazia, *Irresistible Empire: America's Advance Through Twentieth-Century Europe* (Cambridge, MA, 2005); H. Schröter, *The Americanization of the European Economy: A Compact Survey of American Economic Influence in Europe since the 1880s* (Dordrecht, 2005), pp. 105–22.
3. L. Cohen, *A Consumers' Republic: The Politics of Consumption in Postwar America* (New York, 2004), pp. 292–331.
4. On the history and managerial style of JWT, see, among others, D. West, 'From T-Square to T-Plan: The London Office of the J. Walter Thompson Advertising Agency, 1919–70', *Business History* 29 (1987), pp. 199–217; P. Kreshel, 'The "Culture" of J. Walter Thompson, 1915–1925', *Public Relations Review* 16 (1990), pp. 80–93.
5. K.W. Buckley, 'The Selling of a Psychologist: John Broadus Watson and the Application of Behavioral Techniques to Advertising', *Journal of the History of the Behavioral Sciences* 18 (1982), pp. 207–21; P. Kreshel, 'John B. Watson at J. Walter Thompson: The Legitimation of "Science" in Advertising', *Journal of Advertising* 19 (1990), pp. 49–59.
6. P. Cherington, *Advertising as a Business Force* (New York, 1913), pp. 3–23, 89–94; P. Cherington, *The Consumer Looks at Advertising* (New York, 1928), pp. 41–52.
7. Cherington, *Consumer*, p. 186; P. Cherington, *Elements of Marketing* (New York, 1928), p. 182.
8. P. Cherington, 'Market Statistics in Advertising', *Annals of the American Academy of Political and Social Science* 115 (1924), pp. 130–5.
9. On the role of the A-B-C-D consumer classification system in the emergence of marketing, see S. Schwarzkopf, 'Discovering the Consumer: Market Research, Product Innovation and the Creation of Brand Loyalty in Britain and the United States in the Interwar Years', *Journal of Macromarketing* 29 (2009), pp. 8–20.
10. 'Agency in Action: Learning Our A-B-C-Ds', *Advertiser's Weekly*, 12 Mar. 1936, p. 360.
11. On the history of consumer profiling, see H. Hosoya and M. Schaefer, 'Psychogramming', in C.J. Chung and S.T. Leong (eds.), *Project on the City, 2: Harvard Design School Guide to Shopping* (Cologne, 2001), pp. 558–75.
12. V. Mosco, *The Political Economy of Communication: Rethinking and Renewal* (London 1996), pp. 148–53; I. Ang, *Desperately Seeking the Audience* (London, 1991), p. 33.

13. 'Agency in Action: A Day in the Life of Mrs Green', *Advertiser's Weekly*, 30 Apr. 1936, p. 130.
14. R. Marchand, *Advertising the American Dream: Making Way for Modernity, 1920–1940* (Berkeley, CA, 1985), pp. 37–8; S.W. Davis, *Living Up to the Ads: Gender Fictions of the 1920s* (Durham, NC, 2000), pp. 36–41, 87–122.
15. *Advertiser's Weekly*, 30 Apr. 1936, p. 131.
16. D.C. Jones, *Social Surveys* (London, 1949); E.P. Hennock, 'The Measurement of Urban Poverty: From the Metropolis to the Nation, 1880–1920', *Economic History Review* 40 (1987), pp. 208–27; D. Englander and R. O'Day (eds.), *Retrieved Riches: Social Investigation in Britain, 1840–1914* (Aldershot, 1995); M. Bulmer (ed.), *Essays on the History of British Sociological Research* (Cambridge, 1985); M. Bulmer and K. Kish Sklar (eds.), *The Social Survey in Historical Perspective, 1880–1940* (Cambridge, 1991).
17. 'Lux Flakes—3,295 Consumers' (Apr. 1928), History of Advertising Trust Archive, Norwich [henceforth HAT Archive], J. Walter Thompson Collection, Box 688.
18. 'Memorandum—Lux Plan 1931' (undated, c. 1930), HAT Archive JWT Collection, Box 687.
19. 'Lux Investigations' (Spring, 1934), HAT Archive JWT Collection, Box 688.
20. 'Some Possibilities of Increasing the Total Consumption of Soap in England' (undated, c. 1928), HAT Archive JWT Collection, Box 693.
21. 'Lux Shampoo' (15 Aug. 1931), HAT Archive JWT Collection, Box 693.
22. 'Lux Toilet Soap Shampoo' (8 Feb. 1930), HAT Archive JWT Collection, Box 693.
23. 'Considerations of Possible Methods of Improving the Technique of Asking Questions' (10 Apr. 1934), HAT Archive JWT Collection, Box 294.
24. J. Walter Thompson Co., *Population Handbook of Great Britain and Ireland* (London 1924); 'Draft Plan for an Adventure Serial and Premium Scheme to Be Transmitted from Radio Luxembourg—Sponsored by Rowntree Elect Cocoa' (24 Feb. 1949), HAT Archive JWT Collection, Box 294.
25. 'Extension of Radio Advertising 1937' (18 Aug. 1936), HAT Archive JWT Collection, Box 294.
26. Memo from JWT Media Department, 'Cocoa' (12 July 1934), HAT Archive JWT Collection, Box 294.
27. A. Bingham, *Gender, Modernity, and the Popular Press in Interwar Britain* (Oxford, 2005), pp. 29–37, 86–93.
28. This was a concern for working-class consumers throughout much of the nineteenth and twentieth centuries. See F. Trentmann and V. Taylor, 'From Users to Consumers: Water Politics in Nineteenth-Century London', in F. Trentmann (ed.), *The Making of the Consumer: Knowledge, Power and Identity in the Modern World* (Oxford, 2006), pp. 53–79.
29. 'Short Brand Histories' (July 1952), p. 136, HAT Archive JWT Collection, Box 694.
30. S. Street, *Crossing the Ether: British Public Service Radio and Commercial Competition, 1922–1945* (Eastleigh, 2006), pp. 85–94, 103–14.
31. 'Sam Meek's Blue Book', John W. Hartman Center for Sales, Advertising and Marketing History, Duke University, North Carolina (henceforth Hartman Center Archive), J. Walter Thompson Collection, New Business Records, Box 7.
32. 'Letter from New York Office to Mr Rae Smith' (23 June 1933), HAT Archive JWT Collection, Box 693.
33. 'London Office Scheme Interests British Census Officials', *J.W.T. News*, Mar. 1931, p. 5.

34. 'From the Statistics Supplied to Us' (Oct. 1927), HAT Archive JWT Collection, Box 688; 'Principles behind the 1929 Campaign' (undated, c. late 1928), HAT Archive JWT Collection, Box 687; 'Creative Staff Meeting' (25 May 1932), Hartman Center Archive, Information Center Records, Box 5.

35. M. Abrams, 'The Gold and Silver Thread Monopoly of James I.'. PhD dissertation, University of London, 1929.

36. M. Abrams, *Money and a Changing Civilisation* (London, 1934).

37. Mark A. Abrams Papers, Churchill Archive Centre, Churchill College, University of Cambridge, Box 2.

38. M. Abrams, *A Survey of Reader Interest in the National Morning and London Evening Press* (London 1934), Part IV.

39. D. Starch, *Principles of Advertising* (Chicago, 1923), pp. 306–66; D. Starch, *Measuring Advertising Readership and Results* (New York, 1966), pp. 7–15; B. Lipstein, 'An Historical Perspective of Copy Research', *Journal of Advertising Research* 24 (Dec. 1984), pp. 11–14.

40. For contemporary debates in the American context, see, for example, R. Lynd, 'The Consumer Becomes "a Problem" ', Annals of the American Academy of Political and Social Science 173 (1934), pp. 1–6.

41. G. Harrison and F.C. Mitchell, *The Home Market: A Handbook of Statistics* (London, 1936); M. Abrams (ed.), *The Home Market: A Book of Facts about People* (London, 1939).

42. Harrison and Mitchell, *Home Market*, p. 59; Abrams, *Home Market*, p. 61.

43. Abrams, *Home Market*, pp. 98–103.

44. *Ibid.*, p. 145.

45. Abrams's and JWT's consumer classification not only conflicted with the Registrar General's classification system but also provided a competing system to the contemporary tax schedule which had five brackets, A, B, C, D, and E. See M. Abrams, *The Condition of the British People, 1911–1945* (London, 1946), p. 75.

46. Abrams, *Home Market*, p. 93.

47. M. Abrams, *The State of the Nation: An Economic Survey in Pictorial Form* (London, 1947); M. Abrams, *Social Surveys and Social Action* (London, 1951).

48. M. Abrams, *The Teenage Consumer* (London, 1959).

49. M. Abrams, *Beyond Three Scores and Ten: A First Report on a Survey of the Elderly* (London, 1978); M. Abrams, *The Elderly Consumer* (London, 1982); M. Abrams, *People in Their Late Sixties: A Longitudinal Study of Ageing* (London, 1983).

50. Labour Party, *Report of a Commission of Enquiry into Advertising* (London, 1966), paras. 54–5.

51. See J. Thompson's chapter in this volume and T.M. Porter, *Trust in Numbers: The Pursuit of Objectivity in Science and Public Life* (Princeton, NJ, 1995), pp. 41–3, 148–59.

52. S. Nixon, 'Apostles of Americanization? J. Walter Thompson Company Ltd., Advertising and Anglo-American Relations, 1945–67', *Contemporary British History* 22 (2008), pp. 477–99.

53. For a more in-depth discussion of this, see S. Schwarzkopf, 'Transatlantic Invasions or Common Culture? Modes of Cultural and Economic Exchange between the American and the British Advertising Industries, 1951–1989', in M. Hampton and J. Wiener (eds.), *Anglo-American Media Interactions, 1850–2000* (London, 2007), pp. 254–74, and S. Schwarzkopf, 'Turning Trade Marks into Brands: How Advertising Agencies Practiced and Conceptualised Branding, 1890–1930', in T. da Silva Lopes and P. Duguid (eds.), *Trademarks, Brands and Competitiveness* (London, 2010), pp. 165–93.

Part III
Numbers and Public Trust

9 Suspect Figures
Statistics and Public Trust in Victorian England

Tom Crook

Do we really trust statistics—or, to quote the title of one of Theodore Porter's books, do we really 'trust in numbers'?[1] It would seem that we do and do not. On the one hand, the very prevalence of statistics in today's public sphere would suggest that we do trust them, and emphatically so. To give but one example, newspapers brim with numbers and statistically derived numerical rates: immigration figures, price indices, and trade balances. And we trust them because we believe they are (objective) facts, as opposed to (subjective) opinions, generated by experts or institutions with claims to technical neutrality. Statistics seem non-political, beyond the realm of interests and ideologies. But on the other hand, it is also apparent that we distrust statistics. Politicians accuse newspapers of selectively highlighting certain statistical facts for political reasons, whilst newspapers accuse politicians of doing the same. Crime figures, among others, are traded between MPs, who often, after critical questioning, have to add caveats regarding the particular measurements used and what the figures do and do not encompass. Meanwhile, the saying 'Lies, damned lies and statistics', popularized by Mark Twain at the start of the twentieth century, continues to enjoy currency. It even features in the titles of books dedicated to unravelling the myriad ways numbers are manipulated for political gain.[2]

This is no bad thing, of course. In a democratic society it is surely right that citizens remain suspicious of numbers emanating from experts and the state. But if this is the case, then another question arises: what, precisely, is the function of statistics? Statistics play a number of roles and one of the great virtues of recent scholarship is that it foregrounds the *multiple* uses of statistics within modern governance. The work of Porter, Nikolas Rose and Edward Higgs suggests that statistics have no intrinsic purpose, but rather lend themselves to various uses depending on time, place, and culture.[3] Evidently one aspect of the versatility of statistics is that they can be used as instruments of both trust and distrust. After Foucault, we should certainly affirm that one of the purposes of statistics is to provide a certain kind of disciplinary truth, one which homogenizes and normalizes its object or referent, and allows for the identification of the normal and the pathological (as with various statistical 'rates' against which members of the public can compare themselves or their place of residence). And to the extent that statistics provide truth, they also provide authority and allow for the generation of trust.

Yet it is also true that, in a democratic society, statistics perform another crucial function, one which works in the other direction: bottom-up, so to speak, rather than top-down. That is to say, statistics also allow for the scrutiny of the state: they provide accountability and transparency, and equip those who are the object of government with a means of contesting government. In short, a crucial function of statistics is to facilitate distrust of the state. They allow for political engagement and for expressions of opinion regarding the performance, cost, and extent of government. Overall, then, it would seem that within a democratic public sphere statistics can be wielded in various ways and bear no necessary relation to either trust or distrust. It all depends on circumstance and function. At one moment, in one situation, statistics provide trust; at another moment, in another situation, statistics arouse distrust. Furthermore, it is possible to trust statistics while also wielding them in a combative, distrustful fashion against institutions like the state. It is also possible to pit statistics against statistics, trusting their general veracity, and providing some of one's own, but distrusting those produced by another agent or institution.

This chapter traces something of the prehistory of the present in the context of Victorian England. One aim is to complicate received narratives of the transformations of trust and governance in the wake of modernity. For all their sophistication, the likes of Anthony Giddens and Niklas Luhmann present a linear story in which trust, once vested in face-to-face relations and the social standing of superiors, comes to be placed in anonymous experts, whose claims to authority are grounded in professional codes of conduct and the use of particular technologies (laboratories, statistics, and computers).[4] Modern trust is placed in what Giddens terms 'abstract systems, especially expert systems', and is functionally related to the need to manage complex urban societies in which older forms of authority (kinship ties and property ownership) have collapsed.[5]

The complexities surrounding trust and the use of statistics today should already give us pause when considering this narrative. Crucially, it overlooks the distrust which, as has been noted, is intrinsic to democracy. This is a central aspect of Piotr Sztompka's account of trust in which he writes of the way modern democracy is sustained by an ongoing interplay of trust *and* distrust.[6] The 'pre-commitment', as he puts it, to periodic elections and the guarantee of public accountability institutionalizes distrust. Paradoxically, however, institutionalized distrust also creates conditions of trust; or more precisely, a kind of 'spontaneous' or implicit trust in democratic mechanisms in general. 'The emphasis on accountability and pre-commitment', he writes, 'means that trust in a democratic regime is due precisely to the institutionalization of distrust in the architecture.'[7] Sztompka's account provides a useful corrective to the analyses of Giddens and Luhmann. It highlights the fact that whatever trust is generated by experts must none-theless exist within a critical democratic milieu which citizens consent to (or trust in) precisely because it allows for expressions of distrust in institu-tions of authority.

One can see something of this interplay of trust, distrust, and public accountability at work in the Victorian period and in the use and circula-tion of statistics. Yet the Victorian period remains distinctive. For what we find is the persistence and refinement of older forms of trust (such as those vested in property and gentlemanly status) mixing with newer forms of trust (such as that provided by statistics), all the while existing in a political culture increasingly committed to public accountability yet still far from democratic. The second aim of this chapter is therefore to demonstrate that relations of trust, authority and governance are highly complex and contin-gent; that they exist in the form of peculiar, multifaceted amalgams that are always changing and evolving, and as such also weaving together different aspects of the old and the new, the traditional and the modern.

It is for this reason that the chapter opts for a broad understanding of the term 'trust'. In the substantial literature that now exists on the subject, trust is defined in various and conflicting ways. However, many of these definitions refer to forms of knowledge that are historically contingent and whose authority is far from universal. Giddens, for instance, states that 'Trust may be defined as confidence in the reliability of a person or sys-tem, regarding a given set of outcomes or events, where that confidence expresses a faith in the probity or love of another, or in the correctness of abstract principles (technical knowledge).'[8] Yet, as we shall see, technical knowledge, of the kind associated with experts, was treated with suspi-cion for much of the Victorian period. It seems sensible, then, to adopt the broad definition of trust provided by the *Oxford English Dictionary*: 'firm belief in the reliability, truth, ability, or strength of someone or some-thing—acceptance of the truth of a statement without evidence or further investigation.'[9] With this in mind, the chapter deals solely with trust in relation to institutions and practices of governance—with public trust, in short—and it begins with a broad sketch of the governmental culture into which statistics ventured, at first tentatively, later more boldly, but always amidst much dispute and hostility.

TRUST, PUBLIC SERVICE, AND GENTLEMANLY STATUS

We still await a focused study of trust and Victorian governance. No doubt such a study would reveal incredible complexity, not least because, amidst much innovation, it would also find multiple reworkings of traditional sources of trust (though hardly surprising given that Victorian society, while increasingly oriented towards the future, was also profoundly rever-ential of the past). However, on the basis of recent scholarship, it is possible to identify a new ethos of elite governance in which a concern to foster public trust assumed a key place.[10] Indeed, ethos, rather than ideology, is the right term, for what emerged was less a new set of specific prescriptions or ideas, and more a new disposition, which, if not unchallenged, received support from most sections of the elite for most of the period.

This ethos, which might be described as a patrician ethos of disinterested governance, inherited at least three elements from earlier centuries. First, it inherited the ethical ideal of the gentleman, which drew on an eclectic repertoire of moral impulses, from notions of knightly honour through to classical humanist conceptions of virtue and Christian ideals of asceticism.[11] The figure of the gentleman was much discussed during the Victorian period, but it was always associated with trust and moral probity.[12] Second, the ethos inherited a hierarchical conception of society in which those fit to govern were those who possessed sufficient property and independence. Here one's capacity for truth was linked to one's capacity for free action: free, that is, of social dependencies and economic interests. Finally, the ethos excluded women, who, it was thought, were dependent on men and concerned solely with the administration of the material (or 'lower') realm of the household.

All of these elements vested public trust largely in social status and in the lofty detachment thought to be the natural complement of property ownership, especially the ownership of land. However, the Victorian period also inherited the idea that government ought to be systematically distrusted. Such a sentiment can be found in the work of John Locke, David Hume, and Adam Smith, all of whom recommended that government should be regarded with distrust. It also featured in the work of Jeremy Bentham. In his 'Essay on Political Tactics', composed in 1791 but published in 1843, Bentham outlined a plan for a rigorous system of governmental transparency. After detailing its many benefits, he entertained the objection that a 'regime of publicity' also amounted to a 'system of distrust'. 'This is true', he affirmed, 'and every good political institution is founded upon this base. Whom ought we to distrust, if not those to whom is committed great authority, with great temptations to abuse it?'[13] Of course, what for Bentham was an essential working assumption of government was for radicals a basic premise of their political platform. From the end of the eighteenth century through to the 1840s, the language of 'Old Corruption' was deployed by radicals to condemn an aristocratic system of government which, they believed, was 'rotten' to the core and awash with extravagant salaries, pensions, and sinecures.

Yet, as Philip Harling has argued, by the 1850s the radical critique of aristocratic corruption had lost much of its force, principally because the elite had embraced an ethos of disinterested governance in which older forms of authority were fused with a new sense of public service and accountability—in short, an ethos in which public office was no longer the private property of the officeholder but a 'public trust' (the term was often used) which should be enacted accordingly, in the interests of the people.[14] Disinterested governance constituted a kind of enlightened aristocratic outlook: it was sensitive to radical conceptions of open, elective government, yet it was still confident of the virtues of hierarchy, property and gentlemanly leadership.

One facet of this ethos was a commitment to representative, as opposed to democratic, governance, something which involved a more attentive disposition towards 'public opinion' and a conception of parliament as a national body whose purpose was to recognize and integrate the many interests over which it presided. Accordingly, another facet was a commitment to ending taxes and state-sponsored privileges that were seen to benefit some groups but not others, such as the Corn Laws (repealed in 1846), and some of the constitutional privileges of the Anglican Church. Finally, disinterest entailed a commitment to financial probity, retrenchment and openness. This was reflected in various developments: the gradual curtailment of sinecures and excessive pensions; the adoption of modern, 'double-entry' accounting methods by government departments; and the consolidation of all tax revenues into one pool of money, subject to annual scrutiny by parliament.[15]

Much more might be said about the ethos of disinterested, patrician governance. Its complexities—its nuances of temperament as much as broad principle—are difficult to characterize. It was underpinned by a still vibrant Burkean sensibility, which was practically oriented, averse to abstract formulations of political morality, and in favour of only modest, yet timely, adaptations of England's constitution. Yet we might also point to a widely shared Newtonian outlook, which viewed both the natural and the social worlds as governed by universal laws of balance, harmony, and repetition. Or again, though this ethos encouraged individual self-improvement within all classes, it maintained strong, almost instinctive, strains of aristocratic prejudice. Throughout the century sections of the elite continued to think of the lower classes in terms inherited from antiquity: that is, as 'mean', 'narrow-minded', 'petty', and 'deceitful'. Indeed, there was widespread distrust on the part of the elite towards the idea of democracy, which was often equated with anarchy and mob rule.

A kindred kind of complexity is apparent outside of the political elite, in the world of the reformed civil service and the professions. Here a similar ethos of public service prevailed, but it was one less dependent on substantial property ownership and family ties, and more on educational attainment and moral character. Even so, traditional sources of trust remained decisive. This is most apparent in the case of the reformed civil service, which emerged gradually in the wake of the Northcote-Trevelyan Report (1854). As is now widely recognized, civil service reform was about refashioning, rather than rejecting, the ideal of the gentleman administrator.[16] The new gentleman was to be harder working and more efficient than his predecessor, yet he was still to possess the time-honoured qualities of reserve, reticence and tact, coupled with a noble sense of self-sacrifice and duty.

A sense of higher calling pervaded the Victorian professions, especially the established ones such as law and medicine.[17] Many, if not the majority, of these professionals attended public schools, where a self-conscious effort was made to prepare pupils for a life of public service.[18] The subordination of personal to group interests formed one of the guiding principles of public school pedagogy, and pervaded school life, from the cult of games through to the prefectorial system. Great store was also placed on the curriculum, which was of a broad, liberal nature, concerned to foster general qualities of mind and perception, rather than narrow intellectual interests. Oxbridge too embraced the values of liberal pedagogy, whose study at this level, it was thought, freed the mind to range beyond mere technical concerns to contemplate nothing less than civilization as a whole.[19]

The professional gentleman was thus able to distinguish himself from two other figures, which, by contrast, were looked upon with suspicion. On the one hand, he was able to distance himself from the businessman, defined by his greed and financial self-interest. On the other hand, the professional gentleman was able to distinguish himself from the expert, defined by his preoccupation with only specialized, technical fields of knowledge. Suspicion of precisely this form of knowledge had played an important part in shaping the Northcote-Trevelyan agenda of the 1850s, and it remained strong even at the dawn of the twentieth century. 'Nothing would be more fatal than for the Government of States to get in the hands of experts', wrote Winston Churchill in 1902. 'Expert knowledge is limited knowledge, and the unlimited ignorance of the plain man who knows where it hurts is a safer guide than any rigorous direction of a specialized character'.[20]

STATISTICS, PUBLIC ACCOUNTABILITY, AND THE EXCLUSION OF OPINION

In Victorian England, public trust failed to gravitate in a linear fashion from aristocrats to experts. Nor do we find a linear shift to democratic forms of accountability. Instead, a complex synthesis of the old and the new emerged; or rather, a series of syntheses, whose specificity is easily repressed in retrospect. The introduction of statistics needs to be seen in the same light: as a form of authority which simultaneously introduced new elements of trust while also mixing with older ones. Neither should we take key terms for granted, including the term 'statistics'. As the introduction to this volume has noted, prior to the twentieth century, when it came to be associated with numerical information, the term tended to connote both form (empirical, though not exclusively numerical, information) and content (knowledge of society or the state); and as we shall see in the next section, its precise epistemological status as a science was greatly contested.

Statistics had been generated prior to the Victorian period, and there was a steady accumulation from at least the 1790s.[21] The early Victorian period represents something of a watershed nonetheless, partly on account of the sheer increase in the amount of statistical information. The War Office, the Home Office, and the Board of Trade all placed their information-gathering activities on a more orderly footing during the 1830s, the latter with the establishment in 1832 of a specialized Statistical Department. The enhanced use of royal commissions and the establishment of various state inspectorates during these years further served to increase the flow of statistics. Crucially, the 1830s also witnessed the establishment of various voluntary statistical associations, including, most notably, the Manchester (1833) and London (1834) statistical societies, and the statistical section (Section F) of the British Association for the Advancement of Science (BAAS, 1834). Naturally, these associations were concerned to collect and collate statistics, but they also formed arenas where the nature of statistics, as a nascent science, was articulated with unprecedented self-consciousness.

A variety of factors informed the formation of statistical associations and state bureaus during the 1830s. Certainly there was a concern to ensure that Britain kept up with her continental neighbours, especially France, in amassing statistics. Another concern was to reformulate the basis of public trust in light of the political turbulence surrounding the Great Reform Act of 1832. Consider the argument put forward in 1831 by William Jacob, comptroller of corn returns, while lobbying for the establishment of the Board of Trade's Statistical Department:

> The best mode of allaying disquietude and of diffusing contentment on the subject of public affairs is an open and clear disclosure of their conditions and management . . . A more general diffusion of accurate knowledge regarding the state of public affairs would tend to check that excitement and party spirit which has often been created by misrepresentation or exaggeration, and which has produced an annoyance to the government and at least a temporary disaffection to the public mind.[22]

Even in the private associations formed outside the formal channels of government, membership was overwhelmingly drawn from the ruling classes, whether national or civic—precisely those whose authority had been shaken by the events of the early 1830s and who looked towards re-establishing popular faith in the elite.

Thus, whatever trust might be generated by statistics, it was always related to the trust already vested in the figure of the gentleman. The importance of this variant of trust in terms of national elite leadership has already been noted, but it also formed the basis of the culture of authority associated with scientific inquiry. Gentlemanly status remained important even in a body like the BAAS, which was formed as a reaction against the perceived dilettantish amateurism of the Royal Society; and it remained crucial to scientific endeavour right down to the end of the century.[23] Both the London and Manchester statistical societies should be seen as part of this broader culture of gentlemanly knowledge production. The London Society proclaimed that it consisted solely of 'Noblemen and Gentlemen', and members included a number of earls, knights and lords, as well as eminent scientists and economists (Thomas Malthus, Charles Babbage, and Richard Jones).[24] The members of the Manchester Society were not quite so distinguished, but all were considered gentleman. 'Its members', stated its first report published in 1834, 'are gentlemen accustomed for the most part to meet in private society, and whose habits are not uncongenial.'[25]

Statistical societies could thus project a public image of gentlemanly integrity. Yet, as the first report of the Manchester Society suggests, gentlemanly status was also crucial in terms of facilitating its *private* workings, as embodied in conversations, agreements, and the raising of annual subscriptions. This traditional source of trust further featured in the making of its investigations into the condition of Manchester's working classes. A report published in 1838 took care to note that the data collected by paid agents had been double-checked against the 'personal knowledge of different gentlemen'.[26]

Still, the use of statistics was of decisive importance, even if, as a form of knowledge, it remained intimately bound to considerations of social status. In particular, the science of statistics, or so its gentlemanly practitioners claimed, was resolutely fact-based. It followed that it was free from opinion and situated beyond the unruly domain of politics: not insignificant, given the highly charged context of the 1830s and 1840s. The gentlemen of the Manchester Society declared that their work would be carried out to 'the total exclusion of party politics', while the London Society stated in its opening *Prospectus* (1834): 'The Society will consider it to be the first and most essential rule of conduct to exclude carefully all Opinions from its transactions and publications—to confine itself to facts—and, as far as may be possible, to facts which can be stated numerically and arranged in tables.'[27] Facts as opposed to opinions: this binary distinction was crucial to the legitimation of statistics, and entailed that the disinterest which arose from a gentleman's economic independence was supplemented with a form of epistemological disinterest.

Statistical knowledge was crucial in other ways, not least the manner in which it enabled the generation of *general* knowledge. That is to say, it represented an empirical, or inductive, variant of abstraction, which enabled the practitioner to proceed from agglomerations of facts to general laws, regularities and principles. To be sure, this was decidedly not the form of knowledge—idealist, metaphysical—traditionally associated with the liberal education of a gentleman. Yet, to the extent that it enabled empirical states of affairs to be grasped as a whole, it could lay claim to a certain liberality of mind. 'Like other sciences,' stated the London Society in the first edition of its journal (1838), 'that of Statistics seeks to deduce from well-established facts certain general principles which interest and affect mankind; it uses the same instruments of comparison, calculation, and deduction: but its peculiarity is that it proceeds wholly by the accumulation of facts, and does not admit of any kind of speculation.'[28] Furthermore, the 'laws of large numbers' which statistics revealed gelled with the Newtonian providentialism which, as has been noted, was a key facet of the elite mentality of the Victorian period.

In basic terms, then, statistics could be trusted because they were facts. From another perspective they could be trusted because the form of knowledge they enabled seemed to point to realms of immutable generality, which complemented the lofty detachment seen as intrinsic to a gentleman's position. But if, in one sense, the science of statistics was politically aloof, it was also—indeed because of this—politically engaged, albeit in a particular kind of way. Given its intrinsic concern with society, it was thought to be an eminently 'useful' or 'practical' form of knowledge, terms which connoted pragmatic, hands-on neutrality: that is, sensitivity to things as they were, something which resonated with the Burkean elements of the ethos of disinterested governance. The London Society sought 'only to collect and arrange that class of facts which alone can form the basis of correct conclusions with respect to social and political government'. It went on: 'They [statistics] are, as it were, the link which connects them with the practical purposes of life.'[29] Elsewhere, the Society referred to statistics as 'the science of the arts of civil life', noting that the 'body politic', just like the 'human frame', required attentive empirical treatment.[30]

During the mid-century the disinterest associated with statistics continued to be championed by bodies such as the National Association for the Promotion of Social Science, formed in 1857. Like the first statistical associations, it was composed of gentlemen, all with links to national and civic office. The basic, yet all important, distinction between numerical fact and opinion was often affirmed by its members. 'Opinion means ignorance more or less', declared one keynote speaker in 1871. 'I may be "of opinion" it will rain today, but "I know" two and two make four'.[31] But it was the Victorian state which did most to champion the authority of statistics, simply by publishing masses of numerical information. The crucial development here was the systematic publication, via Her Majesty's Stationery Office, of 'blue books' containing the findings of royal commissions and parliamentary select committees. Some of these blue books proved immensely popular—the 1842 royal commission report on the employment of children in mines sold over 10,000 copies—and extracts, sometimes extensive, would appear in sections of the press.[32]

Developments like this, together with the greater financial transparency effected by fiscal reform, meant that for the first time statistics constituted an essential part of the public sphere and could be used, quite systematically, to critique and assess government. This seems to have occurred without much in the way of elaborate theorization or constitutional reflection. Only Bentham, in his massive and uncompleted *Constitutional Code*

(1822–32), sought to connect the existence of facts with the exercise of public opinion: one of the principal functions of his 'public opinion tribunal', which formally enshrined popular scrutiny of government, was a 'Statistic or Evidence-furnishing function.'[33]

But despite the absence of widespread reflection, statistics emerged as an essential tool of accountability and to this extent governmental distrust. This is certainly apparent in the work of the General Register Office (GRO), established in 1837, which was perhaps the most prodigious generator of statistics during the Victorian period. Edward Higgs's chapter in this volume demonstrates that the GRO self-consciously sought to promote local debate regarding the efficacy of public health measures; and as Simon Szreter has argued, one means, among many, through which the GRO fostered critical scrutiny of government was to circulate 'crude death rates' (CDRs) indicating the average number of people dying in a given town, city or district as a proportion of a thousand (15 per 1,000, 30 per 1,000).[34] The measure was indeed crude, and intricate life tables were far more accurate. What distinguished the CDR was its user-friendliness and ease of comprehension. CDRs featured in the GRO's first *Annual Report* (1839) and all those thereafter, and by the 1860s their systematic quarterly circulation was sometimes referred to as the 'national system of computation'. 'By means of these figures', suggested a pamphlet published in 1863, reflecting on the early use of CDRs by the GRO, 'we could at once see the amount of mortality occurring in any particular place, and compare it in this respect with any other places; or mark how far it departs from any ideal standard of health which we might have fixed upon'.[35]

The impact of CDRs on the consciousness of local authorities was profound. One of the first cities to react to its national statistical exposure—its numbering and shaming—was Liverpool. According to one of its historians, Liverpool's consistent ranking in the early *Annual Reports* of the GRO as one of the unhealthiest cities in Britain was a significant factor in prompting its authorities to undertake their own private public health act in 1846, two years before a general act was introduced.[36] The constant circulation of CDRs in fact produced a normalized, disciplinary culture of civic consciousness. For some authorities, an abnormally high CDR was a cause of considerable embarrassment, a real blow to civic pride and self-esteem. A paper delivered in 1888 by the doctor Arthur Ransome, a member of the Manchester Statistical Society, revealed the bad news that Manchester and Salford were losing, by some margin, what he termed the 'race after health'. Referring to a table ranking cities by their death rates, Ransome noted: 'I fear that the patriotic, or perhaps more correctly the civic, feelings of many of us will be shocked at seeing the position now held by Manchester and Salford in this table . . . Manchester is now the worst town in the kingdom, and nearly 60 per cent of the inhabitants die, over and above, the average lost in 29 other towns'.[37]

There is also evidence of CDRs empowering members of the public to engage ruling elites in a combative fashion. In 1867, a magistrate, William

Dawbarn, sent a clutch of letters, subsequently published in pamphlet form, to Liverpool's mayor, castigating the city's sanitary administration. The first letter began in a cautious fashion. Although part of the city's governing elite, Dawbarn acknowledged that he knew nothing of the details which guided the work of the city's Health Committee; he also acknowledged that the Committee was made up of diligent 'gentlemen': 'My hesitation arises not only from the fact that these gentlemen are men of capability, but from the fact that I am not on the Health Committee and so cannot be acquainted with all the various reasons that direct the counsels of this body.'[38] Yet, equipped with the measure of public certainty bequeathed by CDRs, he was able to adopt a confident, bullish posture. He was essentially concerned that, despite further spending, the city's health seemed to be getting worse: 'I have now in my hands a report for 1866 giving us the awful death rate of 41.7 to a 1,000 . . . Now, Mr Mayor, what I particularly want to draw your attention to is to the fact that in 1860 we had arrived at a good normal point for Liverpool, when we had arrived at a death rate of say, in round numbers, 25 per 1,000.' With reference to the death rate of 1860, he then added: 'Why has not this been our average death rate? Have we not spent enough on officers and all kinds of imaginary useful appliances to obtain a better state of things?'[39]

STATISTICAL SCEPTICISM AND MORAL CRITIQUE

It is possible to discern, then, a twofold movement within the context of a patrician culture of disinterested governance. On the one hand, statistics emerged as a new form of trust, seemingly free from the taint of opinion and partisan politics. On the other hand, statistics facilitated a critical culture of governmental distrust and accountability. Wielding statistics as a means of political scrutiny, of course, involved trusting their general veracity. Yet such trust was not always forthcoming, and right from the beginning this nascent science was beset by epistemological doubt and confusion. Statisticians themselves were by no means confident of its status as a science. The formation of Section F of the BAAS proved controversial, prompting anxieties that statistics did not constitute a proper science, and would, given its concern with society, invariably involve political considerations of some sort.[40]

One of the most devastating critiques emerged in 1838 in the pages of the radical *London and Westminster Review*. It was written by G. Robertson, subeditor of the journal, and took the form of an extensive examination of the published *Transactions* of the London Statistical Society. The principal target of Robertson's critique was the Society's explicit repudiation of opinion and theory. He not only argued that it was impossible to divorce 'fact' from 'theory', but also that doing so would render useless and unscientific any resultant knowledge:

> No mere record and arrangement of facts can constitute a science. Facts are evidence. Science is not evidence, but the results of evidence—the things which it proves, that in relation to which it is what it is, the inferences from the premises. To separate the facts from the propositions they support, the evidences from the thing they prove … is to destroy and annihilate their nature as evidence—and by stripping them of that for the sake of which they are noticed at all they are rendered utterly meaningless.[41]

For Robertson, scientific facts existed only in relation to theories, hypotheses and opinions; to veto the latter meant, by definition, that statistics could never attain the status of a science. To claim otherwise was an exercise in deception: ' … while this rule [the exclusion of opinion] lasts the Statistical Society may be an efficient instrument of *charlanterie*—may present specious tables and columns of figures to impose upon the many and gain the purpose of the hour, but to all the ends of science and usefulness it is a mockery and a lie.'[42] He ended by offering an alternative characterization of statistics, one which reduced it to a mode of representation: 'But statistics is not even a department of human knowledge; it is merely a form of knowledge—a mode of arranging and stating facts which belongs to various sciences.'[43]

Of course, it is very unlikely that critiques of this sort—highly technical and, ultimately, philosophical—registered with the public at large, if in fact they registered at all. There were, however, other criticisms directed at statistics, ones of a more accessible sort to the extent that they undermined both the epistemology and morality of statistics—indeed, yoked the two together, so that it was the character of the statistician that was rendered suspect. Clearly, statistics worked two ways, depending on one's perspective: that is, they might complement *and* detract from the moral credentials of their gentlemanly users. In his essay 'Chartism', published towards the end of 1839, Thomas Carlyle dedicated a brief chapter to statistics, disputing their ability to diagnose what, famously, he dubbed 'the condition of England question'. His principal criticism related to their abstract nature: numbers were simply unable to get to grips with the complexities of life. 'Tables are like cobwebs', he wrote, 'beautifully reticulated, orderly to look upon, but which will hold no conclusion. Tables are abstractions, and the object a most concrete one, so difficult to read the essence of.' Happiness, like misery, could not be quantified or assessed via statistical representations. They missed so much, including nuances of feeling and subtleties of temperament: 'The labourer's feelings, his notion of being justly dealt with or unjustly; his wholesome composure, frugality, prosperity in the one case, his acrid unrest, recklessness, gin-drinking, and gradual ruin in the other—how shall figures of arithmetic represent all this?'[44]

For Carlyle, there was an intrinsic connection between the abstraction of statistics and the brutal, ruthless logic, as he saw it, of industrial capitalism. They were part of the same mindset which reckoned with man in a utilitarian, mechanical fashion. Far from complementing an ethos of dis-interested, patrician governance, statistics were its very antithesis: if any-thing, an expression of mean self-interest rather than magnanimous public service. These same associations also featured in the work of Charles Dick-ens, where, as Maeve Adams also notes in this volume, they were developed in characteristically satirical form. In an early piece, published in *Bentley's Miscellany* in 1837, Dickens caricatured an annual meeting of the BAAS, including a session of its statistical section. The impression generated by Dickens is of a science at once absurd and useless, and intensely sancti-monious. Mr Slug, for instance, is depicted giving a paper on 'the state of infant education among the middle classes in London'. Slug 'proves' its corrupting nature, and when it is put to him that a story like Jack and Jill might have some edifying properties, he replies that, in any case, its key defect is that it is a work of fiction rather than fact. This is followed with a paper by Mr Ledbrain detailing the ratio of human legs belonging to the manufacturing population of a Yorkshire town to the number of chair and stool legs.[45] For Dickens, as for Carlyle, statistics expressed a certain meanness and cruelty of spirit: a petty, small-minded disposition entirely at odds with traditional gentlemanly virtues. In *Hard Times*, published in 1854, Dickens developed these associations still further, via the character of Thomas Gradgrind, who believed 'facts alone are wanted in life', and who was always 'ready to weigh and measure any parcel of human nature and tell you what it comes to'.[46]

The forms of distrust discussed above, which targeted both the neutral-ity and morality of statistics, prospered throughout the Victorian period and were expressed at various levels and in various ways. During the 1850s Benjamin Disraeli was reported to have declared: 'This, I believe, is the age of statistical imposture'.[47] By the turn of the century, terms such as 'blue-booky', 'bluebookish' and 'bluebookishness' circulated among the political elite to denote dry, tediously factual texts and individuals.[48] Members of the public, meanwhile, were not averse to voicing profound scepticism. Some even lambasted statistics as the very worst in scientific 'humbug'. So began a letter to London's *Morning Chronicle*, published in 1848, which sought to dispute some statistics provided by the recently convened Metropolitan Sanitary Commission: 'Every pursuit, every science, has its attendant hum-bug; medicine had ever its quacks . . . mesmerism has its clairvoyance; but of all the sciences, if such it may be termed, statistics is the very stronghold and citadel of humbug; it affords safe covert into which charlatanism and empiricism of every kind delight to thrust themselves.'[49]

Distrust also compromised the logistics of statistical research. The agents employed by statistical societies to conduct house-to-house surveys often met with resistance, as did those agents employed by the GRO to gather information for the decennial censuses. Most often in these instances mem-bers of the public were concerned to protect their privacy from the prying eyes of government. Sometimes suspicion was so great that it occasioned special public meetings. Such was the case in 1835, when the Manchester Society conducted a survey of Liverpool's schools, which were strictly divided along sectarian lines. 'In many cases', the Society explained in its report, 'it was suspected that the enquiry emanated from Government who meditated the adoption of measures on the subject of education which might affect the interests of those connected with existing establishments.' It was feared, the report stated, that the information gathered might be used 'in effecting some political or sectarian purpose', adding that the 'party spirit' aroused by the investigation had been 'excited by a large meeting held 29th October, 1835, followed by other proceedings.' It seems that the investigation was only able to proceed after a protracted process of negotiation and persuasion. 'Distrust,' the report concluded, 'even when rendered more intractable from a mixture of party spirit, was generally found to yield to the simple and persevering disavowal of all objects but one, the investigation of the truth.'[50]

STATISTICS AND THE CONTAGIOUS DISEASES ACTS

The complex relations of statistics and public trust can be further illustrated by using a brief case study of the Contagious Diseases Acts (CDAs) and the opposition they aroused. The CDAs were implemented between 1864 and 1869, and provided for the forcible detention of women suspected of practising prostitution; if found to suffer from venereal disease, they could be further detained for up to nine months. Initially applied to only four naval and garrison towns, by the early 1870s the CDAs were in operation in eighteen selected districts. In general, support for the CDAs emanated from military and medical professionals, whose principal concern was the health of soldiers. Opposition to the acts mobilized a more eclectic social constituency and included evangelical Christians, sanitary professionals, political radicals, and civil libertarians. Their assault was impassioned and thorough, and generated a mass of pamphlets, petitions, and public meetings. Eventually, following the successful lobbying of the Liberal party, the CDAs were suspended in 1883 and then abolished in 1886.

The very fact that opposition to the CDAs was able to emerge at all, and on such a scale, is testament to the increased openness that characterized Victorian governance and the varied expressions of distrust which this permitted. Opponents of the CDAs publicly proclaimed a number of grievances, including the charge that the CDAs embraced a 'double-standard' of sexual morality in which only women were punished for an act which disgraced both sexes. Criticisms were also levelled at the statistics provided by the military establishment to demonstrate the sanitary efficacy of the CDAs. For some, however, regardless of whether one trusted them or not, statistics were an irrelevance, a distraction from more decisive political and moral arguments: 'I now come to the facts and statistics of the question, on which I am not solicitous to base any argument', stated one pamphlet, 'for the simple reason that, if these acts are morally indefensible, no facts, nor statistics, can affect our opinions of them.'[51] Indeed, for others, the effects of the CDAs were simply 'incalculable': 'The fact of the widespread moral detriment and the political hardships caused by these acts cannot be contested, while the quality of that detriment is such that it can be neither weighed, counted, named nor measured by any known process whatsoever.'[52]

Yet many within the opposition lobby were prepared to contest the statistics used in support of the CDAs and viewed this as crucial to winning the argument for abolition. Their rhetoric was decidedly strong: 'unfair', 'false', 'misleading', and 'untrustworthy' were some of the terms used to characterize the numbers marshalled in favour of the CDAs. At times, even the gentlemanly status of those within the pro-CDAs camp was invoked ironically. In a speech to the House of Commons made in 1870, the radical MP Jacob Bright quoted the views of William Acton, a high-profile doctor who supported the CDAs. Yet Bright used Acton's views to undermine, rather than support, the case for regulation, stating before he did so: 'Mr Acton is probably the most illogical man who ever put pen to paper, but he is a gentleman of character, and therefore his statements will be accepted.'[53]

Even so, beyond all the rhetoric and posturing, it is clear that members of the opposition lobby did dedicate time to carefully critiquing the statistics which ostensibly told in favour of the CDAs. Here distrust was not directed against statistics per se, but only against those generated by the state, or in this case the War Office and the various official committees which looked into the operation of the CDAs. The attention to statistical detail recalls that of today: tables were picked apart; dates, times and places of enumeration were questioned; and classificatory schemas were deemed outdated or inadequate. The precise details are best spared the reader, but it is worth noting the two points which were made with the most frequency: that venereal disease among the military population had gone into decline *prior* to the advent of the CDAs; and that the number of diseased prostitutes had increased under the operation of the CDAs.[54]

However, those who made such arguments might also, in the very same pamphlet, raise points which rendered inadequate any kind of statistical reasoning. For instance, it was claimed that both troops and prostitutes regularly moved in and out of the areas covered by the CDAs, making accurate assessments of the population all but impossible. It was also claimed that the most likely effect of the CDAs was to increase the amount of 'clandestine prostitution', which by definition could not be counted. Perhaps on account of their passionate hatred of the CDAs, the critique of state statistics mounted by abolitionists was at once total and contradictory: by turns they claimed that statistics were irrelevant; that the statistics which existed proved against the sanitary effectiveness of the CDAs; and that accurate statistics could not be had in any case.

It seems that no decisive blow was struck in the dense exchange and counter-exchange of statistics that characterizes the fractious history of the CDAs. That there was dispute regarding the statistics provided by the state no doubt helped the abolitionist case, but it is not precisely clear what role this played in prompting the suspension and eventual abolition of the CDAs. Nonetheless, it is possible to identify the most rigorous and adept statistical critic within the abolitionist camp: the radical MP and onetime minister, James Stansfeld. He made his most decisive intervention in 1876, in the shape of a paper presented before the London Statistical Society.[55] The paper aimed not to prove the negative sanitary effects of the CDAs, only to disprove the validity of those statistics which had been used to demonstrate their positive effects. Stansfeld set about his task in a ruthlessly systematic fashion and, in addition to the two key points noted above, he added the following: that government statistics wrongly began in 1864, when in fact 1867 was the earliest legitimate starting point; that it was impossible to prove the beneficial effects (or otherwise) of the CDAs on 'constitutional' or 'hereditary' syphilis; that the valid statistics which did exist showed no impact on gonorrhoea or 'secondary syphilis'; and that any reduction in the number of brothels was part of a nationwide trend and was not peculiar to the designated districts.

Stansfeld's critique was precise and devastating, and he was evidently aware that he risked impugning the gentlemanly character of those who had collated the statistics which supported the CDAs. He thus reminded his audience, which included representatives of the War Office, that he 'had not the slightest intention to suggest the cooking of figures'; he had no doubt of the 'good faith' in which they had been initially presented.[56] However, on other occasions Stansfeld was decidedly less circumspect. Speaking at a public meeting in Birmingham in November 1883, just six months after the CDAs had been suspended, he declared, with no little hubris: 'I have never found any difficulty in detecting elements of falseness in statistics produced to prove the success of the Acts in times past'; and should any more be forthcoming, 'I have the most perfect and the calmest confidence . . . [that] I shall be able to detect the same elements of unfairness and of falsehood'.[57] As this example suggests, expressions of distrust could well depend on context and a sense of public performance.

CONCLUSION

The relations and transformations of public trust and statistics in Victorian England resist neat characterization. To be sure, statistics did emerge as a new source of public trust; yet even if trusted as such, they might be wielded as an instrument of distrust and critique. Furthermore, it is also apparent that statistics were distrusted in themselves, on account of their dubious epistemology and morality. Finally, statistics existed in—and by turns complemented and contested—a political culture which, while increasingly representative, remained dominated by a patrician ethos still wedded to a hierarchical view of society and traditional figures of authority such as the gentleman. It is decidedly unhelpful to think in terms of linear trajectories, or even of the coexistence of different forms of authority. It is more useful to think in terms of complex entanglements of function and context on the one hand, and hybrid forms of authority on the other. This cannot be emphasized enough: as Theodore Porter has demonstrated, even the late Victorian statistical pioneer Karl Pearson was no advocate of narrow, technocratic expertise. Rather, Pearson envisaged statistics as part of a new culture of elite-based administration, comprised of men of broad scientific learning, all of whom would be emphatically committed to collective welfare. It amounted to a kind of socialist, scientific aristocracy, but one not entirely at odds with the Northcote-Trevelyan agenda established during the 1850s.[58]

Evidently, there is no single relationship between statistics, public trust, and governmental authority. Statistics are multifunctional tools which can serve any number of different agendas and interests. Indeed, public trust is now subject to statistical polling and survey analysis. Today we trust that statistics will provide an accurate index of public trust. And yet it would seem that trust in statistics is by no means increasing, including in those which emerge from independent bodies such as the Office for National Statistics (ONS). Statisticians themselves remain profoundly suspicious of what are often referred to as 'official statistics'. In 1999, the Labour Government published a white paper entitled *Building Trust in Statistics*, which outlined new arrangements for checking the accuracy of official statistics. The white paper, however, immediately prompted the publication of a critical press release from the Royal Statistical Society. It complained that the white paper concerned only those figures produced by the ONS and not those produced by government departments. The Society felt that the white paper was 'deeply flawed': its definition of official statistics was far too narrow. Nor were the proposals to be enshrined in legislation: 'It will be open to the present or any future government to alter the [new] arrangements should statistical integrity become inconvenient'.[59] If statistics are multifunctional, it is also clear that they are subject to multiple forms of distrust emanating from multiple locations. 'Lies, damned lies, and statistics': it seems this popular phrase will continue to enjoy currency for some time to come.

NOTES

1. T.M. Porter, *Trust in Numbers: The Pursuit of Objectivity in Science and Public Life* (Princeton, NJ, 1995).
2. Twain popularized the saying in 'Chapters from My Autobiography', published in 1907, where he also wrongly (it seems) attributed it to the English prime minster Benjamin Disraeli. See D. Huff's still popular *How to Lie with*

Statistics, first published in 1954, and more recently W. Hutton, *Damned Lies and Official Statistics* (London, 1993) and J. Best's *Damned Lies and Statistics: Untangling Numbers from the Media, Politicians, and Activists* (Berkeley, CA, 2001) and *More Damned Lies and Statistics: How Numbers Confuse Public Issues* (Berkeley, CA, 2004).

3. Porter, *Trust in Numbers*; N. Rose, *Powers of Freedom: Reframing Political Thought* (Cambridge, 1999), ch. 6; E. Higgs, *The Information State in England: The Central Collection of Information on Citizens since 1500* (Basingstoke, 2004).

4. A. Giddens, *The Consequences of Modernity* (Oxford, 1990); N. Luhmann, *Trust and Power: Two Works by Niklas Luhmann* [1973/1975, trans. H. Davis, J. Raffan and K. Rooney] (Avon, 1979). A useful summary of this narrative can be found in the epilogue to S. Shapin's *A Social History of Truth: Civility and Science in Seventeenth-Century England* (Chicago, 1994).

5. Giddens, *The Consequences of Modernity*, p. 83.

6. P. Sztompka, *Trust: A Sociological Theory* (Cambridge, 1999).

7. *Ibid.*, p. 140.

8. Giddens, *The Consequences of Modernity*, p. 34.

9. *The New Oxford English Dictionary* (Oxford, 1998), p. 1988.

10. Works which have informed this section include J. Parry, *The Rise and Fall of Liberal Government in Victorian Britain* (New Haven, CT, 1996), pp. 1–20; R. Price, *British Society, 1680–1880: Dynamism, Containment and Change* (Cambridge, 1999); and P. Mandler (ed.), *Liberty and Authority in Victorian Britain* (Oxford, 2006).

11. A useful discussion of traditional sources of gentlemanly authority can be found in Shapin, *A Social History of Truth*, chs. 2 and 3.

12. For differing conceptions of the gentleman, see R. Gilmour, *The Idea of the Gentleman in the Victorian Novel* (London, 1981), ch. 3.

13. J. Bentham, 'An Essay on Political Tactics' [1791], in M. James, C. Blamires and C. Pease-Watkin (eds.), *The Collected Works of Jeremy Bentham: Political Tactics* (Oxford, 1999), p. 37. The text was not published until 1843, when it appeared as part of John Bowring's complete edition of Bentham's works.

14. P. Harling, 'Rethinking "Old Corruption"', *Past and Present* 147 (1995), pp. 127–58. See also P. Harling, *The Modern British State: An Historical Introduction* (Oxford, 2001), ch. 3.

15. M. Daunton, *Trusting Leviathan: The Politics of Taxation in Britain, 1799–1914* (Cambridge, 2001), ch. 3.

16. P. Gowan, 'The Origins of the Administrative Elite', *New Left Review* 162 (1987), pp. 4–34; L.M.E. Goodlad, *Victorian Literature and the Victorian State: Character and Governance in a Liberal Society* (Baltimore, 2003), ch. 4.

17. D. Duman, 'The Creation and Diffusion of a Professional Ideology in Nineteenth-Century England', *Sociological Review* 27 (1979), pp. 113–38.

18. R. Wilkinson, 'Political Leadership in the Late Victorian Public School', *British Journal of Sociology* 13 (1962), pp. 320–30.

19. B. Knights, *The Idea of the Clerisy in the Nineteenth Century* (Cambridge, 1978), ch. 6.

20. Quoted in H. Perkin, *The Rise of Professional Society: England since 1880* (London, 1989), p. 169.

21. D. Eastwood, '"Amplifying the Province of the Legislature": The Flow of Information and the English State in the Early Nineteenth Century', *Historical Research* 62 (1989), pp. 279–94.

22. Quoted in M.J. Cullen, *The Statistical Movement in Early Victorian Britain: The Foundations of Empirical Social Research* (New York, 1975), p. 20.

23. M. Berman, '"Hegemony" and the Amateur Tradition in British Science', *Journal of Social History* 8 (1975), pp. 30–50.
24. V.L. Hilts, '*Aliis Extrendum*, or The Origin of the Statistical Society of London', *Isis* 69 (1978), pp. 21–43.
25. *First Report of the Statistical Society* (Manchester, July, 1834), p. 1. Manchester Central Reference Library. MS f 310.6 M5. Doc. 11.
26. *Report of a Committee of the Manchester Statistical Society on the Condition of the Working Classes in an Extensive Manufacturing District, in 1834, 1835 and 1836* (London, 1838), p. 4.
27. *First Report of the Statistical Society*, p. 1; *Prospectus of the Objects and Plan of the Statistical Society of London* (London, 1834), p. 1.
28. 'Introduction', *Journal of the Statistical Society of London* [hereafter *JSSL*] 1 (1838), p. 3.
29. *Ibid.*, pp. 1–2.
30. 'Sixth Annual Report of the Council of the Statistical Society London', *JSSL* 3 (1840), pp. 2, 6.
31. G. Godwin, 'Address on Health', *Transactions of the National Association for the Promotion of Social Science: 1871* (London, 1872), p. 97.
32. O. Frankel, 'Blue Books and the Victorian Reader', *Victorian Studies* 46 (2004), pp. 308–18.
33. F. Rosen and J.H. Burns (eds.), *Jeremy Bentham: Constitutional Code, Volume One* (Oxford, 1983), p. 36.
34. S. Szreter, 'The GRO and the Public Health Movement in Britain, 1837–1914', *Social History of Medicine* 4 (1991), pp. 435–63.
35. A. Ransome and W. Royston, *Remarks on Some of the Numerical Tests of the Health of Towns* (Manchester, 1863), p. 4.
36. B. White, *A History of the Corporation of Liverpool, 1835–1914* (Liverpool, 1951), chs. 4 and 5.
37. A. Ransome, 'On the Vital Statistics of Towns', *Transactions of the Manchester Statistical Society* (Mar., 1888), p. 90.
38. W. Dawbarn, *Letters Addressed to the Mayor, John Grant Morris Esq., on the Sanitary Condition of Liverpool* (Liverpool, 1867), pp. 1–2.
39. *Ibid.*, p. 3.
40. M. Poovey, *A History of the Modern Fact: Problems of Knowledge in the Sciences of Wealth and Society* (Chicago, 1999), pp. 309–13.
41. [G. Robertson], 'Exclusion of Opinion', *The London and Westminster Review* 7 (1838), pp. 68–9.
42. *Ibid.*, p. 68.
43. *Ibid.*, p. 70.
44. T. Carlyle, 'Chartism' [1839], in A. Shelston (ed.), *Thomas Carlyle: Selected Writings* (London, 1986), pp. 157, 159–60.
45. C. Dickens, 'Report of the First Meeting of the Mudfog Association', *Bentley's Miscellany* 2 (1837), pp. 409–11.
46. C. Dickens, *Hard Times* [1854] (London, 1995), pp. 9–10.
47. Quoted in an excerpt from *The Lancet* dated 7 Nov. 1857, in T. Fisher (ed.), *Prostitution and the Victorians* (Stroud, 1997), p. 70.
48. Frankel, 'Blue Books and the Victorian Reader', p. 316.
49. The letter appears in *Health of Towns' Bill: The Opinion of the Public Journals, Part One* (London, 1848), p. 32.
50. *Report of a Committee of the Manchester Statistical Society, on the State of Education in the Borough of Liverpool in 1835–1836* (London, 1836), pp. 4–5.
51. Revd C.S. Collingwood, *Some of the Religious and Moral Aspects of the Contagious Diseases Acts* (London, 1871), p. 13.

52. S. Amos, *The Present State of the Contagious Diseases Acts Controversy* (London, 1870), pp. 7–8.

53. J. Bright, *The Contagious Diseases Acts: Speech of Jacob Bright, Esq., MP* (Manchester, 1870), p. 5.

54. See, for example, W. Fowler, *Speech of William Fowler, Esq., M. P., in the House of Commons on May 24th, 1870, on the Contagious Diseases Acts* (London, 1870); D. McLaren, *Facts Respecting the Contagious Diseases Act: Substance of a Speech by Duncan McLaren, Esq., M. P.* (Manchester, 1870); Managers of Metropolitan Female Reformatories, *An Exposure of the False Statistics of the Contagious Diseases Acts (Women)* (London, 1873).

55. J. Stansfeld, 'On the Validity of the Annual Government Statistics of the Operation of the Contagious Diseases Acts', *JSSL* 39 (1876), pp. 540–72.

56. *Ibid.*, pp. 564, 572.

57. J. Stansfeld, *Repeal of the Contagious Diseases Acts Relating to Women: Speech by the Rt. Hon. J. Stansfeld M.P.* (London, 1883), p. 5.

58. T.M. Porter, 'Statistical Utopianism in an Age of Aristocratic Efficiency', *Osiris* 17 (2002), pp. 210–27.

59. www.rss.org.uk/Docs/Building trust on shaky foundations.doc. Accessed 2 Nov. 2009.

10 Numbers, Character and Trust in Early Victorian Britain

The Independent West Middlesex Fire and Life Assurance Company Fraud

James Taylor

In 1836, William Hole and Thomas Knowles, two friends from Kent, decided to set up an insurance company. They teamed up with George Williams, a solicitor, and James Hustler, a physician, and together they formed the Independent West Middlesex Fire and Life Assurance Company (IWM). The firm rented plush office space on Baker Street in London's West End, and in January 1837 it began advertising for customers in an aggressive publicity campaign, taking out space in many leading newspapers, from *The Times* to the *Morning Chronicle* in London and the *Scotsman* and the *Glasgow Herald* north of the border.[1] It also advertised extensively in the radical press, in titles like the *Northern Star* and the *Charter*. It promoted itself as a people's champion, offering 'IMMEDIATE BENEFITS' and 'DEEDS, not WORDS' to the public. It proclaimed its independence from 'any of the combined monopolising companies' in the insurance business who were all overcharging the public. It had a large capital of £1 million, and its life and fire insurance rates were apparently based on 'equitable principles', undercutting other firms by 30 percent.[2]

The company's business grew through 1837 and 1838, but in March 1839 an obscure weekly Glasgow newspaper, the *Scotch Reformers' Gazette*, owned and edited by Peter Mackenzie, published an article accusing the firm of being a '*fictitious* Insurance Company', run by a 'parcel of swindlers'.[3] The exposure caused a stir in Glasgow: hundreds wrote to Mackenzie seeking more information; the company's Glasgow office was besieged by investors demanding to know the truth.[4] The company robustly denied the accusations of the *Gazette*, dismissing them as the result of the 'envy' of the company's rivals, and eventually taking out libel actions against Mackenzie. These legal cases rumbled on through 1839 and 1840, during which time the company continued to do business, albeit on a diminishing scale. They began contesting fire and life insurance claims, which added to the suspicion.[5] But customers who stopped by the company's London office at Christmas 1840 were surprised to find it closed, with no sign of the directors or clerks. It soon transpired that Knowles and his colleagues had stripped the offices bare, and absconded to the Continent.[6]

The collapse was a major news story over the following months. Mackenzie wrote to Sir Peter Laurie, chief magistrate of the City of London, urging him to act. Though the company, based as it was in Middlesex rather than the City, was outside of Laurie's jurisdiction, he invited those who had information on the case, including some of the victims, to the Mansion House courtroom to give evidence and thus to publicize the fraud. Through Laurie's interviews with victims and other witnesses, details gradually emerged. Hole and Knowles were emphatically *not* gentlemen. They both had colourful pasts, holding a variety of positions, ranging from shopkeepers, shoemakers, footmen, house agents, and (in some accounts) smugglers, and had both been declared bankrupt more than once. By the time Hole came to establish the IWM he had gained a couple of properties from his time as a house agent, but was hardly well off. Their friends Hustler and Williams were in similar positions: the former was 'a poverty-stricken apothecary', who had ended up in the King's Bench prison 'in a state of utter destitution', where he was known as 'Poor Jemmy'.[7] The company did not have any capital to speak of, certainly not the £1 million advertised, for it had no shareholders; the majority of the directors listed in company advertisements did not exist, but bore the same names as well-known businessmen in the capital. Before the company failed, it had succeeded in taking somewhere between £160,000 and £240,000 from its customers, in annuities and in life and fire insurance premiums. Although it had paid out on some claims, at least initially, and had operated fire engines in some parts of the country, much of this revenue had been abstracted by Hole and his colleagues, and spent on carriages, horses, servants, fine wine, concerts, and properties in London.[8]

The case of the IWM gives an insight into many aspects of the relationship between numbers, character, and trust in early Victorian Britain. What made the fraud possible was the growing enthusiasm for the joint-stock company. Whereas this form of business organization had existed for centuries, it was the nineteenth century that saw the company become a fixture of the British economy, from railways to steamships, from cemeteries to banks. In 1843, one contemporary calculated that the capital invested in companies quoted on the London Stock Exchange totalled over £210 million.[9] The rapid extension of the joint-stock company in this period led to new processes of trust formation. Given the scale of company operations, it was unlikely that investors would enjoy direct knowledge of, or contact with, boards of directors. Reputation and appearance were thus crucial to a company's success. Directors needed to project an image of trustworthiness to reassure investors that their money was safe, but undermining these efforts was a longstanding suspicion of this form of enterprise, fuelled by frequent scandals—such as the South Sea 'Bubble' of 1720—which exposed directorial negligence or worse.[10] Increasingly, therefore, mechanisms were developed to foster trust between directors, shareholders, and customers: publication of balance sheets; audit of accounts, first by amateurs, then by paid professionals; and the development of a financial press to scrutinize the goings-on in the City. Such mechanisms were the product of a faith in the power of numbers to express the soundness or otherwise of a company: a belief in the superiority of numbers to traditional sources of trust. As a result, the rise of the joint-stock company is associated with the development of recognizably modern business practices.

However, it is only through case studies that we can examine in detail how the public actually formed trust in the companies they chose to invest in. This was an environment in which investment opportunities were rapidly multiplying, along with the supplies of information, reliable or otherwise, about these opportunities. How the public operated in the face of these exciting and bewildering circumstances is still imperfectly understood by historians, with too much emphasis placed on the contemporary—and seductive—rhetoric of speculative 'manias'. More recently, Mary Poovey has surveyed the vast range of literature which aimed to make the nineteenth-century financial system intelligible to the public.[11] But much more needs to be done to explore how people actually used such types of information, alongside others, in order to form trust in companies.

In the nineteenth century, newer sources of trust, particularly statistical data, came to rival traditional sources of trust, such as character and reputation. The case of the IWM suggests that decisions to invest were made on the basis of a fusion of old and new forms of trust, but with the old very much dominant. The company lured investors with cut-price rates. Trust in these rates was generated by questioning the motives of the company's rivals who charged higher rates, and, most importantly, by reassuring the public that the company's directors were gentlemen: affluent, solid, and respectable. The scandal generated by the fraud is particularly interesting because, by exposing the unreliability of traditional sources of trust, it prompted the state to intervene by attempting to improve access to objective information, particularly statistical data, on companies. The chapter ends by examining the reasons for the limited effectiveness of these reforms.

NUMBERS, CHARACTER, AND COMPANIES

In the months after the fraud, the plight of the victims was covered extensively in the press. Those who had insured property or lives lost their premiums, but the biggest sufferers were those who had plunged all their savings into the company to buy annuities, and who lost everything. The owner of the company's Baker Street premises witnessed 'heartrending' scenes as annuitants flocked in large numbers to try to find out what had happened to their money.[12] These included a laundress who had scraped together £400 with the help of friends and invested it in the company, and who was now 'in a state bordering upon madness', and a gentleman representing a man in Limerick, who had invested £700 and had 'attempted self-destruction' as a result of the loss of the money. The landlord decided that he would shut up the premises, as he could not endure such desperate scenes of distress.[13] Reports of annuitants who had ended up in the workhouse or had died of 'broken hearts' were rife.[14] Even a generation later, the devastation caused by the collapse was vividly remembered: 'If the disappointment and ruin which this one fraudulent scheme occasioned could be truly depicted, there is nothing in the realms of fiction which could equal it', wrote one barrister in 1867.[15]

Contemporary characterizations of the victims were often shot through with moral censure, however. They were frequently presented as greedy fools who, blinded by the prospect of great savings, failed to spot what should have been obvious, that this was a fraudulent company. According to one observer the case confirmed the old saying 'that there is no end to the gullibility of mankind.'[16] Another concluded that there was 'always a large ignorant class ready and willing to be duped'.[17] According to most commentators, sufficient evidence had existed for any potential investor to judge the company unsafe. Most fundamentally, the company's numbers did not add up. It was 'a mathematical impossibility' that the company could survive at these rates, when hitherto the greatest variation between rates offered had been 1.5 percent.[18] The 'first thing which attracted suspicion was the low rate at which the company undertook to transact business'.[19] The 'rate of benefit which they offered was so extravagantly high, as of itself to excite great suspicion . . . persons who were conversant with such matters said that it was impossible to grant such rates with safety.'[20] Laurie, though responsible for drawing attention to the fraud by giving its victims a public platform, expressed contempt for those who failed to realize that the company promised unrealistic rates of interest. Referring to the many Scottish victims of the swindle, he thought it 'very odd that the Scotch, who generally saw their way pretty clearly where money was concerned, were, in regard to the West Middlesex Company, very blind.'[21] He argued that 'caution enough was not exercised by those who embarked their money in this speculation, and who ought to have known that so large an interest could not have been afforded by any *bona fide* concern.'[22]

Even if they had not suspected the figures, the argument continued, investors should have looked more carefully at the men behind the company before entrusting their money. They would have learned that they were not established men of business, but rogues, and would have avoided disaster. The arguments used underline Margot Finn's claim that, by the Victorian period, 'the idea of character pervaded English society and culture', underpinning the credit economy and constituting 'an essential form of social capital'.[23] *Bell's Life* thought the case 'ought to impress on the public, and especially those in distant parts of the kingdom, the necessity of strict enquiry into the nature and credit of these offices before they risk perhaps their little all'.[24] '[T]he public should look well to the true character' of the office before they entrusted their cash, urged the *Satirist*: 'again—and yet again—we emphatically warn all people to beware, and to make due, and full, and scrupulous inquiry before they select.'[25] Laurie argued that: 'When one company held out very superior advantages to others, the public ought to make particular inquiry into the character of the promoters, of their wealth, and the length of time they had borne a good reputation.'[26]

However, Laurie, as a member of the metropolitan elite, did not have to make such an inquiry—he had long known all about the company. He told the Commons select committee established in 1841 to investigate the fraud that 'there was not a man *living in my neighbourhood* who did not know the character of this company . . . we all knew that those names were not names of men that had any existence; I had known that ever since it was established'.[27] But what about those not fortunate enough to live in Laurie's neighbourhood: the uninformed investing public, especially those outside the capital, and therefore not privy to city gossip? Did they stand a chance of finding out the truth about the company?

SELLING INSURANCE

The central problem facing the life insurance societies that began to form at the end of the seventeenth century was how to minimize risk in an era when the nature of commerce was rapidly changing. With face-to-face dealings becoming rarer, 'a commanding knowledge of personal reputations was virtually impossible'.[28] Historians have documented the ways in which companies, beginning with the Equitable Assurance in 1762, sought to manage risk by applying probability theory to mortality records, and by carefully appraising their customers so as to insure only 'select lives'.[29] Much less has been written on the flow of trust in the opposite direction, on how customers managed risk by assessing the solidity of the companies which competed for their money. The difficulties they faced by the 1830s were immense. In the eighteenth century, the insurance industry was in its infancy, and life insurance in particular was viewed as a form of gambling. As a result, the number of life assurance companies was small—there were only six by 1800—but they gradually managed to build a reputation for stability and trustworthiness, partly through their adoption of statistics and calculation.[30] However, in the early nineteenth century, the large profits made in the sector attracted rivals, some of them rather speculative, so that by the middle of the century there were around 150 such companies.[31] This rendered the insurance market a perilous environment: in the financial crisis of 1825–26, five insurance companies collapsed; by 1840 a further ten had failed.[32] In fire insurance too, failures were initially rare, but became more common from the late 1820s.[33]

With insurance a relative novelty, it has been noted that 'by the early nineteenth century there remained much ignorance about the purpose and nature of insurance'.[34] This ignorance was complemented by a lack of knowledge about the financial world in general. It was very difficult for investors who did not have access to privileged information to penetrate the mystery shrouding City finance and to distinguish the good companies from the bad. The press represented one of the chief sources of information for such investors, but as Poovey has stressed, financial reporting was still in its infancy, with the *Morning Chronicle* the first newspaper to publish a daily financial column in 1821, and *The Times* following suit in 1825.[35]

Just as important as editorial comment were the countless advertisements for companies carried by newspapers, which formed an integral element of the promotional strategy of most insurance companies.[36] Readers were likely to linger over the advertisements for insurance companies in particular because in the second quarter of the century they were being subjected to an increasing tide of propaganda urging them to take out life insurance policies. In 1839, *Chambers' Edinburgh Journal* was disappointed to find that only 80,000 individuals had insured their lives, estimating that as a result, just one in sixty-two families was protected by life insurance. Only when he had insured his life, the journal claimed, could a man be 'said to do the whole of his duty towards his family, instead of, as is generally the case, only doing the half of it'.[37] Around the same time, the *Church of England Magazine* highlighted the plight of widows and orphans, calling upon every father to bear in mind 'that he is imperatively called upon, on every principle of Christianity as well as of common humanity, to make as ample a provision as he can' for those he would leave behind.[38] The press carried short tales dramatizing the perils of delay: in one such story, Mark Willoughby thought there was 'no hurry' to insure his life, and was always telling his wife he would 'think about it'. Eventually, he dies of apoplexy after dining at a city feast, leaving his family unprovided for: 'He never did insure his life . . . he only "thought about it".'[39]

Such propaganda stimulated demand for insurance; the main obstacle was that life insurance was not cheap, and this lay behind many people's reluctance to invest. The high cost of insurance was largely a result of the reliance of the early companies on inaccurate mortality tables which seriously underestimated the life expectancy of the kinds of people who bought policies, thus inflating premium rates and company profits.[40] The most influential of these was Equitable Life's 'Northampton tables', and despite growing numbers of entrants to the industry in the early nineteenth century, most of the new companies followed the lead of these tables, which 'set the general level of British Whole-Life premium rates until the 1860s'.[41]

Any competition which did exist tended to revolve around the reversionary bonuses granted to policyholders every five or seven years.[42] High rates were regarded as a badge of respectability and stability. In 1841, the actuary of the Atlas Assurance Company claimed that in the twenty years he had held that post, there had been no material alteration in the rates charged by the company.[43] This, he stressed, was typical of the sector as a whole: 'A great number of them, among the leading companies especially, charge identically the same [rates], and others very nearly so.'[44]

As a result, the social base of the early companies' policyholders was very restricted.[45] Conditions were therefore favourable for the entry of new firms willing to undercut the old ones, and the IWM was just one of a new wave of companies in the 1830s offering lower rates and thus seemingly democratizing access to insurance. Readers of the *Examiner* in 1834 would have seen an advertisement from the Promoter Life Assurance and Annuity Company stating that its premiums were 'lower than any offered to the Public', and immediately below this, one from the Argus Life Assurance Company which promised 'Lower Rates of Premium than in any other Office'.[46] The Britannia Life Assurance Company, formed in 1837, promised a 'most economic set of Tables . . . presenting lower rates of premium than any hitherto offered'.[47] The IWM's advertisements raised the stakes still further, offering 'Fire and life insurance rates reduced 30 percent per annum, being a saving to the public of £500,000 per annum.'[48] The adverts used numbers in devious ways to generate trust. The nominal capital of the IWM—£1 million—was larger than many of its rival companies, and was set at a level designed to represent solidity and inspire trust. The power of this figure was enormous: Laurie pointed out to the subsequent select committee that 'when a poor widow looks at the sum of £1,000,000, she thinks she must be very safe'.[49] The share denomination—£50—was fixed at a rate which suggested the respectability of the concern. The value of the shares was widely thought to determine a firm's 'character': if they were set too low, labourers and servants would buy shares, to the detriment of the company's reputation and soundness.[50]

The advertisements also prominently displayed tables of insurance premiums and interest paid on annuities, inviting readers to calculate the costs and returns of investing. The adverts skilfully interwove the moral case for insurance and the economic sense in choosing the IWM. Men were appealed to as husbands and fathers with the company highlighting 'the melancholy fact, that last year, in England, TWENTY THOUSAND WIDOWS, and upwards of ONE HUNDRED THOUSAND ORPHANS, were reduced from a state of comparative ease and comfort to ruin, want, and misery'. But such a calamity was easily averted, because 'a man thirty-four years of age may secure for his wife, or any branch of his family, the sum of FIVE HUNDRED POUNDS, payable at his death, by the annual payment of 10*l*'.[51]

The response to the new companies was mixed, with their promises generating alarm in some quarters. Whereas economic theory dictated that 'competition will ensure good management', the anonymous author of a pamphlet published in 1837 on life assurance and banking companies argued that competition could be 'carried to excess', with managers induced 'to undertake more than they can perform' by the hunt for customers.[52] In 1838, the *Spectator* warned anyone thinking of insurance against trusting 'any of these newly-established societies, until he has satisfied himself not only of the soundness of the principles which they profess to act upon, but also of the prudence with which their business is conducted'. It acknowledged that economies could be made, but there were still grounds for 'suspicion that the premiums asked by some of the new companies are too low'.[53]

In 1839, the IWM began to be mentioned by name, as in the series of articles in the *Scotch Reformers' Gazette*. The accusations were followed up in the *Town*, a semi-pornographic newspaper established by the controversial figure Renton Nicholson, though the mainstream press generally refrained from commenting.[54] An exception was the *Quarterly Review*, which dedicated a lengthy article to what it saw as an increasingly dangerous market for life insurance at the end of 1839. While not accusing the company of fraud, it singled out the IWM for particular criticism, reprinting 'its oft-repeated and almost daily notice in the newspapers', and subjecting its figures to a minute and contemptuous dissection. It pointed out that, with the rates offered, a thirty-four-year-old customer could, for £100, buy an annuity paying £8 per annum, and insure his life for £100 at an annual premium of £2, receiving a guaranteed £6 per annum. 'Can this', the *Review* asked, 'deceive any one with comprehension beyond that of an idiot?'[55] The same month, Barber Beaumont, founder and resident director of the County Fire Office, and magistrate for Middlesex and Westminster, wrote a cautionary letter, and with an obvious nod to the slogan of the IWM, advised investors to make careful inquiries 'before they throw their dependence into the hands of strangers, who look only to their own "immediate benefits" '.[56]

What effect did this very public questioning of the viability of the IWM have? Some heeded the cautions and took their money elsewhere. Beaumont received 'numerous letters of thanks' after his warning letters 'from parties who had been preserved from ruin by his timely caution'.[57] Mackenzie, of the *Scotch Reformers' Gazette*, also claimed that his warnings saved many from the clutches of the IWM.[58] While it seems that the company's business was quite badly affected in Scotland, the company kept trading through until late 1840. The sums they enrolled for annuities received even rose from £39,000 in 1838 to £43,000 in 1839, though they did fall to £14,000 in 1840.[59] It is clear that despite the rumours and denunciations, the company could still find many willing customers.

SIMULATING GENTILITY

Although it is tempting to view these customers as fools who would not help themselves, we should take into account the variety of powerful techniques used by the IWM to reassure the public, enabling it to carry on the fraud for several years. Criticisms of its numbers were countered by endorsements inserted into newspaper editorials or 'answers to correspondents' columns. These endorsements, known as 'puffs', carried more weight than simple advertisements, as they had the appearance of objectivity, even though they were usually paid for by the company in question.[60] Puffs for the IWM appeared in several journals in which the company advertised extensively, including the *Farmers' Journal*, the *Satirist*, and *Freeman's Journal and Daily Commercial Advertiser*. These dismissed doubts cast on the affordability of the annuities paid as sour grapes from the company's competitors. They gave the 'unbiased opinion' that the company was 'a most valuable institution', which deserved 'to be patronized by the public at large'.[61] It was based on 'sound principle[s]', and was able to offer lower rates because of the 'rigid economy' with which its affairs were conducted.[62]

The company was able to discredit criticisms of its numbers by using its advertisements to project an image of gentility. The company's numbers could be trusted because the men who calculated them were respectable and wealthy businessmen. Hole and Knowles 'concoct[ed] a directory of gentlemen' and reproduced this list in most of the company's advertisements. It contained the names of wealthy metropolitan businessmen: 'there was scarcely a banker, a brewer, or a merchant whose patronymic, with different initials, was not used by these ex-smugglers to forward their views. Drummonds, Perkins, Smith, Price, and Lloyd were all produced as fancy directors'.[63] The perceived gentility of these names was crucial in engendering trust: one victim subsequently noted that after seeing several 'distinguished personages in the list of the patrons and supporters of the society, he did not hesitate to purchase an annuity'.[64]

In addition, Knowles and Hole managed appearances very carefully at the London head office on Baker Street. These premises were 'very good': a parliamentary agent later commented that 'if I had had no suspicion, I should have taken the company to be respectable, from the appearance of the office'.[65] The porter in the entrance hall 'was dressed as if he had been the Lord Mayor's state attender'.[66] Hole and Knowles dressed up their friends and relatives as directors to be seen by customers on board days. Hole's brother-in-law, Edward Taylor, who was a bellhanger, came over every Friday afternoon to sign policies, and was told to wear his Sunday best with a brooch on his shirt and rings on his fingers—he was fined if he forgot any of this apparatus, or if he turned up drunk. To entrench the illusion of solidity, the directors lived extravagantly. They 'kept carriage-horses and saddle-horses; servants in gorgeous liveries waited on them; they fared ... sumptuously every day'.[67] Hole, who lived at the offices, 'gave large evening parties, and collected some of the most respectable people in the neighbourhood to visit him; he had parties of 100 people, musical parties and dancing'.[68] Money bought the company 'all the outward show of respectability ... all the appearance of rank'.[69]

Given the trustworthy appearance thus manufactured, criticisms appearing in the press were not likely to be automatically accepted as fact. Instead, investors put the claims to the directors, who, as gentlemen, were given the opportunity to deny them. That some of the exposures appeared in newspapers of dubious repute made it easier for the directors to discredit them. An anonymous 'elderly gentleman, who had been a Vice-Consul in a foreign country', purchased an IWM annuity and 'placed the greatest confidence in the company till in 1840 he by accident took up a paper called the *Town*, and in its pages beheld the most frightful exhibition of the directors'. The annuity holder went to see George Edward Williams junior, son of one of the directors, who was able to successfully discredit the source of the allegations. He claimed that Nicholson, the proprietor of the *Town*, had tried to extort £100 from the directors in return for withdrawing the story, but they had refused. Williams also mentioned (truthfully) that Nicholson had recently been in prison for twelve months, casting further doubt on the credibility of his reports.[70] Though the *Scotch Reformers' Gazette* was a more respectable source, the company could also successfully cast doubt on its accusations. H.B. Walker, a policyholder in Kent, had been sent a cutting from the Glasgow paper, and wrote to the company in some distress. Williams replied, with reassurances which obviously had the desired effect: the customer wrote back in October 1840 wishing the office 'every success in their prosecution of the Editor', and stating that he had paid his half-year's premium.[71]

Of course, investors were not dependent solely on the reassurances of the company's board: they could also rely on local business networks, asking the opinion of bankers, solicitors, and insurance agents, as well as business associates, family members and friends. But these did not always help in getting at the truth. A Mr Wallace, who had bought an annuity for his niece for £500, claimed that he had made 'what is considered every necessary inquiry. I consulted a solicitor and a broker, and I heard that the parties mentioned in the list of directors were highly respectable. I entertained not the slightest doubt of the solvency and good character of the company'. Just before it closed its doors, he had met Knowles face-to-face and decided to invest more in the company, 'having heard so high a character of the company' and learning nothing from the experts to change his opinion.[72]

Another source of information was the local agent—often a solicitor—who transacted business for metropolitan insurance companies outside London. But this was also a flawed source, because the agents were not impartial advisers. The practice was controversial, with the author of one book on actuarial techniques published in 1810 condemning the commission that agents were paid as a form of bribery: it was in their interests to drum up as much business for their company as possible, regardless of whether this was in the interests of their clients.[73] As a result, a small number of companies, including the largest—the Equitable—eschewed agents, instead dealing with all premiums directly at head office. However, as Robin Pearson has suggested, an agent 'with the right social and business connections was regarded as indispensable' by most firms, who were happy to pay the accepted commission of 5 percent on the business thus attracted.[74]

The IWM relied heavily on agents and offered unusually high rates of commission—up to 25 percent—to lure them into the service of the firm.[75]

As a result, the company seems to have had little trouble attracting respectable agents into its service. Laurie told the select committee in 1841 that the company had agents in, among others, 'Hull, Bath, Glastonbury, Chester, Oswestry, Bristol, Nottingham, Exeter, Weymouth, Gloucester, Kidderminster, Dover, Waterford, Plymouth, Armagh, Newberry, Lancaster, Falkirk, Devon, Chelmsford, Edinburgh, Cheltenham.'[76] These agents were instrumental in the success of the fraud: as Laurie commented, 'giving the agents 25 percent was a great stimulus to them to say all they could in favour of this company'.[77] For most customers, the agents represented the public face of the company, and they played a major part both in attracting custom, and then keeping it. In early 1840, doubts were spreading through Exeter as to the stability of the company, but the agent wrote to a sceptical policyholder assuring him that all was well: 'I have been to London purposely to examine the affairs of this society, and I can assure you that the reports issued against them are wholly without foundation; the principal part of them are gentlemen living on their own property.' He went on to list the substantial assets held, which, he asserted, included £375,000 paid-up capital.[78]

POLICY, POLICYHOLDING, AND THE STATE

The IWM had a range of critics willing to cast doubt on the company's calculations. But without a reliable means of assessing such claims against the persuasive arguments presented by the IWM and its supporters, investors were likely to conclude that the company's rates were a bargain rather than a snare. The extreme vulnerability of investors that the case exposed, and the fear of similar frauds in the future, led to calls for legislative intervention. Accordingly, after much lobbying by backbenchers, and agitation in the press, Lord Melbourne's Whig government agreed in April 1841 to appoint a select committee which would 'inquire into the state of the law respecting joint-stock companies, with a view to the prevention of fraud'.[79] After interviewing half a dozen witnesses about the IWM case, and a handful of other companies which had failed in dubious circumstances around the same time, the committee lapsed, a victim of the demise of the Whig government, and lay moribund for two years until William Gladstone, then a crusading young president of the Board of Trade in Robert Peel's Conservative administration, decided to revive it. In its new incarnation, the committee interviewed many more witnesses, with a view to devising general rules making the joint-stock sector as a whole more stable.

Legislation followed in 1844 in the form of a Joint-Stock Companies Act, the centrepiece of which was a Joint-Stock Companies Registrar under the authority of the Board of Trade. The aim was to reduce the reliance placed by the public on the outward signifiers of gentility, which the IWM had manipulated so successfully, on to more objective and numerical methods of verifying the soundness and honesty of a business.

Improving the quality of information available to the public would create a community of informed investors. To this end, the main principle of the act was publicity. Henceforth, all companies would have to register their existence, sending to the registrar details of the company's business, its capital, the value of the shares, how much had been subscribed, the names of the shareholders and the shareholdings of each, and the names of the directors.[80] Companies would also have to make annual returns of balance sheets, and of auditors' reports on these balance sheets, to the registrar.[81] Any member of the public could visit the registry and inspect any of the returns, paying one shilling for each inspection, and sixpence for each folio sheet copied.[82] Legislators were infused with an idealistic faith in the power of publicity to protect the public—the report of the select committee argued that full disclosure of information about a company 'would baffle every case of fraud'.[83]

The legislators' faith in the power of publicity chimed with the wider intellectual climate of the time. Compulsory publicity, enforced by law, had been urged even before the smash as the cure for fraud. 'Fairness and open dealing are the true and wholesome sources of legitimate credit', wrote one anonymous author in 1837: firms which dreaded publicity and scrutiny must be 'rotten'.[84] Complementing compulsory publicity were publishing initiatives in the early 1840s, including volumes published under the auspices of the Society for the Diffusion of Useful Knowledge, which made annuity, mortality and life assurance tables available to the public, with the intention of allowing customers to judge for themselves the soundness of the claims made by insurance companies.[85] The author of one of these texts acknowledged that the 'abstract nature of the doctrine of probabilities', combined with the 'technical and scientific' terminology used in existing texts, had rendered the subject unintelligible to general readers, but still thought that the 'simple information required' by members of the public could be provided in an accessible format.

The power of the new legislation and the new sources of information to create an army of rational investors was limited, however. Although we can date the beginnings of the modern system of corporate regulation from the act of 1844, fraud was not checked. There was no mechanism for ensuring that the returns made to the registrar were genuine: the information held at the registry was no more reliable than that which could be found in newspapers and prospectuses.[86] By requiring the registration of balance sheets but not taking any steps to ensure these were accurate, the legislature was, in the view of the Assistant Companies' Registrar in 1850, actually *facilitating* fraud.[87] More generally, the process of registration added a gloss of authenticity to unsound companies, who could announce to the world that they were 'empowered by Act of Parliament'. The Board of Trade, rather than stamping out fraud, had been rendered, according to one critic, a 'convenient . . . vehicle for the operations of some of the greatest villains London can produce'.[88]

Undercutting the government's faith in numbers was a countercurrent of public scepticism. Some doubted the power of numbers contained in balance sheets to convey the truth, and the ability or willingness of amateur auditors to spot errors or frauds in these accounts. There was a deep-seated cynicism about even the most basic numbers issued by companies, nicely captured by Charles Dickens in *Martin Chuzzlewit*, written after the exposure of 1841. Readers are shown the process by which the rogue Montague Tigg establishes the fraudulent Anglo-Bengalee Disinterested Loan and Life Assurance Company, which echoes the formation of the IWM: he tells his secretary that the capital, according to the next prospectus, will be '[a] figure of two, and as many oughts after it as the printer can get into the same line.'[89] The extent to which the mysteries of insurance could be rendered transparent by objective data was doubted, even by those who called for such data. In 1839, the *Quarterly Review* had written that no author could 'serve society more essentially than by affording the public at large some distinct *data* for making a prudential choice among so many rival Insurance Offices'; yet in the same breath it admitted that 'the attempt would be extremely invidious; and we are sensible, moreover, that *we* could not, if we would, do the thing completely and satisfactorily'. So, whilst the article provided data to the reader in the form of a list of assurance offices arranged into four categories by date of formation, named 'experimental', 'probationary', 'salutary state' and 'general stability', it also noted that some newer companies might be very well conducted, and some older companies might not deserve patronage. This amounted to a disavowal of the relevance of numbers to forming trust and an affirmation of traditional sources of trust. Readers were told '[p]erhaps the safest general rule is, to look well at the list of directors', and to try to find 'men of known integrity, of aptitude for business . . . and of substantial property'.[90] Similar lessons were drawn by the *Scotsman* after the IWM's collapse:

> The soundness or unsoundness of an assurance company is a matter of which comparatively a small number are able to judge . . . Even where no fraud is contemplated, a slight inaccuracy in the construction of the tables may involve ultimate ruin, and no one but an experienced accountant, furnished with pretty extensive data, is qualified to judge on the matter.[91]

This conclusion was supported by the companies themselves. Industry insiders rejected the idea that the public could be rendered perfectly safe by the dissemination of data or the establishment of statistical laws: in the final analysis, they needed to trust in the gentlemen who ran the companies. Theodore Porter has highlighted how, at a parliamentary investigation into the insurance industry in the 1850s, '[t]he government sought a foundation for faith in numbers, while the actuaries demanded trust in their judgement as gentlemen and professionals.'[92]

CONCLUSION

In the preceding chapter, Tom Crook argues for the persistence of traditional forms of authority in the nineteenth-century public sphere, and the continuing importance of the figure of the gentleman.[93] This chapter has suggested that a similar situation pertained in the early Victorian financial market. At a time when the financial data available to the public were opaque, contested and ultimately unreliable, investment decisions rested upon perceptions of character, which themselves were easily manipulated. This was something that Dickens clearly understood. Take his description of the Anglo-Bengalee offices, 'resplendent in stucco and plate-glass':

> Within, the offices were newly plastered, newly painted, newly papered, newly countered, newly floor-clothed, newly tabled, newly chaired, newly fitted up in every way, with goods that were substantial and expensive, and designed (like the company) to last . . . Solidity! Look at the massive blocks of marble in the chimneypieces, and the gorgeous parapet on the top of the house! Publicity! Why, Anglo-Bengalee Disinterested Loan and Life Assurance company is painted on the very coal-scuttles.

This simulation of solidity and respectability was all that was needed to part investors from their cash: they will 'trust us as if we were the Mint', boasts Tigg.[94] The emergence of the impersonal joint-stock company, then, did not diminish the centrality of character in business. Investors relied on a synthesis of old and new forms of trust, but with the emphasis remaining on traditional mechanisms for building trust. They looked at the numbers presented by companies, but attempted to gauge the reliability of these numbers by evaluating the character of those who published them. Company strategies for encouraging trust therefore focused on proving the gentility and respectability of the directors.

The case of the IWM illustrates how the spread of the joint-stock company had made it easier to simulate gentility, but did not provide compensating mechanisms for detecting such simulations. This highlighted the need to develop superior methods of trust formation, a project enthusiastically embraced by the state in the 1840s. Yet the optimism of legislators faded in the face of frequent commercial scandals which seemed to prove the inability of parliament to ensure the dissemination of reliable numbers to investors.[95] Disillusion with numbers was a common refrain. *The Times* reflected that 'Balance-sheets are untrustworthy things. Even the Arabic numerals themselves have turned traitors, and lend themselves to most discreditable frauds.'[96] The failure of the act of 1844 was acknowledged with the passage of further legislation in 1856 and 1857 which retreated from the requirement to register balance sheets and auditors' reports.[97] The second half of the century saw renewed attempts to give investors alternatives to relying on the gentleman, the most important of which was the development of the accountancy profession and the innovation of the professional audit. However, these represented not so much a new science of numbers but a fusion of old and new forms of trust, suggesting the resilience of notions of character in business. After a series of banking scandals in 1856 and 1857, the *Observer* hoped that from now on, shareholders in all companies, 'no matter how high the standing of those undertakings', would insist on a full audit 'by professional accountants, whose standing, position, and character shall place them beyond all suspicion'.[98] In other words, rather than trusting in numbers, investors were being invited to trust in the character of the accountant. It may have been an improvement on trusting directors such as Hole and Knowles, but statistics could not be entirely divorced from the men who produced them.

NOTES

1. *Scotsman*, 4 Jan. 1837.
2. *The Times*, 22 June 1837; *The Times*, 1 Oct. 1838; *The Times*, 29 Dec. 1838.
3. *Scotch Reformers' Gazette*, 9 Mar. 1839. See also 2 Mar. and 30 Mar. 1839. It had a circulation of 2,300 in 1839: *Waterloo Directory of Scottish Newspapers and Periodicals, 1800–1900* (2 vols., Waterloo, 1989), II, p. 1119.
4. *Scotch Reformers' Gazette*, 9 Mar. 1839.
5. P. Mackenzie, *Reminiscences of Glasgow and the West of Scotland* (Glasgow, 1866), p. 601; D. Pugsley, 'Sham Insurance Companies: Dickens, Thackeray and the West Middlesex Company in Devon, 1837–1841', *Devonshire Association Report and Transactions* 123 (1991), pp. 149–65.
6. *Bristol Mercury*, 23 Jan. 1841; *The Times*, 19 Feb. 1841.
7. *Town*, 30 Jan. 1841, reprinted in J.L. Bradley (ed.), *Rogue's Progress: The Autobiography of 'Lord Chief Baron' Nicholson* (London, 1966), p. 232.
8. For more on the company's legitimate fire operations in Devon, see Pugsley, 'Sham Insurance Companies'.
9. R. Harris, *Industrializing English Law: Entrepreneurship and Business Organization, 1720–1844* (Cambridge, 2000), p. 222.
10. For a detailed discussion of traditional antipathy to joint-stock enterprise, see J. Taylor, *Creating Capitalism: Joint-Stock Enterprise in British Politics and Culture, 1800–1870* (Woodbridge, 2006), part I.
11. M. Poovey (ed.), *The Financial System in Nineteenth-Century Britain* (Oxford, 2003).
12. *The Times*, 28 Jan. 1841.
13. *The Times*, 19 Feb. 1841.
14. *Scotsman*, 24 Feb. 1841; *The Times*, 18 Mar. 1841.
15. C. Walford, *The Insurance Guide and Hand Book* (London, 1867), p. 49.
16. *Trewman's Exeter Flying Post*, 3 Feb. 1841.
17. J. Francis, *Annals, Anecdotes and Legends: A Chronicle of Life Assurance* (London, 1853), p. 229.
18. *Ibid.*, pp. 228, 241.
19. *Bristol Mercury*, 23 Jan. 1841.
20. *Select Committee to Inquire into the State of the Laws Respecting Joint Stock Companies*, Parliamentary Papers 1844, VII, pp. 71–2.
21. *The Times*, 19 Feb. 1841.

22. *The Times*, 31 May 1841.
23. M. Finn, *The Character of Credit: Personal Debt in English Culture, 1740–1914* (Cambridge, 2003), p. 20. For the importance of trust in an earlier period, see C. Muldrew, *The Economy of Obligation: The Culture of Credit and Social Relations in Early Modern England* (Basingstoke, 1998).
24. *Bell's Life in London and Sporting Chronicle*, 24 Jan. 1841.
25. *Satirist*, 14 June 1846.
26. *The Times*, 28 July 1842.
27. *Select Committee on Joint Stock Companies*, p. 5. Emphasis added.
28. R. Pearson, 'Moral Hazard and the Assessment of Insurance Risk in Eighteenth- and Early Nineteenth-Century Britain', *Business History Review* 76 (2002), p. 7.
29. Pearson, 'Moral Hazard'; T.M. Porter, 'Precision and Trust: Early Victorian Insurance and the Politics of Calculation', in M.N. Wise (ed.), *The Values of Precision* (Princeton, NJ, 1995), pp. 173–97; G. Clark, *Betting on Lives: The Culture of Life Insurance in England, 1695–1775* (Manchester, 1999).
30. R. Pearson, 'Thrift or Dissipation? The Business of Life Assurance in the Early Nineteenth Century', *Economic History Review* 43 (1990), p. 237; Porter, 'Precision and Trust', p. 174.
31. In approximately the same period, the sums insured by these companies increased from £10 million to £150 million. Pearson, 'Thrift or Dissipation', p. 237.
32. R. Ryan, 'The Early Expansion of the Norwich Union Life Insurance Society, 1808–37', *Business History* 27 (1985), p. 172.
33. Pearson, 'Moral Hazard', pp. 13–14; Ryan, 'Norwich Union', pp. 170–1.
34. R. Pearson, *Insuring the Industrial Revolution: Fire Insurance in Great Britain, 1700–1850* (Aldershot, 2004), p. 264.
35. Poovey, *Financial System*, p. 28. The public had to wait till 1843 for *The Economist*, a weekly paper dedicated to business affairs.
36. Pearson, *Insuring the Industrial Revolution*, p. 264.
37. *Chambers' Edinburgh Journal*, 23 Mar. 1839, reprinted in *Newcastle Courant*, 10 May 1839.
38. *Church of England Magazine*, reprinted in *Derby Mercury*, 20 Dec. 1837. See also *Age*, 8 Sept. 1839.
39. *Sunbeam*, reprinted in *Derby Mercury*, 13 June 1838.
40. Pearson, 'Moral Hazard', pp. 13–14; Ryan, 'Norwich Union', pp. 170–1; I. Hacking, *The Taming of Chance* (Cambridge, 1990), p. 49.
41. Ryan, 'Norwich Union', p. 171.
42. *Ibid.*, p. 172.
43. *Select Committee on Joint Stock Companies*, p. 46.
44. C. Ansell, *Select Committee on Joint Stock Companies*, p. 50.
45. Pearson, 'Thrift or Dissipation'.
46. *Examiner*, 19 Jan. 1834.
47. Though the company did note that there were 'two exceptions' to this claim: Brighton Patriot and South of England Free Press, 12 Sept. 1837.
48. *London Dispatch and People's Political and Social Reformer*, 3 June 1838.
49. *Select Committee on Joint Stock Companies*, p. 8. For more on popular numeracy, see J. Thompson, 'Printed Statistics and the Public Sphere: Numeracy, Electoral Politics and the Visual Culture of Numbers, 1880–1914', in this volume.
50. J.B. Jefferys, 'The Denomination and Character of Shares, 1855–1885', *Economic History Review* 16 (1946), pp. 45–55; M. Freeman, R. Pearson and J. Taylor, *Shareholder Democracies? Corporate Governance in Britain before 1850* (Chicago, 2011, forthcoming).

51. *London Dispatch and People's Political and Social Reformer*, 3 June 1838.
52. Anon., *Thoughts on the Means of Preventing Abuses in Life Assurance Offices and Joint Stock Banks* (Norwich, 1837), pp. 6–7.
53. *Spectator*, reprinted in *Hampshire Telegraph and Sussex Chronicle*, 1 Oct. 1838.
54. Bradley, *Rogue's Progress*, pp. 230–9.
55. Anon., 'On Life Assurance', *Quarterly Review* 64 (1839), p. 292.
56. *Morning Chronicle*, 5 Oct. 1839. He had written anonymously earlier in the year: *Morning Chronicle*, 25 Mar. 1839.
57. J.A. Beaumont, *Thoughts and Details on Life Insurance Offices* (London, 1842), p. 29.
58. Mackenzie, *Reminiscences of Glasgow*, p. 607.
59. Laurie argued that these figures were unreliable, as the sums the company actually received were greater than the amounts they declared at the Enrolment Office: *Select Committee on Joint Stock Companies*, p. 5.
60. For more on puffs, see T. Nevett, 'Advertising and Editorial Integrity in the Nineteenth Century', in M. Harris and A. Lee (eds.), *The Press in English Society from the Seventeenth to Nineteenth Centuries* (Rutherford, NJ, 1986), pp. 149–67.
61. *Farmers' Journal*, 6 Apr. 1840. The puff was reproduced verbatim in *Freeman's Journal and Daily Commercial Advertiser*, 8 May 1840.
62. *Satirist*, 3 May 1840.
63. Francis, *Annals, Anecdotes and Legends*, pp. 226–7.
64. *The Times*, 31 May 1841.
65. J. Connell, *Select Committee on Joint Stock Companies*, p. 72. The importance of the physical presence of insurance company offices is discussed in L. McFall and F. Dodsworth, 'Fabricating the Market: The Promotion of Life Assurance in the Long Nineteenth-Century', *Journal of Historical Sociology* 22 (2009), pp. 30–54.
66. Mackenzie, *Reminiscences of Glasgow*, p. 599.
67. Francis, *Annals, Anecdotes and Legends*, p. 231.
68. T. Farquhar, *Select Committee on Joint Stock Companies*, p. 86.
69. *Ibid.*, p. 37.
70. *The Times*, 31 May 1841.
71. This was printed, gloatingly, by the *Scotch Reformers' Gazette*, 6 Feb. 1841.
72. *The Times*, 27 May 1841.
73. Ryan, 'Norwich Union', p. 173. Another, Augustus de Morgan, condemned the system as one of '*bribery and corruption*': cited in Anon., 'On Life Assurance', p. 303.
74. Pearson, 'Thrift or Dissipation', p. 239; Francis, *Annals, Anecdotes and Legends*, p. 229.
75. The agent system was extensively deployed in other fields, such as emigration to the colonies. For a case study of the New Zealand Company and its agents, which stresses the importance of advertising, see P. Hudson, 'English Emigration to New Zealand, 1839–1850: Information Diffusion and Marketing a New World', *Economic History Review* 54 (2001), pp. 680–98.
76. *Select Committee on Joint Stock Companies*, p. 6.
77. *Ibid.*, p. 5.
78. *Ibid.*, p. 5.
79. H. Labouchere, *Hansard's Parliamentary Debates* 57, c. 842 (2 Apr. 1841).
80. 7 & 8 Vict. c. 110, art. 7.
81. 7 & 8 Vict. c. 110, art. 43. Auditors were typically shareholders elected at the general meeting.

82. 7 & 8 Vict. c. 110, art. 18.

83. *Select Committee on Joint Stock Companies*, First Report, p. v.

84. Anon., *Means of Preventing Abuses*, p. 14.

85. L. Pocock, *A Familiar Explanation of the Nature, Advantages, and Importance of Assurances upon Lives* (London, 1842); D. Jones, *On the Value of Annuities and Reversionary Payments* (2 vols., London, 1843–4); E. Baylis, *The Arithmetic of Annuities and Life Assurance or Compound Interest Simplified* (London, 1844).

86. Taylor, *Creating Capitalism*, p. 170.

87. *Ibid.*, p. 147.

88. The words are J. Hooper Hartnoll's, editor of the *Post Magazine*. He was referring to a spate of speculative insurance companies which were established in the late 1840s and early 1850s. See Taylor, *Creating Capitalism*, p. 146.

89. C. Dickens, *Martin Chuzzlewit* [1843–44] (Oxford, 1994), p. 370.

90. Anon., 'On Life Assurance', p. 294.

91. *Scotsman*, 24 Feb. 1841.

92. T.M. Porter, *Trust in Numbers: The Pursuit of Objectivity in Science and Public Life* (Princeton, NJ, 1995), p. 111.

93. T. Crook, 'Suspect Figures: Statistics and Public Trust in Victorian England', in this volume.

94. Dickens, *Martin Chuzzlewit*, pp. 372–3, 410.

95. G. Robb, *White-Collar Crime in Modern England: Financial Fraud and Business Morality, 1845–1929* (Cambridge, 1992); J. Taylor, 'Commercial Fraud and Public Men in Victorian Britain', *Historical Research* 78 (2005), pp. 230–52; J. Taylor, 'Company Fraud in Victorian Britain: The Royal British Bank Scandal of 1856', *English Historical Review* 122 (2007), pp. 700–24.

96. *The Times*, 20 Feb. 1861. The remark was prompted by the embezzlement of £67,000 by the ledger clerk of the Commercial Bank.

97. Instead, the legislation conceded limited liability to shareholders: 19 & 20 Vict. c., 20 & 21 Vict. c. 47.

98. *Observer*, 3 May 1857.

Part IV
The Politics of Statistics

11 'Population Combined with Wealth and Taxation'

Statistics, Representation and the Making of the 1832 Reform Act

S.J. Thompson

In twenty-first-century Britain we take it for granted that parliamentary constituencies contain roughly equal numbers of eligible voters, and that constituency boundaries are subject to periodic review by the Boundary Commissions for England, Scotland, and Wales. Indeed, within the last decade, steps have been taken to ensure greater equality of representation between England and Scotland in the aftermath of devolution. The English 'electoral quota'—obtained by dividing the number of electors on the electoral register by the number of parliamentary seats—was applied to Scotland from 2005, with the effect that Scottish representation at Westminster fell from seventy-two seats to fifty-nine.[1] The electoral quota provides a benchmark statistic for the Boundary Commissioners so that 'the electorate of any constituency shall be as near the electoral quota as is practicable'.[2] The British electoral system is governed, as far as possible, by the principle of an equal representation of the people, irrespective of individual voters' willingness to participate in elections at the ballot box.

In the late eighteenth and early nineteenth centuries, campaigners for parliamentary reform focused on the *inequality* of the representative system. For moderate reformers—who form the subject of this chapter—correcting, or at least improving, the underrepresentation of populous northern and western counties and fast-growing industrial cities, such as Manchester, Birmingham, and Leeds, was a more pressing concern than extending the franchise. Motions for parliamentary reform were discussed sporadically in the House of Commons from the 1780s, but it was not until the passage of the 1832 'Act to amend the representation of the people in England and Wales' that measures were taken to re-draw the electoral map, extend county voting rights to copyholders and tenants-at-will, and introduce a uniform borough franchise.[3]

In recent decades, historians have emphasized how little changed after 1832, at least in terms of the exercise of power. It has long been recognized, for example, that nineteenth-century cabinets before and after 1832 were dominated by a small number of aristocratic families, and Peter Mandler has argued that 'England witnessed a reassertion of *aristocratic* power in the 1830s and 1840s'.[4] Much ink has been spilt on the psephological impact of reform, in terms of the size and behaviour of the electorate.[5] Yet, as Jonathan Parry has noted, for the leading Whig reformers themselves—notably Earl Grey, Viscount Althorp, Lord John Russell, Viscount Duncannon, Lord Durham, and Sir James Graham—the Act's 'bold redistribution of seats' was 'much more important than its franchise provisions.'[6] Nonetheless, historians' persistent focus on the right to vote—before, during, and after the reform crisis—means that we still lack a coherent account of why, and on what empirical basis, the Whigs favoured a 'bold redistribution'.[7]

This chapter offers a new perspective on the first Reform Act by re-examining the parliamentary debates on seat redistribution. It argues that the initial framing of the redistribution plan reflected constraints imposed by the trajectory of parliamentary information gathering during the early nineteenth century. Specifically, the institution of decennial census taking from 1801 provided Whig ministers with spatially and temporally consistent population data for every parish and township in Britain. This enabled them to draft the redistribution clauses of the first bill in secret and without recourse to time-consuming empirical investigations into the number of voters in different counties and boroughs. Yet the statistical controversy generated by these clauses—resulting in the abandonment of the first two Reform Bills—forced the government to revise its reform scheme in a conservative direction in late 1831.

STATISTICS AND REFORM

Before turning to the debates of 1831–32, it is worth considering whether there is any necessary connection between 'reform', conceived more broadly as political and social progress, and statistics. Previous historians of early Victorian Britain have certainly thought so. In the 1970s, Oliver MacDonagh drew attention to the accumulation of 'a vast mass of information and statistics' by select committees and royal commissions after 1830, which served to expose 'the bare facts of the extent of suffering, waste, dirt or disease'. Integral to this mid-nineteenth-century 'revolution in social administration' was the 'assisting force' of the 1832 Reform Act.[8] In other words, political reform paved the way for the social reforms of the 1830s, including the Factory Act (1833), the Poor Law Amendment Act (1834), and the Civil Registration Act (1836). Each of these measures generated an array of social statistics that could be used to support the case for further reform.

Michael Cullen, meanwhile, described the 1830s' statistical movement as one of the 'distinguishing features of the period'. Interest in statistics was at such a pitch that provincial societies sprang up across the country, the most prominent in London and Manchester.[9] Yet the use of statistics was not confined to learned societies. George Richardson Porter became the first superintendent of the Board of Trade's statistical department in 1832. For Cullen, the statistical department was 'a central agency for the generation of statistics demanded to support arguments over the necessity or otherwise of particular reforms.'[10] One consequence of MacDonagh's and Cullen's stress on the novelty of the early Victorian period has been a tendency to neglect Georgian innovation in public numbers. Cullen certainly acknowledged limited progress in official statistics prior to the 1830s, paying particular attention to the collection of demographic, criminal, and educational statistics, but he regarded these exercises as 'spasmodic and of little value.' According to Cullen, it was thanks to the 'growing wave of reform', which first repealed the Test and Corporation Acts in 1828 and then overhauled the electoral system in 1832, that one of the 'key institutions of the statistical movement', namely the General Register Office, could be established.[11] Reading Cullen's account, there is no sense that the political and constitutional reforms of 1828–32 might have been facilitated by statistical data. Rather, political reform provided the impetus for the systematic collection of social statistics, which in turn produced social reform.

Twenty years ago, David Eastwood observed that the half-century before 1830 was characterized by the English state's 'growing appetite for information'. This appetite was particularly voracious within Westminster, where several hundred select committees collected evidence, both qualitative and quantitative, on a wide variety of social questions.[12] Much of this information is preserved in the House of Commons' parliamentary papers, colloquially known as 'blue books'. At the end of every session the printed papers were bound up in large blue volumes, arranged under four headings: bills; select committee reports; commissioners' reports; and accounts and papers. The accounts and papers contain a rich seam of empirical data and it is here that parliament's desire for information is most evident.[13]

Because Grey's government convened neither a select committee of enquiry nor a royal commission on parliamentary representation before introducing the first Reform Bill, we must look to the accounts and papers for evidence of statistical inputs into electoral reform. Between the introduction of the first bill on 1 March 1831 and the passage of the Reform Act on 7 June 1832, ninety accounts and papers relating to some aspect of parliamentary reform appear in the blue books. This figure represents just over 9 percent of all accounts and papers printed by the Commons during this period. In terms of sheer physical volume, these documents occupy nearly 3,500 pages. Rather than attempt to analyze each individually, the content of them can be ascertained, in broad terms, from their titles. Table 11.1 illustrates the extent to which demographic and fiscal statistics informed MPs' deliberations.

Information on population and houses, obtained from the census enumerations of 1821 and 1831, feature prominently. Twenty-eight (31 percent) of the accounts and papers dealing with parliamentary reform made use of census data without reference to fiscal data. An additional twenty-seven (30 percent) papers collated demographic information with returns of assessed taxes. In short, more than three-fifths of the accounts and papers analyzed

Table 11.1   Accounts and Papers Relating to Parliamentary Reform, 1831–32

Type of data	Session						TOTAL	
	1830–31		1831		1831–32			
	n	pages	n	pages	n	pages	n	pages
Census	12	69	8	531	8	308	28	908
Assessed taxes	3	20	3	14	3	24	9	58
Census and assessed taxes	3	18	4	86	20	1,816	27	1,920
Other (electors, boundaries, petitions)	1	44	9	154	16	384	26	582
Sub-total	19	151	24	785	47	2,532	90	3,468
Average number of pages per account / paper	-	7.9	-	32.7	-	53.9	-	38.5
Total number of accounts / papers for session	279	-	187	-	496	-	962	-

Note: Each paper only counted once.
Source: P[arliamentary] P[apers], 1830–31, (200–4, 216, 220, 300, 338–9, 349, 352–3, 362, 372–4, 382–3) x–xi; 1831, (64, 68–9, 84, 108, 110–12, 121, 134, 144, 149–50, 178, 183, 185, 200, 207–9, 213, 233, 258, 348) xvi, xviii; 1831–2, (17–21, 31–2, 41–2, 44, 60, 67–9, 81, 92, 107, 109, 112, 126, 141, 151, 178, 180, 182–4, 190, 198, 207, 209, 218, 222, 232, 357, 408–9, 435, 442, 444, 493, 506, 519, 522, 550, 0.36, 0.39) xxxvi–xliii.

the electoral system in terms of the demographic characteristics of boroughs, unrepresented towns, and counties. On 1 March 1831, for example, four accounts were ordered to be printed, tabulating the population of represented and unrepresented places in Great Britain in 1821; the population of several metropolitan parishes; the number of houses assessed at more than £10 annual rental; and the number of houses and electors in different constituencies.[14] The increasing complexity of statistical information should also be noted. Whereas in the 1830–31 session accounts and papers were relatively short, with an average length of just under eight pages, those produced during the 1831–32 session were over six times longer, on average, and were more likely to combine fiscal and demographic data, rather than treat them in isolation from one another.[15]

This finding casts doubt upon two existing orthodoxies. First, it forces us to reconsider the intentions of Whig ministers in 1831–32 because their dependence upon demographic data may indicate a more radically democratic agenda than has previously been assumed. It is widely accepted that the unreformed parliament represented the interests of property, whether measured by franchise qualifications, the social status of MPs, or the content of statutes. The census lacked data on the wealth and property of different communities. Why then did population data play such an influential role if the Whigs proposed, in Russell's words, 'to give to the real property and to the real respectability of the different cities and towns the right of voting for Members of Parliament'?[16]

Secondly, the collection of demographic, fiscal, electoral, and boundary data during the reform debates suggests that far from being the progenitor of social statistics in public policymaking, the 1832 Reform Act was the child of them. By itself, however, this table sheds little light on why counting people was preferred to other statistics, or why demographic and fiscal data together had become the largest single category by 1831–32, having been relatively insignificant in 1830–31. To explain why these statistics were produced it is necessary to re-examine the theory of moderate parliamentary reform, and the Tory critique of it. What, and who, in other words, did the Whigs want the House of Commons to represent?

PARLIAMENTARY REFORM BEFORE 1832

What moderate reformers did not want was the continued representation of 'pocket' and 'rotten' boroughs, whose representatives were elected either by a handful of voters, or nominated by one aristocratic family. Fifty years before the first Reform Act, William Pitt the Younger attacked the persistence of boroughs which 'had no existence in property, in population, in trade, in weight', and he later recommended the abolition of thirty-six nomination boroughs in favour of the metropolis and populous counties.[17] Although Pitt abandoned his youthful enthusiasm for parliamentary reform in light of the French Revolution, support for the redistribution of seats became a totemic policy of the Foxite opposition. Charles (later Earl) Grey proposed a radical redistribution of borough seats in 1797 that would have introduced equal electoral districts based exclusively on the distribution of population.[18] In 1800 Grey declared '*Ex vi termini*, then, the representation of the British constitution is one that supposes population to be a principal basis of representation', and argued for the abolition of forty of the most rotten English boroughs to accommodate the influx of one hundred Irish MPs following the Act of Union.[19]

A younger generation of Whigs, including Thomas Brand, John Lambton (later Lord Durham) and Lord John Russell, repeatedly attacked the borough system in the period after 1810.[20] Russell made speeches in favour of general parliamentary reform on six occasions (December 1819, May 1821, April 1822, April 1823, April 1826, and May 1830). Such credentials made him an obvious candidate for the 'Committee of Four' that drafted the first Reform Bill in late 1830.[21] Although Russell was not a member of the cabinet, it fell to him to introduce the measure on 1 March 1831, having been the principal draftsman of the bill.[22]

Grey's government lacked neither ideas nor enthusiasm to push through moderate parliamentary reform in 1830, but decades in opposition had excused the Whigs from committing to anything more than general statements in favour of redistribution. Because speeches rarely led to bills—due to the scale of opposition to parliamentary reform—reformers had limited opportunities to explain precisely how a redistibution of seats would be achieved. When Pitt, who had the advantage of being in power, proposed a seat redistribution in 1785, he thought that the number of houses should be taken as 'the criterion, by which he should judge what boroughs were decayed.'[23] Pitt was attempting, however partially, to establish a novel principle of parliamentary representation, namely population.

It was novel because the unreformed electoral system had arisen organically over several centuries. The right of a borough to return a member of parliament owed more to custom than size (whether measured by acreage, taxation, electors, or population). The great majority of boroughs returned two members, irrespective of the number of inhabitants. In the notorious case of the uninhabited Old Sarum, Wiltshire, two MPs sat entirely at the discretion of the borough patron. All counties, meanwhile, returned two members, giving Lancashire the same number of representatives as Rutland.

Pitt faced a serious empirical obstacle when he proposed to make the number of houses the criterion for judging if a borough was rotten. Until 1801 Britain had no national census, so Pitt proposed to obtain the necessary data from house tax returns. Because Pitt's motion was defeated, the relevant statistics were never compiled. The young Charles Grey, on the other hand, did not concern himself with the technicalities of measurement. When, in 1797, he proposed to increase the county representation from ninety-two to 113 MPs, giving preference to counties 'where the present representation was not proportionate to the extent of soil and population', he offered no clear indication of how the extent of soil and population might be established. Grey 'did not conceive that it would be difficult in the present, as it had been found easy in other instances, to ascertain the various proportions of population in the different counties.'[24]

By December 1830, when Russell and his colleagues began to draft the first Reform Bill, the statistical landscape had changed dramatically. Three censuses had been taken in Britain, the most recent dating from 1821. However, unlike the United States, whose decennial census was mandated by the Constitution with the explicit purpose of apportioning representatives and direct taxes among the several states, regular census taking in Britain developed with no such ambition.[25] Indeed, it is highly unlikely that Pitt, who in 1800 opposed parliamentary reform, would have lent his support to the first census had he suspected that its results might subsequently be appropriated by reformers. In stark contrast to the United States, the 1801 census in Britain was a short-term expedient intended to provide data on the number of consumers during a period of acute food scarcity.[26]

For half a century before 1830, then, the electoral system was increasingly challenged by critiques that highlighted the disproportionate numerical relationship between population and representation in different parts of the country. The abolition of rotten boroughs and the enfranchisement of populous counties and towns was favoured by reformers of all stripes. Extending the franchise, by contrast, was far more controversial, and drove a wedge between aristocratic Whigs and radical reformers like Major John Cartwright and Sir Francis Burdett. Yet the failure of even the mildest schemes of reform to overcome the first legislative hurdle of securing leave to bring in a bill meant Grey's government had to devise the empirical criteria for redistribution from scratch in December 1830. This had important consequences during 1831 because there was no pre-existing consensus, even among ministers, on how many boroughs ought to be abolished, how many might be salvageable through boundary extension, or which unrepresented towns were most deserving of enfranchisement.

THE FIRST REFORM BILL AND THE 1821 CENSUS

The Committee of Four initially planned to redistribute 150 seats. Russell thought this could be achieved by abolishing fifty boroughs 'of the smallest population, according to the census of 1821', and halving the representation of a further fifty.[27] Rather than rank the smallest hundred boroughs by population, the committee chose to draw two lines of disfranchisement: boroughs containing fewer than 2,000 inhabitants in 1821 would be abolished altogether, and those with fewer than 4,000 would lose one seat. The seats would then be allocated to towns of over 10,000 inhabitants and counties of over 150,000.[28] Applying a population 'test' meant that when the committee drew up schedules A (boroughs under 2,000) and B (boroughs under 4,000), the numbers originally mooted by Russell altered in line with the actual state of affairs prevailing at the time of the 1821 census.[29] As a result, schedule A of the first bill contained sixty boroughs and schedule B contained forty-seven, disfranchising a total of 168 seats, or 30 percent of the unreformed Commons.[30]

Russell had considerable experience of applying census evidence to the reform question. In his speeches during the 1820s Russell consistently drew attention to the rapid growth of unrepresented towns. Although he generally related population growth to the growth of wealth and political knowledge, not least among the middle classes, it was the unmistakeable *fact* of population change which Russell thought demanded the attention of the House.[31] Moreover, population was Russell's preferred criterion for judging which places should lose representation, and which places should gain it. What distinguished Russell's arguments in the 1820s from those of the older generation of Whigs was his extensive use of statistics to emphasize the inequality of the representative system. Referring in December 1819 to the claims of Manchester, Leeds, Birmingham, and Halifax for representation, Russell highlighted their rapid population growth, not their manufacturing output, or fiscal contributions. He compared a variety of eighteenth-century population estimates for each town with the results of the 1811 census to demonstrate their growth 'up into importance':

> Thus, Manchester, which in 1778 had only 23,000 inhabitants, is now supposed to have 110,000. Leeds had, in 1775, 17,117; in 1811, 62,534. Birmingham had in 1700, 15,032; in 1811, 85,753. Halifax had, in 1764, 41,000; in 1811, 73,000 ... Now, Sirs, it is very evident that these places suffer a serious inconvenience from the want of representatives.[32]

Russell recommended that towns of more than 15,000 inhabitants should receive the elective rights of corrupt boroughs.[33] By May 1830, six months before the Whigs entered office, Russell argued for a halving of the representation of all small boroughs under 2,500 inhabitants, and capping their number at sixty.[34] While the scale of the seat redistribution proposed by Russell on 1 March 1831 took many in the Commons completely by surprise, the mode of redistribution should have been less startling, given Russell's earlier efforts to re-establish the representative system according to population criteria.

Why did the Committee of Four rely on the 1821 census to redistribute seats, given how out-of-date it was? This question was asked repeatedly during the course of 1831, but the first person to raise doubts regarding the statistical basis of the plan was William IV. Upon reading the cabinet's scheme of reform, the king quickly grasped that the 'foundation' of the plan was 'the amount of population'. Given this, he thought it expedient to take a new census so as 'to remove all possibility of objection and doubt'.[35] The Population Act authorizing the 1831 census was passed in June 1830 but the enumeration was not due until 30 May 1831.[36] In his reply to the king, Grey argued that waiting for the results of a new census would 'occasion an inconvenient delay' which might give rise to 'increased agitation and the propagation of dangerous theories.' Furthermore, if ministers declared their intention to use the results of the 1831 census, 'the accuracy of the new returns might be affected', whereas the 1821 returns might be used 'without the possibility of a suspicion that any inaccuracy can have crept into it from interested motives.'[37] Grey took the view that putting off the ministry's *raison d'être* would risk either the fall of the government, or having a more radical measure pressed upon it by public opinion. Perhaps naïvely, he assumed that opponents of the bill would accept that the census of 1821 was, as he put it, 'a tolerably just estimate of the present state of population.'[38]

The first bill's redistribution clauses not only introduced the idea of linking representation to population, but did so on a quasi-proportional basis. Certainly ministers did not propose equal electoral districts, but the disfranchisement test implied a broadly symmetrical relationship between population and representation, at least for small boroughs, of one MP per 2,000 inhabitants. Similarly, the original enfranchisement proposals assigned one MP to previously unrepresented towns of 10,000 inhabitants, and two to towns of 20,000 inhabitants. The logic of this was quickly challenged by Tory MPs. One of the government's most determined opponents, John Wilson Croker, wondered why 'the noble Lord's system of arithmetical proportion treats 2,000 inhabitants on the same footing as 10,000; and 20,000 or 30,000 inhabitants received from his impartial hands exactly the same measure as 4,000.' Croker playfully imagined how Russell must have sat down with 'the population returns of 1821 . . . as the guide and manual of a new Constitution', to remodel 'all the institutions of the empire by the four rules of arithmetic'.[39]

Before the first bill received its first reading, ministers also had to defend the accuracy of census data. The ultra Tory Colonel Sibthorp advised the government on 7 March to wait until a new census had been taken, unwittingly echoing the king's private view.[40] William Peel thought the 'returns made for the purposes of this question ought to have been returns of the number of houses, and not of inhabitants'. He noted that Tamworth (in schedule B) had more houses than Tavistock (a Whig-controlled rotten borough which escaped unscathed), but fewer people.[41] The bill's supporters were caught off guard by these criticisms. Grey's son, Lord Howick, denied that it had ever been the government's intention 'to make the Representation proportional to the population', a sentiment echoed by Russell on 9 March: 'they [ministers] had never put the measure of Reform on a footing of such perfect symmetry and regularity as to reduce the Representation of the country to exact proportions, so that a certain and fixed number of persons should return a certain number of Members.'[42] Yet this claim was not entirely consistent with Sir James Graham's comments the previous day, when he had declared that ministers 'had the authority of Mr Pitt' for their 'doctrine of deciding Representation with reference to population'.[43] Although Graham was not suggesting that Pitt had proposed reducing the representation 'to exact proportions', his remarks nevertheless suggest that the Committee of Four had failed to agree upon a common rationale for their redistribution scheme. Graham's appeal to Pittite precedent and Russell's denial of ministerial pretensions to establish 'perfect symmetry' reveal the extent to which the technicalities of reform took second place to the imperative to act quickly and decisively.

Criticism of the schedules continued unabated during the latter part of March, forcing the cabinet to make various concessions in cases where the boundaries of parish and borough were not co-extensive.[44] Sir Robert Peel's discovery that the 1821 returns did not always distinguish between the populations of parishes and boroughs embarrassed the government and did not instil confidence in the reliability of the information on which the bill was constructed.[45] Although the government won the second reading debate by just one vote, the bill was set upon in committee.

The MP for Liverpool, General Gascoyne, adopted a new line of attack which proved considerably more effective than the arguments of either Croker or Peel. Gascoyne highlighted the anti-English implications of the bill. He exploited widespread fears of Irish nationalism, noting on 12 April 1831 that 'The Bill would give additional Members to Ireland and in the conduct of its inhabitants he saw nothing to deserve such a mark of favour.'[46] Gascoyne buttressed this with an appeal to English fiscal grievances, declaring that the changes were being made 'at the expense of the people of England'. Specifically, he objected to the demographic rules of redistribution because Ireland, though populous, contributed 'not more than one-tenth of taxes in proportion to its population as compared with this country; so that if population were taken as the ground for adding to the Representatives of that country, it ought also to be made the basis of a more equal taxation.'[47] The success of Gascoyne's amendment—that there should be no reduction in the number of English and Welsh MPs—effectively killed the first bill and forced Grey to seek the dissolution of parliament.[48] Thus it was the bill's redistribution provisions, and particularly the demographic means by which they would be effected, that provoked the greatest opposition from the very beginning of the reform crisis.

THE SECOND REFORM BILL

The resulting general election not only increased Grey's Commons majority substantially, but also confined the Tories overwhelmingly to the rotten boroughs threatened with extinction under schedules A and B.[49] No doubt buoyed by the extent of popular support for reform, ministers were in no mood for concessions of principle. When Russell introduced the second bill in June 1831, he was emphatic that population remained the best test of disfranchisement, especially when compared with tax-office or stamp-office returns. Ministers, Russell declared, had taken their 'measure from a well known statistical book, as free from error and doubt as could be expected.'[50]

During the first few weeks of the second bill's committee stage (12 July–2 August), the statistical basis of schedules A and B dominated proceedings. Russell repeatedly reminded MPs that 'the returns of 1821 were those by which the framers of the Bill had been guided'.[51] Undeterred, William Mackinnon moved an amendment on 19 July to instruct the committee to use the 1831 population returns to determine the composition of schedules A and B.[52] In the debate on this amendment the MP for the condemned borough of Corfe Castle, George Bankes, suggested that 'if the adoption of the population census as a criterion was taken from America' then ministers ought to follow the American practice of using the most recent decennial census to alter representation 'in accordance with the alterations in the population.'[53] The size of the government's Commons majority meant that this amendment, along with numerous others, served only to delay, rather than derail, the bill's progress.

The second bill passed the Commons on 22 September 1831 with a majority of 109. When it reached the Lords, opponents of the measure focused more on the principle embodied in the redistribution clauses than the reliability of the statistics upon which the plan was constructed. Lord Wharncliffe, who would become leader of the so-called 'waverers'—those peers whose support was vital in securing the second reading of the third (and successful) bill—objected on 3 October 'to the number of great towns' due to be enfranchised. For Wharncliffe this was clear evidence 'that the principle of the Bill was not property, but population'.[54]

The following day, another future waverer, the earl of Harrowby, wondered if the bill might be improved in committee. He concluded that this was impossible because the principle of the bill, 'that population, taken by itself must be the basis of Representation', was simply too objectionable to allow constructive amendment of the measure. This principle, he suggested, had only ever been tried in the United States, and even 'in the wildest times of the French Republic, population and taxation combined were considered as the essential basis of the system of Representation.'[55]

On each of the five nights of the Lords' debate, the opposition objected in the strongest terms to the principle of redistribution. The earl of Haddington, for instance, read extracts from an article in the *North American Review*, published anonymously in London as a pamphlet in August 1831, which suggested that 'we [i.e. the Americans] shall give back the tide of life to the frame of our political parent'.[56] Haddington argued that the ministerial rule of disfranchisement, which bore more than a passing resemblance to the US Constitution's apportionment clause, 'was making very rapid progress among the philosophic inquirers of Birmingham and elsewhere, and it was evidently a principle which could only be settled by the division of the country into electoral districts.'[57] For the earl of Carnarvon, 'the basis of population was no ingredient in the basis of the British Constitution', and 'must, as a matter of course, lead to revolution.'[58]

The ministerial response to these objections was anaemic at best. Viscount Melbourne flatly denied that population was the basis of the measure; it was rather a 'practical rule' for disfranchisement. Property, different interests, different classes, and population together had been looked to by the government.[59] The Colonial secretary, Viscount Goderich, thought 'the population of a borough was taken merely as an indication of its decay or of its importance'.[60] Lord Chancellor Brougham said it was 'a gross fallacy' to assert that population, and not property, was the basis of representation in the bill.[61] He collapsed the distinction between property and population, arguing that the population criterion was 'the general test of wealth, extent, importance; and therefore substantially, though not in name, it is really the test of property.'[62] Grey, closing the debate, seized upon this interpretation, declaring that ministers had taken population 'only as *primâ facie* evidence of wealth and importance.'[63] During the debate, ministers shifted from a position of denying that population was more important than property in the framing of the bill, to one that simply conflated them. The contrast with Russell's dogged defence of the 1821 census in the Commons, made during the debates on the first and second bills, could not be more striking.

Peers remained unconvinced by these claims, however, and the second reading was lost by forty-one votes. Population statistics had provided the empirical foundations of the schedules of both Reform Bills, but were also their undoing. The urgency of the reform question forced ministers to rely on out-of-date census returns because they feared that waiting for the results of the 1831 census would risk provoking unrest in the country at large, which not only expected reform, but demanded it. Despite protestations to the contrary, ministers could not effectively rebut claims that they wished to make population the sole basis of representation whilst still retaining their commitment to census data.

THE PASSING OF THE REFORM ACT

Negotiations with Wharncliffe and Harrowby began shortly after the second bill's defeat. Although these discussions failed to produce agreement on a new measure, the cabinet did at least discover which aspects of the bill were most objectionable.[64] Wharncliffe's plan for a revised bill reluctantly acknowledged that disfranchisement was non-negotiable, but demanded in return for this concession 'a more correct mode of ascertaining the propriety of disfranchisement'. He proposed, as a new criterion, 'the number of houses and the amount of direct taxation in each place'. Grey's marginal note on the plan indicates that this proposal was originally his, not Wharncliffe's, and was suggested at their first meeting on 16 November.[65] In other words, even before Grey met Wharncliffe, ministers had resolved that something had to be done to counter objections to the redistribution clauses.

In an undated memorandum, Russell set out the arguments in favour of abandoning the lines of disfranchisement and settling upon a given number of 'say 56, or 60, or 64 or 66.' There were three advantages in this method: 'First, It is more conformable to the proceedings of the two Unions, & Mr Pitt's plan in 1785. 2dly It puts an end to all the jargon which the *North American Review* has put forth, respecting the rule of population—3dly It brings on an early vote on the number of boroughs to be disfranchised.'[66] Whether or not this was written before or after Grey's meeting with Wharncliffe is to some extent immaterial. That Grey appreciated the weakness of the earlier disfranchisement criteria is evident from his marginal note. What Russell's memorandum demonstrates is that the attacks against the principle of disfranchisement during the Lords' second reading debate—led by the waverers Wharncliffe, Harrowby, and Haddington—had succeeded. Moreover, the 'jargon' of the *North American Review* was identified as having been especially damaging.

The cabinet rejected Wharncliffe's plan on 26 November, but in the meantime had already set to work on drawing up new versions of schedules A and B, based on the number of houses at the time of the 1831 census, and the amount of assessed taxes.[67] On 24 November Melbourne instructed the chairman of the Boundary Commission, Lieutenant Thomas Drummond, to 'ascertain the relative importance of the smaller Boroughs in England and Wales'.[68] This was the origin of the 'Drummond Scale', a ranking of 120 boroughs, comprising all the boroughs in the original versions of schedules A and B, together with an additional twenty-three small boroughs. Drummond calculated a series of index numbers which gave equal weighting to the number of houses and amount of assessed taxes paid. To ensure the greatest possible accuracy, and to avoid the embarrassments that had arisen over the 1821 population totals, Drummond collated information from four different authorities, namely the boundary commissioners, the returning officers of individual boroughs, the surveyor of taxes, and the census taker John Rickman.[69] If there was disagreement between these sources, Drummond proceeded on a case-by-case basis, giving his reasons for each individual decision.[70]

In practical terms, it might be argued that the Drummond Scale changed little. The new disfranchisement test, based on houses and assessed taxes rather than population alone, affected only a small minority of boroughs in schedule A. Fifty-two of the sixty boroughs originally slated for abolition in March 1831 ceased to return members after 1832. Its impact on schedule B was more extensive (fewer than half of the boroughs in the original schedule B eventually lost one member), although the pruning of schedule B also reflected the cabinet's decision to maintain the Commons at its pre-Reform size of 658 MPs.[71]

Its real significance, however, was theoretical. William IV, for example, regarded this alteration, above all others proposed by ministers, as 'the *very essential one* . . . which goes to the establishment of the principle on which the King from the first laid so much stress, *that it should be a representation of property as well as of numbers*, and the adoption of the census of 1831 instead of that of 1821'.[72] When he moved the third—and ultimately successful—bill on 12 December, Russell tried to portray the new test as a matter of practical expediency, which simply used the more up-to-date population returns of 1831. He explained that ministers had decided, recalling Pitt's 1785 scheme, to combine the test of houses with that of assessed taxes in order to 'give a more correct view of the importance of the boroughs.'[73] Significantly, however, Russell chose not to characterize the test as uniting measures of population and property. He was not prepared to admit publicly the force of the arguments put forward in the House of Lords in October, even if he did so in private.

In terms of principle, however, the Drummond Scale was a major concession, and was immediately recognized as such by opponents of the bill. In reply to Russell, Peel remarked that 'there was scarcely an amendment which had been offered from that [the Opposition] side of the House, which had not been adopted', and at the very top of the list, 'the principle of population was abandoned—the census of the present year preferred to the census of 1821'.[74] Croker demanded that the information used by Drummond be laid before the House without delay because he understood that the bill was 'formed upon a new principle'.[75] Sir Robert Inglis, meanwhile, noted on 17 December that, notwithstanding ministerial protests to the contrary, Melbourne's instruction to Drummond confirmed that the government had indeed 'determined to found the Reform Bill on a new basis.'[76]

To a large extent, however, the continued opposition of 'diehards' such as Croker and Inglis was not a major cause of concern for ministers. Only sixty-nine MPs voted against the third bill's second reading on 18 December, a far cry from the 301 MPs who had voted against the first bill's second reading on 23 March. The Drummond Scale was devised for the benefit of the House of Lords, not John Wilson Croker, who continued to denounce it long after the Reform Act had been passed.[77] When Grey introduced the third bill into the Lords on 26 March 1832, Harrowby and Wharncliffe made two of the most influential speeches in favour. Despite their reservations, both declared their willingness to vote for the second reading. Harrowby noted that the new bill differed from the previous one, especially in respect of the mode of disfranchisement:

> In the first place, in the Bill which was before them in the course of the last Session, the leading principle of disfranchisement was founded on population, or on the depopulation of the places to which the disfranchisement was to attach. In the present Bill, that principle had been abandoned, and a different principle, that of population combined with wealth and taxation, was substituted.[78]

This, then, was the significance of the Drummond Scale. It provided the necessary political cover for the waverers to pursue their strategy of constructive engagement with the government. By itself, the scale self-evidently failed to persuade a sufficient number of peers to give their wholehearted support to the third bill. Once it reached its committee stage, ministers were ambushed by Lord Lyndhurst's amendment to defer consideration of the disfranchisement schedules.[79] This prompted the resignation of the government and the infamous 'Days of May' when Wellington tried and failed to form an administration. When Grey returned to office, determined to pass the 'whole Bill' and backed by the monarch's promise of an unlimited creation of peers, opposition in the Lords crumbled.

CONCLUSION

The Drummond Scale was certainly not what mobilized the political unions in Birmingham and London during May 1832. Few histories of the reform crisis make more than a passing reference to it; some have ignored it altogether.[80] Yet, in the face of peers' opposition to census data, ministers were forced to abandon their population lines, the principle of which they had never convincingly defended, either arithmetically or intellectually. Indeed, the government's apparent inability to justify the statistical logic of the seat redistribution implies that the initial preference for demographic data had more to do with the convenience and accessibility of census returns than any genuine commitment to Jeffersonian constitutional theory. Nonetheless, the *perception* of a link between the Whig plan and the US Constitution, however tenuous, was sufficiently alarming to produce a ministerial retreat in the closing months of 1831. Arguably, however, the Drummond Scale was only a partial concession. By defining the 'importance' of the smallest boroughs in wholly numerical terms, the Whigs introduced a form of rationality which had hitherto been lacking in the British electoral system.

For far too long historians have studied the 1832 Reform Act in terms of its impact upon the electorate: that is, as the first stage in a century-long process of franchise extension. It is therefore not surprising that it has been seen as disappointing. But this approach is profoundly anachronistic because it assumes that the Whigs' principal concern was the representation of individuals. As this chapter has demonstrated, the greatest controversy arose over the representation of place, and the criteria for judging which boroughs, towns, and cities deserved a voice at Westminster. Moreover, the census and the fiscal statistics used to determine representation pertained to entire communities, not simply the minority of the population entitled to vote. The failure of both the first and second bills was a direct consequence of objections to the redistribution proposals, and it was only when the government compromised on this aspect of reform that progress could be made in parliament.

Viewed from a longer term perspective, the debates of 1831–32 may also help to explain why it is that parliamentary representation in Britain is still not determined by census data. It was earlier noted that the electoral quota used by the Boundary Commission is calculated by dividing the number of electors on the electoral register by the number of parliamentary seats. As the commissioners noted in their *Review of Parliamentary Constituencies in England* (2000):

> The Commission do not base their recommendations on forecast or projected electorates or on populations, actual or projected. The

Commission are required to base their recommendations on the numbers of electors on the electoral registers at the start of a review and they are unable to take account of any under-registration or over-registration of electors which is sometimes claimed in some districts.[81]

In other words, the American practice of using the census to re-apportion representation never took hold in the United Kingdom. Although Britons like to think that they live in a representative democracy, the reality is less clear-cut. If parliament is meant to represent the *demos*, then there is a case for saying that the electoral quota should measure the ratio of population—rather than registered voters—to seats. Otherwise, the equality or otherwise of the representative system is dependent upon householders choosing to return their electoral registration forms. Political representation, it would seem, is only as comprehensive as the statistics upon which it is based.

NOTES

1. Fifth periodic report of the Boundary Commission for Scotland, 2004/05, Cm 6427, pp. 6, 10.
2. Rules for redistribution of seats, schedule 2, Parliamentary Constituencies Act, 1986, c. 56. At the time of going to press, these rules were due to be amended by the passage of the Parliamentary Voting System and Constituencies Bill, 2010/11.
3. 2 & 3 Wm. IV c. 45. Similar acts were passed for Scotland and Ireland: 2 & 3 Wm. IV, c. 65, 2 & 3 Wm. IV, c. 88.
4. P. Mandler, *Aristocratic Government in the Age of Reform: Whigs and Liberals, 1830–1852* (Oxford, 1990), p. 1.
5. P. Salmon, *Electoral Reform at Work: Local Politics and National Parties, 1832–1841* (Woodbridge, 2002), pp. 3–11, provides a useful overview of recent historiographical trends.
6. J. Parry, *The Rise and Fall of Liberal Government in Victorian Britain* (New Haven and London, 1993), p. 72.
7. C. Hall, 'The Rule of Difference: Gender, Class and Empire in the Making of the 1832 Reform Act', in I. Blom, K. Hagemann and C. Hall (eds.), *Gendered Nations: Nationalisms and Gender Order in the Long Nineteenth Century* (Oxford, 2000), pp. 107–35. Hall's chapter is typical of the tendency to view parliamentary reform principally through the prism of individual citizenship and voting rights, with the effect that representation is defined narrowly in participatory terms.
8. O. MacDonagh, *Early Victorian Government, 1830–1870* (London, 1977), pp. 1, 5–6.
9. M.J. Cullen, *The Statistical Movement in Early Victorian Britain: The Foundations of Empirical Social Research* (Hassocks, 1976), p. ix.
10. *Ibid.*, p. 19.
11. *Ibid.*, pp. 14–15. For a different perspective on the origins of the General Register Office, see E. Higgs, *Life, Death and Statistics: Civil Registration, Censuses and the Work of the General Register Office, 1836–1952* (Hatfield, 2004).

12. D. Eastwood, '"Amplifying the Province of the Legislature": The Flow of Information and the English State in the Early Nineteenth Century', *Historical Research* 62 (1989), pp. 291, 285.
13. For a discussion of trends in parliamentary information gathering, see S.J. Thompson, 'Census-Taking, Political Economy and State Formation in Britain, c. 1790–1840' (PhD thesis, University of Cambridge, 2010).
14. *Parliamentary Papers* [hereafter *PP*], 1830–1, (201), (202), (203), (204), x.
15. E.g. Instructions . . . on parliamentary representation: V (Number of houses and amount of assessed taxes in boroughs and towns), *PP*, 1831, (21) xxxvi [44 pages].
16. Hansard's *Parliamentary Debates* [hereafter *PD*], 3rd ser. ii. 1069–70.
17. Cobbett's *Parliamentary History* [hereafter *PH*], xxii. 1418; *PH*, xxv. 441.
18. *PH*, xxxiii. 649–50.
19. *PH*, xxxv. 90.
20. Brand's motion of 1810 followed Pitt in proposing compensation for borough owners, whereas Lambton's motion in 1821 did not. Russell vacillated on this issue during the 1820s.
21. The other members were Lord Durham, Viscount Duncannon, and Sir James Graham.
22. John, Earl Russell, *Recollections and Suggestions* (2nd edn., London, 1875), pp. 84–5.
23. *PH*, xxv. 441.
24. *PH*, xxxiii. 649.
25. United States Constitution, Art. 1, Sec. 2.
26. D.V. Glass, *Numbering the People: The Eighteenth-Century Population Controversy and the Development of Census and Vital Statistics in Britain* (Farnborough, 1973), pp. 96–8.
27. Russell, *Recollections and Suggestions*, pp. 84–5.
28. 'Report on Reform', in Henry, earl Grey (ed.), *The Reform Act, 1832: The Correspondence of the Late Earl Grey with His Majesty King William IV* (2 vols., London, 1867), I, pp. 462–3.
29. M. Brock, *The Great Reform Act* (London, 1973), p. 137.
30. *Ibid.*, pp. 138–9.
31. For Russell's comments on the rise of wealth, trade and manufactures in unrepresented towns, see *PD*, xli. 1096; N.S. v. 613; N.S. vii. 55–6; N.S. xxiv. 1223–4; on education, knowledge and intelligence, see *PD*, xli. 1098–99; N.S. vii. 56–9; N.S. viii. 1271–2; N.S. xv. 652, 656; N.S. xxiv. 1223.
32. *PD*, xli. 1097.
33. *PD*, xli. 1106.
34. *PD*, N.S. xxiv. 1225. Russell moved four resolutions on moderate reform during the debate on O'Connell's plan for radical reform based on universal suffrage.
35. William IV to Grey, 4 Feb. 1831, in *Reform Act, 1832*, I, pp. 103–4.
36. 11 Geo. IV c. 30.
37. Grey to William IV, 5 Feb. 1831, in *Reform Act, 1832*, I, pp. 106–7.
38. *Ibid.*, p. 107.
39. *PD*, 3rd ser. iii. 93, 95.
40. *PD*, 3rd ser. iii. 123.
41. *PD*, 3rd ser. iii. 146.
42. *PD*, 3rd ser. iii. 145, 307.
43. *PD*, 3rd ser. iii. 226.
44. Brock, *Great Reform Act*, pp. 183–4.
45. *PD*, 3rd ser. iii. 939–41. See also corrected return of the population of each city and borough in England from the population returns of 1821, *PP*, 1830–1, (339) x.

46. *PD*, 3rd ser. iii. 1236.

47. *PD*, 3rd ser. iii. 1528.

48. Brock, *Great Reform Act*, pp. 186–92.

49. Cannon, *Parliamentary Reform*, p. 221.

50. *PD*, 3rd ser. iv. 343–4.

51. *PD*, 3rd ser. iv. 1262; cf. *PD*, 3rd ser. iv. 1297, 1353, 1355, 1358–9; v. 39.

52. *PD*, 3rd ser. v. 36–54. The amendment was lost by seventy-five votes.

53. *PD*, 3rd ser. v. 41.

54. *PD*, 3rd ser. vii. 975.

55. *PD*, 3rd ser. vii. 1157–8. The Montagnard constitution of 1793, which was never implemented, decreed that population was the sole basis of representation, and that there should be one deputy for every 40,000 inhabitants: J.M. Roberts and J. Hardman (eds.), *French Revolution Documents* (2 vols., Oxford, 1966–73), II, pp. 142–8.

56. [E. Everett], 'The Prospect of Reform in Europe', *North American Review* 32 (1831), p. 177.

57. *PD*, 3rd ser. vii. 1380–2. The next day, the ultra Tory earl of Falmouth read additional passages from the pamphlet, calling it a 'republican book' which showed how reform would eventually undermine the Monarchy, House of Lords and the established Church: *PD*, 3rd ser. viii. 70.

58. *PD*, 3rd ser. viii. 100–1.

59. *PD*, 3rd ser. vii. 1182.

60. *PD*, 3rd ser. vii. 1372.

61. *PD*, 3rd ser. viii. 237.

62. *PD*, 3rd ser. viii. 240.

63. *PD*, 3rd ser. viii. 325.

64. Brock, *Great Reform Act*, pp. 260, 263; *Reform Act, 1832*, I, pp. 464–78 for the discussions between Grey and Wharncliffe in November 1831.

65. Lord Wharncliffe's plan for the alteration of the Reform Bill, 23 Nov., 1831, in *Reform Act, 1832*, I, p. 473.

66. Kew, The National Archives, Russell Papers, PRO 30/22/1B, f. 296.

67. Brock, *Great Reform Act*, pp. 260, 265.

68. Instructions . . . on parliamentary representation I, *PP*, 1831–2, (17) xxxvi.23. The Boundary Commission was established in November 1831 to determine the limits of the new English and Welsh constituencies.

69. For Drummond's methodology, see *PP*, 1831–2 (17), xxxvi.23–25.

70. Instructions . . . on parliamentary representation VIII, *PP*, 1831–2, (44) xxxvi.189–96.

71. *PD*, 3rd ser. ii. 1077–78; 2 & 3 Will. 4, c. 45.

72. Sir Herbert Taylor to Grey, 2 Dec. 1831, *Reform Act, 1832*, II, pp. 5–6. Emphasis original.

73. *PD*, 3rd ser. ix. 160–2.

74. *PD*, 3rd ser. ix. 174.

75. *PD*, 3rd ser. ix. 257.

76. *PD*, 3rd ser. ix. 432; cf. *PP*, 1831–2, (17) xxxvi.23.

77. [J.W. Croker], 'The Present and Last Parliaments', *Quarterly Review* 49 (1833), pp. 255–81.

78. *PD*, 3rd ser. xi. 859.

79. For Grey's objections to the amendment, see Grey to Sir Herbert Taylor, 7 May 1832 in *Reform Act, 1832*, II, pp. 391–2.

80. See, for example, Brock, *Great Reform Act*, p. 265; Cannon, *Parliamentary Reform*, pp. 229, 253n. I. Newbould, *Whiggery and Reform, 1830–41: The Politics of Government* (London, 1990), p. 74, describes the changes as 'minor' and, like J.R.M. Butler, *The Passing of the Great Reform Bill*

(London, 1914), p. 325, refers only to use of the 1831 census, omitting any reference to the inclusion of a test based on assessed taxes.

81. *Review of Parliamentary Constituencies in England* (Boundary Commission for England, 2000), ch. 4, para. 14, reprinted in C. Turpin and A. Tomkins, *British Government and the Constitution* (6th edn., Cambridge, 2007), p. 502.

12 A 'Naked Strength and Beauty'
Statistics in the British Tariff Debate, 1880–1914

Edmund Rogers

Few areas of policy debate in Victorian and Edwardian Britain were as contentious and as markedly awash with numerical information as that over the taxation of imports. Free trade was a central pillar of Britain's economic experience during this time. Repeal of the protectionist Corn Laws and the mercantilist Navigation Acts, alongside the abolition of imperial preference in the 1840s, was followed by Britain's transformation into a ravenously hungry consumer of imported food. Agriculture shrank in economic importance, whilst urban communities and the manufacturing sector expanded rapidly.[1] The class politics that resulted from these socio-economic changes prompted Gladstone's class-sensitive fiscal policies of the 1850s and early 1860s, including the reduction of import duties to the point where they were imposed only on goods unproduceable in Britain, such as tea and tobacco.[2]

As Britain prospered in the 1850s and 1860s, critics of free trade shrank into the background. From around 1873, however, they became increasingly numerous and outspoken. British crop producers suffered through world-wide deflation and the structural transformation of global trade, whilst manufacturers began to feel threatened by emerging industrial nations such as Germany and the United States. 'Fair trade' emerged in the 1880s as an alternative to free trade. Its backers argued that retaliatory tariffs ought to be imposed on goods from protectionist nations, and preferential duties used to encourage greater commercial interdependence between Britain and the Empire. In 1903, Joseph Chamberlain and the Unionist party unleashed this formula into Edwardian electoral politics as 'tariff reform', prompting the Liberal party to rally in defence of free trade. Even after the latter's victory in the 1906 election, however, the fiscal question remained a defining political issue on the eve of war.[3]

Historians have readily noted the contribution of statistics to this long-running contest between free trade and fiscal reform in Britain. The Board of Trade's Statistical Department provided the empirical foundations for the initial Peelite fiscal departures of the 1840s.[4] The current author has elsewhere observed that the fiscal debate conducted between the 1870s and the First World War demonstrates the emerging importance of economic statistics in British public debate. The increasing availability of price, wage, and employment data, particularly by the Edwardian period, facilitated international comparisons and took public discourse beyond theoretical generalities towards a 'more empirically informed stage'.[5] In a fascinating account of 'Free Trade' in early twentieth-century Britain and its decline as a popular creed of patriotic and consumerist values, Frank Trentmann pays welcome attention to the use of economic statistics and their presentation to the public in campaigns that involved all the trappings of today's mass politics: posters, presentations, and publicity stunts.[6]

The intention here is not to provide a comprehensive and definitive account of the role of statistics during the fiscal controversy of these years, but rather to use the tariff debate in late Victorian and Edwardian Britain to highlight a number of broader historical points relating to the presence of statistics in the public sphere. First, it demonstrates how statistics contributed to the formulation of international perspectives within public debate at the national level. Ironically, for a debate over the curbing of imports, the international flow of statistics went unimpeded, and Britain provides a particularly interesting case due to its imperial ties in this period. As will be shown, the fiscal politics and pioneering statistical efforts of the Australian colonies had a unique impact on the British tariff debate, whilst the experience of Britain's industrial competitors under protection fuelled the political campaigns over the country's fiscal direction.

Secondly, the tariff question prompts us to recognize that statistics have historically existed within a public sphere more heterogeneous in nature than Habermas posited.[7] Tariff policy represented a major political issue in which a formidable grouping of weighty statistical themes—trade, unemployment, prices, and wages—appeared in two contexts. On the one hand, they appeared in the ideologically driven, partisan discussion carried out in print among the highly educated and politically and academically involved. On the other, they appeared in the field of mass democratic politics so colourfully portrayed by Trentmann, in which both sides in the fiscal debate also used statistics to persuade working-class voters, as well as unenfranchised citizens whose interests and opinions could bear on the enfranchised (e.g. wives). In covering the period from 1880 to the First World War, this chapter permits a contrast between these two contexts. Whilst published appeals to the working class on the tariff issue certainly existed prior to 1903, they were not produced or consumed in the context of a forthcoming electoral contest featuring a choice of alternative tariff platforms.[8]

The final theme relates to the presentation of statistics to a popular electorate. Free trade and tariff reform feature heavily in James Thompson's recent article on political posters, in which he rescues popular visual campaigning methods from perceptions of a 'debased politics of the image' in the late Victorian and Edwardian periods. Political parties and organizations were coping with an increasingly complex electorate, and using a variety of media to communicate with its constituent parts.[9] The chapter explores this use of visual forms to present statistics to the electorate, but also addresses several key points relating to free traders and tariff reformers' use of statistics in the context of mass political participation. From where did they derive their figures? How did the two sides challenge the reliability and validity of each other's numbers? And how did they deal with those challenges, and with the rival side's statistics?

The first part of the chapter focuses on the fiscal 'contest' or 'experiment' of the 1880s and 1890s involving two Australian colonies: free trade New South Wales and protectionist Victoria. The physical juxtaposition of these rival fiscal regimes was perceived in Britain as a unique empirical opportunity to observe the relative effects of each policy. Crucially, the colonies were also highly precocious producers of economic statistics. The chapter then moves into the electoral context of the early twentieth century. A concluding section highlights the commonalities in the two contexts of statistical debate presented here, and reflects more deeply on the broader observations about statistics in the public sphere which can be drawn from Britain's fiscal controversy.

NEW SOUTH WALES VERSUS VICTORIA

Free trade came under increasing attack in Britain from the 1870s, as the country endured the pains of structural economic adjustment and increased competition from foreign agricultural and industrial producers. During the 1880s, the 'fair trade' movement emerged to campaign for retaliatory tariffs, and fiscal reform also became linked to visions of imperial unity. This questioning of free trade was reinforced by a seismic shift in economic thought in the British Isles. *Laissez-faire* and the orthodoxies of Ricardian political economy were coming under attack from the 'historical economists', whose ranks included prominent tariff reform economists such as William Cunningham, W.J. Ashley, and W.A.S. Hewins. Historical economists criticized classical political economy for its overemphasis on generalized theory and deductive methodology. All economic theory, they argued, was only relevant to certain times, places, and points of economic and social development. The historical economists advocated an *inductive*, scientific, and historically informed approach to studying the economy, which would draw on empirical findings and take account of a nation's particular circumstances. In their view, free trade might not necessarily be suited to all nations at all times.[10]

This 'historist' critique of free trade actually benefited from the ideas of one of the great Liberal intellectual heroes, John Stuart Mill.[11] In his *Principles of Political Economy*, originally published in 1848, Mill rejected protection and staunchly defended free trade, but in one controversial passage he made a theoretical concession to protectionism. In what has become known as the 'infant industries argument', he suggested that protection might be 'defensible' when 'imposed temporarily (especially in a young and rising nation)' to establish an industry suited to the country's circumstances but facing the uphill struggle of competing against long-established foreign competitors.[12] Inspired by Mill, the 'new countries', as the white settler societies in the New World were commonly known, were indeed pursuing industrialization with the aid of tariffs. The United States imposed heavy and long-lasting tariffs during the Civil War, protectionism thrived amongst the Australasian colonies, and Canada enacted its 'National Policy' in 1879.[13] Free traders usually criticized the 'infant industries argument' on the grounds that protection distorted investment and led to the misallocation of labour and capital, which was especially harmful in new countries.[14] But the conspicuous prosperity of new countries protecting their infant industries threatened to undermine the idea of free trade as a universal economic good. Conceding that protectionism was fine for new countries would be the thin end of the wedge for free trade.

Not all new countries had opted for protectionism, however. New South Wales bucked the trend in 1866, adopting a low revenue tariff (5 percent) with extra duties on a select few items such as tea and coffee. In eschewing differentiated duties to protect specific domestic industries, New South Wales abided by the essential principles of free trade. This fiscal model benefited from its ideological appeal, the backing of numerous commercial interests, and buoyant land revenues, and in 1873 the general *ad valorem* tariff was abolished altogether. But for a short protectionist turn in the early 1890s, the colony maintained a reputation as an unusual bastion of free trade in the New World.[15] By contrast, in 1866 neighbouring Victoria adopted a broad-based revenue tariff that satisfied protectionist demands, before moving to a more explicitly protectionist fiscal policy in the 1880s.[16] This juxtaposition of free trade in New South Wales and protectionism in Victoria on the 'clean slate' of Australia offered free traders in Britain what they saw as the perfect opportunity to discredit the infant industries argument, the most mild and caveat-laden form of protectionism. Furthermore, it would give their claims of the universal applicability of free trade an empirical, scientific basis. George Baden-Powell, a passionately imperialist free trader employed as private secretary to the governor of Victoria in the late 1870s, brought the duel between New South Wales and Victoria to public attention in the early 1880s. It was, he pronounced, 'a unique case—a test case—the first that history has given us, of the actual recorded results of high and low tariffs in two similarly circumstanced communities, specially interesting because they are young communities, where, if anywhere, Protection is allowed theoretically.'[17]

What made comparisons of New South Wales and Victoria especially useful to free traders as they fought inductivist critics in the final two decades of the nineteenth century was the advanced state of Australian economic statistics. Through the work of official statisticians like William Archer and Henry Hayter in Victoria, and T.A. Coghlan in New South

Wales, the Australian colonies were international pioneers in economic statistics, producing the world's most advanced economic data in the pre–Second World War period. Statistical innovation sprung from the colonies' desire to measure their progress as they competed with each other to attract immigrants and capital, and the needs arising from the developmental role of the state in the antipodes. New South Wales had decided to employ a government statistician in the 1880s in order to match the statistical output of rival Victoria. Consequently, Coghlan, who pioneered national income estimates (albeit crudely), began his official work in 1886.[18]

Free traders were by far the most eager to seize upon the figures as proof of the similar, often greater, levels of prosperity and growth under free trade in New South Wales as under protection in neighbouring Victoria.[19] Baden-Powell celebrated 'the great practical use of statistics . . . brought to substantiate, by the cold logic of recorded acts and facts, the reports and rumours that have been rife in these two colonies.'[20] For the economist Edward Charles Robinson, this was 'an *experimentum cruces*' that would finally squelch speculation about whether Britain would have performed even better under protection. These were ideal experimental conditions, and he wished to let the 'naked strength and beauty' of the favourable statistics for New South Wales speak for itself.[21]

The figures found their way into Britain's public sphere through a number of routes. Baden-Powell's position no doubt familiarized him with the colonies' official publications, but these were publicly available documents, and interested parties in Britain could access them through governmental or bibliothecarial means. The press was also a significant transmitter. Journalists in Sydney and Melbourne would produce material relating to newly released statistics and their relevance to the tariff issue. British newspapers either employed these men as special correspondents, or they would reproduce stories and articles which had previously appeared in Australian newspapers such as the *Sydney Morning Herald*. British economists and opinionated colonists would pen letters to the editors of British newspapers, thus placing hard figures from colonial statistical departments before the general educated readership of the imperial metropolis. None of these paths for the transmission of statistics were, of course, exclusive to Britain's imperial relationships. However, the case of the Australian fiscal contest certainly relates to the burgeoning literature on 'networks' and 'webs' as a means of conceptualizing Britain's empire. Information, like people, capital, and goods, flowed through these networks, and the prominent role of intra-imperial exchanges via the press chimes with the important work of Simon Potter and Alan Lester.[22]

The Canadian economist Craufurd D.W. Goodwin has portrayed British views of Australian protectionism as symptomatic of how colonial economic policies were measured against accepted *laissez-faire* orthodoxy rather than the objectives of industrial development and urban employment in those young communities. He bemoans that 'the statistics of this employment' were not examined when Britons evaluated Australian tariff policy, and that a 'wide range of information which now seems important to a fair appraisal of national policies . . . was rejected or ignored.'[23] Goodwin's judgment is unfair, however. The nature of the debate was often constrained by the available statistics, but more importantly, free traders claimed that lower tariffs in New South Wales had encouraged industrial employment without needing to mimic Victoria's recourse to protection. This contradicted common free trade arguments that by abandoning tariffs new countries would obtain greatest benefit by specializing in agriculture. Nevertheless, free traders happily adduced New South Wales as proof that protection had not been responsible for Victoria's development, arguing that its growth had in fact been due to capitalists and entrepreneurs discerning commercial advantage in establishing manufacturing there.[24] In other words, market players had independently done what protectionists claimed the state had to encourage them to do. Free trade, not protection, was therefore the true infant industries policy.[25]

Due to the relative comprehensiveness and reliability of the Australian census, its figures for population growth, both natural and through immigration, were the crude main indicator of national prosperity. Population growth was itself considered to be a sign of increasing welfare and the engine of economic expansion, especially in new countries.[26] In addition, import and export statistics were readily available, and free traders adduced greater increases in New South Wales' trade volume compared to Victoria's as indicative of greater wealth and welfare under free trade.[27] Coghlan compiled *A Statistical Account of the Seven Colonies of Australasia* from 1890, which allowed comparisons between the colonies. His income statistics also developed over time, benefiting enormously from the information gathered for New South Wales' income tax, introduced in 1897.[28] Consequently, the statistics which British free traders utilized began to go beyond population, both human and sheep. When the Australian Liberal C.H. Chomley updated the late Lord Farrer's *Free Trade Versus Fair Trade* for its 1904 edition, he included a judicious helping of comparative statistics for the Australian colonies, including per capita income, consumption of various goods, and factory output, employment, and wages.[29] Elsewhere, Chomley drew on Coghlan's *Statistical Account* and Australian trade magazines to show Britons that New South Wales outstripped Victoria in population, wages, trade, output per head, and consumption, and enjoyed lower prices.[30]

Not all free traders embraced the Australian contest with such passion. Sir Charles Dilke, Liberal imperialist and popularizer of the term 'Greater Britain', rejected the idea that petty victories in inaccurately compiled statistics relating to population and public revenue could possibly provide cast-iron proof of free trade's superiority. At most, he concluded, 'all that can be asserted is that a protective system is by no means so disturbing an element in national finance and national prosperity as was imagined, before the colonies had tried their experiments, to be the case'—a point not unlike that made by tariff reformers.[31] Dilke's imperialist leanings rendered him deeply sympathetic to the developmental aims of the colonies, and less inclined to use Australia to support the free trade case.

Robert Giffen, the chief statistician at the Board of Trade and a dedicated free trader, also resented his fellow free traders' partisan and inaccurate application of Australian statistics. Rather than arguing that New South Wales had out-industrialized Victoria under free trade, he explained that neither colony had developed substantive manufacturing industries other than those which had a purely local application and required no protection, such as tanneries and brickyards. Neither protection nor free trade had helped either new country to sustain viable factory-based industries, said Giffen, for the crucial factor was the size of a country's domestic market; in both New South Wales and Victoria this was relatively small.[32] Giffen had long been convinced that free trade had been responsible for Britain's economic growth and improved living standards, and he did not need squabbles over Australian development to prove it. By 1903, however, he was prepared to accept tariff reform on political and imperial grounds, even whilst lambasting Chamberlain for his uses of statistics. In January 1910 he backed the Unionists, finding himself more willing to support import duties than the confiscatory direct taxation contained in Lloyd George's budget of the previous year.[33]

THE EDWARDIAN TARIFF CONTROVERSY

The statistical battle between free trade New South Wales and protectionist Victoria had been carried out primarily in newspapers, periodicals, and specialist publications intended for a middle-class audience. Although regarded as a unique case, it certainly reflected an international statistical perspective that, as will be shown, would continue to play a prominent role in the early twentieth-century tariff debate. By the Edwardian period, statistical comparisons between Britain and protectionist countries were now facilitated by the development of national statistics, particularly relating to labour, including wages. The United States had been particularly quick off the mark in this field, establishing a Bureau of Labor Statistics in 1884, eight years before a similar agency was set up in Germany, and nine years in the British case.[34] However, the advanced state of Australian statistics to some extent compensated for Britain's deficiencies in other areas. The difficulty of debating the economic worth of rival fiscal systems without statistics for industrial output was a prime motivation behind David Lloyd George's Census of Production Act 1906. Indeed, the Welshman singled out America and Australia as successful practitioners of industrial production figures.[35] In the electoral battle between free trade and tariff reform from which he and his fellow Liberals had just emerged victorious (but which was to continue), statistics were forced to play a markedly different role than previously. Statistics retained their place in 'high-brow' Edwardian discussion of economic matters.[36] But following Chamberlain's reopening of the tariff issue in 1903, they were now also to be used to persuade a mass electorate, which included many less-educated working-class voters, of the merits of one fiscal system over another.

As Trentmann has explained, 'Free Traders realized that Tariff Reform would not be defeated by statistics alone'. Whilst tariff reform promised to benefit particular industries, and therefore had immediate appeal to voters connected with those industries, it was more difficult to organize 'collective action' in support of free trade. Its supporters consequently saw that they had to communicate economic matters to the electorate in a comprehensible, educational, yet entertaining way.[37] As G. Wallace Carter of the Free Trade Union remarked in 1910, '[s]ince nobody can think statistically in millions . . . the ordinary man must be helped to think by contrasts, and in pictures.'[38] Statistics and visual imagery went hand in hand in an effort to persuade voters, and tariff reformers themselves countered with their own visual campaigning methods. International comparisons were central to the cases made by both sides. Through the media of posters, exhibitions, and shows, statistics relating to British and foreign living standards and other economic indicators were presented for popular consumption.

The Board of Trade's 1903 blue book on British and foreign trade became a central text of the tariff controversy, providing free traders with statistics which they incorporated into the primary visual and rhetorical component of their campaign: the big free trade bread loaf and its small tariff reform counterpart. The loaf imagery, Trentmann notes, was used to represent not just the difference in prices under free trade and protection, but also purchasing power: how much more British workers could buy with their wages than workers in protectionist countries. In November 1903, the pro-free trade *Daily News* responded to Chamberlain's stunt of presenting two identical loaves representing free trade and tariff reform by baking its own loaves based on the blue book statistics: the free trade loaf was, of course, much bigger. In the 1905–6 election campaign, one Liberal candidate presented voters with images of the two loaves alongside 'facts from the Government Blue Book 1903', which compared wages for skilled workers, wheat prices, and weekly working hours in Britain and Germany (see Figure 12.1).[39]

In the tariff reform camp, there were initial doubts that statistics would be suitable for mass consumption and comprehension. Chamberlain told Hewins that workingmen and public audiences would not be swayed by facts and figures; indeed, one of his main arguments for imperial preference was an emotional, rather than material, appeal to the higher calling of empire.[40] Tariff reformers were more prone to rely on nationalistic, rather than statistical, imagery: John Bull, Uncle Sam, and the German bogeyman, 'Herr Dumper', a moustachioed individual who took advantage of

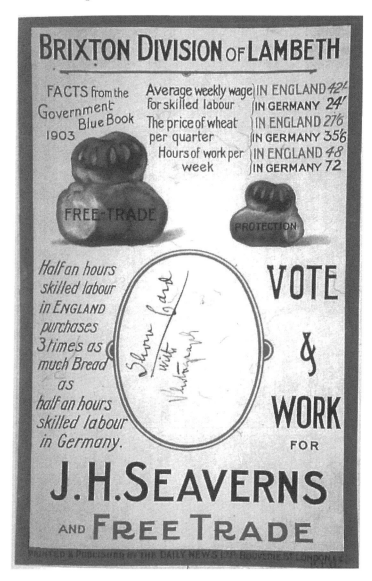

Figure 12.1   A 1905 election card. Reproduced by kind permission of the National Archives, London.

Britain's free trade to flood its market with underpriced goods. However, tariff reformers did make heavy use of statistics. T.A. Brassey, arguing in favour of tariff reform before Tunbridge Wells farmers in 1904, spoke of 'the great Blue Book which is being quoted by speakers on both sides'.[41] The Tariff Reform League had a discernible appetite for verbal argument, and statistics made for an enlivening condiment. Its *Speaker's Handbook*, originally published in 1903 and updated annually, sought to provide tariff reform campaigners with ready responses to free trade jibes, and to supply them with ample figures to bolster their arguments. The 1903 *Handbook* drew on the blue book's statistics for individual trades—a different perspective from aggregate economic matters such as prices, and one which made sense given the selective nature of protectionism. An eclectic range of other sources offered further facts. The *Musical Trade Review Directory*, for instance, provided statistics relating to musical instruments; perhaps not the 'index of national manufacturing capacity' that iron was, but apparently helpful to the tariff reform cause all the same.[42]

Concerns immediately arose in 1903 regarding the inaccurate use of statistics by advocates of both free trade and tariff reform. As in the contest between New South Wales and Victoria, when Giffen counselled against hyperbolic statistical claims, perhaps the most stinging remarks came from pro-free trade statistical experts. 'So many writers and speakers are making use of statistical arguments, in dealing with the current fiscal controversy, to support such inconsistent and confusing conclusions', bemoaned the London School of Economics' Liberal statistician, A.L. Bowley. 'A writer publishes a theory based on his own interpretation of history and political economy, and fits it with some partly relevant and incomplete figures.'[43] Many of Bowley's professional exhortations, including the need to account for alterations in price indices, were disregarded. When they were, it could be meat and drink to the opponents of the offending side. As Trentmann has discussed, the use of statistics prompted crucial questions about fair comparisons and the trustworthiness of sources.[44]

Free traders and tariff reformers were engaged in a decade-long fight to discredit each other's statistical arguments in the eyes of the public. The Cobden Club's riposte to Chamberlain published in 1904 aimed to show 'how delusive and unscientific his statistics' were, and how he had engineered a 'distortion of figures and facts to fit in with his new theories and schemes.' It attacked his 'statistical jugglery', through which he claimed a rise in the price of bread after Repeal in the 1840s but included several years of war and protected prices in his chosen time frame. No mercy was given to his 'audacious manipulation of figures', whereby he was said to have dishonestly compared a boom year of the 1870s with a lean year of the 1900s, and ignored altogether the significant deflation of the period which lowered the nominal value of British exports.[45]

To help counter these attacks, the *Speakers' Handbook* provided Tariff Reform League activists with figures from blue books, the Board of Trade's *Labour Gazette*, Tariff Commission Memoranda, and French official returns, among many other sources. The League was particularly keen to belittle free traders' emphasis on exports per head. 'Of all the fallacious tests of comparative prosperity applied by Cobdenism', the 1908 *Handbook* asserted, this was 'the most absurd.' Statistics from Berlin's *Deutsche*

Industrie Zeitung showed that the proportion of population employed in mining and manufacturing compared to agriculture was far lower in Britain than in Germany or the United States, whilst protectionist Belgium's exports per head surpassed Britain's: in other words, Britain's rivals were manufacturing with tremendous efficiency under protective tariffs. The *Handbook* also defended the figures relating to the relative performance of specific industries such as iron and steel, in which German production had leapt far ahead of Britain's and there were 'statistics of production in this country which permit of a trustworthy comparison with the record of our leading industrial competitors.' Speakers were given the tools to challenge the free trade defence that British and German unemployment figures were incomparable: if British figures were recorded on the German basis, the *Handbook* informed activists, unemployment would appear to be even higher.[46] However, when appropriate, the League certainly pointed out where British and foreign unemployment statistics *were* incomparable and worth ignoring.[47]

Statistical credibility in the fiscal debate was about more than pleasing scholars like Bowley. In this most popular of political campaigns, citing the provenance of figures demonstrated less a concern for scientific accuracy than an appeal to working-class ideas of trustworthy sources of information. These included trade unions, themselves prodigious statistical machines, which accrued and generated the data that shaped and facilitated a number of late Victorian and Edwardian social reforms. Union strike figures fed state interventionism in industrial disputes, whilst National Insurance co-opted trade unions, with their own existing actuarial systems, as 'approved societies'.[48]

Tariff reformers were understandably eager to reconcile a working-class electorate with the cold hard numbers of industry and trade. However small and unsuccessful the Trade Union Tariff Reform Association was as a genuinely working-class force for converting working-class voters to Chamberlainite fiscal policy, it is noteworthy that the association's trade unionist speakers received training and materials from the Tariff Reform League to which it was increasingly beholden.[49] Following their landslide victory in 1906, the Liberals increasingly appealed to anti-aristocratic class sentiments in their fiscal and social policies, encouraging the League to step up its efforts to appeal to workers. It organized a number of 'working men's tours' of Germany in 1910: a calculated exercise to scotch the myths propagated by free traders of an impoverished, oppressed German working class forced to eat black bread and horseflesh because of protection.[50] The published reports provide a useful window into the statistical politics surrounding working-class audiences.

In addition to experiencing German life firsthand, many of the delegates on these tours gathered statistics from town halls, labour exchanges, trade unions, and individual firms, including the industrial giant Krupps. But why, given that the League's *Handbook* was already packed with blue book statistics, were these tours deemed necessary? As the preface to the first volume of reports observed, '[a]ccurate statistical information is always available in Government publications'.[51] It was not therefore the case that tariff reformers distrusted official figures, but rather that workingmen's reportage, combining acquired statistics with anecdotal evidence, could provide them with something more:

> We have in these pages the opinions set forth of Liberals, Conservatives, Socialists, and of men without political bias at all. The reports are not the narratives of expert sociologists, but of British working men writing for their fellows to read. Discrepancies there may be in the setting-out of figures received, but it is in the consensus of individual opinions that the main value of the reports consists . . . the information found in this volume has a value distinct from that of Blue Books, and will prove useful, we have every confidence, where the contents of many Blue Books would be worthless.[52]

Such informal and 'unscientific' categories of knowledge were usually perceived to lack the impartial authority of formally, professionally, and methodically acquired information.[53] But above the probity of statistical professionals, the League prized an authentic statement of working-class approval for German protectionism. By presenting the firsthand 'consensus' view of a broad section of workingmen, tariff reformers laid claim to a 'truth' about living standards under protection that, they suggested, the cold hard figures of the blue books did not reveal. The workingmen's tours were the League's attempt to introduce information with working-class credentials to the fiscal debate in order to combat progressive mythmaking. This was evidence obtained *by* workingmen *for* workingmen, something with presumed appeal to that constituency. Yet it is debateable, or simply unclear, how 'working class' many of the delegates who dealt with statistics actually were: some were 'ex-socialist' journalists and writers—hardly coal miners—whilst (perhaps suspiciously) the occupations of an entire, and particularly statistically minded, delegation were not listed as they were in other cases.[54]

There were, however, important linkages between the use of official statistics in popular campaigning and the 'higher-level' debate of economic and social scientists. The trust of the average workingman in the veracity and reliability of statistics was not taken for granted by either the free trade or the tariff reform organizations. Deference and authority were strong components of Edwardian society, and the judgments of more educated minds upon the use and abuse of economic statistics were therefore important to free trade and tariff reform rhetoric. Academic research and writing therefore permeated the oratory of popular soapbox politics. For instance, the Tariff Reform League encouraged speakers to look at a paper on food taxation in the United Kingdom, France, Germany, and the United States appearing in the Royal Statistical Society's journal. Tea and coffee, speakers were urged to note, enjoyed free entry to the American republic; a useful point, given the tariff reform scheme to reduce tea duty as compensation for a duty on corn.[55]

The United States was the most heavily protectionist rich country, and free traders usually emphasized the high cost of tariffs to the average American consumer, backing up these claims with facts and figures.[56] These could be articulated in visual form, as in the Free Trade Union's *Perils of Protection* pamphlet series of 1909, which presented images of the American home and workingman labelled with the costs imposed on everyday goods by tariffs, along with visual demonstrations of the American consumer's diminished purchasing power (see Figure 12.2).[57] However, whilst free traders had taken a boost from the international comparisons in the 1903 blue book, they were less comfortable with the Board of Trade's 1911 report on working-class conditions in American industrial towns. Prosperous, high-wage, protectionist America was ever the awkward case for free trade, and the Board's report laid down in stark facts and figures that tariffs seemingly did the American worker little harm.[58] Tariff reformers happily amalgamated these official statistics with entertaining visuals in their publications. One Tariff Reform League cartoon from 1911 showed an American workman and a British workman admiring a poster quoting the Board of Trade report. American wage earners, the British workman who had backed free trade might have been surprised to learn, took home earnings two-and-a-half times greater than he did (see Figure 12.3).[59] Whilst free traders had benefited from the unique conditions of the New World in the contest between New South Wales and Victoria, they now argued that the differences between old and new countries negated comparisons between Britain and America. Previous Board of Trade reports on France, Germany, and Belgium had shown lower wages, longer hours, and higher rent and costs than in Britain, but, said *The Economist*, 'when we come to the New World it would indeed have been surprising if the comparison had been in our favour'.[60]

Numbers, then, were not unquestionable in their authority. If statistics, even from a source respected for its reliability, did not affirm one's policy preferences, the facts and figures could be excused for one reason or another. Because statistics were simply a selected means of illustrating positions already held, the implications of contrary figures were minimal. As Giffen had posited in the early 1880s, no set of comparative statistics for free trade and protectionist countries could ever settle the fight for definite: ultimately, each creed's followers had a favoured fiscal system for reasons that went beyond material benefits, and therefore 'political and moral considerations must come in.'[61] To its supporters, free trade represented political purity, preventing the state and fiscal policy from being captured by narrow and selfish commercial interests. To its enemies, it meant the erosion of Britain's 'productive power', empire, and international position for the sake of narrow and selfish 'cosmopolitan' interests.[62] Statistics were thus used to reinforce these political and moral

Figure 12.2 'Wages, food prices and savings', part of *Perils of Protection* series in Free Trade Union, Miscellaneous Pamphlets, 1909. © The British Library Board.

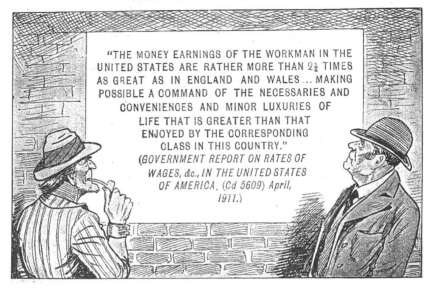

*Figure 12.3   American workman: "Yes, Sir, that's what the tariff does for me."
British workman: "Well, I'm blowed!—and to think I've been shouting for Lloyd
George and voting Free Trade."* 'The truth at last', *Monthly Notes on Tariff Reform*,
14, 5 May, 1911. © The British Library Board.

standpoints. For the free trade cause, figures relating to American prices
simply strengthened its scaremongering rhetoric about tariffs as the 'foster-
mother' of monopolies.[63] Contrary to Alain Badiou, who is cited in the introduction to this volume, statistics did not necessarily push out abstract ideas
from public debate, but could in fact reinforce notions of liberty and justice.
It is unlikely that we shall ever know the extent to which statistics persuaded
Edwardian voters one way or the other. But it seems that their greatest impact
was in adding some degree of 'authority' to those rhetorical and visual planks
of the fiscal debate concerned with securing justice for the masses: the big and
small loaves, the 'theft' of jobs, and the 'demon' of monopoly.

CONCLUSION

Britain's tariff debate provides an illuminating historical example of the
same arguments and challenges involved in using statistics in intellectual
and political discourse today. It saw wide-ranging public discussion of an
economic issue that contemporaries perceived to be of supreme importance,
taking place in a mature economy and an increasingly democratic society. Statistics added a 'scientific' dimension to intellectual debate among

educated Britons and found their way into electioneering at an early stage of mass political participation. The Edwardian fiscal debate was perhaps unusual in the extent of its incorporation of statistical information into popular political campaigning. However, there are other examples of statistics in public policy debates which point to the increasing importance of numbers, including the debates over industrial relations and old-age pensions in the 1890s and 1900s.[64]

The main themes of this essay point towards some broader observations relating to statistics and the public sphere. First, the Australian tariff 'contest' and the Edwardian fiscal controversy demonstrate the significant role of international statistics in the public sphere. To some extent, this was endemic to discussion of tariff policy: concerned with imports, exports, and international competitiveness, it was by nature an internationalized topic. But statistics themselves are inherently disposed to transnational migration and use. Numbers, unlike words, are more capable of transcending linguistic and cultural boundaries. Yet it is also noticeable how preconceived notions, or rhetorical definitions, of other economies can be used to validate or invalidate statistics relating to those same economies. It has been demonstrated here that the concept of 'new countries' and their unique qualities fulfilled both of these roles. The characterization of Australia as a *carte blanche* environment underpinned the notion of experimental conditions, whilst the New World's abundance invalidated the awkward fact of American prosperity under protectionism.[65]

Secondly, there is something to be learnt about Habermas's notion of the public sphere itself. In his terms, the use of statistics in the Edwardian tariff debate represented the task of 'integrating' the masses 'with the help of new methods' in order to win their votes. Habermas described this 'systematic propaganda' as having 'the Janus face of enlightenment and control; of information and advertising; of pedagogy and manipulation.'[66] James Thompson's nuanced analysis has shown the shortcomings of this suspicious view of the politics of early twentieth-century mass consumer society.[67] Similarly, the example given here of the workingmen's tours in Germany demonstrates that the modern public sphere does not necessarily entail the degree of public passivity suggested by Habermas.[68] Nevertheless, he was essentially correct that in an age of mass political participation competition for votes meant embracing 'new methods', of which statistics, and their presentation to the public, was one.

Confirmation is also found for Theodore Porter's observations regarding social scientists and statisticians, and their engagement with the public sphere of the nineteenth century. 'Objectivity' for these practitioners was not, as it is for their present-day counterparts, a matter of demonstrable neutrality towards the subject of investigation. In the fiscal debate, Giffen best represents the kind of Victorian social scientist described by Porter: a government employee, bound by certain standards of political neutrality, but certainly active in defending and promoting free trade within civil society. His position was not without tensions, however. His double life as a journalist, which had included stints at Liberal bastions the *Daily News* and *The Economist* in the 1860s and 1870s, meant that he found some difficulty in abiding by those standards of political neutrality expected of civil servants.[69]

Giffen is also noteworthy for his confidence in the utility and application of statistical evidence. But just as Whiggish views of British history were sustained by an upward economic and geopolitical trajectory, so too, perhaps, was it relatively easy for free traders to rely on statistics prior to the First World War. Britain was still an industrial behemoth, facing increasing competition perhaps, but unquestionably an advanced economy. The free trade case was that there was little to worry about. But in the 1920s and early 1930s, when national economic problems were indisputable, economic statistics were arguably of less importance in the public sphere. In the context of Keynes's challenge to traditional assumptions regarding a self-equilibrating economy, economic principles, rather than figures, tended to dominate public debate. Statistics certainly contributed to the formulation and discussion of economic theory at an academic level: the period witnessed attempts to accurately measure unemployment, national income, and the business cycle. But broader public discussion was characterized less by a comparative battle of numbers than by arguments over fundamental economic principles. For instance, would public investment to reduce unemployment simply 'crowd out' private-sector activity and generate inflation?[70] Shorn of persuasive figures and the need to compare one fiscal policy with another, the remaining rump of committed campaigners for free trade now relied upon abstract principles and emotional appeals; comparative consumer prices were out, whereas 'Economy' and national character were in.[71]

NOTES

1. A. Howe, 'Britain and the World Economy', in Chris Williams (ed.), *A Companion to Nineteenth-Century Britain* (Oxford, 2004), pp. 17–33. The author would like to thank Frank Trentmann for commenting on an early version of this essay.
2. H.C.G. Matthew, *Gladstone, 1809–1874* (Oxford, 1986), pp. 120–8; R. McKibbin, 'Why Was There No Marxism in Britain?', in *idem.*, *The Ideologies of Class: Social Relations in Britain, 1880–1950* (Oxford, 1990), pp. 31–2.
3. S.H. Zebel, 'Fair Trade: An English Reaction to the Breakdown of the Cobden Treaty System', *Journal of Modern History* 12 (1940), pp. 161–85; B.H. Brown, *The Tariff Reform Movement in Great Britain, 1881–1895* (New York, 1943); A. Sykes, *Tariff Reform in British Politics, 1903–1913* (Oxford, 1979); E.H.H. Green, *The Crisis of Conservatism: The Politics, Economics, and Ideology of the British Conservative Party, 1880–1914* (London, 1995); F. Trentmann, *Free Trade Nation: Commerce, Consumption, and Civil Society in Modern Britain* (Oxford, 2008).

4. L. Goldman, 'Victorian Social Science: From Singular to Plural', in M.J. Daunton (ed.), *The Organisation of Knowledge in Victorian Britain* (Oxford, 2005), p. 101.
5. E. Rogers, 'The United States and the Fiscal Debate in Britain, 1873–1913', *Historical Journal* 50 (2007), p. 622.
6. Trentmann, *Free Trade Nation*, pp. 86–91. Trentmann capitalizes 'Free Trade', as contemporaries often did, to emphasize that it was a totemic political and cultural creed, not just an economic policy and theory. However, capitalization, and also hyphenation, were employed inconsistently during this period. As a matter of personal preference, free trade and tariff reform appear in decapitalized form throughout this essay.
7. C. Calhoun, 'Introduction: Habermas and the Public Sphere', in *idem*. (ed.), *Habermas and the Public Sphere* (Cambridge, MA, 1992), pp. 33–9.
8. For instance, H.J. Pettifer, *John Bull and Jonathan: Or Free Trade v. Protection. An Address to Working Men* (London, 1889).
9. J. Thompson, '"Pictorial lies"?—Posters and Politics in Britain c. 1880–1914', *Past and Present* 197 (2007), pp. 177–210.
10. A.W. Coats, 'The Historist Reaction in English Political Economy, 1870–90', *Economica* 21 (1954), pp. 143–53; S. Collini, D. Winch, and J. Burrow, *That Noble Science of Politics: A Study in Nineteenth-Century Intellectual History* (Cambridge, 1983), ch. 8; G.M. Koot, *English Historical Economics, 1870–1926: The Rise of Economic History and Neomercantilism* (Cambridge, 1987); Green, *Crisis*, ch. 5.
11. Although the two terms are often used interchangeably, 'historist', as employed by A.W. Coats, is a preferable term to 'historicist' in the English context—see Koot, *English Historical Economics*, pp. 1–2. On the different definitions attached to the equivalent German terms, see S. Berger's response to Ulrich Muhlack, in *German Historical Institute London Bulletin* 23 (2001), p. 28f.
12. J.S. Mill, *Principles of Political Economy* (1st edn., 2 vols., London, 1848), II, book 5, ch. 10, sec. 1.
13. F.W. Taussig, *The Tariff History of the United States* (New York, 1914); G.D. Patterson, *The Tariff in the Australian Colonies, 1856–1900* (Melbourne, 1968); S.J. McLean, *The Tariff History of Canada* (Toronto, 1895); C.D.W. Goodwin, *Canadian Economic Thought: The Political Economy of a Developing Nation* (Durham, NC, 1961), pp. 42–3.
14. 'The Canadian Protective Tariff', *The Economist*, 25 Sep. 1858, p. 1064.
15. Patterson, *Tariff in the Australian Colonies*, chs. 3, 6, 9, 12; A. Howe, *Free Trade and Liberal England, 1846–1946* (Oxford, 1997), pp. 120, 127, 140; Cobden Club, *Protection in New Countries* (London, 1886).
16. Patterson, *Tariff in the Australian Colonies*, chs. 2, 5, 8.
17. G. Baden-Powell, 'Protection in Young Communities: Recorded Results in Victoria and New South Wales', *Report of the British Association for the Advancement of Science, 1881* (1882), pp. 760–1. See also *idem*., 'The Results of Protection in Young Communities', *Fortnightly Review* 31 (1882), pp. 369–79; *idem*., *State Aid and State Interference* (London, 1882).
18. H.W. Arndt, 'A Pioneer of National Income Estimates', *Economic Journal* 59 (1949), pp. 616–25; P. Studenski, *The Income of Nations—Part One: History* (New York, 1958), pp. 135–7; C. Forster and C. Hazlehurst, 'Australian Statisticians and the Development of Official Statistics', *Year Book Australia 1988* (Canberra, 1988); P. Groenewegen and B. McFarlane, *A History of Australian Economic Thought* (London, 1990), ch. 5; S. Macintyre, *A Colonial Liberalism: The Lost World of Three Victorian Visionaries* (Oxford, 1991), pp. 112–14; I. Castles, 'Australian Official Statistics, 1822–1945:

From Blue Book to White Pages' (paper presented at International Statistical Institute, 55th Session, Sydney, Australia, 2005).

19. 'Free Trade v. Protection in Australia', *The Colonies and India*, 6 Oct. 1882, p. 13; 30 Mar. 1883, p. 9; 20 Apr. 1883, p. 12; and 4 May 1883, p. 14; Lyon Playfair, *Subjects of Social Welfare* (London, 1889), pp. 170–1; letter from E.C. Robinson, 'The M'Kinley Tariff', *The Times*, 13 Oct. 1890, p. 14.
20. Baden-Powell, *State Aid*, pp. 133–4.
21. Robinson, 'The M'Kinley Tariff'.
22. S.J. Potter, *News and the British World: The Emergence of an Imperial Press System, 1876–1922* (Oxford, 2003); *idem.*, 'Webs, Networks, and Systems: Globalization and the Mass Media in the Nineteenth- and Twentieth-Century British Empire', *Journal of British Studies* 46 (2007), pp. 621–46; A. Lester, *Imperial Networks: Creating Identities in Nineteenth-Century South Africa and Britain* (London, 2001). For an excellent summary of this literature, see A. Lester, 'Imperial Circuits and Networks: Geographies of the British Empire', *History Compass* 4 (2006), pp. 124–41.
23. C.D.W. Goodwin, *The Image of Australia: British Perception of the Australian Economy from the Eighteenth to the Twentieth Century* (Durham, NC, 1974), p. 108.
24. 'Free Trade v. Protection in Australia', *The Colonies and India*, 6 Oct. 1882, p. 13; 30 Mar. 1883, p. 9; 20 Apr. 1883, p. 12; 4 May 1883, p. 14; C.W. Dilke, *Problems of Greater Britain* (2 vols., London, 1890), II, p. 345.
25. M. Davitt, *Life and Progress in Australasia* (London, 1898), pp. 145–6.
26. See, for instance, D. Syme, 'Restrictions on Trade from a Colonial Point of View', *Fortnightly Review* 13 ns (1873), p. 463.
27. Baden-Powell, *State Aid*, pp. 127–8.
28. Arndt, 'A Pioneer', pp. 617–18.
29. Lord Farrer, *Free Trade Versus Fair Trade* (London, 1904), pp. 239–40.
30. C.H. Chomley, 'Free Trade New South Wales and Protected Victoria', *Contemporary Review* 85 (1904), pp. 172–85.
31. Dilke, *Problems*, II, pp. 340–5; T.A. Brassey, *Problems of Empire* (London, 1904), p. 129.
32. R. Giffen, 'Protection for Manufactures in New Countries', *Economic Journal* 29 (1898), pp. 3–16.
33. R.S. Mason, 'Robert Giffen and the Tariff Reform Campaign, 1865–1910', *Journal of European Economic History* 25 (1996), pp. 171–88; A.C. Howe, 'Giffen, Sir Robert (1837–1910)', *Oxford Dictionary of National Biography*, online edn., Jan. 2008, http://www.oxforddnb.com/view/article/33396. Accessed 27 Feb. 2010.
34. M.O. Furner, 'Knowing Capitalism: Public Investigation and the Labour Question in the Long Progressive Era', in M.O. Furner and B. Supple (eds.), *The State and Economic Knowledge: The American and British Experiences* (Cambridge, 1990), pp. 246–7.
35. *Hansard*, 4th ser., clvii, col. 500 (16 May 1906), and clxii, col. 1174 (1 Aug. 1906). Joseph Chamberlain wished to highlight that British manufacturers would be more averse than their New World counterparts to 'disclosing any particulars with regard to their business.'
36. A.W. Coats, 'Political Economy and the Tariff Reform Campaign of 1903', *Journal of Law and Economics* 11 (1968), pp. 205–8.
37. Trentmann, *Free Trade Nation*, pp. 87–8.
38. Quoted in *ibid.*, p. 81.
39. *Ibid.*, pp. 88, 90–1.
40. *Ibid.*, p. 188; Sykes, *Tariff Reform*, pp. 59–60.
41. Brassey, *Problems of Empire*, pp. 180–1.

A 'Naked Strength and Beauty' 243

42. Tariff Reform League [hereafter TRL], *Speakers' Handbook* (London, 1903), p. 43; TRL, *Speakers' Handbook* (London, 1908), p. xi.
43. A.L. Bowley, 'Statistical Methods and the Fiscal Controversy', *Economic Journal* 13 (1903), p. 303.
44. Trentmann, *Free Trade Nation*, p. 90.
45. Cobden Club, *Fact Versus Fiction: The Cobden Club's Reply to Mr. Chamberlain* (London, 1904).
46. TRL, *Speakers' Handbook* (1908), pp. xi, 17–18, 43–4, 52–3.
47. *Ibid.*, pp. 52–3.
48. R. Davidson, *Whitehall and the Labour Problem in Late Victorian and Edwardian Britain: A Study in Official Statistics and Social Control* (Beckenham, 1985); B.B. Gilbert, *The Evolution of National Insurance in Britain: The Origins of the Welfare State* (London, 1966).
49. K.D. Brown, 'The Trade Union Tariff Reform Association, 1904–1913', *Journal of British Studies* 9 (1970), pp. 141–53.
50. TRL, *Reports on Labour and Social Conditions in Germany, Volume One: Working Men's Tours* (London, 1910), pp. iii–iv. On these myths, see Trentmann, *Free Trade Nation*, pp. 95–100.
51. TRL, *Reports on Labour*, p. v.
52. *Loc. cit.*
53. There are similar issues of comparative regard for 'tacit knowledge' and formal knowledge. See M. Daunton, 'Introduction', in *idem., Organisation of Knowledge*, p. 8.
54. TRL, *Reports*, pp. vi–xi.
55. TRL, *Speakers' Handbook* (1908), p. 36.
56. On the level of American protectionism, see A. Estevadeordal, 'Measuring Protection in the Early Twentieth Century', *European Review of Economic History* 1 (1997), pp. 89–125.
57. Free Trade Union, miscellaneous pamphlets (1909), British Library.
58. Rogers, 'The United States', p. 609.
59. 'The Truth at Last', *Monthly Notes on Tariff Reform* (May, 1911), p. ii.
60. 'The American Working Man', *The Economist*, 22 Apr. 1911, p. 831.
61. R. Giffen, 'The Use of Import and Export Statistics', *Journal of the Statistical Society of London* 45 (1882), pp. 226–7.
62. Sykes, *Tariff Reform*, pp. 59–60, 288.
63. Rogers, 'The United States', p. 622.
64. E. Rogers, 'The Impact of the New World on Economic and Social Debates in Britain, c. 1860–1914' (PhD thesis, University of Cambridge, 2009), chs. 8–9, p. 253.
65. On the dichotomy between old and new countries, and its impact on the public sphere, see Rogers, 'The Impact of the New World'.
66. Jürgen Habermas, *The Structural Transformation of the Public Sphere: An Inquiry into a Category of Bourgeois Society* [1962, trans. T. Burger with the assistance of F. Lawrence] (Oxford, 1991), p. 203.
67. Thompson, 'Pictorial Lies'.
68. See introduction to this volume.
69. He was temporarily suspended from his position at the Board of Trade in 1881 for his 'injudicious journalism'. See Howe, 'Giffen'.
70. The classic history of Keynes's interwar thought, and the public debate on policy responses to unemployment, is P. Clarke, *The Keynesian Revolution in the Making, 1924–1936* (Oxford, 1988).
71. P. Clarke, 'The Treasury's Analytical Model of the British Economy between the Wars', in Furner and Supple, *State and Economic Knowledge*; Trentmann, *Free Trade Nation*, ch. 7.

13 Polling Public Opinion before Opinion Polls

The Conservative Party and Election Prediction between the Wars

Laura Beers

The Conservative party was the largest party in parliament for all but thirty-eight months of the twenty-seven years between the end of the First and the end of the Second World War. Despite the existence of genuine three-party competition for much of the period, at no point did the Conservatives poll less than a third of the popular vote. The 1924 and 1931 elections were both landslides for the party: the Conservatives increased their representation by 154 seats in October 1924, and by 210 seats in October 1931. In his classic essay 'Class and Conventional Wisdom', Ross McKibbin ascribed the dominance of the interwar Conservative party to its ability to marshal effectively so-called conventional wisdoms about the fractious and self-interested nature of trade unionism against its Labour opponents, while simultaneously presenting itself as the guardian of national interests.[1] Over the past two decades, McKibbin's thesis has become a conventional wisdom of its own. The effectiveness of the electoral strategy based on anti-socialism and one-nation Toryism pioneered by Stanley Baldwin in the early 1920s is viewed as crucial to the breakup and eventual disintegration of the Liberal party, and to the ultimate capture of a majority of ex-Liberals by the Conservative camp.[2]

Given the historical consensus around the genius of interwar Conservative electoral strategy and the strength of Conservatism's hold over the public after 1931, it is surprising to read records from the party's archive indicating an extreme uncertainty and nervousness as to their hold over public opinion, especially in the 1930s. While the interwar Conservative leadership appreciated the impact of the 'national crisis' of August 1931 in converting Liberal voters to the Conservative cause at the election of that October, they were less ready than subsequent scholars to believe that 1931 marked a turning point in British politics after which 'the once great Liberal party became, in reality if not in name, an adjunct of the Conservative party.'[3] Retrospective analyses of Labour's by-election and general election performances from 1931 to 1935 have led scholars to conclude that 'in by-elections and in the 1935 general election Labour's recovery was both patchy and uneven'; and that 'Labour never really secured gains in *middle-class* seats from 1931 to 1935 ... [In 1935] much of the Liberal vote either stayed Conservative or stayed home. The middle ground of British politics was lost by Labour.'[4] Labour's by-election gains in the early 1930s in constituencies such as Rutland, Norwood, Rusholme or, most strikingly, East Fulham have been retrospectively dismissed on the grounds that '[i]t cannot be too strongly emphasized that these were by-elections. The fate of the government was not at stake.' From the perspective of hindsight, with the knowledge that neither Rutland, Norwood, nor Rusholme fell to Labour in 1935, and that East Fulham was lost to the party two years after it was regained, it is easy to conclude that, in the mid-1930s, 'Liberals would [not] risk voting Labour at a General Election.'[5] The same dismissive attitude has been taken towards Labour's post-1935 by-election gains. David Butler downplayed the significance of Labour's success in winning thirteen seats from the government between 1935 and 1939 by emphasizing that by-elections tend to be more 'agin' the Government' than general elections. The political scientists Mark Franklin and Matthew Lander have gone so far as to suggest that such a conversion did not even occur during the Second World War, but that Labour owed its 1945 victory to the introduction of new voters on to the electoral register.[6]

Retrospective analyses of by-election data are bolstered by statistical sampling and opinion polling of the electorate carried out by the political parties and later by the Nuffield psephology group. In May 1950, the Conservative Research Department commissioned a survey of Liberal and ex-Liberal voters which determined that approximately 40 percent of former Liberals who were not intent on voting Liberal again planned to vote Conservative, whereas only 20 percent planned to vote Labour and 20 percent remained undecided.[7] Butler and Donald Stokes's 1963 survey of voters whose earliest political preferences were Liberal found that 'despite the fact that the Labour party succeeded to the Liberals' place as the Conservatives' main opponent in the British party system, only a minority of historic Liberal support went to Labour.'[8]

All of this data, of course, was not available to Conservative strategists in the 1930s. Nonetheless, the available indicators should arguably have given them less anxiety than they did, particularly after the general election of 1935. However, the party remained hesitant to accept that the seeming conversion of former Liberals to the Conservative cause in 1931 represented a permanent and reliable shift in voter allegiance. The Conservatives' uncertainty can only be understood by taking into account the specific circumstances of interwar politics—circumstances that rendered election prediction exceptionally difficult.

In the nineteenth century, a limited franchise, smaller parliamentary constituencies, and (until 1872) the public ballot meant that parties were able to ascertain the opinions of electors with comparative certainty. In the first half of the twentieth century, by contrast, public opinion was incomparably inscrutable. As a result of the franchise expansions of 1884, 1918, and 1928, the British electorate grew by a factor of ten in less than half a century. Franchise reform combined with redistricting meant that the average constituency grew from 10,000 to 50,000, making most too large to canvass effectively. In addition to the impact of these reforms, the first decades of the twentieth century saw the emergence on the political scene of the Labour party, which by 1922 was contesting over 400 constituencies. The growth of Labour would ultimately cause a dramatic realignment of British politics, with Labour replacing the Liberals as the dominant party of the left in a two-party system. But in the decades between the war, and in particular in the 1920s, Britain witnessed an anomalous period of genuine three-party politics—a situation which rendered election prediction exceptionally tricky. As a journalist for *The Economist* wrote in 1935, in apology for his inability to offer firmer predictions as to the result of the upcoming election: 'Since the unromantic progress of Democracy, by the instrumentality of the Corrupt Practices Act many things have changed; and a General Election in the United Kingdom is nowadays about as far away from precise scientific calculation and as closely akin to a game of chance as anything in the world of politics could well be.'[9]

The unpredictability of modern politics was thrown into repeated relief in the 1920s, as pundits, punters, and parties repeatedly misread the intentions of the newly expanded electorate. The arrival of opinion polling in the late 1930s, and the subsequent development of focus-group research, enabled parties to quantitatively and qualitatively identify supporters, opponents and undecided voters and to adjust their political and electoral strategies accordingly.[10] In the 1920s, however, election prediction remained more an art than a science, and most of those who tried their hand at it found that they were exceptionally talentless artists. The unpredictability of politics in the 1920s had carry-on implications for politics in the 1930s, in that it made politicians less willing to trust either their instincts or other available indicators that had so recently proved dangerously faulty.

Thus it is unsurprising that, despite the seemingly optimistic evidence of the landslide towards Conservatism in October 1931, party leaders remained reluctant to rely on the constancy of public support for the Conservative-dominated National Government in the 1930s, and showed a retrospectively unwarranted fear that former Liberal supporters would gravitate towards the Labour party. These voters were not seen as Conservative converts, but as 'floating voters' whose political allegiance remained up for grabs.[11] This pessimism had a direct impact on Conservative policy and propaganda in the 1930s, as party organizers sought to avoid alienating the ex-Liberal vote. New Labour's electoral success owed much to its ability to locate marginal constituencies and to focus its message and its resources at those groups.[12] The interwar Conservative party, in contrast, could not feel confident in ignoring large sectors of the population and targeting its energies so selectively. Its lack of confidence in the depth of its support dictated an electoral strategy that was exceptionally cautious, conciliatory, and broad-based.

THE 1923 AND 1924 GENERAL ELECTIONS

The return of 412 Conservative MPs in 1924, which has conventionally been attributed to the success of the Conservative party in rallying the 'constitutionalist' or 'anti-socialist' vote, was perceived by contemporaries as by no means a foregone conclusion. Whereas prime minister Stanley Baldwin professed his party to be 'in good heart' going into the campaign, he was unwilling to prophesy on the election outcome—a cautiousness which reflected a more general wariness after the surprise outcome of 1923, when the Conservative government had failed to retain its majority.[13] Though several political observers, including the king, had foreseen the possibility of a government collapse in 1923, the Conservative leadership had remained bullishly optimistic.[14] In the week before the election, a Conservative agent had predicted to the *Daily Mail* that the party would return 332 MPs, compared to 157 Liberals and 120 Socialists. The Conservative candidate for Barnard Castle, Cuthbert Headlam, recorded 'a feeling of confidence in the air' after a trip to Unionist headquarters two weeks before the election.[15] J.C.C. Davidson, at that point Baldwin's principal confidant and personal advisor, as well as a key party strategist, not only overestimated the government's chances generally but erroneously believed his own seat to be 'absolutely safe.'[16] (He was defeated by seventeen votes in a three-cornered contest.)

Such optimistic assessments were buttressed by the predictions of the London Stock Exchange. At least since 1906, the Stock Exchange's members had run an informal futures market in 'Government Majorities' before each general election. Futures prices were tied to the expected size of the government majority. Prices rose and fell over the course of an election campaign with changing perceptions of the parties' political strength, and hence served as a barometer of perceived shifts in public opinion. For example, on 11 November 1923, the market in Conservative Majorities closed at 38–45, implying that, on the evening of 11 November, the collective wisdom of the market believed that the likely election outcome would be a Conservative majority of between thirty-eight and forty-five. Over the course of the campaign, the spread moved up and down as traders adjusted their views on the likely election outcome; at one point the spread dipped to 20–23, before settling in the mid-30s on the eve of the election.

Although there is no record of the number of brokers participating in this market, or in the number of investors on whose behalf these men were buying and selling, the figure of £100,000 which was reported to have changed hands in settling these contracts after the December 1923 election indicates that Majorities trading was a substantial phenomenon. As *The*

Economist reported on 1 December 1923, the market was watched closely by political organizers, and 'the closing prices were telephoned, regularly every afternoon, to several hundred [local election] committee and other political headquarters.'[17]

After the election, the king chided Davidson for 'ha[ving] been rather too optimistic,' to which Davidson admitted himself guilty.[18] The right-wing and anti-government *Daily Express* was less tactful, arguing after the election that '[t]his overthrow is due to the stupidity and miscalculations of Mr Baldwin and the little ring which surrounds and advises him.'[19] The Secretary of State for Air, Samuel Hoare, notably blamed the defeat on the 'credulity of the women'—an assessment which casts doubt on conventional wisdoms about the supposed conservatism of the interwar women's vote.[20] But more than the women, Conservatives blamed the Liberals. The 1923 election left Conservative strategists with a lasting fear of the Liberal electorate—a fear whose implications were evident in the conduct of the 1924 'Red Scare' election campaign, which was designed to alienate both women and wavering Liberals from the Labour party.[21]

Only four Liberal candidates formally withdrew in order to leave the field open for a Conservative to oppose Labour in a straight fight in October 1924; and nearly two-thirds of Liberal candidates (223 out of 339) stood in three-cornered contests.[22] Conservatives such as the former MP for South Croydon, Sir Ian Malcolm, may have publicly expressed their 'conviction that, in triangular fights, thousands of Liberals will vote Conservative rather than risk the return to parliament of a party, however small, which after the last election proved to be nothing more useful than a crutch to enable Labour to hobble into seats upon the front bench.'[23] However, this bluster overlay a significant degree of anxiety.[24] After the 1923 defeat, Davidson had articulated the need for 'more drive and enthusiasm' at Central Office, and, in October 1924, Conservative headquarters produced more leaflets and pamphlets than any party at any previous election.[25] Nevertheless, the *Daily Express*, which was fanatically alarmed about the possibility of Liberal candidates splitting the 'constitutionalist' vote and leading to the return of another Labour government, urged Baldwin's party on to more vigorous action, warning that:

> Conservative headquarters do not realize completely what is going on in the constituencies . . . It is a mistake to suppose that because the big political guns are talking about the lawyers' quarrel over the Campbell case or the Russian Treaty that the unreported Socialist speaker is bothering even to mention these joints in the Ministerial harness . . . That the Liberals realize these facts is shown by the immense efforts of the party machine to 'boom' the policy of Liberalism on coal, or agriculture, or housing as a real alternative to Socialism. If Conservatism remains absolutely blind to these signs and portents it may suffer some surprises at the polls.[26]

It was difficult for the Conservative leadership to discount such warnings, as, other than the impressionistic sense gained from canvassers, the political parties had few reliable mechanisms for gauging public opinion in 1924.

The difficulty of obtaining an objective measure of public opinion in a country with 20 million registered voters was thrown into relief by an attempt to do just that. As a pre-election publicity stunt, the department store Selfridges launched Britain's first 'Straw Ballot' in October 1924. The company sent out one million ballot cards—one to each twentieth voter on the registers—and asked recipients to record both their planned vote on the 25 October and their vote in the previous year's election. It described the poll as 'perhaps the most ingenious and authentic way of looking into the future that the wit of man has ever devised.' The Selfridges poll, it boasted, would likely 'obtain a greater accuracy' even than similar polls which had been conducted in the United States—'which have in the past shown a 90 percent accuracy'—as it was based on actual electoral registers, whereas the US polls had been conducted using lists culled from telephone directories.[27] Yet, though nearly 400,000 cards were completed and returned, the distribution of respondents was so skewed as to render the results suspect. The results are reprinted in Table 13.1.[28]

Clearly, a disproportionate number of Conservative supporters had returned their ballots, while those who had supported the Liberals in 1923 were significantly underrepresented. Although the company sought to explain the comparative exaggeration of Conservative support by arguing that 'it is quite conceivable that Conservatives would reply more rapidly and more in the course of their everyday business than the Labour partisans who are not perhaps so accustomed to receiving and dealing with correspondence', they could offer no explanation for the underrepresentation of Liberal votes.[29] Perhaps Liberals were too sensible a lot to comply with what was essentially a department store publicity stunt. It is difficult to speculate, though the scale of the poll strongly suggests that the discrepancy was not the result of random bias. Given the systematic underrepresentation of Liberal voices, the department store quietly scaled back its claims on the poll's behalf in the weeks before the election (although, if the

Table 13.1 Returns of Selfridge Million Straw Ballot, 1924

Party voted/plan-ning to vote for	1924	1923 (Reported)	1923 (Actual results)
Conservatives	56.05	51.02	38.0
Socialist	28.33	27.42	30.7
Liberal	15.32	21.33	29.7
Others	.30	.33	1.6

results are weighted to reflect the distribution of votes in the 1923 election, they actually yield a not excessively inaccurate prediction). [30]

Ultimately, the Liberals polled less than 70 percent of their 1923 votes in the 1924 election—about 4 percent less than the result predicted by the Selfridge poll. But the poll was taken before the publication of the infamous Zinoviev letter, which allegedly revealed the operation of Bolshevist agitators in Britain during the Labour administration, and the election was held just four days after its publication. Though the *Daily Mail*'s editor Thomas Marlowe had had the letter in his possession for several days, he only decided to publish it after consultation with the Conservative Central Office—a decision which suggests the depths of the Conservatives' uneasiness about the likely election outcome. [31] The fear that Liberal votes would again lead to a decisive number of Labour victories in three-cornered contests in 1924 arguably explains the decision to publish the letter four days before the poll. Over the next five years, the impact of the letter—particularly on the Liberal and female vote—remained an uncertain, though politically significant, question. [32] The *Daily Mail*'s owner, Viscount Rothermere, never ceased to believe that his paper's intervention had had a decisive impact on the election outcome, and, according to Lord Birkenhead, Baldwin's public dismissal of the role played by the 'press stunt' in 1924 went a long way towards explaining the animosity between the two men in the 1920s. [33] If wavering Liberal voters had been panicked into voting Conservative by the eve of poll publication, the Conservatives' base was much less reliable than the scale of their victory might initially suggest.

THE 1929 GENERAL ELECTION

Despite the party's uncertainty in the run-up to the 1924 election, Conservative leaders became increasingly confident as the decade wore on of the reliability of those voters who had voted Tory for the first time in 1924. By the end of the decade, the Conservative leadership believed that the solid majority of middle-class voters were tending towards Conservatism as the only alternative to Socialism. Conservative candidates, it was believed, now stood a solid chance even in those constituencies where Liberals had voted Tory in the absence of a Liberal candidate in 1924, but where Conservative candidates would likely face a Liberal as well as a Labour challenge in the upcoming election. In February 1929, discussing the Battersea South by-election, Neville Chamberlain crowed to his sister that 'I am pleased to see that of the Liberal revival there is no sign anywhere. In my opinion the sooner they disappear the better, for they dont [sic] seem to me to serve any useful purpose ... Also the bye-elections do not indicate any landslide against us so I am not disposed to be pessimistic.' [34] Davidson took a similarly dim view of the Liberals as a political force. He believed that the party 'had a far greater nuisance value than they really deserved. They had no policy, they had—so far as one could tell—no political principles different from ours, and yet they were determined to split the vote in order to get Labour in.' Consequently, Davidson's campaign strategy focused on delegitimizing the Liberals in order to ensure that the anti-Socialist vote coalesced around Conservative candidates.[35] Central Office's strategy was evident in a party election broadcast by the Secretary of State for War, Sir Laming Worthington-Evans, which concluded with an appeal to traditional Liberals: 'I know this advice will be unpalatable, it will be called impertinent by ardent Liberals accustomed in previous years to party fights, but nevertheless, the elector of to-day has to deal with the conditions of to-day. The real and substantial division of parties is for or against nationalization. My last words to you in saying Good-night shall be these: If you are against nationalization, Safety First! Vote for Baldwin and the Conservatives!'[36]

Whilst the Conservative leadership accepted that Labour might benefit on the margins from the large number of three-cornered contests in 1929, they did not perceive a serious threat of a repeat of 1923. In March 1929, Chamberlain recorded a conversation with Park Goff, Conservative MP for Darlington, in which the latter told him that he had 'been studying the constituencies rather carefully and informed me with great confidence where we should lose seats and to whom. For what it is worth his view was that the Liberals would increase their numbers from 37 to 70 or 80 but that we should have a majority over both the other parties of something between 35 and 55'—an analysis which suggested that the Labour party would return between 200 and 220 MPs.[37] As the phrase 'for what it is worth' suggests, Chamberlain was sceptical of Goff's analysis, though more for its assessment of Liberal strength than for its overly sanguine view of the Conservatives' prospects. In a letter to his sister two months later, he noted that 'no seriously minded student of politics seems prepared to give them [the Liberals] more than 60–70 seats and a good many are doubtful whether they will even increase their present total of 46. On the other hand the average opinion in our party seems to range round a majority of 40 to 50 over the other two . . . But I have a feeling that we may come out better than that. This is a women's election and I think the Baldwin legend appeals pretty strongly to women.'[38] Chamberlain's optimism was matched by that of Baldwin and the Central Office leadership.[39] Though backbenchers such as Cuthbert Headlam believed Baldwin 'quite mad to have the election in May . . . [as] we may quite likely go out with as big a thud as we did in 1906 and become as futile and feeble a party in the House of Commons as the Liberals are today', even Labour supporters such as Sidney Webb believed that the Conservatives would retain a plurality of seats—although potentially not a plurality of the popular vote.[40]

Once again, the confidence of Conservative party headquarters was bolstered by the forecasts of the London Stock Exchange. Although political betting on the exchange had been a regular feature of British elections for the past several decades, the 1929 election saw an enormous increase in interest in the practice, both in the City and around the country. Given the uncertainty about which (if any) party would attain a majority, there was no market in 'Majorities' contracts per se, but instead separate markets in Conservative, Labour, and Liberal seats. When the market opened on 22 February, the average price for Conservatives was 294; for Labour 253; and for the Liberals 65. In other words, the market was predicting a Conservative plurality, but not an absolute majority for the governing party. The following two months saw the launch of Lloyd George's final push to revive the Liberal party's fortunes, culminating in the publication of 'We Can Conquer Unemployment' in late April. The result was a long steady slump in Conservative prices and an offsetting rise in the price of Liberals, as traders erroneously bet on a Liberal revival at the expense of the Conservative party. By the start of the general election campaign, on 12 April, the Stock Exchange odds were Conservatives 273–277; Socialists 253–57; Liberals 83–87; and Independents 5–7. Liberal contracts continued to gain in value over the course of the campaign, though, from 23 March on, the party gained ground at the expense of the Labour party, not at the expense of the Conservatives, as the punters came to the conclusion that the Liberal programme was more likely to appeal to Labour sympathizers than to Tories. On the eve of the election, the markets were trading at Conservatives 272, Labour 245, and Liberals 97.[41]

The market predictions proved to be significantly off the final result, which was: Labour 287, Conservatives 260, and Liberals 59. One doubtless significant reason for the failure of the London Stock Exchange to foresee the Labour plurality was the impact of the newly enfranchised 'flapper voters', whose unquantifiable political preferences added a new degree of uncertainty to the election. Additionally, the oddsmakers both overestimated the likely success of the Liberal party and failed to gauge correctly the direction in which disaffected Liberals voters would turn.

The reasons for the election outcome, and for the experts' failure to predict it, were hotly contested within the Conservative party after the election. Many failed candidates attributed their defeat to the intervention of Liberal candidates, believing that the Liberals split the anti-Socialist vote, leading to their defeat. The former Conservative MP Headlam attributed his defeat at Barnard Castle to the intervention of Emmanuel Spence—'this fat, unctuous Town Councilor from Middlesboro'—arguing: 'the Liberals did the trick. Their wretched man polled over 4,000 votes, the majority of which in a straight fight would have come to me . . . as things were Lawther won by about 800 votes. . . . I honestly think even the Labour people were rather upset by the result: they realized that but for the Liberal I should have won hands down.'[42] If Headlam's analysis of the opinion of 'Labour people' is dubious, so too is his analysis of Liberal opinion. Chamberlain wrote to his sister in the wake of the defeat that he had 'had some very nice letters from MPs to whom I had written to condole on their defeat. Nearly all ascribe their misfortunes in the first place to Liberal intervention, but I fear they assume that in the absence of a Liberal candidate, Liberal votes would have been given to them, which seems to me very doubtful.'[43] Chamberlain's doubts probably contain significant substance. Whilst Winston Churchill may have believed that the Conservatives were defeated by the Liberal theft of rightfully Tory votes—a process which he dubbed 'maddogging'—in all the Tories won 150 seats on a minority vote and Labour 118, suggesting that Liberal candidates were, on average, more likely to split the progressive vote.[44]

As in 1923, the second most popular scapegoats for the election outcome were the new women voters. Lord Rothermere had taken the view going into the election that the 'flapper vote' would be the Conservatives' undoing. He claimed that the *Daily Mail*'s 'shrewdest electioneering prophets' had indicators that these 5.5 million 'irresponsible young women' 'will poll largely for the Socialists', not 'from a sense of conviction for Socialism . . . [but] out of an impulse of audacity.'[45] Adrian Bingham has suggested that Rothermere's fears were ultimately unsubstantiated, and outside the political mainstream.[46] However, in the aftermath of the election, many Conservatives shared his pessimism about the impact of the women's vote.[47] In a memorandum written three days after the election, the king's private secretary, Lord Stamfordham, explained to His Majesty that 'the votes of the people, enormously increased by he himself having given the Women's Franchise, shows again that the country has refused to place its confidence in [Baldwin].'[48]

The shock of the 1929 defeat had long-term consequences for the Conservatives' thinking about the electorate in the 1930s, and in particular for Conservative Central Office's confidence in the innate conservatism of the British public. The adoption in 1929 of the slogan 'Safety First,' which had been recommended to Central Office by the Bensons advertising agency, was premised on the belief that the majority of the country was fundamentally 'small-c' conservative.[49] As Davidson admitted in retrospect, he had been unwilling to 'accept at the time the criticisms that it was not a daring enough slogan and that the country wanted something more exciting.' The 1924 election, it was believed, had been won because the country feared the radicalism of socialist programmes, and in 1929 Central Office trusted that the party could again secure victory by 'impress[ing] upon the public the necessity of no wild-cat schemes.'[50] To an even greater extent than the 1923 election, the 1929 defeat profoundly shook the confidence of Conservative strategists in their ability to read the interwar electorate.[51]

THE CONSERVATIVES AND THE ELECTORATE IN THE 1930S

The general election of 27 October 1931 was one of the great landslides in British political history. After the Labour government led by Ramsay

MacDonald failed to agree to a programme of budget cuts necessary to keep the pound on the gold standard and secure a loan from the Americans, the cabinet resigned, and MacDonald went on to form a new 'National' coalition government, composed primarily of Conservatives. The new government was not able to keep the country on gold, but it nonetheless staked a claim to govern, and went to the country requesting a 'Doctor's Mandate' to fix the mess allegedly caused by its Labour predecessors. The disappearance of Liberal candidates in a majority of constituencies after 1929 meant that former Liberal voters were left with the choice between abstaining or switching their votes to either Labour or the 'National' candidate (in nearly nine cases out of ten, a Conservative).

The general agreement of contemporary observers and subsequent scholars is that, in 1931, 'the overwhelming bulk of the Liberal vote clearly went to the National Government.'[52] Andrew Thorpe's analysis of the poll results in the 236 seats in which there had been three-cornered contests in 1929, but which saw a straight fight between Labour and Tory candidates in 1931, indicates that: 'even here, the Labour vote fell, on average, by 10.2 percent, while the Conservatives' increased by 79.7 percent. Thus in seats where Labour needed to gain new [ex-Liberal] votes to be successful, it was unable even to poll its 1929 strength.'[53] Overall, the National Government won 551 seats (473 of which were held by Conservatives).

The extent of the Liberal swing to Conservatism in 1931 was appreciated by both the Labour and Conservative parties at the time. According to Arthur Henderson, Labour's poll in 1931 represented 'our sheet anchor ... our minimum basic vote in the country.'[54] In the view of Tory strategist Herbert Brooke, the ex-Liberal vote was 'almost entirely attracted to candidates supporting the National Government . . .; the total Socialist vote at that election represents the hard core of the electorate on which no anti-Socialist candidate is likely to make any impression.'[55] Yet, the Conservatives were not as confident going into the contest as the results suggest that they should have been. For one consequence of the Conservatives' profound insecurity post-1929 was a lasting scepticism of impressionistic reports of popular opinion. In March 1931, Charles Bridgeman 'pointed out [to Baldwin] that election agents' opinions, especially collective ones, were almost invariably wrong, and instanced the fact that they had foretold our victory in the 1929 election.'[56] In the weeks after the formation of the National Government, Chamberlain, now head of Conservative Central Office, recorded his belief that though 'our idiotic party thinks it has the game in its hands and wants us to fight on party lines', they could not count on a truly solid majority if they went to the country without National Liberal and National Labour support.[57] His hesitancy was shared by his colleagues at Central Office. The head of the party's research department forcibly argued in favour of going to the country on a National platform on the grounds that, whereas 'many of our supporters think that an immediate General Election, even on the old three-party lines, would inevitably result in a complete and overwhelming victory for the Conservatives, . . . there is and can be not conclusive evidence that victory on these lines is certain.'[58]

The party leadership's unwillingness to trust impressionistic evidence of the mood of the country was mirrored in the Stock Exchange Majorities prices offered in the run-up to the 1931 election. These were even more inaccurate than the 1929 odds, although this time the gamblers overestimated Labour's performance at the polls. In his party election broadcast two weeks before the polling day, Lloyd George noted that 'the Stock Exchange is betting on a Protectionist majority of over 150.'[59] By the eve of the poll, the predicted government majority had risen to 198–201, but remained significantly less than half of the National candidates' actual majority of 493.[60] If we assume that those investing in the election stock market in 1931 had the same metropolitan conservative biases as those investing in 1929, the excessively low estimates of the government majority are indicative of the unwillingness of the Conservative establishment to trust in their luck after the unexpected defeat two years earlier.

Another consequence of the 1929 defeat was the establishment of a more systematic approach to psephelogical analysis within Central Office. A chastened Central Office established a new Conservative Research Department (CRD) with the ostensible remit to 'conduc[t] research into . . . modern industrial, Imperial and social problems.'[61] However, the appointment of Stuart Ball, the party's former head of publicity, to run the new office indicated that the department also intended to concern itself with the saleability of potential policy solutions. Although the Conservatives would not set up a separate public opinion research unit until 1949, the CRD in the 1930s devoted considerable attention to an analysis of political opinion, particularly Liberal opinion.

Almost no one believed that the Liberals had an independent political future after 1931. The chairman of the National Liberal Federation, Ramsay Muir, wrote in 1934 that the party was 'beaten in advance by the public's idea that we are done for' and that, 'if we put up 400 candidates [in the next general election] (which I think impossible), we shall forfeit at least 200 deposits.'[62] But though Central Office no longer realistically had to worry that three-cornered contests would take 'anti-socialist' votes away from National candidates, the eventual distribution of the Liberal vote remained very much an open question, especially in the early 1930s. In 1934, Lord Lothian expressed his conviction that ex-Liberal voters would hold the balance of power between the government and Labour candidates in between 200 and 300 constituencies.[63] The Liberal leader Sir John Simon's de facto defection to the Conservatives suggested that a significant contingent of Liberal supporters might see Conservatism, even Conservatism openly wedded to a policy of protection, as preferable to Socialism. In contrast, the former Liberal prime minister Lloyd George's strident denunciations of the National Government from August 1931 onwards, the defection of Herbert Samuel's followers—the so-called Liberal Nationals—in 1933, and the criticism of the government by the rump Liberal party, now headed by Archibald Sinclair, during the 1935 election campaign raised questions about the reliability of former Liberal supporters.[64]

The Liberals in the 1930s had effectively become, as Herbert Brooke put it, 'the "floating vote", which so largely determines the result of elections', and the CRD became increasingly obsessed with the evidence as to which direction this vote was floating.[65] The problem was that the CRD lacked modern statistical methods for polling ex-Liberal voters to determine which way this vital constituency was leaning. In the absence of statistically representative sampling, the CRD had to rely on the scattershot evidence of by-election data to determine what was happening to the Liberal vote in the country.

Although subsequent scholars have analyzed by-election results from this period to conclude that the Conservative dominance was not under threat, the evidence could be interpreted from many angles, and the CRD analysts chose to see the worst in these off-cycle contests. The CRD began with the assumption that 1931 was an aberrant election. Though the Conservative organization did not necessarily share the Conservative MP Leo Amery's conviction that 'the Socialists will no doubt come in after 1939', they did not see 1931 as indicative of a long-term setback for Labour.[66] Chamberlain himself suspected that it was 'probable' that 1931 represented not a conversion of voters to Conservatism, but an aberrant situation in which (a) 'many socialist voters had abstained', and (b) 'many people who did not vote at all in 1929 voted National in 1931.' It was not clear to Chamberlain that these men and women could be relied upon either to vote again, or, if they did vote, to vote Conservative.[67] Ball shared Chamberlain's scepticism, though his own anxieties focused on the fate of the Liberal vote in 1931, as did those of his CRD colleague Herbert Brooke. Brooke noted that the Socialist (Labour) share of the vote had only fallen 17 percent in the English county seats between 1929 and 1931, as compared with 26 percent in London seats, and 22 percent in English borough seats. He rejected the analysis that 'Socialist feeling was less affected in the Counties than in the Town by the events of 1929–31', inclining instead towards the belief that the comparatively slight drop in the Socialists' county poll owed to a conversion of Liberal voters in 'county constituencies where there was a Liberal candidate in 1929 but not in 1931.'[68]

Given their belief that the Liberal landslide towards the National Government in 1931 could not be relied upon, the CRD analysts compared by-election results in the early 1930s not to the 1931 results but to those in 1929. Martin Ceadal has characterized the interwar period as 'an age that was innocent of the concept of "swing" for comparing electoral performances.'[69] This is simply untrue. The Central Office analysts were both aware of, and dispirited by, the extent of the swings away from the government in several of the by-elections held in the early 1930s. Brooke devoted considerable attention to the outcome of the Rusholme and Rutland by-elections in the autumn of 1933, despite the fact that both seats were retained by the government: 'The Rusholme result was almost as unsatisfactory as East Fulham, except that the seat was not actually lost. Rutland was serious for its very large increase in the Socialist vote, which appears to be due to nearly all the Liberals in the division having been induced to vote Socialist in the absence of a Liberal candidate.'[70] Chamberlain similarly kept an eye on the size of swings against the government, although he took a more sanguine view of such tendencies. On 10 February 1934, he wrote to his sister in respect of the Cambridge by-election, in which the government majority fell from 14,795 to 2,720 on an 18.5 percent swing:

> Cambridge was none too good after one has said all there is to be said about the candidate and the weather and the rest of it. But . . . no one knows to begin with how the Conservative poll was made up. It may have contained very large elements of Liberal or non-party men and it may easily have been the Conservatives who were lazy. With our gigantic majority and everything going along pretty comfortably I must say I can see little reason why people should get into a state of excitement over a by-election.[71]

Such sangfroid notwithstanding, by late 1934 Chamberlain was concerned enough about the coming general election to ask Ball to prepare an additional set of recommendations 'as to the government's election programme generally', above and beyond what had been requested from the department by the Conservative Campaign Committee, and to undertake a full survey of the party's general election prospects.[72] In analyzing the party's prospects, the CRD took into consideration not only the by-election data mentioned above, but the impressionistic reports of observers, such as an organizer in Leicester who reported to the party's chief publicity officer Sir Patrick Gower in late 1934 that, whereas the working classes remained largely loyal to the government, middle-class support was much shakier. 'The middle class,' he believed, 'are the puzzle of the political situation.' These wavering middle-class voters, who can be presumed to have been disproportionately ex-Liberals, were, according to this observer, wary about low wages and job security and hence drawn towards the municipal corporation model of local government: 'These people believe they can secure security by securing Municipal posts [for themselves], or for their children, consequently I believe they are voting Socialist at Municipal Elections. This I feel sure is the reason why the Socialists are able to make headway at the Municipal Elections.'[73] Gower forwarded the report on to Ball with a covering note suggesting that the man's conclusions were 'very interesting.'[74]

After the March 1935 by-election in Lambeth Norwood, Baldwin received a report from the Conservative politician Lord George Lloyd suggesting that at recent by-elections the government candidates had received few Liberal votes.[75] Sir Reginald Topping, the party's principal agent, looked into the situation further and reported to Lloyd that 'the Liberals did not vote, but we had a telephone canvas of every elector in the Division whose name appeared in the telephone directory. Two-thirds of the Liberals so canvassed promised to vote for the Conservative candidate, and our records show that most of them carried out their promise . . . We polled the type of individual who was likely to be found in the telephone directory; those with more left-wing tendencies voted against us.'[76] Telephone polls, reaching as they did a disproportionately middle-class cross section, were susceptible to the same unrepresentative biases as straw polls, or stock market forecasts, a fact which the principal agent fully appreciated.

Though historians and psephologists can look back at the 1935 election and conclude that those Liberals who had voted Labour in by-elections in the early 1930s 'would [not] risk voting Labour at a General Election', the likely direction of Liberal votes was less clear to politicians at the time.[77] When, in August 1935, Baldwin wrote to Gower asking him for a memorandum laying out the pros and cons of an autumn versus a winter election, Gower advised Baldwin to bide his time on the grounds that 'the policy of frightening the electors may not be entirely successful. It is not easy to frighten the electorate twice running, and one's efforts in this direction may be made difficult owing to the fact that the Socialists have spent three years in trying to persuade them that the fears that were created last time were largely due to scaremongering.'[78] To the anxiety that voters would no longer fear a Labour government in charge of domestic affairs was added the fear that even the government's cautious commitment to rearmament would alienate a significant proportion of wavering voters. Whilst the League of Nations Union's Peace Ballot, whose results were announced on 27 June 1935, was about as scientific a measure of public opinion as the Selfridges straw poll, it nonetheless impressed upon the government the strength of pacifist sentiment in the country, the lack of enthusiasm for rearmament, and the reluctance to support the League with military force.[79]

CONCLUSION

Although few actually believed that Labour might secure a victory in 1935, nearly all observers predicted a better showing by the opposition. Hugh Dalton estimated that Labour should 'have . . . nearer 240 than 200. The Liberals less than 20.'[80] The *Daily Express* conducted its first random-sample election survey during the campaign and on 9 November announced: 'Daily Express Election Survey Gives The Government Majority of 169'. The survey overestimated Labour's returns by over fifty, though it actually underestimated the Liberal performance, giving the Sinclair Liberals only fifteen. The actual result was National 429 (Conservatives 387), Labour 154, and Liberals twenty-one, resulting in a government majority of over 240. As the *News Chronicle* wrote in the wake of the poll, the results indicated that 'The floating vote, that is to say, has not deserted the Government to vote Labour.'[81]

It is impossible to know whether wavering voters came around to the government on the eve of the election, whether Labour's limited success was the result of anxieties about the recent splits within the parliamentary party and the change of party leadership, or whether politicians and interested observers had simply misgauged public opinion once again. However, one could argue that the government's unexpectedly large victory was, at least partially, a result of Conservative party strategists' assiduous effort to court the 'floating vote.' For another ramification of the 1929 election upset was that it instilled in the Conservative leadership the importance of keeping party policy in touch with perceived public opinion. Stanley Baldwin's reputation has suffered from his admission in 1936 that he could not have pushed forward with a programme of rearmament in November 1933 because there was 'at that time . . . probably a stronger pacifist feeling running through this country than at any time since the war,' and 'I cannot think of anything that would have made the loss of the election from my point of view more certain.'[82] Though the statement was at best ill-conceived, it was essentially a confession of the reality of 'government by the polls,' or—in the age before opinion polling—government by perceived public opinion. The unreliability of available measures of public opinion rendered the Conservative party excessively pessimistic about the depth of its public support. This in turn led it to spend large sums on propaganda efforts, such as the establishment of the National Publicity Bureau to advertise the government's achievements, and also, when necessary, to adjust its policies in line with what was seen to be the public mood.[83]

In subsequent decades, Conservatives, Labour, and the Liberals would repeatedly trim their sails in line with shifts in public opinion. What distinguished Conservative policy in the 1930s was the uncertainty of the political environment in which the party operated. The political dislocation caused by the rise of Labour and the breakup of the Liberal party, combined with the expansion of the electorate—and in particular the influx of over ten million new women voters between 1918 and 1928—served to destabilize the existing political order. In the era of smaller franchises and open ballots, election agents could literally account for each voter on the rolls. The existence, for more than half a century, of a clear two-party system meant that voters established comparatively stable political identities on which party operatives could largely rely in weighing the consequences of policy decisions. As Gilbert and Sullivan memorably put it in 1882, 'Nature always does contrive/That every boy and every gal/That's born into the world alive/Is either a little Liberal/Or else a little Conservative!'[84] The formation of the Labour party and the arrival of universal suffrage conspired to wipe away these old certainties.

Ultimately, the existence of a quantifiable but individually unknowable electorate would push parties towards the use of new techniques of opinion polling and focus group research that would allow them to categorize, quantify, and stratify their approach towards the new democratic public.[85] The period between the wars was a unique interval in which the old electoral strategies had been superceded, but new approaches to assessing the mood of the public had yet to be developed. It was also a period in which a large percentage of voters were forced to redefine their political allegiances. The above discussion illustrates the insecurity that this unprecedented uncertainty engendered in even the most seemingly dominant and secure of parties.

NOTES

1. R. McKibbin, 'Class and Conventional Wisdom', in *idem.*, *The Ideologies of Class: Social Relations in Britain, 1880–1950* (Oxford, 1991), pp. 259–93.
2. See P. Williamson, *National Crisis and National Government: British Politics, the Economy and Empire, 1926–1932* (Cambridge, 1992); *idem.*, *Stanley Baldwin* (Cambridge, 1999); D. Jarvis, 'Mrs Maggs and Betty: The Conservative Appeal to Women Voters in the 1920s', *Twentieth Century British History* 5 (1994), pp. 129–52; *idem.*, 'British Conservatism and Class Politics', *English Historical Review* 111 (1996), pp. 58–84; S. Nicholas, 'The Construction of a National Identity: Stanley Baldwin, "Englishness" and the Mass Media in Inter-War Britain', in M. Francis and I. Zweiniger-Bargielowska (eds.), *The Conservatives and British Society, 1880–1990* (Cardiff, 1996), pp. 127–46; E.H.H. Green, 'Conservatism, Anti-Socialism and the End of the Lloyd George Coalition', in *idem.*, *Ideologies of Conservatism: Conservative Political Ideas in the Twentieth Century* (Oxford, 2002), pp. 114–34.
3. J. Stevenson and C. Cook, *Britain in the Depression: Society and Politics, 1929–1939* (London, 1994), pp. 113–14.
4. C. Cook, 'Liberals, Labour and Local Elections', in G. Peele and C. Cook (eds.), *The Politics of Reappraisal, 1918–1939* (London, 1975), p. 171; Stevenson and Cook, *Depression*, p. 139.
5. *Ibid.*, cf. M. Ceadal, 'The East Fulham By-Election', in C. Cook and J. Ramsden (eds.), *By-Elections in British Politics* (London, 1997), p. 104.
6. D. Butler, 'Trends in British By-Elections', *The Journal of Politics* 11 (1949), pp. 396–407; M. Franklin and M. Lander, 'The Undoing of Winston Churchill: Mobilization and Conversion in the 1945 Realignment of British Voters', *British Journal of Political Science* 25 (1995), pp. 429–52.
7. 'Survey of Liberal Voters', distributed July 1950, CRD 2/21/3, Conservative Party Archive. Bodleian Library, Oxford.
8. D. Butler and D. Stokes, *Political Change in Britain: The Evolution of Electoral Choice* (London, 1974), p. 168.
9. 'Electoral Mathematics', *The Economist*, 9 Nov. 1935, pp. 897–8.
10. On the impact of opinion polls on British party politics, see M. Abrams, 'Public Opinion Polls and Political Parties', *Public Opinion Quarterly* 27 (1963), pp. 9–18; *idem.*, 'Opinion Polls and Party Propaganda', *Public Opinion Quarterly* 28 (1964), pp. 13–19; A. Taylor, '"The Record of the 1950s Is Irrelevant": The Conservative Party, Electoral Strategy and Opinion Research, 1945–1964', *Contemporary British History* 17 (2003), pp. 81–110; L. Beers, 'Whose Opinion? Changing Attitudes Towards Opinion Polling in Britain', *Twentieth Century British History* 17 (2006): pp. 177–205. For a recent discussion of

the emergence of the political focus group, see J. Moran, 'Mass-Observation, Market Research, and the Birth of the Focus Group, 1937–1997', *Journal of British Studies* 47 (2008), pp. 827–51.

11. The term 'floating voter' had been used at least since the 1935 general election. See, e.g., '"Floating Vote" Will Decide', *Daily Express*, 28 Oct. 1935; *News Chronicle*, 16 Oct. 1935.

12. I. Crewe, 'Elections and Public Opinion', in A. Seldon (ed.), *The Blair Effect* (London, 2001), pp. 67–96. On Conservative attempts to counter Labour strategy in this respect, see C. Pattie and R. Johnston, 'The Conservatives' Grassroots Revival', *Political Quarterly* 80 (2009), pp. 193–203.

13. Stanley Baldwin to Louisa Baldwin, 12 Oct. 1924, reprinted in P. Williamson and E. Baldwin (eds.), *Baldwin Papers: A Conservative Statesman, 1908–1947* (Cambridge, 2004), p. 160.

14. Memorandum by King George V to Stanley Baldwin, 12 Nov. 1923, in *ibid.*, pp. 128–9.

15. *Daily Mail*, 3 Dec. 1923; Cuthbert Headlam diaries, 27 Nov. 1923, reprinted in S. Ball (ed.), *Parliament and Politics in the Age of Baldwin and MacDonald: The Headlam Diaries, 1923–1935* (London, 1992).

16. R.R. James (ed.), *Memoirs of a Conservative: J.C.C. Davidson's Memoirs and Papers, 1910–37* (London, 1969), p. 189.

17. L. Beers, 'Punting on the Thames: Electoral Betting in Interwar Britain', *Journal of Contemporary History* 45 (2010), pp. 282–314.

18. James, *Memoirs of a Conservative*, p. 191.

19. *Daily Express*, 8 Dec. 1923.

20. Hoare to Davidson, 8 Dec. 1923, in James, *Memoirs of a Conservative*, p. 190. See also Sir Daniel T. Keymer to Stanley Baldwin, 11 Dec. 1923; Sir M. Archer-Shee to S. Baldwin, 7 Dec. 1923, in Baldwin Papers, Vol. 35, ff. 122–3, 159, Cambridge University Library.

21. See Jarvis, 'Mrs Maggs and Betty'; and L. Beers, 'Counter-Toryism: Labour's Response to Anti-socialist Propaganda, 1918–1939', in M. Worley (ed.), *The Foundations of the Labour Party: Identities, Cultures and Perspectives, 1900–1939* (Aldershot, 2009), pp. 231–49.

22. A. Taylor, 'The Effect of Electoral Pacts on the Decline of the Liberal Party', *British Journal of Political Science* 3 (1973), p. 245.

23. I. Malcolm, letter to the editor, *The Times*, 27 Oct. 1924.

24. A series of articles on three-cornered constituency contests published in *The Times* in the run-up to the election suggests the degree of Conservative anxiety about the impact of Liberal interventions on the 'constitutional' vote. E.g. 'Unionist Withdraws at Paisley' and 'The Election Campaign', *The Times*, 14 Oct. 1924; 'Hackney Outlook', *The Times*, 17 Oct. 1924.

25. James, *Memoirs of a Conservative*, p. 191; *Daily Express*, 18 Oct. 1924.

26. *Daily Express*, 23 Oct. 1924.

27. *The Times*, 15 Oct. 1924; 21 Oct. 1924.

28. *Daily Express*, 24 Oct. 1924.

29. *The Times*, 21 Oct. 1924.

30. *Loc. cit.*

31. J. Ferris and U. Bar-Joseph, 'Getting Marlowe to Hold His Tongue: The Conservative Party, the Intelligence Services and the Zinoviev Letter', *Intelligence and National Security* 8 (1993), pp. 100–37.

32. While scholars have subsequently questioned the importance of the letter to the election outcome (e.g. James, *Memoirs of a Conservative*, p. 199), contemporary observers believed that its impact had been significant, if not decisive. See K. Martin, 'The Influence of the Press', *Political Quarterly* 1 (1930), p. 163; R. Graves and A. Hodge, *The Long Week-End* (New York,

1963), p. 157, B. Donoughue and G.W. Jones, *Herbert Morrison* (London, 2001), p. 110.

33. Davidson memorandum of conversation with Birkenhead, n.d. [1927], in James, *Memoirs of a Conservative*, p. 201.
34. Neville Chamberlain to Ida Chamberlain, 9 Feb. 1929, in R. Self (ed.), *The Neville Chamberlain Diary Letters* (4 vols., London, 2005), III, p. 122.
35. James, *Memoirs of a Conservative*, pp. 301–2.
36. Sir Laming-Worthington Evans, Party Election Broadcast, 8 Apr. 1929. Reprinted in *The Listener*, 17 Apr. 1929.
37. Neville Chamberlain to Ida Chamberlain, 9 Mar. 1929, in Self, *Chamberlain Diary Letters*, III, p. 128.
38. Neville Chamberlain to Hilda Chamberlain, 5 May 1929, in *ibid.*, p. 136.
39. Ramsay MacDonald diary, 7 May 1929, in *Baldwin Papers*, p. 217; James, *Memoirs of a Conservative*, p. 301.
40. Headlam diary, 21 Mar. 1929, in *Parliament and Politics*, p. 168; Tom Jones to Eirene Jones, 24 May 1929, in Keith Middlemas (ed.), *Whitehall Diary, Volume Two* (New York, 1970), p. 185.
41. Beers, 'Punting on the Thames'.
42. Headlam diary, 31 May 1929, in *Parliament and Politics*, p. 175.
43. Neville Chamberlain to Hilda Chamberlain, 9 June 1929, in *Chamberlain Diary Letters*, III, p. 145.
44. Middlemas, *Whitehall Dairy, Volume Two*, p. 187; James, *Memoirs of a Conservative*, p. 302.
45. *Daily Mail*, 6 Apr. 1929; 11 Apr. 1929.
46. A. Bingham, 'Stop the Flapper Vote Folly: Lord Rothermere, the *Daily Mail*, and the Equalization of the Franchise, 1927–28', *Twentieth Century British History* 13 (2002), pp. 17–37.
47. A. Thorpe, *The British General Election of 1931* (Oxford, 1991), p. 31.
48. Lord Stamfordham memorandum to the king, 2 June 1929, in *Baldwin Papers*, p. 220.
49. P. Williamson, '"Safety First": Baldwin, the Conservative Party, and the 1929 General Election', *Historical Journal* 25 (1982), pp. 385–409. The view that voters, and especially women, were sceptical of change had a long history within the Conservative party. Cf. Sir Daniel T. Keymer to S. Baldwin, 11 Dec. 1923, Baldwin Papers, Vol. 35, f. 159.
50. James, *Memoirs of a Conservative*, p. 302.
51. Williamson, '"Safety First"', p. 409.
52. Stevenson and Cook, *Britain in the Depression*, p. 139.
53. Thorpe, *General Election of 1931*, p. 263.
54. 'Report on the General Election', 10 Nov. 1931. Filed in minutes of the National Executive Committee, Labour Party Archive, Manchester.
55. Herbert Brooke, '6 Recent By-Elections', memorandum, 30 Nov. 1933, CRD 1/7/16.
56. William Bridgeman diary, Mar. 1931, in P. Williamson (ed.), *The Modernisation of Conservative Politics: The Diaries and Letters of William Bridgeman, 1904–1935* (London, 1988), p. 244.
57. Neville Chamberlain to Hilda Chamberlain, 19 Sept. 1931, in *Chamberlain Diary Letters*, III, p. 279.
58. Stuart Ball, memorandum, 16 Sept. 1931, CRD 1/7/15.
59. Lloyd George, Party Election Broadcast, reported in *The Listener*, 21 Oct. 1931.
60. Beers, 'Punting on the Thames'.
61. Quoted in J. Ramsden, *The Age of Balfour and Baldwin* (London, 1978), p. 33.

62. Quoted in T. Stannage, *Baldwin Thwarts the Opposition: The British General Election of 1935* (London, 1980), p. 103.
63. *Ibid.*, pp. 103–4.
64. Lloyd George famously advised Liberals to vote for the Labour candidate at the North Hammersmith by-election in Apr. 1934.
65. Herbert Brooke memorandum, 30 Nov. 1933, CRD 1/7/16.
66. Leo Amery diary, 16 Nov. 1935, in J. Barnes and D. Nicholson (eds.), *The Leo Amery Diaries: Empire at Bay* (London, 1980), p. 403.
67. Handwritten note by Neville Chamberlain on p. 9 of report titled 'General Election 1931: Analysis', complied by Herbert Brooke, CRD 1/7/15.
68. Hebert Brooke, 'General Election 1931: An Analysis', CRD 1/7/15.
69. Ceadal, 'East Fulham', p. 104.
70. Brooke, '6 Recent By-Elections'.
71. Neville Chamberlain to Ida Chamberlain, 10 Feb. 1934, in *Chamberlain Diary Letters*, IV.
72. Minutes of interview with Neville Chamberlain in House of Commons, 26 Nov. 1934, CRD 1/7/17.
73. Report of Leicester organizer, n.d. [c. Oct./Nov. 1934], CRD 1/7/7.
74. Gower to Ball, 9 Nov. 1934. CRD 1/7/7.
75. Stannage, *Baldwin Thwarts the Opposition*, p. 122.
76. Topping to Lord George, 8 Apr. 1934, quoted in *ibid.*, ch. 4, fn. 45.
77. Stevenson and Cook, *Depression*, p. 139.
78. Quoted in Stannage, *Baldwin Thwarts the Opposition*, p. 119.
79. Whereas over 10 million respondents evinced a willingness to use sanctions and other non-military measures to punish aggressor countries, only 6.8 million supported the use of military measures.
80. Dalton diaries, 28 Oct. 1935, in B. Pimlott (ed.), *The Political Diary of Hugh Dalton, 1918–1940* (London, 1986), p. 191.
81. *News Chronicle*, 16 Oct. 1935.
82. Quoted in Ceadal, 'East Fulham', p. 96.
83. Stannage, *Baldwin Thwarts the Opposition*, p. 123.
84. W.S. Gilbert and A. Sullivan, "When all night long a chap remains", from *Iolanthe, or the Princess and the Peri* (London, 1882).
85. The term 'stratified electioneering' was first used by Sidney Webb in 1922 to refer to the targeted approach to voters of different socioeconomic classes ('Labour and the Middle Class', *London Labour Chronicle*, Dec. 1922).

14 Towards New Histories of an Enumerated People

Tom Crook and Glen O'Hara

At least three themes arise from the preceding studies of Britons' engagements with statistics as they have developed since the turn of the nineteenth century. The first is the sheer depth and array of numbers generated in the modern British Isles. From the late 1700s onwards, there were few elements of national life that were not counted in some way, whether by gifted amateurs, professional learned societies, scientific experts, or by governments themselves. The second theme is the political disputation and conflict generated by statistics. Whether it was local health reforms, the question of tariffs, the aspirations of consumers, or the strength of European economies after World War Two, numbers were continuously invoked and disputed as a critical part of public debate. The third and overriding impression to emerge from this collection is the intense complexity that characterized the generation, application, and reception of statistics. Companies, political parties, Whitehall, Westminster, the press, members of the public: all inched forwards into a vast and ever expanding world of numbers that confounded as much as it enlightened. But these themes are all part of a more wide-ranging abundance, for it was the multifarious, multifunctional nature of statistics which allowed them to become and remain so contested; and it was their rich density that made the nature of the world 'outside' any given institution, party, or group of people seem by turns alien and familiar, uncertain and dependable.

The first theme is the most obvious. Numbers poured forth on an ever growing range of topics and with ever greater temporal regularity. All our authors attest to this in one way or another. They also demonstrate the multifunctional nature of numbers, and their many and varied uses. Just as their field of application expanded, so too did the range of purposes they served. Ample confirmation can be found in this volume for the idea that numbers have no intrinsic or essential governmental function. But whether the exponential growth of numbers made for a clearer and more accurate picture of the social world and national life is a moot point. The sheer quantity of data was enough to necessitate extremely schematic representations of reality, as Edward Higgs in particular has argued in this volume. Yet, as Higgs's argument suggests, this 'reduction of complexity'—which proceeded according to certain logistical and economic constraints, as well as preconceived ideas regarding what should and should not be counted—was the necessary precondition for the production of statistical representations in the first place. Furthermore, as Maeve Adams and Stefan Schwarzkopf have highlighted, there was an inherent epistemological tension between the abstraction of statistics and the unique particularities of individual lives. It would seem that the very generation of statistics and statistical representations demands a certain partiality of perspective, one which obscures as much as it illuminates, regardless of how such data then feed into the public sphere and into processes of governance.

Our second theme builds on the first, for, however partial their initial generation, numbers were then subject to uncertain and fragmented appropriations by members of the public, politicians, parties, and various interests groups. Among other examples, population censuses were at the heart of the debates leading up to the Great Reform Act of 1832; and government blue books and colonial statistics provided the framework within which tariff reform was debated during the late Victorian and Edwardian periods. Numbers were always subject to political appropriation, and as such they were often greeted by public scepticism. It is a situation which prevails today, of course. The general election of 2010 was marked by sharp exchanges regarding the validity of statistics. Gordon Brown's assertions about immigration reform were immediately challenged on the basis of the figures they contained. Teenage pregnancy statistics provided by the Conservatives—which missed the mark by a factor of ten—were also fiercely criticized.[1] Criticisms of this sort have been an established feature of British public life since the Victorian period. It was during this era when numbers were first institutionalized as a means of scrutinizing government. Yet, at the same time, these very same numbers were probed and contested by the public, politicians, and professionals alike. Then, as now, numbers were held to account in the public sphere.

These observations feed into the third theme: the sheer complexity that characterized the generation, application, and reception of statistics. The rise of statistics is often associated with the emergence of state or governmental rationality. Taken together, the essays contained in this volume should give us pause when making equations of this sort. The multifunctional nature of statistics—not least their use as instruments of state power *and* critiques of state power—suggests that we should at least speak of rationalities in the plural; they serve much more than one agenda. But it is also evident that statistics have been a source of confusion and contestation as much as clarity and consensus. The essays in this volume have described myriad forms of resistance and scepticism, from opposition to the reform and improvement of statistics within government to those which accompanied their eventual circulation outside of government in the public sphere. To be sure, as James Thompson noted in his chapter, we still know too little about popular numeracy and the ways numbers were actually understood and consumed by members of the public. Yet anecdotal evidence would suggest that statistics might confound and frustrate even the well-educated. In 1902, the Cambridge graduate and later Liberal MP Charles Masterman wrote an article reviewing Charles Booth's monumental survey *Life and Labour of the People of London*, published at various points during the 1880s and 1890s. At the end of reading 'nine bulky volumes', comprising 'mazes of statistics, ordered and classified', what was left, wrote Masterman, was a 'general impression . . . of something monstrous, grotesque, inane: something beyond the power of individual synthesis; a chaos resisting all attempts to reduce it to orderly law.'[2]

Beyond this, there is the question of simply living in a world teeming with numbers and how this affects both the public and politicians. Fears regarding what we now term 'information overload' were voiced as early as the mid-Victorian period, when members of the public began to confess astonishment at the sheer profusion of numerical 'facts' that seemed to characterize modern life.[3] By the middle of the twentieth century excessive amounts of information were becoming ever more problematic within government, and at the highest levels. When Harold Macmillan served as prime minister in the late 1950s and early 1960s, he often mused in his diary about what he termed 'the economic situation'; quite what was going on seemed elusive. The burden of dealing with complex numerical information and various interlocking crises constantly told on ministers, and at the end of the 1957 parliamentary session Macmillan wrote that 'everyone is so exhausted . . . nothing is right; everyone is wrong'.[4]

The great whirl of data that characterizes modern life seems unlikely to abate. The growth of the World Wide Web, with its online databases, self-generated content, and interactive links between different clusters of pages, has made gathering—let alone dealing with and understanding—numerical information still more daunting. In February 2010, *The Economist* ran a front-page headline highlighting an impending 'data deluge'. The magazine detailed how quickly numerical information was proliferating. Global information amounted to around 750 exabytes (that is, 750 billion gigabytes) in 2009; it was likely to build to some 1,750 by the end of 2011.[5] *The Economist* noted the two-faced nature of this data explosion in a wide-ranging editorial: 'It has great potential for good—as long as consumers, companies and governments make the right choices about when to restrict the flow of data, and when to encourage it.' But it also noted the risk of 'Big Brotherishness of various kinds, particularly when governments compel companies to hand over personal information about their customers'. It concluded: 'the process of learning to cope with the data deluge, and working out how best to tap it, has only just begun'.[6]

It is difficult to disagree with *The Economist*. Quite how, as a democratic society, we handle and dispose of vast swathes of data regarding our everyday lives seems certain to become a matter of long-standing debate. Indeed, it could be that we stand on the threshold of another step-change with respect to the sheer volume of numerical information—another 'avalanche' of numbers like the one that fell in the early nineteenth century, only this time of a digital rather than a printed kind. Yet there is still much for historians to debate and research, and this volume by no means exhausts the historical problematic of statistics and the public sphere in modern Britain. As has been noted, much work remains to be done on the question of reception and how numbers were utilized and understood by the public. In a similar vein, as the introduction suggested, we still know too little about the presentation of numbers in popular graphical and tabular forms: James Thompson's chapter in this volume is only a start. Many other fields of empirical research lie fallow, not least the great postwar explosion in the party-political use of opinion polling data and focus-group research.[7] Even with respect to the Victorian period, relatively well-documented compared to the twentieth century, there are neglected areas. Still only a small amount of work has been done on the reception and contestation of crime figures, for instance.[8]

Doubtless more empirical areas of neglect might be highlighted. But there is also the question of how we think about statistics and the public, as well as the manner in which we theorize their interrelations and mutual transformations. Three areas might be highlighted which deserve greater theoretical attention. First, there is the question of statistics and time. The introduction to this volume noted the growing temporal regularity with which numbers were collected and disseminated during the nineteenth century, something which intensified further in the twentieth. We take this for granted today, living as we do in a world where numbers appear everyday in our newspapers detailing fluctuations in prices, growth rates, crime figures, and so on. Yet this relentless public circulation is only of nineteenth-century origin, and it enabled the relations of past, present, and future to be mapped and experienced in new ways: for example, as a 'time-series' of statistical changes involving quantitative increases, decreases, and plateaus. How, then, have statistics altered professional and public perceptions of time, change, and even crisis? Here historians might benefit from engaging with the work of Anthony Giddens, Niklas Luhmann, and Reinhart Koselleck, all of whom understand modernity in terms of the institutionalization of more reflexive, future-oriented temporal practices.[9]

The second question is the related one of risk and the role that statistics play in rationalizing the future on a probabilistic basis. Trust is also at stake here, to the extent that where there is less risk, trust increases (and vice versa), whether in relation to a person or a particular environment. Statistics, of course, might be trusted or distrusted, as the chapters by Tom Crook and James Taylor have demonstrated. Yet it is also evident in light of today's statisticalized 'risk society' that numbers have played a fundamental role in shaping what we understand by trust in the first place. But when, and how, did ideas and practices relating to trust, risk, and the future begin to change at the popular level? Probability theory dates back to the seventeenth century and there are now a number of different ways of theorizing probability, from the logical and mathematical to the more empirical. The more inductive, statistical variants, however, are of nineteenth-century origin and emerged alongside—and as part of—the modern (and statistically sophisticated) insurance industry. It could be that the Victorian period witnessed the emergence of new public conceptions of trust, and new appreciations of risk, understood now in terms of the relative probability of given future events (robbery, ill-health, death, and so on). Once again, the work of Giddens and Luhmann is likely to be of use here, but so too that of Ulrich Beck and François Ewald.[10]

Finally, and not least, there is the question of power. What kind of power is at stake in the circulation of statistics in the public sphere? Should we speak in fact of only one form or field of power? There would seem to be an evident tension between statistics on the one hand, and the public sphere on the other. Statistics, as Foucauldian scholars like to note, are objectifying and normalizing, and provide the epistemological basis for various forms of disciplinary and bio-political management. The public sphere, by contrast, is supposed to provide a place for free discussion, where autonomous individuals can participate in open debate regarding their collective existence. Statistics, then, seem to constrain freedom—they objectify, classify, and monitor. The public sphere, on the other hand, would seem to enable freedom and allow for the expression of public sovereignty. How, then, to think of the field of power created by the profound entanglement of statistics and the public sphere?

Perhaps we should recognize that power lies in neither, but rather takes place at precisely the fraught and ever-shifting points where the two meet. Never a consistent theorist of power, Foucault himself encouraged just this view. In a lecture delivered in 1975 at the Collège de France, for a course entitled 'Society Must Be Defended', he stated:

> From the nineteenth century until the present day, we have then in modern societies, on the one hand, a legislation, a discourse, and an organization of public right articulated around the principle of the sovereignty of the social body . . . ; and we also have a tight grid of disciplinary mechanisms that actually guarantees the cohesion of that social body . . . A right of sovereignty and a mechanics of discipline. It is, I think, between these two limits that power is exercised. The two limits are, however, of such a kind and so heterogeneous that we can never reduce one to the other. In modern societies, power is exercised through, on the basis of, and in the very play of, the heterogeneity between a public right of sovereignty and a polymorphous mechanics of discipline.[11]

The essays in this volume provide at least some credence for this view, premised as it is on the inherently diverse and intrinsically fractious nature of power. It also has the virtue of acknowledging the reality of both freedom and discipline in modern Western societies. One is thing certain, however: any attempt to theorize or generalize about the form of power manifest in the circulation of statistics in the public sphere must refrain from privileging either its disciplinary or its democratic dimensions. Somehow the two must be thought together.

NOTES

1. A. Travis, 'Immigration Is Not Out of Control, Says Gordon Brown', *The Guardian*, 31 Mar. 2010; L. Penny, 'Our Sex Lives, Their Agenda', *The Guardian*, 29 Mar. 2010.
2. Quoted in A. Briggs, 'The Human Aggregate', in H.J. Dyos and M. Wolff (eds.), *The Victorian City: Images and Reality, Volume One* (London, 1973), pp. 96–7.
3. R. Menke, *Telegraphic Realism: Victorian Fiction and Other Information Systems* (Stanford, CA, 2008), pp. 15–21.
4. H. Macmillan, *Riding the Storm: 1956–1959* (London, 1971), pp. 661, 663.
5. K. Cukier, 'Data, Data Everywhere', *The Economist*, 'Special Report on Managing Information', 27 Feb. 2010, p. 4.
6. 'The Data Deluge', *The Economist*, 27 Feb. 2010, p. 13.
7. Research of this sort is not entirely absent, it should be emphasized. See, for instance, J. Moran, 'Mass-Observation, Market Research and the Birth of the Focus Group, 1937–1997', *Journal of British Studies* 47 (2008), pp. 827–51.
8. See, for instance, H. Taylor, 'Rationing Crime: The Political Economy of Criminal Statistics since the 1850s', *Economic History Review* 51 (1998), pp. 569–90; C. Emsley, *Crime, Police and Penal Policy: European Experiences, 1750–1940* (Oxford, 2007), ch. 7.
9. See especially A. Giddens, *The Consequences of Modernity* (Cambridge, 1990); N. Luhmann, *Observations on Modernity* [trans. W. Whobrey] (Stanford, CA, 1998); and R. Koselleck, *Futures Past: On the Semantics of Historical Time* [trans. K. Tribe] (Cambridge, MA, 2004).
10. See especially U. Beck, *Risk Society: Towards a New Modernity* [trans. M. Ritter] (London, 1992) and F. Ewald, 'Insurance and Risk', in G. Burchell, C. Gordon, and P. Miller (eds.), *The Foucault Effect: Studies in Governmentality* (London, 1991), pp. 197–210.
11. M. Foucault, *'Society Must Be Defended': Lectures at the Collège de France, 1975–76* [trans. D. Macey] (London, 2003), pp. 37–8.

Contributors

Maeve E. Adams recently completed her doctorate at New York University. Her dissertation was entitled 'Printed Evidence and the Scientific Networks of Literary Realisms, 1774–1900'. Her next project will address the 'politics of modesty', c. 1700–1900.

Laura Beers is Assistant Professor of British History at American University in Washington, DC. She was previously a Junior Research Fellow at Newnham College, Cambridge, and an ERSC Postdoctoral Research Fellow in the Faculty of History, Cambridge University. She is the author of *Your Britain: Media and the Making of the Labour Party* (2010).

Tom Crook is Lecturer in Modern British History at Oxford Brookes University. He has published in *Social History*, *Urban History* and *Journal of Victorian Culture*. He is currently completing a book-length study entitled *Time and the Social Body: Public Health and English Modernity, 1830–1914*.

Edward Higgs is Professor of History in the Department of History at the University of Essex. He has written widely on the history of state censuses and information gathering. He is currently writing a book on personal identification from 1500 to the present, and helping to create an integrated digital dataset of the British census returns, 1851 to 1911.

Steven King is Professor of Economic History and Medical Humanities at the University of Leicester. He has published widely on the histories of industrialization, poverty and welfare, marriage, and medicine. His current research projects include work on sickness and poverty, 1750–1850; the economics of overseeing; and the history of corsets as artefacts and evidence.

Glen O'Hara is Senior Lecturer in Modern History at Oxford Brookes University. He is the co-editor of *The Modernisation of Britain? Harold Wilson and the Labour Governments of 1964–1970* (2006), and the author of *From Dreams to Disillusionment: Economic and Social Planning in 1960s Britain* (2007), and *Britain and the Sea since 1600* (2010). His next book, *Governing Post-War Britain: The Paradoxes of Progress*, will be published in 2011.

Theodore M. Porter is Professor of History at the University of California, Los Angeles. His books include *The Rise of Statistical Thinking* (1986), *Trust in Numbers* (1995), and most recently *Karl Pearson: The Scientific Life in a Statistical Age* (2004). In 2008 he was elected to the American Academy of Arts and Sciences.

Edmund Rogers completed his PhD in History at the University of Cambridge in 2009, before taking up an Ulster-Scots Postdoctoral Research Fellowship at the University of Guelph. He now holds an SSHRC Postdoctoral Fellowship at the University of Toronto, through which he is researching the Irish dimensions of the nineteenth-century tariff debate.

Stefan Schwarzkopf is Associate Professor in Business History at Copenhagen Business School. His work on the history of advertising, marketing and political propaganda in twentieth-century Europe has appeared in *Contemporary British History*, *Management and Organizational History*, and *Journal of Cultural Economy*.

James Taylor is Senior Lecturer in History at Lancaster University. His first book, *Creating Capitalism: Joint-Stock Enterprise in British Politics and Culture, 1800–1870* (2006), won the Economic History Society prize for best first monograph in economic and/or social history published in 2006–7. He is currently writing a book on fraud and the law in nineteenth-century Britain.

James Thompson is Lecturer in Modern British History at the University of Bristol. He has published widely on the history of political communication in Britain, 1850–1950, including an article on political posters in *Past and Present*. He is currently completing a book on the idea of public opinion and modern British political culture.

S.J. Thompson is a Junior Research Fellow in History at St John's College, Cambridge. He recently completed his ESRC-funded doctoral dissertation at the Cambridge Group for the History of Population and Social Structure on 'Census-Taking, Political Economy and State Formation in Britain, c. 1790–1840'.

Index

An environmentally friendly book printed and bound in England by www.printondemand-worldwide.com

This book is made entirely of sustainable materials; FSC paper for the cover and PEFC paper for the text pages.

#0033 - 200513 - C0 - 229/152/15 [17] - CB